Language
Development

Language Development
Knowledge and Use

Paula Menyuk
Boston University

Scott, Foresman/Little, Brown College Division
Scott, Foresman and Company
GLENVIEW, ILLINOIS BOSTON LONDON

Library of Congress Cataloging-in-Publication Data

Menyuk, Paula.
Language development.

Includes index.
1. Language acquisition. I. Title.
P118.M42 1987 401'.9 87-17063
ISBN 0-673-39740-8

1 2 3 4 5 6 7 8 9 10 – KPF – 93 92 91 90 89 88 87

Printed in the United States of America

Acknowledgment

Entry on page 279 from Webster's *New World Dictionary,* College Edition (World Publishing Company). Copyright © 1966 by Harper & Row, Publishers, Inc. Reprinted by permission of Harper and Row, Publishers, Inc.

This book is dedicated
to my grandchildren.

Preface

This book is about language development, but not simply about the facts of language development that have been gathered thus far. Rather, it focuses on those questions that researchers, teachers, and clinicians ask about the process of language development. These questions cluster into four categories:

- Questions about *why* the child acquires this knowledge.
- Questions concerning *how* this process takes place from birth to adulthood.
- Questions about the *differences* that occur in this process among groups of children or individual children.
- Questions about language development and learning.

This book is organized around these questions.

This Preface is designed to act as a guide to the reader. Chapter One presents a description of what children know when they acquire a language, as well as an overview of the topics that are discussed throughout the book. The four chapters that follow (Two through Five) are concerned with the *why* of language development. Chapters Six through Nine deal with the question of *how* the process of development takes place by examining children's acquisition of the components of language — namely pragmatics, lexicon, semantax (semantics and syntax), and morphophonology (morphology and phonology). Chapter Ten is concerned with language acquisition in children who are considered to be different because of their biological makeup (dysphasic children, for example). Chapter Eleven examines the same process in children different because of their experience in general and their language experience in particular. Finally, in Chapter Twelve, the use of language in learning and the development of written language knowledge are examined.

The chapters that follow the introductory chapter are all concerned with explanations of language development. The first of these, Chapter Two, presents an overview of some theories of language development. The theories represent strong positions concerning the causes for — or the *why* of — the entire process of language acquisition from infancy to adolescence. The chapters that follow, Chapters Three, Four, and Five, present a different view of how to explain language development. This view is the one espoused by the author, that language development results from particular cognitive, biological, and social readinesses, and continues to develop due to other particular factors. Further, this view holds that different aspects of the components of language are particularly influenced by certain factors. The chapters that follow this first section of the book provide further support for this view.

A large part of each of the chapters on the acquisition of the components of language is a presentation of general aspects of development. Each of these chapters briefly describes the *categories* and *rules* in that particular component of the language (pragmatics, lexicon, semantax, or morphophonology) and then traces the development of categories and rules in that component during infancy, early childhood, and middle childhood and adolescence. Finally, the reasons for developmental change are presented. Whenever available, findings concerning individual variation in both the rate and the order of development are discussed.

The final section of the book discusses topics that are of particular interest to educators and clinicians. Although these chapters could be thought of as dealing with applied problems and previous chapters as dealing with theoretical issues, this would be incorrect. Information generated by research on the questions of *what* is acquired when language is acquired, *why* it is acquired, and *how* the process of acquisition takes place is of obvious importance in understanding differences in language development and the role of language development in learning. Conversely, information gathered on differences in patterns of language development due to biological and environmental differences and the role of language in learning has obviously equal importance for developing adequate theories and descriptions of the *why, what,* and *how* of language acquisition. Evidence that *theory* and *application* are interdependent is an underlying theme of the entire book.

The author wishes to thank Mary and Peter Salus of Oakland, California, formerly of Dominican College; William Stokes of Lesley College; David Bloome of the University of Michigan, Ann Arbor; Noel Jones of the University of North Carolina, Wilmington; Barbara C. Palmer of Florida State University; Donald Richgels; and Nancy Hansen-Krening for their careful reading of the draft version of the book and for their suggestions for revision. Some of these suggestions are now part of the book.

Contents

Chapter Eight Semantax Development *160*

Chapter Nine Development of Morphophonology *188*

Chapter Ten Language Disorders *216*

Chapter One
Overview

What Is Acquired?

The Grammar of the Language
The Use of Language
Differences Among Languages and Dialects

Why Is Language Acquired?

Theories of Language Acquisition
Cognition and Language
Capacity to Acquire Language
Input and Language Development

How Is Language Acquired?

Pragmatics
Lexicon
Semantax
Morphophonology

Differences in Language Development and Learning

Language Disorders
Language Differences
The Role of Language in Learning

Why is language acquired? How does language acquisition take place? What are the patterns of language development in children with language disorders and those who are said to exhibit marked differences in their language development? How is language used to learn? These main questions and many others, and some of the answers to them, make up the content of this book. The purpose of this chapter is to introduce the topic of language development and to preview the contents of the book.

The introduction to the topic of language development is a presentation of linguistic descriptions of the content and structure of language. A discussion of what the child is in the process of acquiring and what the adult presumably knows introduces the linguistic terminology that is used in the book and some of the descriptions of language knowledge and use that are the bases for theoretical and experimental investigations of language development. Following, there is a brief summary of the main topics in the chapters that are concerned with the questions posed above. This summary provides different terminology, that concerned with theorizing and experimentation in the area of language development. Finally, although, language development is discussed in much greater detail in many chapters of the book, a brief summary of language development trends is presented in the discussion of those chapters concerned with the question: How is language acquired?

What Is Acquired?

A language is said to be a *system* of *arbitrary symbols* that is used to *communicate*. The word *symbol* means something that stands for or represents another thing. The word *arbitrary* means that the symbols used are based on preference or notion rather than on intrinsic characterizations of the things represented. (A nonarbitrary representation would be photographs of the things represented.) The word *system* means a set of things so related or connected as to form a unity or organic whole. The word *communicate* means to impart, make common, or share information, signals, or messages. Roughly, then, a language is a set of things making up a whole that preferentially represents other things and is used to make common, impart, or share information, signals, and messages.

If we substitute linguistic terms for the generally used terms, we come up with this definition of language: Language is a grammar (system) that is made up of a set of categories and relations among categories (set of symbolic and arbitrary things) that are used to produce and comprehend messages (to communicate). Categories can be further defined as units that make up the system. In spoken language these units are sounds, words, utterances, and discourse. In a manual language, sounds are replaced by particular hand gestures. Relations among categories are defined by the ways in which the categories are combined or organized.

Understanding the meaning of the terms "arbitrary" and "symbolic" is particularly important in understanding what a language is. Arbitrariness and symbolism are indicated in both spoken and manual language by the fact that different languages or dialects within each type of language have somewhat different categories or units. For example, Spanish speakers say "casa" and English speakers say "house" to represent the same kind of object. To change a positive statement into a negative one, not only are different words used in French as compared to English, but also the words are arranged differently: "Il *n'est pas* mon ami" as compared to "He'*s not* my friend."

The descriptors that have been used to define a language (arbitrary, symbolic, and systematic) make human language distinct from any animal's native communication system (Sebeok, 1972; 1981). Although a controversy exists as to whether some subhuman primates (such as chimpanzees) can acquire all aspects of a human language (a sign language), there is much less argument about important distinctions between human languages and animal communication systems. This will be discussed at greater length in Chapter Four, Capacity to Acquire Language.

One of the principal explanations given for the distinction between animal and human communication systems is that human language is composed of a set of categories and relations (grammar) that are used in infinitely different ways by making substitutions among them. Additionally, language is used by humans in ways that are vastly different from the ways in which animals use their communication systems. These differences are crucial to a full definition of language.

The Grammar of a Language

The speech sounds — or phonemes — in oral language and the signs — or cheremes — in manual language are put together to make words. These words — or morphemes — are put together to make utterances, and utterances are put together in discourse or conversation. There are, then, several levels of arbitrary symbols — from sound to sentence — that make up the grammar of a language. Sentences are used and combined in particular ways to make up conversation and discourse.

The sounds that make up the morphemes or words in a language have no meaning when they are in isolation unless a single sound forms a morpheme, as does the article "a." The word "upon" is composed of four sounds (/ə/, /p/, /a/, /n/). Each of these sounds is meaningless in isolation but when put together, they form a meaningful unit. Each language has a particular repertoire of sounds. Many sounds are shared across languages (for example, some of the nasal sounds, /m/, and /n/), while others are unique to particular families of language (for example, click sounds). Each sound has a number of articulatory features that differentiates it from the other sounds in the language. For example, /s/ is different from /k/ because /s/ is produced in the front of the mouth with the tongue tip up and the teeth together while air is being continuously expelled, whereas /k/ is produced in the back of the mouth with the mouth open, the back of the tongue up, and with a brief explosion of air. The sound /s/ has the features +anterior (front), +coronal (tongue tip up), +continuant (continuous sound), while /k/ has the features −anterior (back), −coronal (tongue tip down), and −continuant (a burst of sound).

Each morpheme in a language usually has two kinds of meaning, semantic and syntactic. Semantically, the word "upon" describes a relation of location between objects. Syntactically, it appears in certain places in an utterance to describe that relation. In the sentence "The book is upon the table," the two kinds of meaning of "upon" become clear; "upon" describes the location of the book in relation to the table, and it does this by beginning a prepositional phrase. The fact that the word "upon" appears before the phrase "the table" indicates to us that the book is on top of the table rather than the table being on top of the book. To indicate the latter, the sentence would be "The table is upon the book" and the meaning of the utterance would be changed. We can change meaning in the following ways:

1. By combining the same words in the sentence in different ways (as in the example using the word "upon").
2. By adding words to the sentence.
3. By changing words in the sentence by combining sounds in different ways.

For example, we can change the meaning by adding the word "not," as in "The book is not on the table," or by adding a plural marker to the word "book," as in "The book*s* are upon the table." We can change it by changing some of the words to different phoneme sequences, as in "The book is under the couch." In each of these examples, we changed the meaning of the original sentence by combining or organizing the categories of the language in different ways — but *always* according to the rules of the language.

We could take all of the same examples and combine language categories in nongrammatical or nonmeaningful ways. For example, we could (1) change the order of the words in our example sentence to "The upon book table the is." We could (2) add the word "not" and (3) the plural marker *s* and come up with "The*s* upon not book table the is." We could (4) come up with word changes such as the "The love is into the liberty." Finally, we could (5) combine sounds to come up with words such as "tsable" and "srouch." What we have done in these examples is to violate the rules of the grammar of our language. In example (1) we've not followed syntactic rules of order. In addition, in examples (2) and (3) we have violated syntactic rules for placement of negative and plural markers in a sentence. In example (4) we have violated semantic/syntactic vocabulary or lexical selection rules, and in example (5) we've not followed the rules of our language for sound combination.

The examples given of both well-formed and improperly formed sentences show that a language has categories and rules for combining these categories that operate at three different structural levels; the sound level, the word level, and the utterance or sentence level. The combinatory rules that operate on the sound level are called *phonological rules,* and the categories are called *phonemes.* The rules that operate on the word level are called *morphophonological* and *lexical rules,* and the categories are called *morphemes.* The rules that operate on the utterance level are called *semantic* and *syntactic* (or *semantax*) rules, and the categories are called *phrases* or *clauses.* The levels of categories and rules are nested into each other. As we said at the beginning of this section, sounds are combined into words and words (morphemes) are combined into sentences. We have now added the fact that phrases and clauses are combined to make sentences. Some examples are given in Figure 1-1. Examples A and B in Figure 1-1 are sentences that are made up of phrases. Examples C and D are sentences that are made up of clauses, which in turn are made up of phrases.

Earlier it was stated that human language and animal communication systems are considered to be distinct from each other on the basis of at least two factors. The first was the symbolic and arbitrary nature of the categories of human language and the fact that these categories are used to create unique utterances that can be infinitely variable. That is, we can, potentially, create totally new utterances all the time and not ever have to say exactly the same thing twice. Yet speaker-listeners of the same language or dialect are able to understand each other because they share the grammar of that language or dialect. It is this factor (grammar) that has been described thus far. The other factor that makes human language different from animal communication — how it is used — will be discussed in the following section.

The Use of Language

Just as there are particular terms that are used to talk about the grammar or structure of language (for example, morphophonology), so is there a term used to talk about the *use* of language. This term is *pragmatics.* The categories and rules of grammar have been described in detailed ways for many years,

A. At the level of the morpheme:

(The) (boy)(s) (kiss)(ed) (the) (girl)(s).

B. At the level of the phrase:

((The boys)) ((did not kiss) (the girls)).

C. At the level of the clause (and sentence):

((The boy went to school) and (the girl went to school)).

D. At the level of the clause (and sentence):

((The boy (who kissed the girl) ran away)).

Figure 1-1 Segments within the sentence at the level of morpheme, phrase, and clause.

although controversy exists about these descriptions. And, the categories and rules of pragmatics have been the domain of philosophers for many years and are just beginning to be described by linguists and psycholinguists.

Categories concerning the use of language are at the sentence level and beyond the sentence level. The categories that operate at the sentence or utterance level have been called "speech acts" and those that operate beyond are called "conversation" and "discourse." Speech acts convey the intents of the speaker. For example, the speaker might want to make a statement about something, to negate a statement, or to make a request or a promise. Speech acts are used in conversational exchanges. Discourse consists of the types of speech acts used in conversation and, also, of different types of acts that are specific to the type of discourse. For example, in story telling, initial utterances convey the speaker's intention to set the stage for the story rather than simply to make statements. The category of discourse is sometimes used to refer to conversation and is sometimes used to refer to a long treatment of a subject, as in a narrative, lecture, or speech. The category called conversation refers to verbal exchange between two or more participants.

Engaging in conversation requires that all participants observe certain rules. For example, there are rules about how to take a turn in conversation. It is insufficient, however, to simply take a turn. One must take a turn appropriately. If one conversational partner were met by silence on the part of the other, this could certainly kill a conversation. However, certain responses to certain queries could, equally, deal a death blow. For example, if one participant were to ask "Would you like to go to the movies?" and the other were to reply by reciting the Gettysburg Address, the conversation would be equally dead.

Referring to unshared information as if it were shared, being ambiguous in reference, or being unintelligible are also potential assassins of conversation. For example, if a friend were to tell you "John and Stella are getting married," when you don't know who John and Stella are, he would be referring to unshared information. An example of the second kind of killer, ambiguity in reference, would be your partner's request that you "get the red book," when there are at least three red books in view. A final type of conversation stopper is unintelligibility, as when a partner continuously speaks softly into his chest. In summary, taking a turn, taking it appropriately, and being clear in reference and in speech are all rules of conversation (Clark & Clark, 1977).

Speech acts (Grice, 1975) are defined as utterances that carry out an intention of a speaker and are understood by the listener as doing that. Just as speaker–listeners of the same language or dialect share the structural categories and rules of that language or dialect, so do speaker–listeners share common speech act rules and pragmatic rules. Intentions are conveyed in speech acts by several means. If the speaker wishes to talk about a proposition (whether the world is flat) and wishes to make a statement about the proposition, negate it, or question the proposition, he or she would use particular structural forms.

To state the proposition, a declarative sentence would be used ("The world is flat"); to negate it, a negative sentence form would be used ("The world is not flat"); and to question, a question form would be used ("Is the world flat?"). The selection of particular sentence forms is one way of conveying intent. If I wanted to inform my conversational partner that the books that he was looking for were on the table, I would probably make a statement, "The books are on the table." If I wanted to let him know that amongst the things he was looking for it was the books that were on the table, I might say "The *books* are on the table," stressing the word "books" to let him know that they and not the spaghetti were on the table. If he had been pestering me about where the books were, I might say "*The books are on the table,*" stressing each word, wearing an annoyed expression, and gesturing emphatically in the direction of the books. In summary, when I say something in a conversation, I usually wish to convey more than the meaning of the words in a certain combination. To do this I will use words in a certain combination, *and* add particular stress and intonation patterns, *and* use particular facial expressions and particular gestures.

Given this description of how a speech act might be carried out, it should be clear that selection of particular speech acts and, certainly, their use in conversation are highly dependent on situational factors. You might not have stressed all the words in the sentence if your conversational partner had not been pestering you. Even though he had been pestering you, you might not have stressed *any* of the words, or used emphatic gestures, if he were your supervisor. You certainly would not have had an annoyed expression. Some of the situational factors that govern how speech acts are conveyed are the conversational history, the physical situation, the nature of the relation among the participants in the conversation, and the social rules of conversation in the language or dialect community.

The last factor mentioned, the social rules of conversation in your language or dialect community, governs not only how speech acts are conveyed but which speech acts you will consider using under what circumstances and with whom. Such rules will also govern broad factors such as topic of conversation and narrow factors such as the degree of politeness you will convey by your selection of particular words and combinations of words. For example, it seems unlikely that you would discuss your personal problems with a casual acquaintance you bump into on the street. Nor would you be likely to first address this person by saying "Hiya blabbermouth!" although you might do both with an old friend.

Figure 1-2 graphically represents those factors that need to be taken into account, by both speaker and listener, to appropriately engage in conversation. There is a need to remember both linguistic and extralinguistic context factors that are taking place and have taken place. This, at least theoretically, places a sizeable memory load on conversational participants.

Such rules of conversation exist in all language and dialect communities,

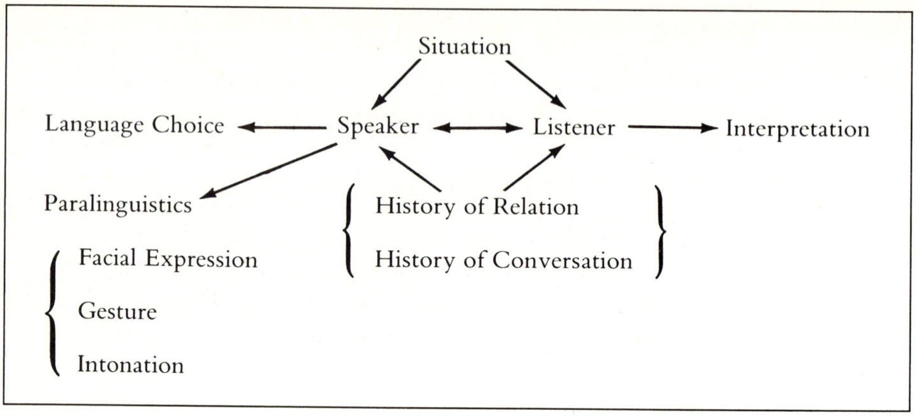

Figure 1-2 Factors that play a role in the generation of speech acts.

but they may vary markedly from community to community. A very well known and discussed example is the degree of politeness that is required in formal and informal exchanges by members of differing communities and how the appropriate degree of politeness is conveyed (Gumperz, 1979). Use of prosodic features (intonation and stress), gestures, facial expressions, and eye contact rules may, in particular, differ markedly from community to community (LaFrance & Mayo, 1976). The structure of conversation or discourse and the rules of turn-taking in conversation may also differ. These differences are usually much more subtle than are structural differences. It is easy to know when someone is speaking a foreign language. It is sometimes difficult to detect the fact that a somewhat different set of conversational rules is being used.

Differences Among Languages and Dialects

Although an important quality in being a human language user is the ability to acquire any language or dialect, it is important to point out that what a child acquires is what the child is exposed to. One possible difference, the number and type of speech sounds or phonemes in a language, has already been referred to. Differences may exist in any level of the categories and rules of both the *grammar* and *pragmatics*; that is, in both *the structure of the language known* and in *the use of this knowledge*. Much of what will be covered in this book will pertain to the American-English-speaking child. However, there are differences among American-English-speaking children that reflect differences in both linguistic and cultural experiences. Such differences are discussed in Chapter Eleven.

Why Is Language Acquired?

Acquiring language is probably not a simple task. The child has to acquire the categories and rules that are used at all levels of the grammar and all the rules used in conversation and discourse. There are many categories and rules, and their uses are variable. However, all normally developing children, apparently, go about acquiring language with ease and success. The explanations for this have been quite varied and, also, have led to heated controversies. These controversies concern the nature of the human as a learner and, therefore, are not limited to the question of language acquisition. The various theories that have been developed to explain language acquisition are presented in Chapter Two and several topics that are important for explanation are discussed in Chapters Three, Four, and Five. Both the theories and the topics have had very important effects on the assessment and teaching of language to children and adults.

Theories of Language Acquisition

Some theorists attribute the child's acquisition of language to his *innate biological* equipment. Others propose that the child's *innate cognitive* abilities account for the process taking place. The distinction between these two sets of theorists is that the first proposes that language development is separate from cognitive development whereas the latter proposes that language development is dependent on cognition. A third group of theorists proposes that language acquisition takes place because of the special interaction between the child's cognitive abilities and the *learnability of language*. Finally, some theorists attempt to explain language acquisition as they explain all other learning, by *Stimulus-Response-Reward* connections, either of the direct kind, S-R-R, or of the mediated kind, S-r-s-r-s-R.

Theorists of these four groups have been categorized as: innatists, S-R-R and elaborated S-R-R theorists, cognitivists, and learnability theorists. Keeping in mind what we know about language, the theories of each of these groups is analyzed in Chapter Two, primarily in terms of three issues: the reasons they provide for the child being able to acquire language; their explanations of the process of development; and their descriptions of what the child knows when the child knows a language. Some of the evidence used to support each theory is also discussed. Again, keeping in mind what we know about language, the possibility that different aspects of language may be accounted for by different theories will also be discussed. Further, the effect that each theory can have on the methodology used to teach language is discussed.

These groups of theories have led to extended research on a number of related topics: the relation between cognition and language, the innate capacity to acquire language, and the role of input in language development. Each of these topics, in turn, has led to certain positions or suggestions about teaching language to populations who develop normally and to populations with developmental disabilities.

Cognition and Language

A very large problem in trying to determine the relation between cognition and language is that there are varying definitions of cognition or cognitive development. In Chapter Three the positions of three developmental psychologists, Piaget, Vygotsky, and Werner, on what cognition is and, therefore, on what the relation between cognition and language is, are presented. These psychologists have had a profound influence on the research being carried out to examine the relationship. The results of this research is presented in terms of sequences in development (which comes first — cognition or language?) and what the sequences can mean in terms of the child's overall development.

An alternative to these views is an information processing model of linguistic and nonlinguistic cognitive development. This model has also been used in examining the relation between cognition and language, particularly the relation between attention, perception, memory, and language development. Some of the theorizing and experimentation in this area has been based on computer modeling of learning.

Views about the relation between cognition and language development have affected views about the capacity of particular populations of children (and adults) to acquire language and, therefore, how language teaching should be approached with these populations. These groups are: the deaf, the mentally retarded, and second language acquirers from low SES (socioeconomic status) backgrounds. Findings with these groups on the relation between cognition and language shed further light on the matter.

Capacity to Acquire Language

There are two ways in which you can think about a human infant's ability to acquire language. One is that he is uniquely biologically preprogrammed to do so. Another is that he is uniquely preprogrammed to take advantage of the special environment that he is presented with. From this point of view, human infants' biological, social, and cognitive readiness *all* contribute to their special ability to acquire language — not simply their biological readiness. It is this view that is explored in Chapter Four.

Under the heading of biological readiness there are several avenues that researchers have explored. One is the comparison of subhuman primates' acquisition of man-made symbol systems (signs, representative plastic chips, written words, and so on) and the similarities and differences between that and language acquisition in the child. Another is the structural and functional uniqueness of the parts of the biological system that go into producing language: a person's brain, hearing system, and vocal tract. The effects of early and late brain damage, deafness, and cerebral palsy, each of which can discretely affect the different parts of the biological system, have been examined to determine the relative necessity of each part for language acquisition. Findings from studies with brain-damaged individuals and adult second-language acquirers are used to discuss the "critical period" hypothesis.

Both cognitive and social readiness to acquire language are areas of research that are receiving a great deal of attention. Researchers have become increasingly aware of the infant's remarkable ability to process auditory and visual information, integrate the two, and remember the resulting information. There is evidence of the social readiness of the infant to communicate and to acquire and use language. This evidence comes from a variety of sources; for example, very early speaker identification, use of non-cry vocalization during the first year of life, early conversational turn-taking, and identification of speaker affect by means of intonation, stress, and facial expression. The biological versus learned bases for these early cognitive and social behaviors will be discussed in Chapter Four.

Input and Language Development

After a number of years during which child language researchers were, apparently, uninterested in the effect of language input on the child's language development, there was an enthusiastic rebirth of such interest.

Three questions on the topic of input and language development will be addressed in Chapter Five.

The first question is: How do caregivers modify their language according to the age of the child they are speaking with? A new term, "motherese," has been coined to talk about the way in which caregivers talk to very young children as compared to older children and adults. The characteristics of so-called motherese and how these characteristics change over the first three years of life will be described. The second question is: Why do caregivers speak in a special way to children? A number of factors have been said to account for this special speech style to young children. These include universal cultural factors, affective factors, communicative factors, and the role that caregivers assume they need to play when talking to a young child; that is, the role of modeler. Which set of factors plays the most crucial role in producing this behavior has been explored in a number of studies that examine communicative interaction between child and caregiver over the early years of life.

The final question covered in Chapter Five is the most relevant one: What effect does this special behavior have on language development? There are findings that suggest that the special language of adults to children is all-important to their development, and there are findings that support the opposite position. These opposing findings, and those of other less partisan researchers, are discussed in light of: 1) what they suggest about the rate and "quality" of structural language development in children who have received varying degrees of the special language, and 2) what they suggest concerning the development of the communicative aspects of language. The results of such studies are most important for the planning of intervention with populations of children who are thought to have language problems. Therefore, the chapter closes with a discussion of the findings of studies that have examined communicative interaction between children of different socioeconomic and cultural groups and their caregivers and between deaf, blind, and mentally retarded children and their caregivers.

How Is Language Acquired?

To answer this question, the sequence of acquisition of aspects of each component of language will be examined. One can then think about possible explanations for the sequence found and come up with possible answers to the question. One cannot do this when there are no data to think about.

Chapters Six, Seven, Eight, and Nine deal with the development of the four components of language that were described previously under the heading "What Is Acquired?" These are:

- pragmatics
- lexicon (or vocabulary)
- semantax (word combinations to express meaning)
- morphophonology (sounds and sound combinations to generate morphemes)

Since the child is in the process of acquiring language, not components of language, it might be more appropriate to talk about periods of language development to get the answer to the question of how the process of language development takes place. However, an argument can be made that the different components of language development require the use of different processing mechanisms and, therefore, to put them all together would hide the developmental processes rather than make them clear. It is this position that is taken in the book. As each component is discussed, the particular processing mechanisms that may be required for acquisition of this component are also discussed. In addition, the way in which each component relates to the others is discussed to make clear similarities as well as differences in processing. Finally, the dependencies of each component on the others is also discussed in order to address the question of interdependencies in development among the components of language.

Various models have been developed to describe the processes of comprehension and production of language. These models can be grossly labelled as "top-down," "bottom-up," and "parallel." Each of these models suggests a certain sequence in the use of linguistic information from each component of the language as shown in Figure 1-3.

It seems reasonable to suggest, and a number of researchers have suggested, that these models describe the sequence of acquisition of various components of the language. That is, some suggest that the language acquisition process begins with morphophonological acquisition because it's a "bottom-

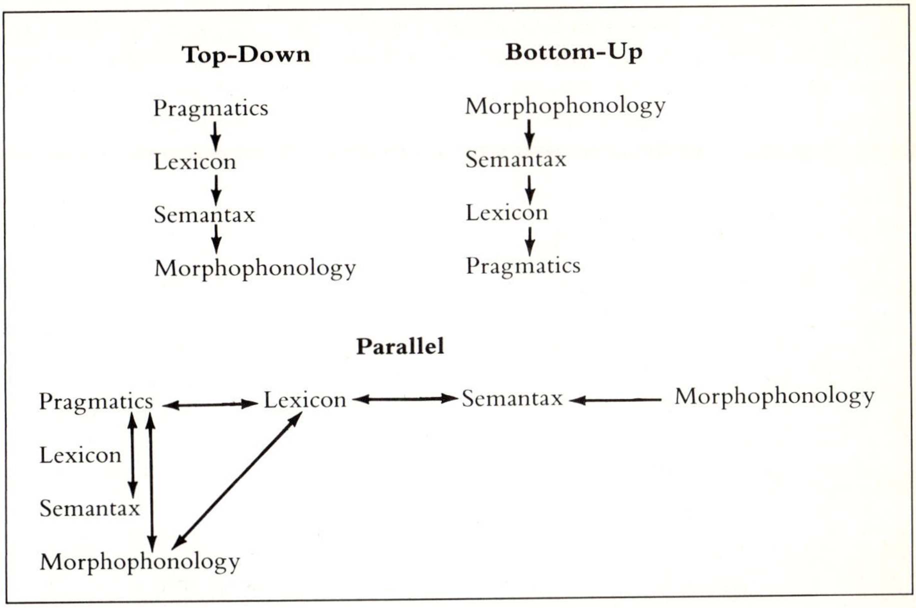

Figure 1-3 Models of processing among the components of language.

up" process, or that it begins with pragmatics because it's a "top-down" process, or that it begins with a little bit of everything because it's a "parallel" process. The parallel position seems to describe most adequately the processes of comprehension and production of conversation and discourse and to describe the acquisition of structural knowledge once the lexical period begins. Therefore, one can think of the process of acquisition as occurring simultaneously within each component of the language and across components.

To capture the notion of interdependencies among components, Chapters Six through Nine address both the question of what special processing mechanisms are required for acquisition of a component's categories and rules *and* the question of what the relations are among the components. The first part of each chapter presents a description of the types of linguistic categories and combinatory rules that characterize each component. This helps clarify the domains of knowledge that are required for each component. This clarification can, in turn, help in understanding what the child has to be able to do in order to acquire knowledge in each component. For example, although morphophonological and lexical acquisition both require discrimination between categories and generalizations about categories, there are different demands placed on memory in the two types of discrimination. Additionally, different cues are used in the two different types of categorization.

The second part of each chapter describes the content and sequence of acquisition of these rules during three developmental periods: infancy, early childhood, and middle childhood and "later." This discussion of developments during the same periods for all components of the language provides further information about relations among the components. In this section of each chapter, the general trends that have been observed in the acquisition (but not *rate* of acquisition) of each component by American-English-speaking children is presented. The general trends provide information about how much and what kinds of linguistic information the child can deal with at varying ages. In addition to general trends, there have been some findings in some components of the language that suggest that groups of normally developing children may display differences in the sequence due to reasons that are importantly related to the processes by which language is acquired. These differences are discussed, along with general developmental trends. The findings for each component of the language are presented in the following order: pragmatics, lexicon, semantax, and morphophonology.

Certain developmental trends seem to mark differences in what the child knows about any aspect of language during differing periods. Rules that appear to be universal are acquired during infancy. It has been hypothesized that the child first acquires surface structure rules for marking categories and relations in the language that are perceptually salient and/or communicatively important. The child acquires some aspects of all the components of language during this period, but those aspects are the ones that are most clearly indicated by the situation and the language. During early childhood the specific rules of the language are acquired and the child becomes a very efficient speaker-listener. However, it is not until middle childhood that the child is able to think and talk about many aspects of language (metalinguize) and see relations among the categories and rules of the language. At the end of each chapter some of the outstanding developmental changes that occur during each period for each aspect are presented in a table. A comparison of the tables for each aspect clearly reveals the trends in development for each period.

Pragmatics

Chapter Six, Pragmatic Development, begins with a restatement of the definition of pragmatic rules: rules for the use of language in contexts. The two categories of rules that have been described and are discussed are rules for conveying communicative intent (or "speech acts") and rules for participating in conversation and engaging in discourse. There are, then, two aspects in which developmental changes occur. As was noted in the description of pragmatic rules, an array of social factors need to be taken into account when one participates in conversation and engages in discourse. In addition, there are cognitive factors that appear to influence the degree of success with which these two types of communication can be carried out. There is an intimate relation between semantax and pragmatic development which suggests that there are, in addition, linguistic factors that play a role in pragmatic development.

The chapter discusses developmental changes in the types of speech acts that are used over time and the developmental changes in how speech acts are realized. What speech acts children use, and how they use them, both change in time. The chapter also discusses developmental changes in the child's ability to effectively engage in conversation and in the child's ability to produce various types of discourse, such as reporting on an event or telling a story. The questions addressed are: What social, cognitive, and linguistic factors account for some of the developmental changes in pragmatic competence? and What aspects of pragmatic development can best be accounted for by each of these factors?

Lexicon

Lexical acquisition, or the development of the understanding of the meaning of words and of word classes, plays a central role in the child's development of language as a whole. Why this should be so and how the process of lexical acquisition takes place are explored in Chapter Seven.

There have been varying views of how words are represented in the mind: as perceptual images, as bundles of different types of features (semantic, syntactic, phonological, and eventually, orthographic features), or as hierarchical and related networks. These different views have different implications for how we understand what children know when they know the meaning of a word and how they acquire such knowledge. Both the process of word acquisition and the product of this acquisition involve knowledge of the fact that one word can represent many instances (for example, the word "chair" represents an array of objects that differ across the dimensions of size and shape) and that more than one word can represent one "thing," as in the case of synonomy (for example, the words "large" and "big" may both be used to represent the same dimensions of an object or person). The big question raised by these views and facts is, How are word meanings encoded and stored in memory over time?

Two aspects of lexical acquisition are the focus of the discussion of lexical developments during infancy, early childhood, and middle childhood and later. One aspect is the semantic fields in which lexical items are acquired. Semantic fields are subdivisions of contentive words — nouns, verbs, adjectives, and adverbs — into classes. For example, two semantic fields of the noun category are "animal" and "furniture." The order in which verbs (words for actions or states) or nouns (words for objects) or determiners such as adjectives (words for attributes) are acquired and the order in which items in these classes are acquired help us to understand the process of lexical acquisition.

The second aspect to be discussed is what we know about the changing nature of the representation of words — from representation for single objects and events to representation for classes of objects and events, and from single representations to multiple ones. Findings on this topic are important in evaluating the validity of the theoretical views discussed first in the chapter and, of course, in understanding the factors that play a role in lexical acquisition. The bases for lexical development appear to be both cognitive and linguistic or, more specifically, conceptual and semantactic. How these factors account for both the sequence and content of lexical acquisition is discussed in the final section of the chapter.

Semantax

Many recent descriptions of the grammar of languages have attempted to convey the notion that the meaning of an utterance (if not a group of utterances) and its communicative intent, as indicated by *form,* are conveyed by the words selected and the arrangement of these words. The term *semantactic* has been coined to refer to these descriptions. How these descriptions attempt to do this is discussed first in Chapter Eight.

Utterances convey a relation among actors, actions, and objects in place, time, and manner, and convey this with a certain intent. For example, in utterances such as "The boy eats the apple" and "Will the boy eat the apple?" the relation expressed by the speaker and understood by the listener is the same, even though the communicative intents of the two utterances are different. Both utterances contain the same relation of actor (boy) and action (eat) as well as object (apple). However, in the first utterance the intent is to make a statement, and in the second it is to ask a question. In distinction to the above, in the two utterances "The boy chases the girl" and "The girl chases the boy," the communicative intent of making a statement is the same. However, the relation expressed (that is, who is doing the chasing and who is being chased, or the actor–action–object relation) is different. As you can see, semantax rules convey both relations and, to some extent, intent. As stated, other aspects of the message also convey intent. The speaker also uses the situation and paralinguistics (intonation, stress, facial expression, and gesture). In addition to conveying relations among the words used, semantax rules make it impossible to put just any words into this kind of actor–action–object utterance. For example, such rules would make unlikely such utterances as "The apple kisses the boy" or "The boy kisses the green."

A number of theoreticians have viewed the process of development of word combination categories and rules as a semantactic process. That is, the child is thought to be *simultaneously* acquiring word knowledge and knowledge of the possibilities for combinations of these words. Research that has examined the interaction of lexical and structural developments is discussed in Chapter Eight. The sequence of structural developmental changes that take place from *holophrases* (single word or phrase utterances) to the development of phrases and simple sentences have been described by a number of researchers. Developments that result in expansion of sentences, during later early childhood and middle childhood and even later, have also been examined. These developmental changes are discussed in terms of the changing forms of the child's semantax knowledge rather than by a simple description of syntactic changes. Findings concerning developmental changes in the use of semantactic knowledge, from *intuitive use* to an *awareness of form,* are also discussed. These abilities have been termed *metalinguistic.*

The bases for the development of semantax knowledge should, at least theoretically, include those factors that play a role in lexical and pragmatic development as well as word combination knowledge. By definition, semantactic knowledge includes all three types of knowledge: word meanings, how to convey different intents by different forms of word combination, and how to combine words to express relations. In addition, research findings concerning developmental changes in short-term memory strategies are reviewed as a possible explanation for developmental changes in semantax knowledge. All of these factors are discussed to examine how the process of semantactic development takes place.

Morphophonology

To understand language, the child must translate what he hears (or sees, in the case of sign language) into units that are recognizable and meaningful. The morphophonological system of the language is the bridge to that translation. How the child goes about acquiring knowledge of that system is the subject of Chapter Nine.

The first section of the chapter describes what the child has to learn in order to have knowledge of the system. This consists of learning the phonological characteristics or sounds that make up the morphemes of the language. For example, the child must learn what sequence of sounds means "boy" versus what sequence means "toy." The child must also learn that some morphemes don't mean anything by themselves but must be bound to other morphemes to convey meaning. The /s/ at the end of "mats" and the /z/ at the end of "bees" are examples of such morphemes. The suprasegmental or prosodic features of the language (intonation and stress), as we have already found in the discussion of pragmatics, also convey meanings. How the sounds of the language are sequenced and how intonation and stress are applied are functions of the rules of the morphophonological system of the language.

In the developmental section of the chapter, what the child appears to know about each aspect of the system during the varying periods of development is discussed. There appear to be three developmental periods that are remarkably different from each other, and the differences between them provide important clues to how morphophonological development takes place. The first stage described is what the child knows about sound production and perception during a large part of infancy. This period is traditionally known as the "babbling" or pre-lexical (before words) period. The shift from processing sounds to processing words and phrases occurs sometime during the second year of life. Findings concerning early word perception and production provide interesting, if incomplete, evidence about the bases for this shift. Later morphophonological development indicates that lexical knowledge plays a crucial role in determining the phonological characteristics of morphemes, both those that are meaningful alone and those that are bound, and the rules for permissible sequences of sounds. A final shift occurs in the child's use of morphophonological knowledge similar to that observed in semantax development: there is, first, an intuitive use of knowledge and, then, an aware use of knowledge. This awareness plays a vital role in learning to read. These are the developmental changes that are discussed in detail in Chapter Nine.

Reasons for some of the developmental changes that occur appear to be biological. For example, the ability to produce some sounds and sound sequences requires greater control of the jaw, tongue, and lips than does the production of other sounds and sequences. Some of the changes seem to be due to developmental changes in memory strategies; that is, the older child can keep in mind three syllables (as in "umbrella") whereas the younger one can only process two syllables (as in "baby"). The order in which both the categories and rules of the system are, in general, acquired sheds some light on some of the factors involved in bringing about developmental changes. As with the other components of the language, some of the factors are based on the relation between this component of the language and other components.

Differences in Language Development and Learning

The last section of the book will deal with some questions very important to clinicians and to educators who are concerned with "special" populations of children. These questions have to do with the effect of differences that are internal, so-called *state differences,* and the effect of differences that are external, *environmental differences*.

Every child is different from every other child in terms of biological equipment. However, there are some biological differences among children that mark one group as developing language normally and other groups, in comparison, as somehow deviating from the norm. The questions that arise about these differences are: What are the effects of different types of biological differences on patterns of language development? How are these differences related to cognitive processing? What kinds of educational intervention are proposed to accommodate for these differences? These questions will be discussed in Chapter Ten, Language Disorder.

Just as children are different from each other in terms of their biological state, so are they different from each other in terms of their environment. So far as language development is concerned, these differences may take the obvious forms of how much and what kind of language the child hears (or sees). These differences could, theoretically, affect the child's knowledge of the structures of the language. Environmental differences may, more subtly, affect what the child knows and thinks about the use of language. Finally, both kinds of difference could affect the child's performance in school. The differences that will be discussed under the heading of language differences (in Chapter Eleven) have received a great deal of attention by researchers: dialect variation, bilingualism, and second language acquisition. The questions asked about these populations are:

- □ What are the patterns of language development in children with different kinds of linguistic experience?
- □ How are these patterns related to cognitive processing?
- □ What kinds of educational intervention have been proposed to accommodate these differences?

The final topic discussed in this text, in Chapter Twelve, is the role of language in learning, specifically, how language is used to learn about the physical and social world both before and after entering school. The relation between acquisition of written language knowledge (reading and writing) is clearly one of the most important special ways in which language is used to learn.

Language Disorders

In Chapter Ten, three themes are presented and discussed. The first deals with defining a language disorder. There are varying views on (1) what a language disorder is and how such a disorder should be defined; (2) whether types of disorder represent steps on a continuum or discrete categorizations; and (3) whether a disorder is a delay or deviance in language development. The role that society plays in developing these definitions is clear in a number of examples of populations that have been labelled language disordered.

The second theme in the chapter is the difference among language disordered children in their patterns of language development, both within and across diagnostically labelled groups. Some of the differences appear to be due to differences in the kinds of information that are available to the child and others to how the input information is processed. These differences point to biological and cognitive factors as playing the most important causal role in affecting language knowledge and use. However, there are some findings that suggest that social factors can have an effect as well. Altogether, recent findings concerning the language development of these children are remarkably different from past findings. The reasons for these remarkable changes shed light on the issue of what a language disorder is and why it occurs.

There have been dramatic changes not only in how the language behavior of varying groups of language disordered children has been described and viewed, but also in the intervention approaches that have been suggested. Throughout Chapter Ten there are references to some of these new approaches to the education of children with a language disorder, approaches that reflect a better understanding of the behavior of these children and the causes of this behavior.

Language Differences

The populations discussed in Chapter Eleven are very different from the populations described in Chapter Ten. There is no evidence that these children differ developmentally from the norm of their *group* as do the children with language disorder. There is no evidence that there is any marked biological variation that distinguishes them from children with whom they are often compared. The three populations discussed are those who have been labelled nonmainstream or minority dialect speakers, bilinguals, and second language acquirers.

Of the three types of difference to be examined, only bilingualism has been studied in children whose families are of middle and upper-middle socioeconomic status (SES). Much of the research on the processes of language acquisition and the learning of language of the other two groups has been done with children whose families are of low SES. Therefore, findings about the patterns of language development in these groups of children are a product not only of their different linguistic experiences, but also of all other factors that make life different for working-class and poor children as compared to middle-class and upper-middle-class children.

Three areas are discussed under the heading of difference. The first is variation in input. Sociocultural variables have been found to affect the amount and the structure of the input that the child receives and the topics of discourse that the child hears and participates in. These variables have also been found to affect the kinds of social pressures exerted through language use.

The second area is the effect of this variation in input on the child's knowledge of the structures of language and the rules of use of language in the culture. Topics in this area concerning structure are: features of Black and Hispanic dialects, language storage and processing in compound and coordinate bilinguals, universals and interference in second language acquisition, code switching, and the development of pidgins and creoles. Topics concerning development of pragmatic rules are: conversational rules, stylistic changes due to situation, organization of discourse, domains of discourse, and metalinguistic abilities.

The third area discussed in this chapter is one that has created a great deal of heat: cognitive development in bilingual children, second language acquirers, and nonmainstream dialect users. Not only has there been a lot of controversy in this area, but also the findings and *interpretation* of findings have been conflicting. Possible reasons for the controversy and conflict are discussed in Chapter Eleven and related to past and present educational intervention programs with these children.

The Role of Language in Learning

The role of language in learning is discussed in the last chapter, Chapter Twelve, for two reasons. First, it is logical to first explain the process of learning language before showing how language is used to learn. Therefore, the what, why, and how of language acquisition are discussed in the first nine chapters. Second, it also seemed logical to present what has been found about the patterns of language learning in two populations that are or have been said to be different from some hypothetical norm in language learning as a prelude. The findings with these two populations make some of the issues clearer. For example, an examination of whether and how bilingualism affects cognitive development helps to specify more clearly the role of language in learning. The process of reading acquisition in speakers of nonmainstream dialects can be better understood after a discussion of sociocultural variables in use of language.

The first section of Chapter Twelve deals with those specific aspects of learning that have been found to be highly dependent on the use of language: obtaining information (through communicative interaction in general and through questioning specifically), focussing attention, discriminating, solving problems, and remembering.

The next section of the chapter examines the role of language development (in particular, metalinguistic processing) in learning to read and write. Four topics are covered in this examination. The first is a discussion of the varying models that have been proposed to describe the relation between reading and oral language knowledge and use. The second is a description of the stages of acquisition of reading from print awareness to comprehending connected discourse. The role that oral language knowledge has been found to play in decoding words, comprehending sentences, and in comprehending and remembering passages is discussed next. For example, there are developmental changes that occur in reading competence that seem to reflect the development of automaticity at the lexical or word recognition level. This automaticity, in turn, is dependent on how quickly the reader can access the meaning of the printed word. Similarly, entrenched knowledge of semantax relations is required for automatic processing of sentences. The fourth topic discussed is the relations between different oral and written language problems. For example, children who are delayed in language acquisition appear to have different reading problems than those who have specific word retrieval problems.

The third section of Chapter Twelve discusses writing. Writing as a process rather than simply a product is now being explored by a number of researchers. Some have examined the relation between reading and writing. Others have examined the relation between speaking, in an interactive situation, and writing, in which no feedback is available. Still others are examining the differences between good and poor writers of the same age.

Throughout this chapter references are made to the implications of recent research in these areas for the teaching of reading and writing — in particular, for teaching children who vary in their rate of development of language, in their linguistic knowledge, and in their linguistic and cultural experience. This chapter, like every chapter in the book, is concerned with the relation between research and educational application.

Chapter Two

Theories of Language Development

The first question that might be asked in a discussion of theories of language development is: Why discuss them at all? Regardless of which theory might best explain language development, all normally developing children acquire language. Therefore, for applied purposes, it seems useless to be concerned with explanatory theory.

The fact is that clinicians and teachers have been very much affected by what theorists have said about the reasons for language acquisition. This has been true in intervention with language disordered children and in the education of normally developing children, and it makes sense that this should be so. Theories of language development contain assumptions about the learning abilities of human learners, the conditions under which learning takes place, and what it is that children learn when they learn a language — all matters that are obviously of concern to clinicians and teachers.

In this chapter four schools of theory on language development are examined. Three of them have been around for some time and all books on language development refer to them. These three schools are roughly labelled as: *innatist, S-R-R,* and *cognitivist.* The fourth and newer theory is labelled here, again roughly, *learnability.* Theorists arguing for each of these theories — from both very different and overlapping points of view — attempt to describe the human learner, the conditions under which learning takes place, and what is learned. In addition, each school of theorists attempts to account for a group of "facts" that have been gathered on language development. The word "facts" is in quotation marks because each group of theorists incorporates a somewhat different subset of facts and certainly interprets these facts in different ways.

The assumptions that each theory makes about the matters of concern are described in this chapter, along with how each accounts for the so-called facts of language development. The relation of each theory to what we know about the language to be acquired will also be examined. Finally, the history of the effect that each theory has had on intervention and education will be presented. To set the stage, the so-called set of facts will be discussed first.

What Theories Need to Account For: The "Facts"

The first fact that is very strongly claimed by three of the four theories is that *language development takes place in a set sequence and that this sequence is universal.* Children throughout the world acquire and use some aspects of language before others. For example, they produce sounds (or signs) before they produce words, they produce words or jargon phrases before they produce sentences, and they produce simple sentences before they produce complex ones. They talk about the here and now before they talk about things removed in space and time. The degree of detail that each theory claims is universal differs from theory to theory. Thus some theories assume a rough universal sequence, such as that described above, whereas others cite detailed evidence of a fixed sequence of phonological, morphophonological, and semantactic structures, pragmatic rules, and lexical acquisitions. The only school of theory that does not refer to a universal sequence is the S-R-R school.

A second fact which theorists attempt to account for is that *a great deal of knowledge about language is acquired over a fairly short period of time.* By age two many children are combining words, by age three they are producing sentences that are complex as well as simple, and by age five, when they enter school, they are sophisticated conversationalists who know, for example, how to bargain as well as how to state and question.

Another so-called fact is that *children hear language that is highly variable, takes place in time in a connected sequence, and then disappears.* Despite these characteristics of the language they hear, children determine the categories and rules in the language.

One of the many aspects of variability of language heard by the child is determined by the acoustic product of speech. Not only are the same words produced somewhat differently by different speakers but the same word may be produced somewhat differently by the same speaker on different occasions and in different contexts. Therefore, the word will sound acoustically different to the hearer on different occasions and in different contexts. This variation alone could cause a great deal of confusion, and yet the child somehow figures out that a sequence of sounds that is roughly like — for example, the word "hat" — is, indeed, always the same word — "hat." In a sentence such as "Put your hat on," each morpheme overlaps its neighbor. The sentence may sound like "Putchuraton." And yet the child figures out that this sequence should be segmented into four morphemes. He does this even though he hears sequences such as this for an extremely brief period of time.

The last fact to be accounted for by any theory is that *the child produces language that he couldn't possibly have heard at all.* These unique productions appear at all structural levels of the language. For example, children have been found to produce speech sound contrasts that do not exist in their language at all, such as the initial sound in "ship" as /ts/. They produce plural nouns such as "childrenziz" and past tense verbs such as "runned." They produce lexical items that do not exist in the vocabulary of their language such as "buggieboo" for ghost. They produce sentences such as "The door closed me."

There are other statements that theorists make that can't be listed as facts since they are open to dispute. These include such statements as the "fact" that language is learned but not taught. The four "facts" discussed in the preceding paragraphs are also open to some dispute. However, there is some evidence that:

1. Some universals exist in the sequence of acquisition of different parts of a language by children throughout the world.
2. A lot of language is acquired by the very young child over a short period of time, and the amount of language learned and the shortness of

the length of time needed to learn it is never matched again during maturation.

3. The language heard by the child is variable, appears in a connected sequence, and disappears as it is being produced.
4. Children produce utterances for which they have had no model.

How each group of theorists has dealt with these facts, as well as with the matters of concern — the learning abilities of children, the conditions under which they learn, and what it is they learn when they learn a language — is discussed below.

Major Theories of Language Development

The schools of theory are presented here in historical order from the earliest to the latest. It is interesting to observe that there have been changes in theoretical positions over time that have come about by major advances in either psychology or linguistics. Each discipline has, in turn, remarkably affected views about this developmental process, and the influence of one discipline has been replaced by the influence of another over a comparatively short period of time — about thirty years.

S-R-R Theory

The S-R-R theory dominated both psychology and linguistics in the 1950s. The name that should immediately come to mind when discussing S-R-R theory in general as well as when it is applied to language development is that of B. F. Skinner (Skinner, 1957). In addition to Skinner, there have been and there continue to be a number of researchers who consider that the processing of language (Osgood, 1966) and the language development process (White, 1970) can best be explained by the tenets of S-R-R theory or mediated S-R-R theory. Very simply stated, the mediated S-R-R theory suggests that external stimuli can elicit an internal response which can elicit internal stimuli that lead to an external response (S-r-s-R). These internal responses and stimuli act as mediators between external stimuli and responses and are the bases for the generalizations made across similar stimuli and responses.

Characteristics of S-R-R Theory. The learning process has been described by theorists of this school as a process of forming stimulus-response-reward chains. These chains come about because of the nature of the environment and, it can be presumed, the nature of the learner. The environment provides the stimuli, in this case language stimuli. The learner provides the responses, either comprehension or production of aspects of language, and the environment then provides the reward. The parameters that lead to the formation of the stimulus-response-reward chains can somehow be extracted and generalizations made that lead to the formation of classes of stimulus-response-reward chains. In the case of language these classes might be word groups or sentence groups.

The characteristics of the human, or nonhuman, learner are the ability to:

- □ Respond to certain stimuli in certain ways
- □ Intuitively evaluate the reward potential of responses
- □ Extract the important parameters that made up the stimulus-response-positive reward chain
- □ Generalize these parameters to similar situations to form classes of S-R-R chains

As to the conditions of learning, clearly the environment plays a major role in the exercise of these learners' abilities since it both provides the stimuli and can shape responses by selectively rewarding some responses and not others. Nevertheless, the learner's part is not trivial. He must respond, extract, and generalize. By definition, then, what the child learns when he learns a language is a set of classes of stimulus-response-reward chains.

This, very generally, is how S-R-R theorists describe the abilities of human learners, the conditions of learning, and what the child learns. There is in addition, however, one other aspect of the human learners' abilities and of the learning conditions that is frequently stressed by these theorists. That aspect is *imitation*. The importance of imitation is that it provides the learner with a repertoire of appropriate productive responses. The learner does not have to generate an original response but rather learns to imitate or approximate the productive responses provided by the environment. This factor obviously increases the role or importance of the environment and reduces the role of the learner. Figure 2-1 summarizes S-R-R theorists' positions on what the learner can do, how learning takes place, and what the learner learns.

S-R-R and the "Facts" of Language Development. Let's now examine how the theory deals with the list of "facts." The first fact, a universal sequence of development, can either be ignored or denied, as it is by many S-R-R theorists. If the conditions of learning are those described by these theorists and the learner is capable of learning the piece of behavior, then there is no fixed sequence in which particular classes of words and sentences are learned. Any order is determined by the particular conditions that exist in the environment (Guess, Sailor, & Baer, 1974). Alternatively, other theorists of this school suggest that if a universal order can be found, this order can be explained by

Learner Abilities	How Learning Occurs	What Is Learned
Imitation and generalization	Shaped by occurrences of S-R-Rs	S-R-R chains

Figure 2-1 The S-R-R position.

similar environmental conditions for very young children throughout the world (Salapatek, 1977). Although on the surface there appears to be some truth to this latter statement, it seems to be much too general to account for the specifics of a universal sequence, such as, for example, the fact that stop sounds (/p/, /t/, and /k/) are mastered before continuant sounds (/s/, /sh/, and /f/).

The position that S-R-R theorists hold about the conditions of learning and the characteristics of learners make some facts difficult to explain. In fact, those who have argued *against* this theory of language development have used the three following facts in their arguments.

First, they suggest that *if language were acquired in the way S-R-R theorists describe it, then the five-year-old could never achieve what he apparently knows in such a short space of time.* If, as S-R-R theorists hold, language behavior requires imitation of a model and storage of rewarded imitations, then language knowledge would consist of a memorized list of words and sentences. In order to memorize all the sentences that we apparently use to understand and speak in the way we do, several lifetimes would be needed. Further, we would not have room in our nervous system to store the lists (Miller, 1962).

Second, *if it is a fact that the speech that a child hears is variable, and that the child is rewarded for imitating a model, then it seems that the environment is creating a very difficult puzzle for the child.* Which of the different models should the child imitate? If the child is rewarded for only "approximating" a model, how does the child determine what parameters of the stimulus should be imitated? And why do children ever change what they are being rewarded for to a "better" approximation? Finally, how do children determine that "this is it" — and they don't have to change anymore?

The process of word acquisition is often pointed to as a good example of how language behavior is shaped by the environment (Stemmer, 1971). Obviously the environment provides the stimulus. If this were not the case then it would be very difficult to explain why French children learn "chaise," Spanish children learn "asiento," and English children learn "chair" as the name of an object that one sits on. However, since the stimulus is provided by different speakers (for example, Mom, Dad, and big brother) and in different contexts (for example, "Sit in the chair," "Here's a chair," "Chair," "Mommy's chair"), the word will sound very different on different occasions. Under those circumstances, what is the model that the child attempts to imitate in order to be rewarded? Further, on the way to saying "chair," the child will probably be rewarded for such approximations as /te/, /shuh/ and /se/ (likely substitutions for the sounds in the word "chair"). Children may also be rewarded for calling likely sittable objects, like a pillow on the floor, one of the above speech sound approximations. At some point in children's development of the meaning and sounds of the word "chair," they will reach a version which will not be substantially changed again.

Clearly, even for a so-called simple example of language acquisition, such as word acquisition, there are some problems for S-R-R theory explanations. These problems become even larger when attempts are made to explain acquisition of "sentence types." For example, the way in which words are combined to convey the same or very similar meaning can be quite varied. You can say things like "The man didn't have any apples" and "The man had no apples." You can say "Mary kissed John" or "John was kissed by Mary." You can say "Yesterday I played ball" or "I played ball yesterday." In these types of instances the "models" are not only somewhat different, as in Mom's production of "chair" as compared to Dad's production of "chair." They are obviously widely different.

The last fact, that the child produces sounds, words, and sentences for which not even variable models are provided and that this is done in "rule-governed" ways, is said to be the death blow for the S-R-R theory of language development. For example, all normally developing children learning American English produce plural forms such as "peopleses" and verb forms such as "singed." They are given no model for this behavior and yet these forms occur. They are quite different from — and, therefore, not approximations to — the models they are given. In summary, the unique forms that children produce in all aspects of language violate the apparent tenets of S-R-R theory: the environment provides models, the child imitates or approximates these models, and is rewarded for this imitation or approximation.

Many S-R-R theorists have argued that the problems that other theorists have pointed to can be eliminated if the ability to generalize is taken into account. This ability to generalize allows the learner to group similar *stimuli,* such as somewhat different productions of the same words. It also allows the learner to group on the basis of similar kinds of *responses* as might be the case with different versions of negative sentence types (Salzinger, 1967). The objection to these explanations is that they do not come to grips with the problem of describing the basis for either stimulus or response generalization about the categories and relations in language except in a post hoc manner when generalization is seen to occur. That is, they do not tell us what the child uses to come to the conclusion, for example, that different sounding "chairs" are in fact the same, but different from "chess." Or that "The man doesn't have any apples" and "The man has no apples" are the same, but that "The man has some apples" is different. It is explanation of the bases for the development of this kind of knowledge that theorists from other schools of thought attempt to express.

Innatist Theory

Toward the end of the 1950s and the beginning of the 1960s a revolutionary theory of language and of language knowledge was being accepted by both linguists and psychologists. The best known proponent of this theory, called *transformational grammar* by some and *generative grammar* by others, is Noam Chomsky (1965). The position held by the generative grammarians was in direct opposition to those of S-R-R theorists, who had dominated both psychological and linguistic theory in the previous few decades.

Characteristics of Innatist Theory. Innatist theorists took the position that the structure (biological makeup) and content (specific language-learning mechanisms) of the learner played the most important role in learning. As we have seen, the S-R-R theorists stated that the structure and content of the environment played the most important role in learning. The arguments between these two schools of theory have been described as the "nature versus nurture" arguments.

What exactly is meant by the innatists when they talk about an innate ability to acquire language is that human beings are genetically preprogrammed to acquire language just as they are preprogrammed to walk upright. The comparison being made between walking and learning language is deliberate. It is held by the innatists that the abilities of human learners, the conditions under which they learn, and what is learned are exactly the same for the two behaviors, language and walking.

If we keep in mind this notion that the two behaviors are alike, then the descriptions and explanations of innate theorists become clear. The reason for children acquiring language is that there are particular structures and functions of their biological makeup that *cause* language acquisition to take place, just as there are particular structures and functions of their biological makeup that cause them to walk upright. Walking upright and acquiring language are two of the products of evolutionary change that resulted in *homo sapiens.* It is for this reason that subhuman primates are incapable of acquiring language. They are not genetically preprogrammed to do so.

All children who are developing normally learn how to walk upright, but they are not taught to do so. The two parts of this sentence capture what innatists believe are the conditions for learning language. That is, all normally developing children acquire language, but they are not taught to do so. The particular environment in which a child grows up has no effect on whether or not he will learn to walk or learn language. This is clearly true since despite obvious differences amongst possible environments all children do both types of learning. The only limits on learning to walk upright or learning language are those imposed by the biological makeup of the child.

This last position is the most important tenet of innatist theorizing. It means that no matter what the environmental conditions are, certain developmental processes will take place so long as the child has the biological capacity required. This does not mean that the environment cannot affect any aspect of development. It might affect, to some narrow extent, the time of onset of the behavior and the rate at which the behavior develops and reaches maturity.

For example, it might be the case that babies who are kept in an upright position on their mothers' backs learn to walk earlier than babies who are kept in prone positions. It might also be the case that babies whose caregivers frequently interact with them verbally begin to comprehend and produce words earlier than those babies whose caregivers infrequently interact with them verbally. In fact, the effect of either of the above environmental conditions on the rate of learning to walk upright and of learning language is unclear. However, the innatist would argue that even if these factors did bring about earlier onset and more rapid development of a behavior, this does not change what is learned.

Another analogy is needed to understand what innatists mean when they state that the environment has no effect on what is learned. There are different characteristics of structure in the makeup of roses as compared to violets. The environment, by providing more or less sunshine and water, can affect the rate at which the flower grows. It can also affect its eventual size and health, but only by bringing about structural changes in its physiological state. However, variation in these or other environmental conditions can neither change the course and sequence of development of the rose or the violet, nor can it change one into the other.

In like fashion, the environment can affect the rate at which language knowledge is acquired, but it cannot bring about differences that affect the course and sequence of development or the structure of what is acquired, the grammar of a language. Only environmental conditions that bring about changes in the physiological state of the child can affect the course, sequence, and structure of what is learned. This position is obviously open to a great deal of discussion and debate. Children are not exactly roses and violets and the care they are given is not exactly comparable to sunshine and water.

In summary, the theoretical assumptions of innatists concerning the abilities of human learners, the conditions under which learning takes place and what the child learns are radically different from those of S-R-R theorists. The innatists hold that human learners are uniquely genetically preprogrammed to acquire language. Therefore, no species not so preprogrammed is capable of acquiring language. This genetic preprogramming causes the onset of language development and then, as the program develops, so does language. Thus, neurophysiological development brings about the course and sequence of language development. This is why the course and sequence are fixed and can only be altered by changes in the neurophysiological state of the child. Finally, what the child learns is the grammar of the language, the categories, and the relations or rules. This grammar has a certain structure, consisting of categories and rules, because of the capacities of the human learner. These positions are summarized in Figure 2-2.

Innatist Theory and the "Facts" of Language Development. The "facts" of language development — the universal sequence, the acquisition despite variability, the production of unique forms, and the speed of development — are plausibly explained by the innatist theorists. However, plausible explana-

Learner Abilities	How Learning Occurs	What Is Learned
Biologically pre-programmed for language acquisition	Biological maturation	Grammar of language

Figure 2-2 The innatist position.

tion, as we shall see, does not mean that satisfactory supporting evidence has been provided.

As you might imagine, the innatist theorists lay heavy emphasis on the "fact" that there is a universal sequence of language development, at least during its early stages. The plausible explanation for this is that since the course and sequence of development is a function of the neurophysiological development of the child, and since all normally developing children's course of neurophysiological development is similar, then the course of language development is similar.

One can talk with some confidence about some general universal sequences. It seems that all children produce words and phrases before sentences. Most children acquire knowledge of concrete nouns before abstract nouns. There is evidence that children produce phonological sequences with repetitive consonant/vowel sequences (CVCV as in "mama") before CVC sequences (as in "cat"). However, when the course of a particular child's language development is examined in detail and compared to another, both similarities and differences in development are apparent. This is true of children acquiring the same language as well as those acquiring different languages or two languages simultaneously (bilinguals). Some of the differences appear to be due to the different learning requirements of the language the child is learning (Slobin, 1973), but others appear to be due to the particular learning conditions the child is exposed to (Nelson, 1973). Further, some of the universals of language development could be attributed to universals of cognitive development.

The innatist theorist's explanation of the child's ability to segment and categorize variable streams of speech or sign seems to be based on a logical argument rather than evidence. The argument is that since the speech stream is fast-fading and variable, the child must come to the language-learning task with some hypotheses about the categories and relations in language (MacNeill, 1971).

We've talked about the problems of categorizing the same words that sound different when they're produced by different speakers in different contexts, and of determining where words begin and end in connected speech.

Innatist theorists often refer to the problem of determining syntactic categories when the child frequently hears sentences in which the same word has very different functions. In the sentences "She is playing" and "I like playing," the word "playing" has two very different functions (verb in the first and object in the second). In the two sentences "She is sick" and "She is playing," the word "is" has two very different functions (copula in one and auxiliary in the other). In order to categorize these words in these sentences into the appropriate syntactic category, it is argued, the child must have a set of hypotheses about the possible relations that can be represented by a language. Although this explanation sounds somewhat magical, it is difficult to come up with a counterargument that is less so. The fact of variability, unlike the "fact" of a universal sequence, is a totally real one.

There is little supporting evidence for some of the alternatives that have been suggested. One suggestion is that the child becomes aware of the distributional occurrences of such forms and somehow comes up with different syntactic categorizations based on such distributional information (Braine, 1971). How the child keeps track of such information is unclear, but it is possible that one of the characteristics that differentiates humans from other primates is their memory capacity (Premack, 1983). Another suggestion, already discussed, is that of S-R-R theorists. Somehow generalizations take place through stimulus and/or response similarity that allow syntactic categorization to take place. Although it is the case that individuals do learn to respond in the required manner in conditioning experiments and do generalize when given the opportunity, it has been suggested that this is because they have figured out the rules of the experimental game, and not because they have been "conditioned." Thus, conditioning provides the motivation for generalization but does not explain it. These alternative explanations seem equally magical.

The next fact, the speed at which language knowledge is acquired, was accounted for in innatist theory by the same argument that was used to explain segmentation and categorization despite variability. Since the child comes to the language-learning task with a set of hypotheses about the possible categories and relations in language, the child doesn't have to go through a process of discovery of the grammar of the language. This might take several lifetimes. Instead the child, like a good detective, uses his or her "little gray cells," and tests the hypotheses, using the data provided.

More recently this position has been modified to the extent that it is no longer held that the child has finished the language acquisition process by age five. Rather, this process may be completed by puberty (approximately age ten to sixteen), but not before. The development of language period has been extended by some innatist theorists because of one factor and one fact. If one hypothesizes that language development is a function of the development of the neurophysiological system, and, simultaneously, that there is development of the nervous system until puberty, then, clearly, language development cannot be complete by age five (Lenneberg, 1966). The fact is that there is clear evidence of substantial changes in language development after age five (Chomsky, 1969). Despite this modification in the developmental time period, it is still strongly held by innatist theorists that the process of language development takes place in the manner previously described, the testing of a set of given hypotheses about the structure of language.

It is clear that innatist theorists place primary emphasis on the biological equipment of the human and its development over time to account for language development. The environment's role, in their view, is limited to providing the data that is needed to test hypotheses about the structure of language. These hypotheses are prelimited by the biological equipment of the child and change as the child matures neurophysiologically. These prelimits and maturational constraints mean that the child does not go through a trial-and-error process, a process that would take generations to result in the kind of knowledge that every adult speaker-listener of a language has. This position, in turn, accounts for all the "facts" of language development: universals, the ability to segment and categorize a highly variable and fast-fading stream of acoustic (or visual) information, and the fixed (and still fairly short) period of development.

Despite the apparent logic of this position there is still a great deal of mystery that surrounds it. For example, there is no explanation of what in the biological equipment accounts for the prelimited set of hypotheses nor what aspects of neurophysiological development account for developmental changes in knowledge of language structure. There is little explanation for a fairly fixed (and fairly short) period of language development, a so-called critical period, and, as we shall see in Chapter Four, Capacity to Acquire Language, there is lots of controversy on this issue.

There are many additional questions about what innatist theorists mean when they talk about the language "knowledge" of the adult speaker-listener. These questions deal with the issue of *competence* and *performance*. The innatist position is that children acquire an abstract set of categories and rules, the grammar of a language. This is what is meant by competence. Other theorists hold that the child acquires not only abstract structural knowledge but also abstract pragmatic knowledge (Hymes, 1971). This latter addition in no way seriously argues against the innatists' notion of competence; it simply is a broader competence. Other theorists, on the other hand, take issue with the existence of competence separate from performance and suggest that the rules of performance are what is actually acquired by the child (Devilliers and Devilliers, 1974).

A final set of questions is concerned with whether or not the unique hypothesis-testing abilities that innatist theorists refer to are just linguistic or, rather, are more generally cognitive. It is the latter position that is, for the most part, held by those who theorize that language development is a product of cognitive development.

Cognitivist Theory

All during the 1970s, modifications of the original descriptions of generative grammar were being introduced by linguists. Many of these modifications addressed what was felt to be a lack of emphasis on meaning in the original descriptions. One such modification was *case grammar* (Fillmore, 1968). This description attempted to modify the generative grammar description to take into account the semantic relations implicit in utterances (such as actor, action, patient, or object) as well as syntactic relations (such as subject, verb, and object). In response to the mysteries left unsolved by innatist theorists and the many questions left unanswered, a group of language development theorists turned to these new linguistic descriptions to describe the early utterances of children (Bowerman, 1973).

Despite the feeling that these descriptions were more adequate, primarily because they included semantics, or meaning, as a component of children's earliest utterances, there was still a lack of satisfaction with the inability to explain development. In the search for explanation, many theorists turned to Piaget's theory of cognitive development, as well as other cognitive theories, for explanations of language development. Cognitive explanations of language development became very frequent in the 1970s and they continue to be frequent in the 1980s.

Characteristics of Cognitivist Theory. Piaget had said a great deal about language in his earliest writings (1926) but very little in his later writings, except to suggest that the growth of logical thinking underlay both linguistic and nonlinguistic developments (1970). This suggestion has been taken seriously by the cognitivist theorists of language development. The principal point of view held by many of these theorists is that the child develops knowledge of the world in general (nonlinguistic knowledge) and then "maps" this knowledge onto language categories and relations.

It is important to understand that Piaget's view of cognitive development bears a great deal of similarity to the innatists' view of language development. Piaget does not claim that cognitive development is genetically preprogrammed but, rather, that it is the product of interaction with the environment. However, he and others who follow his school of thought have claimed that regardless of environment the growth of logical thinking takes place in a fixed sequence of stages. Further, the stages of development of thinking that take place after the sensori-motor period are beyond the capacity of species other than man. This seems quite similar to the innatist theorists' position of a fixed sequence of development determined biologically (that is, unalterable by experience) and the uniqueness of man in the acquisition of knowledge of language. The only difference appears to be the domain of knowledge that is being referred to. The cognitivists talk about *thinking* and the innatists talk about *language*.

The first assumption, then, of cognitivist theorists concerning the learning ability of humans is that they have an innate capacity to develop logical thought. In the development of language the child must have, in addition, the ability to map logical thought onto the categories and relations found in language. The process by which this might occur is one of association.

The Process of Association. The process of association has been used to describe the means by which the child learns to relate what is said to particular objects and events in the environment. The bridge by which such associations are made is *meaning*. This assumes that the child has the ability to:

1. Pick out objects and events in the environment.
2. Categorize these objects and events.
3. Associate particular things that are said (or signed) with particular objects and events.

The things that are said are semantically representative of these objects and events (MacNamara, 1972). Even though it is clear that the extent and accuracy of the associations made are said to change in time as the child matures, it is obvious that cognitivists, like innatists, attribute very powerful abilities to the language-learning child.

The conditions for learning language, say cognitivists, are the same conditions that are necessary for any kind of learning. The environment is needed to provide the material that the child can work on. Cognitivists view the role of feedback in the learning process as generally important, primarily for affective reasons, but noninfluential in terms of modifying or altering the sequence of development (Piaget, 1970). This position, again, seems quite similar to that of innatist theorists and the same claims are made. The environment can speed or delay development, but cannot seriously alter the shape of development.

The differences between cognitivist and innatist theorists concerning the language-learning abilities of humans and the conditions needed for learning language lie in what each school believes is necessary and sufficient for this developmental process. Cognitivists believe the human is uniquely capable of developing logical thought, whereas the innatist believes that the human, in addition, must be uniquely capable of learning language. That is, the development of logical thought alone is insufficient for the development of language. The cognitivist believes that certain aspects of logical thinking must be developed before certain aspects of language can be developed. Innatists believe that the structure of language makes it very clear that the development of knowledge of language is independent of logical thinking. That is, the structures of language and of thinking are radically different (Piatelli-Palmarini, 1980).

Despite the above differences, cognitivist and innatist theorists do agree on what it is that the child acquires when acquiring a language. Both schools assume that the child acquires knowledge of the categories and rules of language. Further, they agree that this knowledge is abstractly represented in the speaker-hearer's mind. Cognitivists have little difficulty with the notion that structures are abstractly represented in the mind, since a primary principle of Piagetian theory is that categories and structures of things in the world are abstractly represented in the mind.

One other factor that does not seem to seriously separate some of the practitioners in the two schools of theory is the issue of having a prelimited set of hypotheses about either linguistic or nonlinguistic things. Most cognitivists assume that there are prelimiting notions about how the world is organized, both nonlinguistically and linguistically. They agree with innatists who hold that language development is not a discovery procedure without any a priori ideas. Overall, there appears to be a great deal of similarity between the two schools in their notions about the learning abilities of humans, the conditions for learning, and about what the child learns when learning a language. Figure 2-3 graphically presents the cognitivist's model of the language acquisition process.

Cognitivists and the "Facts" of Language Development. There is, obviously, a great deal of similarity in how the two groups of theorists account for the "facts" of language development. The first fact, universals in the sequence of development, is probably held to even more adamantly by cognitivist theorists than by innatists. Cognitivists believe that, at least at the early stages of development if not the later, language development is dependent on particular developments of logical thought, which are clearly sequential and clearly universal. Therefore, logically, the sequence of acquisition of language must be universal.

The ability to segment and categorize variable signals is an ability that is needed in nonlinguistic as well as linguistic development. For example, cups that are used by the child may vary in color, shape, and size. Nevertheless, the child is able to determine that there are certain characteristics that make these objects containers for liquid despite the fact that they look different. Given these facts it is clear that cognitivists would have no difficulty in assuming that what the child can do nonlinguistically, he should be able to do linguistically. The only difference between the cognitivist and the innatist in dealing with this fact would be that the former would assume that the child must learn to

Learner Abilities	How Learning Occurs	What Is Learned
Biologically preprogrammed for cognitive development	Map linguistic category onto cognitive category	Grammar of language

Figure 2-3 The cognitivist position.

segment and categorize nonlinguistic variable signals before he can learn to do those tasks linguistically.

The final "fact" — the speed at which knowledge is acquired — is, again, a fact that is accounted for quite similarly by the two schools of theorists. The developmental period during which the child goes through the universal stages of cognitive development is from birth to approximately twelve years or puberty. Given this fact, there is no difficulty in accounting for the acquisition of language over exactly the same period. As we shall see in Chapter Three, many cognitivists have had to rethink their notions of a continuing dependency of language on specific cognitive developments during the later stages — middle childhood and adolescence — of both developments. This is because of the specific type of knowledge that researchers say is acquired in both areas of development during these later stages.

Despite all the similarities between innatists and cognitivists in their beliefs about the language learning process, the differences are really significant in terms of understanding crucial factors in language learning. It is not trivial to hold that the child cannot acquire knowledge of a linguistic category or rule without prior knowledge of a nonlinguistic category or rule. This belief, as we shall see, has obvious implications for education and clinical intervention.

The emphasis on meaning or, more specifically, semantics as the basis for forming associations between nonlinguistic and linguistic things is also an important difference. Most innatists emphasize the central role of syntax in language acquisition. The cognitivists, however, take a position that must, logically, suggest that lexical knowledge, or knowledge of the meaning of words, is crucial to or forms the basis for achieving knowledge of other aspects (syntactic and morphophonological) of language. This position, again logically, implies that the sequence for acquisition of language is from knowledge of nonlinguistic categories of objects and events to semantic categories for objects and events to other aspects of language.

The cognitivist positions seem very reasonable and, to some extent, less mysterious. We can see how a child might learn to associate a thing in the environment and the name for the thing. We can even see why it would be necessary to recognize the reappearance of the thing in order to learn the association between the thing and its name. What seems less explicable is how one gets from names of things to knowledge of the meaning of words for unrecognizable things (for example, abstract nouns), and syntactic and morphophonological structures.

Learnability Theory

All through the 1970s, varying linguistic descriptions were being proposed to describe the structure and content of language. Almost all of these descriptions were modifications of generative grammar that focussed on the role of semantics in the generation of utterances. Further, these linguistic descriptions became more and more concerned with the cognitive basis of linguistic structures; that is, how language can be said to mirror thought (Jackendoff, 1978). Simultaneously, cognitive psychologists were beginning to examine the adequacy of Piagetian descriptions in explaining cognitive development and were turning to *information processing models*. Psycholinguists were talking about the information processing requirements of sentence production and comprehension (Fodor, Bever, and Garrett, 1974). Linguists, psychologists, and psycholinguists seemed to be following similar paths in modifying theories about language, thinking, and the relation between the two. These changes in theorizing about language and cognition have led to new theorizing about explanations for language acquisition. One somewhat new approach to explaining language development is what has been termed *learnability theory*.

Characteristics of Learnability Theory. Many of the basic beliefs of those who argue for a learnability theory account of language acquisition are exactly the same as those of innatists and cognitivists. They share the belief that the human learner has an innate ability to process information in certain ways, that the environment plays no crucial role in *shaping* the knowledge that is acquired, and that what is acquired is an abstract set of categories and rules, the grammar of a language. What is *different* about this theorizing is that it attempts to deal directly with the mysteries presented to us by innatists and cognitivists: *How* could a child possibly acquire a generative grammar when confronted with a variable and fast-fading signal? The innatists have proposed that this takes place because the child comes to the task with a set of limiting hypotheses. The cognitivists propose that the child has the ability to form nonlinguistic categories and rules and relate them to linguistic ones. Both explanations leave us with more questions than answers.

There are two ways in which learnability theory tries to account for the "how" of language acquisition. The first is to adopt a grammar of the language that is presumably learnable (hence the term "learnability theory"). The second is to hypothesize about how this grammar could be learned and to examine some of the accumulated facts to see whether they conform to the hypothesized procedure. One of the grammars that has been quite widely adopted by theorists of this school is some form of a *lexical interpretive grammar* (for example, Bresnan, 1978). This description of grammar suggests that the listener comprehends sentences by analyzing the structure of phrases in sentences and by knowing both the *meaning* of the words in the sentence and the *syntactic roles* that the words may play. Just this kind of "on-line" processing ability is required. There is no need to have knowledge of so-called deep structure transformational rules, the kinds of rules that traditional generative grammar descriptions propose are needed to add, delete, substitute, and permute parts of sentences to express negation, question, passive voice, and so on. This latter condition, the need for only surface structure analysis, makes this grammar easier to use in computer analysis of language, and, theoretically, easier for children to learn.

The hypothesized process by which the learning of this grammar could take place has been described by Pinker (1981). The process is an expansion and clarification of the position held by cognitivists. The language learner first learns the invariant meanings of syntactic elements (for example, subject, verb, and object) by observing the meaning of sentences in context. This does not mean, says Pinker, that the parts of sentences and the relations expressed early are semantic and not syntactic. Rather, contextual information helps fix *both* syntactic and semantic information in the child's mind. Further learning entails determining the possible meanings of lexical items and the possible structures in which these lexical items can play a role. This semantactic learning would not only save time in the acquisition process but also more adequately account for the ability of the listener to rapidly comprehend a fast-fading signal.

It is argued that the learnability theory more adequately explains how the child gets from nonlinguistic categories to lexical items and syntactic (and possibly morphophonological) structures than do cognitivist theories. The child is using contextual information to observe both the semantic and syntactic "meaning" of a lexical item so no leap is required from cognitive categories and relations to linguistic ones. It is also argued that the theory eliminates having to refer to an innate set of hypotheses to account for the ability of the child to come up with an abstract grammar. The child simply uses the data presented in context to come up with lexical meanings and syntactic roles of lexical items. Then, using the knowledge acquired, he or she expands on lexicon and structures. We could argue that the theory does appear to eliminate the first problem but leaves us with many questions about the second. The child would have to have a very remarkable ability to observe and remember the distribution of lexical items and of the structures in which they play a role. Finally, this theory, like the innatist and cognitivist theories, has nothing to say about the acquisition of pragmatic rules.

Theory and Aspects of Language Development

The discussion of theoretical explanations of language development has been limited, thus far, to the question of acquisition of structural knowledge. There has been recent theorizing not only about how the structural rules of language can be acquired, but also about how the pragmatic rules can be acquired.

First, notions of what is meant by pragmatic rules have been expanded a great deal over the past decade. There is now greater emphasis on rules of conversation and discourse rather than on sentence-level speech-act rules. Much greater emphasis has been placed on the differences among cultures in the types of discourse rules that are presented to children to learn and the very important role that a society plays in making children particular kinds of users of language (Scollon & Scollon, 1981). These recent developments in thinking about the importance of the role of the child's society or culture in presenting particular ways in which to communicate are certainly not new. They have their roots in anthropology, sociology, and cognitive psychology. Vygotsky (1962) was talking about the role of society in the child's learning of language and scientific thinking as early as the 1920s.

Views about how the child acquires language or any other system of knowledge have often been likened to the three blind men and the elephant. That is, each school of theory is said to view only one aspect of the process, just as each of the blind men conceived of the elephant as being composed of only the one part he could touch — the trunk or ears or legs. This doesn't appear to be the case any longer. Developmental psycholinguists, those most specifically concerned with theory and research in language development, no longer seem to hold singular points of view of the language-learning process. Rather, they either focus on factors that might affect the acquisition of the different aspects of language (pragmatics, lexicon, semantax, and morphophonology) or on a unified theory of language development.

Acquiring Aspects of Language

Those who hold the view that each aspect of language is best explained by one of the theories that has already been discussed suggest that:

1. Aspects of pragmatics acquisition might best be explained by S-R-R theory.
2. Lexical acquisition might best be explained by cognitivist theory.
3. Semantactic and morphophonological acquisition might best be explained by innatist theory.
4. Lexical, semantactic, *and* morphophonological acquisition might best be explained by learnability theory.

The reason why S-R-R theory is said to best explain pragmatic development is that such development is largely dependent on a specific environment. Each environment provides the models that the child uses to determine what the pragmatic rules are (stimuli). The child's ability to conform to these models (responses) is positively rewarded by the environment. Finally, the categories of pragmatic rules that are often pointed to as examples are very ritualistic and apparently imitated and memorized. These bits of behavior are such things as greetings, partings, politeness formulas, and bargaining. It has been suggested that our communications to others are largely composed of these rituals. This description of pragmatic knowledge as being a repertoire of imitated behaviors certainly fits in with the tenets of an S-R-R theory of language development. However, pragmatic knowledge is clearly not limited to ritualistic behavior. The appropriate use of language requires that one keep in mind very complex aspects of the physical and linguistic and social situation.

Lexical development, it has been stated, must be dependent on cognitive categorizations, since we cannot talk about what we don't know about. Words are representations of perceptual and conceptual categorizations. For example, words that refer to a class of objects such as "table," "chair," and "boy" are based on such perceived characteristics of "chairness," "tableness," and "boyness" as, respectively, objects on which we can sit, objects on which we can place other objects, and objects that are young, male, and human. Other words, such as "good," "unhappy," "liberty," and "freedom," are based on conceptual development. However, still other morphemes, such as markers of tense, conjunction, and disjunction (for example, "-ed," "and," and "but"), represent particular relations among objects and events. Perceptual and conceptual categorizations are necessary for the development of the meaning of words that represent categories, such as "table," "good," and the like. The ability to associate categorizations and words is needed to learn words and their meanings. However, relational terms, such as "and," "-ed," and so on, require an understanding of the structure of the language contexts in which they are found. It is from this source that the meanings of these words are derived, not from perceptual and conceptual categories.

Knowledge of the rules of the language for combining words into sentences is semantactic knowledge. Knowledge of the rules of the language for combining sounds into words is morphophonological knowledge. There are no obvious perceptual or conceptual categorizations of contextual events that the child can use to determine these rules for combining. For example, it would be difficult to conceive of an environmental event that would mark the fact that "Flying planes can be dangerous" is an ambiguous statement and has two possible meanings, or that "John kissed Mary" and "Mary was kissed by John" are paraphrases of each other. These relational meanings are understood by speaker-listeners of the language. There is no environmental event to mark the fact that the most general rule for pluralization is to add the sound /z/ and for past tense to add the sound /d/ — and yet children learning English do this. Given these facts, state the innatists, the child must have the innate ability to determine abstract categories and rules. This innate ability is a set of limiting hypotheses about the structure of language. This set of hypotheses changes in time as the child matures. However, learnability theorists suggest that the ability to determine abstract categories and rules is first dependent on the child's ability to observe words and relations in a context and, simultaneously, develop knowledge of word meanings and the relational roles they play in utterances. Another theory of semantactic development is presented by those who describe the structure of language as a role and function grammar (Foley & Van Valin, 1984). They claim that learning the abstract rules of language can be derived from communication interaction. Finally, the ability to determine the distributional characteristics of semantactic and morphophonological structures accounts for further advancement in language development.

Figure 2-4 illustrates the position that differing aspects of language knowledge and use are best explained by different theories. How learning takes place and what component of language is learned in this way are depicted, as well as the theory that is thought to best explain that aspect of development.

Aspect of Language	How Learning Occurs	Theory to Explain
Pragmatics	Imitation and memorization	S-R-R theorist
Lexicon	Association of word and cognitive category	Cognitivist
Semantax	Hypothesis testing Distributional analysis	Innatist Learnability theorist
Morphophonology	Hypothesis testing Distributional analysis	Innatist Learnability theorist

Figure 2-4 The aspects-of-language position.

The differing explanations for the acquisition of the differing aspects of language might seem, on the surface, very reasonable. However, there are a number of problems with this view. For example, it seems questionable to take the position that pragmatic knowledge is solely a set of memorized behaviors. It also seems questionable to suggest that learning the meaning of all words is dependent on perceptual and conceptual categorizations of what is observed and associating these categorizations to words. Finally, it seems highly questionable that the ability to observe the relation between active and passive sentences — or to recognize that sentences that have the same words in the same order can have different meanings — is solely due to a set of innate limiting hypotheses or the ability to determine distributions of structures. Further, it seems reasonable to suggest that, since there appear to be interrelations among the components of the language, a unified theory might better explain language development.

A Unified Theory

Learnability theory is an attempt at coming up with a unified theory of language development. However, this theorizing deals separately with the acquisition of structural knowledge and the acquisition of pragmatic knowledge.

Learnability theory attempts to describe the acquisition of lexical and structural knowledge by the child. These aspects of knowledge are acquired by initial reliance on context. The child learns the meanings of words and the syntactic relations that these words can express by observing the context in which utterances occur. She or he then uses the lexical and syntactic knowledge that has been acquired (that is, language knowledge per se) to extend this knowledge. Therefore, learnability theorists are quite close to cognitivists when they describe the early stages of acquisition, but they attribute later acquisitions to the child's unique abilities to build on language knowledge and to process the language he or she is presented with. The extension of knowledge is not done by the child having innate limiting hypotheses but, rather, by an ability to observe the language's distributional properties. Thus, this theorizing appears to be an attempt to unify cognitivist and innatist theories and, in addition, to go beyond both in terms of explanation.

Those who are presently theorizing about the child's acquisition of pragmatic knowledge are focussing on:

1. What pragmatic knowledge consists of.
2. The conditions under which the child's *generative* knowledge of this aspect of language might be acquired.
3. The sequence of its acquisition.

Theory and research in this area may have very important implications for those concerned with educating children, since a primary focus of this theory and research is how a society teaches children to use language to interact with others and to learn.

Theory and Education

The history of foreign language teaching in this country over the past three decades provides an example of the impact of theorizing on education. In the 1950s, when it was thought that all learning could be explained by S-R-R theory, the approach to teaching a foreign language was to provide models or patterns. Students would imitate these models and be rewarded for the closeness of their approximations. The terms often used to describe this approach were "pattern–practice drill" or "the audio-lingual method" (Brown, 1980). This approach was expected to produce a speaker who had "correct" knowledge of the grammar of the language and "correct" pronunciation of words. The approach, however, did not always — or even often, it is claimed — result in either knowledge of the grammar of the new language or native-like pronunciation of words.

A similar approach was followed in trying to teach mentally retarded children and adults to speak (Baer & Guess, 1973). It was theorized that if the pupils could imitate models, they could be successfully taught a repertoire of talking behaviors. It was found that some of the pupils' behaviors were generalized to other situations. Many questions were raised by researchers and educators about both the successes and failures of this approach. When the pupils acquired only a repertoire of behavior and did not appear to generalize, it was suggested that this result might be attributable to either the teaching approach — which did not provide enough data for generalizations to be made — or to the subjects' inability to learn rules. When generalizations *did* occur, it was suggested that this was attributable to the pupils' ability to learn — not to the teaching technique. Finally, if no new behavior could be instituted in the pupils, it was suggested that the reason was the subjects' lack of the innate ability to develop any rules of language. An S-R-R theorist might argue that the questions raised, the suggestions made, and the conclusions reached about the teaching technique were simply ones of interpretation of results. There were, nevertheless, successes — of a limited kind — and failures within this population, with no clear explanation for the differences in results. Many educators and clinicians believe that it is crucial, when making decisions about educational interventions for these pupils, that they themselves be able to understand a particular student's ability to learn an oral or signed or other communication system and to understand the conditions under which such learning takes place. Because these teachers and clinicians felt that the theory did not provide explanations, they turned away from the teaching techniques.

Turning away from S-R-R theorists' explanations of language learning and teaching led some educational and clinical researchers to questionable assumptions. Innatist descriptions of the abstract language knowledge that children were supposed to have led some educators to develop teaching materials that would enable children to analyze sentences in the way that generative grammarians would. That is, the children were to be given practice in parsing sentences in terms of transformational rules in the hope that this would expand their language knowledge. These types of materials were also given to deaf youngsters. This approach ignored the innatists' position that the child developed unconscious knowledge of rules, and did so simply by being exposed to the data. The results of such programs were disappointing. No innatist or generative grammarian had ever suggested that the environment *pointed* to the rules that were acquired or that the rules that were acquired were, in fact, those that linguists describe.

Misapprehension of the implications of theory also resulted in the development of programs to stimulate cognitive development in the belief that this stimulation would lead to the development of language. This approach ignored the position of Piaget and Piagetians that both cognitive development and linguistic development are products of the growth of logical thinking, rather than that language is the product of a particular cognitive development (Menyuk, 1975). The results of educational intervention based on both types of misapprehension have been, as might be predicted, less than successful in terms of teaching language.

Summary and Questions

Theories of language development have affected the development of techniques for the teaching of language to a variety of populations and will probably continue to do so. For example, the notion that the student is an active processor of information, capable of drawing from the data the rules of his or her language, has been largely the result of innatist and cognitivist theorizing and research. However, as indicated in the discussion of relevant theories, there are still many questions that have been left unanswered by all of them and gaps in what present theories attempt to account for. Present theories primarily attempt to describe early acquisition of words and sentences, but none gives a fully satisfactory explanation for the development of all the aspects of all the components of language. Additionally, present theories of language development do not attempt to explain individual variation in the acquisition of structural knowledge or in the development of communication skills. It is just this kind of explanation that is crucial to planning language-teaching programs for clinical populations. In addition, theory has not attempted to deal with the effect of context, both situational and linguistic, on language processing. Again, explanations of the effects of context are crucial for program planning. It is entirely possible that educational and clinical researchers, as well as theorists, will provide answers to these questions.

Chapter Three
Cognition and Language

Language development is clearly dependent on the child's mental abilities. Although other factors play a role, the way in which the human infant thinks and develops its thinking explains a large part of the process. One can ask, then, given this very obvious fact, why there is so much controversy about the relation between cognition and language. There are those who state that language is dependent on cognition. Others state that language and cognition are mutually dependent, and still others that cognition is dependent on language. Much of the controversy arises out of the fact that those who hold varying positions also have varying opinions of what cognition is.

In this chapter the positions of three paramount figures in the child development literature on the relation between cognition and language are presented — Piaget, Werner, and Vygotsky. Research findings on language development based on the positions of these three developmental psychologists is discussed. An alternative to these positions — an information processing view — is then presented, and research findings based on this position examined. In this chapter we will also focus on the fairly recent emphasis on the role of the development of *memory* in the acquisition of language.

The last section of this chapter examines the effect of these varying positions on views concerning the development and education of three groups of children: children who in the past were said to have little or no language (the deaf), children who are said to be developmentally delayed across all domains of development (the retarded), and children who acquire more than one language (bilinguals). Children in these three groups, it has been claimed, shed enormous light on the nature of the relation between cognition and language. It is certainly clear that different theoretical positions have had a marked influence on *their* education.

The Relation Between Cognition and Language

There are, at least, three positions concerning the relation between cognition and language. Those who hold these positions often quote from or interpret the words of three developmental psychologists who have had a very marked influence on the thinking of other developmental psychologists and psycholinguists — Piaget, Werner, and Vygotsky. Piaget, it is held, claims that language development is dependent on cognition. Werner, say his followers, would state that cognitive and linguistic development are interdependent. Those who are in Vygotsky's camp affirm the acquisition of knowledge *through* language.

Jean Piaget

Piaget describes cognitive development as taking place in stages (Piaget, 1970); during each stage certain abilities are manifested by the child. For example, during the earliest — sensori-motor — stage, the child develops notions of cause and effect, means–ends, and, finally, object performance. During a later stage of development, the concrete operational period, the child's greatest accomplishment is *conservation*. However, the child is not able to conserve in all domains (weight, volume, and time) at the same time. The child conserves in one domain, and then at a later time in another, and so on. For example, the child is able to conserve weight long before he or she can conserve time. The acquisition sequence of the operation of conservation for each domain is the result of the complexity of the task. Conserving time is obviously a more abstract problem than conserving weight. The final stage of development, formal operations, is characterized by the ability to mentally manipulate a number of actions (or operations) on objects and events and to think about the possible consequences of such actions. The cognitive products of each period are the result of changes in the ways in which the child perceives the world, organizes these perceptions, stores them, and then thinks about objects and events in that world using these stored representations. Language development is considered by Piaget to be one of the products of this growth in logical thinking.

There are three somewhat differing positions that are held by the "Piagetians." In the view of some, both language development*s* and cognitive development*s* are the result of the development of logical thinking, that is, how the child thinks about categories and their relations in the real world (Sinclair-deZwart, 1969). Others claim that certain cognitive developments in logical thought are prerequisite to certain linguistic developments throughout the child's maturation (Beilin, 1975). This position is probably no longer strictly held by any Piagetian. The third position is that certain sensori-motor developments are prerequisite to early or basic acquisition of language. Those who hold this position do not discuss later acquisition. These three positions are graphically represented in Figure 3-1.

Those who hold the three positions described above would (and have) theorized somewhat different sequences of occurrences of cognitive and linguistic developments. Those who hold the first position suggest that cognitive and linguistic developments that are similar should occur at about the same time in a child's development. For example, they argue that logical action schema, such as putting a doll into a crib and covering it, is somewhat similar to producing actor-action, action-object and actor-action-object sentences, and that, therefore, a certain level of development of logical seriation (putting objects into sequential arrays) is required for both. If that is the case, then both behaviors should appear at about the same time and apparently they do (Sinclair-deZwart, 1973). Other examples might be conservation of volume, the production of comparatives (more, less, bigger), and the inclusion of simultaneous attributes (fat and yellow) in sentences. Apparently, this is true as well. Some evidence supports the position that developments that require similar types of thinking in both cognition and language occur at about the same time.

The second position, that certain cognitive developments *always precede*

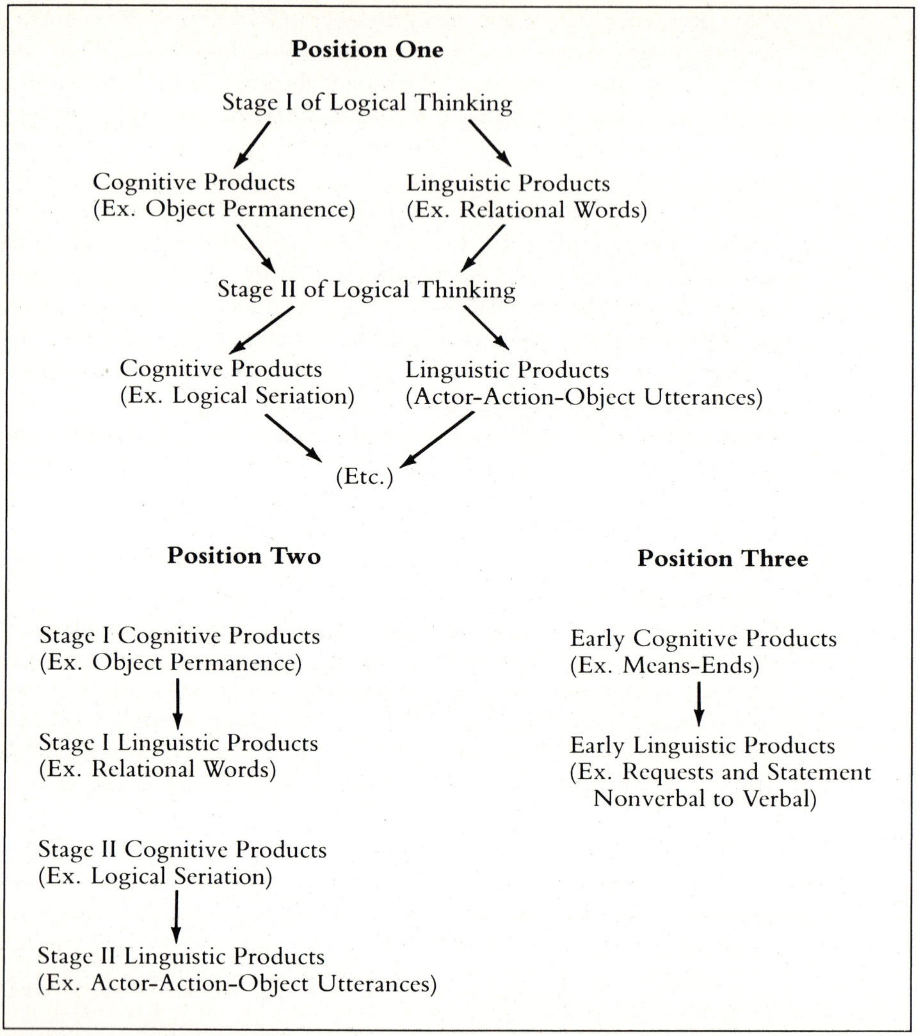

Figure 3-1 Three positions held by Piagetians concerning the relation between cognition and language.

linguistic developments throughout infancy, childhood, and adolescence, is less well supported by the data. For example, it has been argued in the past that object permanence is necessary for word production or, at least, for some kinds of word production (Brown, 1973). The data concerning the sequence of development of object permanence and word production suggests that there is no strict sequence of, first, object permanence and then, word production. Rather, there is a general correspondence between beginning language and the periods of transition from sensori-motor stage five (approximately age twelve to sixteen months) to stage six, object permanence (Corrigan, 1979). This finding seems to better support the previous position, that cognitive developments and linguistic developments that are somewhat similar appear at approximately the same time, than it does the notion that a cognitive product is prerequisite to a linguistic product. In fact, recent research supports the "specificity" argument; that is, that in early development, specific cognitive developments are related to specific linguistic developments (Gopnik & Meltzoff, 1986). For example, it has been found that disappearance words are acquired within a few weeks of the solution of complex object permanence tasks, and success and failure words are acquired within a few weeks of the solution of complex means–ends tasks.

The same conclusion seems appropriate for studies that have examined the relation between symbolic play and word or words production (McCune-(Nicolich, 1981). Although it seems logical to suggest that symbolic play behaviors and the use of words, which are both symbolic acts, are related to each other, there does not seem to be any a priori reason why play should precede language use. In fact, there is no strict sequence of occurrence of symbolic play before word production. Rather, certain levels of play and word production occur at approximately the same time.

These findings all concern the early stages of development. There are comparatively few studies that examine the sequence of development of cognitive and linguistic products at later stages of development. The ability to seriate and the ability to transform an array (completely reverse the position of objects in a matrix) have been found to appear before the use of passive sentences (Beilin, 1975). Since passive sentences in English reverse the usual order of subject, verb, and object — "The girl (object) was kissed by the boy (actor)" — there is a similarity in the processes that are required. Again, the findings indicate that similar behaviors in the two domains of development appear to occur simultaneously. However, this reversal of actor and object for passive constructions does not occur in all languages. Therefore, the co-occurence of these abilities may be limited to those children who are acquiring a language in which these reversals occur.

In all of the studies just cited, the behaviors that appear simultaneously are all *production* behaviors. In many instances, *perception* of language categories has been found to precede their production and, also, to precede the cognitive production. That is, word comprehension precedes not only word production but also the sixth stage of sensori-motor development, object permanence. Comprehension of words and word combinations precedes their production and also precedes symbolic play at the highest levels. The comprehension of passives, or at least of some types of passives, precedes production of passives and the cognitive developments that are said to be similar.

Since it is usually the case that the language perception behaviors appear before the language production and cognitive production behaviors, it is hard to support the argument that cognitive developments are prerequisite to linguistic developments. The data does seem to support the argument that similar behaviors in both domains (thus far all production behaviors) appear simultaneously. If that position is correct, then cognitive perception behavior and language perception behaviors should also appear at about the same time. Information processing models appear to have more to say on this issue than do Piagetian models. Some studies, however, that have used the Piagetian approach do provide hints of perception behaviors occurring simultaneously in both domains.

Long before object permanence is complete, cognitive behaviors occur that indicate development of the recognition of objects and events. It is these very early behaviors that some researchers claim are prerequisite to language development. That is, the cognitive developments of the middle portions of the sensori-motor period are the necessary ones for language acquisition, whereas later ones may not be crucial to the process.

The behavior the infant displays during this period not only indicates recognition of objects and events but also indicates the ability to use knowledge of objects and events in problem solution. These latter behaviors have been labelled "means–ends" and "operational causality" (understanding that certain actions can bring about consequences; for example, that pulling a blanket that an object is on can bring the object nearer). These developments have also been pointed to as being prerequisite to the beginning of communication behavior (Bates, Benigni, Bretherton, Camaioni, & Volterra, 1979). They generally occur over the eight-to-eighteen-month period of development. It is also during this period that infants begin to recognize words and certain two-part relations in words (for example, actor-action and action-object). Although the similarities in the linguistic and cognitive perception behaviors are more difficult to pinpoint than similarities in production behaviors, it is possible that they exist.

Overall, the results of research carried out from the "Piagetian" point of view indicate that early cognitive products, such as means–ends, observation of causality, and object permanence, are not prerequisite to word comprehension and production. Rather, both cognitive and linguistic percepts and products may require similar processing abilities and, therefore, appear at approximately the same developmental time. The same appears to be true of such later cognitive developments as seriation, permutation, and conservation, and such linguistic developments as the use of the passive, comparative markers, coordination, and other so-called transformations of basic structures. Table 3-1 provides an outline of what appear to be simultaneously occurring cognitive and linguistic products during the earliest period of development.

Piaget's position that the development of logical thinking is necessary for both cognitive and linguistic developments seems to be supported by the data obtained thus far. Acceptance of Piaget's view still leaves us with a problem: We still need to determine the changing nature of logical thinking and the bases for the changes. (This is what information processing modelers attempt to do.)

Table 3-1 Sequences of early cognitive and linguistic behavior.

AGE IN MONTHS	LINGUISTIC BEHAVIORS	COGNITIVE BEHAVIORS
1–4	Vocalization Vocalization exchange Voice discrimination	Organized reflexes Hand-mouth coordination Object tracking
4–8	Voice identification Babbling	Object identification Repetition of motor habits
8–12	Attention to word length utterances Reduction of babble length	Observation of causality Means–ends
12–18	Comprehension of two-part utterances Holophrastic utterances	Object permanence

There are still other views of the relation between cognition and language. The claim that development in both domains is dependent on some other higher-order level of thinking does not satisfy all theorists. There are at least two questions that other theorists attempt to address. The first is the role of language in cognitive development. The second is the role of language as a "socialization" tool and its effect on both domains of development.

Heinz Werner

There is a great deal of similarity between Piaget's and Heinz Werner's descriptions of cognitive development, but there are important differences as well (Langer, 1970). In addition to describing stages of development, which are quite similar to the stages described by Piaget, Werner stressed the role of language and the role of society in bringing about developmental changes. Further, development is viewed by Wernerians as a spiral along which retreat to more primitive behaviors because of environmental conditions can occur.

In Werner's view, the early stages of development, both cognitive and linguistic, are dependent on perceptual-motor experiences. These experiences lead to the development of *symbolization* or *representation*. For example, out of such motor acts as reaching and calling are derived pointing and vocal denotation. The later stages of cognitive development, states Werner, are very dependent on language. These later stages, called *conceptual* and *analytical,* require abstract thinking and logico-mathematical operations, respectively. From Werner's point of view, the mental manipulations involved in both types of thinking require an *abstract* symbol system and, therefore, require language. Visual, auditory, and motor imagery (perceptual representations) cannot be mentally manipulated and, therefore, would be insufficient for such thinking.

The research carried out by Werner and Kaplan (1963) supports the notion that the development of abstract concepts is helped through language or at least by the naming process. It is possible, however, that the results of experiments that are said to support this dependency are due to the design of the experiments rather than to language being necessary for such thinking, or for all such thinking. That is, abstract symbol manipulation in the form of words seems necessary when the child is asked to discover the meaning of a word through sentences (Werner & Kaplan, 1952) or when the child is only given words to help him develop a concept. If the situation were different the child might use situational means to discover the meaning of words and visual parameters to develop a concept.

Werner implies in his own writing that both concept development and the use of words to represent class concepts and relations are functions of the child's ability to distance himself from concrete perceptual-motor experiences. This position suggests that cognitive developments that are dependent on similar processing abilities appear at the same time rather than that language use is the only means to concept development.

A stronger case — one based on logical explanation — might be made for the idea that analytical thinking is crucially dependent on language. This form of thought, say Wernerians, is composed of the ability to *think about possibilities* as well as actualities and the ability to be *conscious of one's own thoughts*. Both abilities, hypothesizing and consciousness of thought, absolutely require language, say those who take the position that cognitive development is dependent on language. Although language, obviously, plays a very important role in analytic thinking, as it does in concept development, it is not clear that such thinking cannot take place without language. The only thing that is clear is that one can't *talk* about one's thoughts without language.

Hypothesizing and consciousness have been referred to as *meta-abilities*. These abilities to consciously think about one's thoughts and to plan, reason, and solve problems on the basis of this conscious awareness are considered the highest level of achievement in both the cognitive and linguistic domain. Again, there seems to be more support currently for the notion that like developments in each domain are probably dependent on like developmental progressions in the processing of information than there is for the notion that even these very advanced levels of thinking are totally dependent on language.

Werner sees development as a process that is determined by the child's interaction with the environment. How the child interacts with the environment is a function of the unique biological and psychological characteristics of being human, the physical and social properties of the environment that the child is in, and schemes for interacting determined by the child's *affective* states. It is these affective states that make the child more or less sensitive to certain stimuli or events in the environment.

For example, the child may perceive certain aspects of a sound sequence that another animal would not perceive because the child and the other animal are different biologically. The environment would provide certain sound sequences to the child — and not others — and provide them in certain contexts — and not others — because of the cultural organization of a particular environment. Finally, because the child is relaxed and happy, he or she will be very observant of the important aspects of the sound sequence. If the child were tense and unhappy he might ignore some of the parameters. This view of the developmental process is a marked departure from that of Piagetians. The focus of their research has been the first of the three factors that Werner talks about as being crucial in an interaction, the biological basis of processing information in certain ways and the fixed evolution of this process.

The Wernerians suggest that the roles of the second and third factors in cognitive development, the cultural background of the child and his affective state, can be understood by comparing populations in which these factors vary (Langer, 1970). Comparisons of levels of thinking of various cultural groups (the more or less primitive) and of the normal and the mentally ill shed light on the role of societal structure and its effect on the child's cognitive development. It is not clear that either type of comparison is valid. However, one can see how these two factors could affect developments in cognition and language. What is not clear is how these factors relate the two areas of development, language and cognition. Vygotsky, however, presents a plausible description of how the society in which the child finds himself or herself can play a role in the relation between the two.

Lev Vygotsky

Vygotsky's book *Thought and Language* (1962) best presents his position on the relation between thought and language. He suggests that the child's thought and language take different developmental paths until the child is about two years old. At that time thought and language become overlapping. This process occurs because the environment provides labels for the objects and events that the child is thinking about. These labels then become pointers to or containers for generalizations about objects and events. Words then, states Vygotsky, are crucial for abstract concept development. This view is similar to that of Werner, who also suggested that concept development is dependent on naming.

There is a great deal of evidence in Vygotsky's own research that the use of language plays a crucial role in concept development. Much of this research examines the child's ability to acquire a concept for a set of features (for example, size, shape, and color) that the experimenter is thinking of. Children are much better able to form such concepts when words are provided than when they are not. In addition, it seems logical that being provided with words, and then having words, puts the child on the path of searching for features that categorize objects and events as being the same or different. Word meanings and concepts change as the child develops.

Language plays a crucial role not only in concept development but also in planning and problem solution, stated Vygotsky. He reached this conclusion as a result of examining the situations in which children used so-called egocentric speech. He found that children talked to themselves about what they were doing or should do as they were engaged in tasks. This behavior was particularly prominent in situations where difficulties arose. Many other researchers found that language plays the roles in task solution that Vygotsky claimed, and we are all aware of the fact that we often talk to ourselves as we confront problems. In addition, we are aware of the role of language in remembering, as we rehearse with language to store information, use linguistic mnemonic devices, and cue ourselves with language for recall.

These findings have been interpreted as proving that language is necessary for thinking. However, Vygotsky himself did not take this position nor did his famous colleague Luria in his discussion of higher mental processes (Luria, 1976). Vygotsky describes the relation between thought and language in its mature form (when speech becomes "inner") as two partially overlapping domains. As Figure 3-2 indicates, in Vygotsky's view language and thought overlap for some purposes. For others, language is used without thought (for example, in rote memorization) and thought occurs without language (purely imaginal thinking).

Despite the fact that Vygotsky refers to thinking without language, he and many present-day cognitive psychologists (for example, Wertsch, 1979; Clark, 1978) place a great deal of emphasis on the role of verbalization in Western culture in socializing the child. This is done through communicative interaction in which the ways society solves problems are indicated to the child. In particular, Western societies acculturate children to use language to carry out mental tasks. Clearly this suggests that for children in our society, language does play a crucial role in thinking.

Vygotskyites have examined the development of the way in which lan-

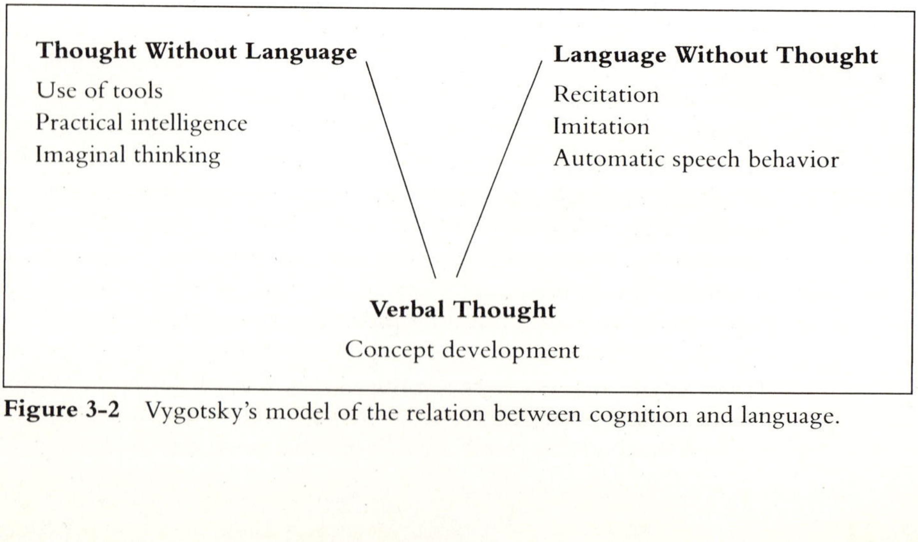

Figure 3-2 Vygotsky's model of the relation between cognition and language.

guage is first used by the environment to direct the child and then used by the child to direct first his actions and then his thoughts. The stages of development are: first, social speech; then, egocentric speech; and then, inner speech. Before age two, speech (or vocalizations) is used to express needs and feelings and to socialize. From about age two to three, the child's actions can be directed by speech presented by others. Further, the child can direct the actions of others through speech and in this way begin to find out about the society's beliefs and customs. Gradually, the child begins to use speech to direct the action he is engaging in. At this point speech appears to be egocentric: that is, not communicative, since the child is talking to himself. Children talk to themselves as they carry out tasks. Finally, overt use of speech during activity no longer occurs, although there is evidence that the child is still "talking" subvocally.

Vygotskyites take the position that language is crucial to cognitive development. However, it may be the case that language is not in and of itself crucial to cognitive development but, rather, that the society in which the child is being reared makes it so. That is, some societies, and ours is one of them, emphasize the importance of verbal interactions and the use of language to solve problems. This becomes a very important issue for understanding the development of children who are socially and/or biologically different from so-called "mainstream" or "normal" children. With these children language may not or cannot play the same role as that described by Vygotsky. Knowing whether or not this is the case is crucial in planning for these children's education.

Summary of Piagetian, Wernerian, and Vygotskyite Theory

The three basic positions concerning the relation between cognition and language are:

- □ Language is dependent on cognition.
- □ Cognition and language are interdependent.
- □ Cognition is dependent on language.

The views of none of the three developmental psychologists that we have discussed — Piaget, Werner, and Vygotsky — appear to fall neatly into any one of these three positions.

Piaget suggests that cognitive and linguistic developments are equally the product of development of logical thinking. Werner believes that early developments in both cognitive and linguistic domains are dependent on perceptual development. Later developments, contemplative and analytic thinking, he suggests, rely heavily on the use of language. However, all developments are a product of three factors; biological state, affective state, and societal conditions. Vygotsky places great emphasis on the role of the society in conveying to the child the ways in which he or she should think about and solve problems. Language and thought are fused in concept development, and language is used in planning and problem solution, and for remembering. However, thinking can take place without language, and language use can take place without thinking.

Putting any of these psychologists into any of the fixed positions seems to be only the product of the imaginations of their interpreters. The three psychologists take far more thoughtful views of the relation between cognition and language than may have been ascribed to them by their protagonists. They still, however, leave us with many questions about what are the best explanations for the relationships between cognitive and linguistic development. One area of current theorizing suggests that these explanations can come from a detailed step-by-step analysis of the way in which information, of any kind, can be processed and stored.

Information Processing and Memory

Information processing models attempt to explain how the sensory information received by the organism is dealt with over time as it is received — so-called "on-line processing." They also deal with how storage and retrieval of information changes over developmental time. Thus, the way or ways in which long-term memory storage is used in processing information in short-term storage is something these models attempt to explain. As you can see, some of the terminology used in these models is identical to that applied in computer models of learning. For example, a recent theoretical discussion of the child's acquisition of language knowledge beyond what is given innately proposed that the child's ability to produce more and more complex language is based on the ability to formulate and execute more and more complex plans. This ability, it was suggested, is based on a process of *compiling* information and then *interpreting* it (Hamburger & Crain, 1984). Despite the frequent analogies, the conclusions that have been reached concerning the development of information processing abilities and of memory are based on studies of children in the process of dealing with information and of remembering.

If we were to draw a picture of the stages in information processing, it would look like Figure 3-3. The first stage is labelled *attention*. All of the various definitions of this term include the fact that attention involves both the concept of attending to sensory stimuli and the fact that the human infant, at birth, is biologically ready to attend to incoming sensations in particular ways. Babies have special ways of looking (Haith, 1980) and of listening (Eimas, 1975). Therefore, even at this first stage in information processing, and even at the earliest stages of development, attention is an active process not a passive one.

Clearly the stages that follow, *discrimination* and *categorization,* are active processes as well. Discrimination requires analysis of the features of the sen-

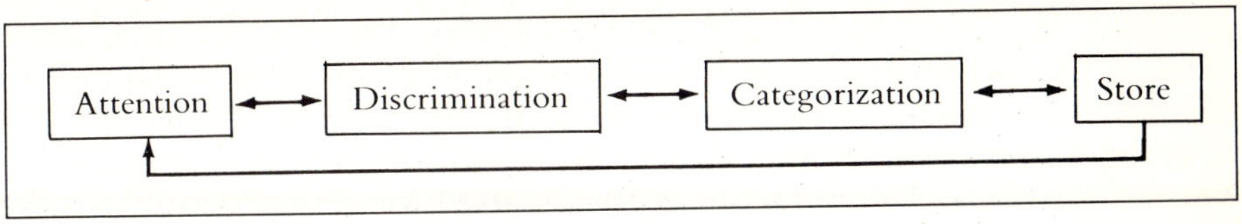

Figure 3-3 Stages in the processing of information.

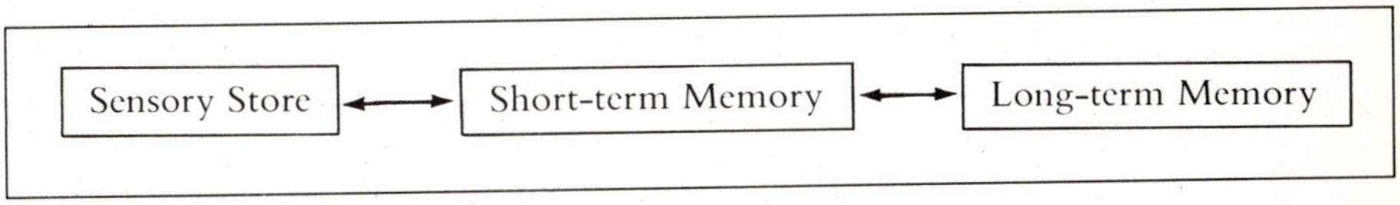

Figure 3-4 Stages in the memorial process.

sory input, and categorization requires inclusion of the sensory input into a class that consists of certain features. *Storage* of the categorization, or — more familiarly — putting it into memory, is the last stage in the information processing model presented in Figure 3-3. This last stage will play a crucial role in further information processing. This fact is represented in Figure 3-4.

As can be seen in Figure 3-4, information that is stored in long-term memory is used to carry out processing in short-term store which, in turn, affects what is placed in long-term store. Obviously, information that gets into short-term store is a product of what the processor has registered in sensory store. In other terms, it is determined by what the organism attends to and how the organism is equipped to, or has learned how to, categorize information.

The aspects of information processing referred to in both Figures 3-3 and 3-4 are crucial to the development of nonlinguistic and linguistic cognitive knowledge. The question of whether or not these two developments impinge on each other is a trivial one from this point of view, since all developments would be based on changes in information processing. These changes, rather than changes in linguistic or cognitive products, underlie development in all areas.

What this means in terms of language development has not been described in any great detail, but certain generalizations can be made. For example, it has been observed that the child can attend to and process, literally, more and more language information and more and more complex language information over time. The models presented above can account for these facts more adequately than can explanations provided by Piaget, Werner, and Vygotsky. Clearly, however, language development is more than perceiving and producing more and more complex information over time. We will take some examples of phonological development to indicate what appear to be the explanatory strengths and possible weaknesses of these models.

From the beginning of development the infant has available two phonetic or speech-sound-processing attentional devices that are crucial for language processing. These are: the ability to discriminate between human speech and other sound events, and the ability to analyze some phonetic features of these sounds. This latter ability allows the very young infant to discriminate between speech-sound contrasts that are found in all the languages of the world. For example, the very young infant is able to discriminate between syllables such as /pa/ and /ba/. The initial sounds in these syllables differ from each other in terms of voicing onset time. The very young infant also discriminates between syllables that have flat and rising or flat and falling fundamental frequency contours (Morse, 1978). These two aspects of speech contrast are universal, and the infant is probably biologically ready to observe these contrasts.

As the infant matures, his or her ability to discriminate between syllables that have more subtle features of difference is observed. The older infant can discriminate between, for example, /la/ and /ra/. These two syllables differ in terms of the transition rate from the consonant to the vowel and this contrast does not appear in all languages. Also, the young infant can only observe differences between speech-sound sequences that are one syllable in length, whereas the older infant can observe differences between those that are three syllables in length (for example, the difference between /pataka/ and /papata/). The older infant's behavior indicates an increase in the complexity and amount of speech information that he or she can process.

At about eight months of age, there is a change in the pattern. There is evidence of a shift in the basis for processing speech information; from perceptual processing to communicative processing. For example, the infant of approximately eight months does not discriminate between utterances with *steadily* rising and falling fundamental frequency but only between those with question and statement intonation contours (Kaplan & Kaplan, 1970). Discriminating between utterances with steadily rising and falling fundamental frequency changes is a perceptual differentiation. Discriminating between utterances with question and statement contours (for example, "See the cat" versus "See the cat?") involves some knowledge of the differences in the communicative intents conveyed by the two contours.

At about ten months, the infant exhibits language-specific patterns of speech sound discrimination (Strange, 1986), and infants of approximately twelve months give evidence of being able to recognize monosyllabic words out of context (Thomas, Campos, Shucard, Ramsay, & Shucard, 1981). A number of pieces of evidence of the infant's perception and production of speech (Menyuk, 1974) indicate that the infant has shifted attention from the speech signal, or the phonetics of what is heard, to the phonology and semantics of what is heard.

This shift in information processing cannot be accounted for by a simple increase in the amount and complexity of the signal that can be processed in time. Some "cognitive leap" occurs and when it does, the basis for the infant's perception of the speech signal is the meaning of the units in the signal, not their acoustic characteristics. The question is: What is the cause of this cognitive leap and, for that matter, others that occur throughout development? Possible sources for such cognitive leaps may be both biological changes (such as an increase in the amount of information that can be stored simultaneously) and experiential changes (such as the information that becomes salient for the child over time.) These factors, biology and input, will be discussed in the next two chapters.

In information processing and memory models that have been developed with the adult in mind, it is now taken for granted that semantic categorization plays a vital role. The question is: How does it become established for the child?

Cognition and Language in "Different" Children

There are three populations of children that have frequently been studied to examine the relation between cognitive and linguistic development. These populations are *deaf, retarded,* and *bilingual* children. These groups were chosen for study by researchers who held very adamant positions concerning the relation between cognitive and linguistic development.

Researchers who worked with the deaf wanted to prove that language was not crucial for cognitive development. If the deaf were found to be similar to hearing children in cognitive development, the researchers theorized, there would be evidence of the independence of cognitive development. Many of those who did research with the retarded were concerned with the relation between degree of mental retardation and degree of language deficit or delay in achieving early Piagetian stages and delay in language development. If such correlations were found, the researchers theorized, there would be evidence of the dependency of language on cognition. In a very different vein, those who did research with bilingual children hypothesized that acquiring more than one language was either a cognitive handicap because it retarded language development or a cognitive advantage because more language knowledge was available to the child.

Deaf Children

For a long time educators of the deaf were primarily concerned with the deaf child's acquisition of oral language. It was thought (and examined experimentally in a number of studies) that deaf children could not develop cognitively in a normal way because they had great difficulty in oral language development.

In response to this position, Furth (1973) and his colleagues undertook a number of studies examining the cognitive development of deaf children from a Piagetian perspective. It was Furth's hypothesis that the deaf children he was studying had no language, either oral or signed. He engaged these deaf children in a number of conservation and formal operation tasks. His findings overall were that deaf children and adolescents were very similar to hearing children and adolescents in their pattern of cognitive growth. He also concluded that, on the whole, deaf children were somewhat delayed, but not remarkably so, in their cognitive development as compared to hearing children of the same ages. He attributed this delay to lack of experience in acting upon the environment. This seemed to be a reasonable conclusion given the fact that many of the children he studied were in residential schools for the deaf.

From these data, Furth also concluded that he had provided evidence that language was not necessary for cognitive development. Furth clearly established the fact that there are overall similarities between deaf and hearing children's cognitive development. However, there are problems with the assumption that these deaf children did not have a language available to them. Anecdotal data indicate that even though deaf children were not exposed to or taught a standard sign language in many residential schools for the deaf in the United States, they nevertheless acquired some form of sign language and used it, often in secret. Further, a careful observational study was made of young deaf children who were not exposed to a sign language because of their hearing parents' wishes. Results of this study indicated that the children developed a system of gestures and use of gestures that was, apparently, lexically and structurally, quite similar to the words and structures used by young hearing children (Goldin-Meadow & Feldman, 1977).

These findings indicate that deaf children are *not* without language and, therefore, that to claim that cognitive development can occur without language — based on research with deaf children — is incorrect. However, Furth's very real contribution was his general finding of "normal" cognitive development in deaf children. This result very clearly points to the fact that the oral language of hearing persons is not necessary for cognitive development. This discovery has been very important for decision making concerning the education of the deaf. Those who teach the deaf no longer hold that oral language must be taught to these children so that they can develop intellectually in a normal way.

Furth's findings obviously did not resolve the question of the relation between cognition and language. Nevertheless, one could hypothesize from his findings, and the findings concerning the acquisition and use of sign language by deaf children, that having the capacity to develop in both cognition and in language is not dependent on being able to hear or, in other words, on having all five senses.

Mentally Retarded Children

The language development of mentally retarded children should, it is thought, accurately describe the relation between cognitive and linguistic development. In this population certain cognitive limitations exist that can be determined by standard tests or experimental measures. Therefore, the effect of these cognitive limitations on language development should be evident. The research examining this issue, however, does not lead to easy conclusions.

From an information processing point of view, having all five senses but not having the normal ability to process the information from these senses because of attention, discrimination, categorization, and storage problems, would seriously affect one's development in both cognition and language. Mentally retarded children have been found to have problems in any one or all areas of information processing and, therefore, studies of their development should shed light on the relations between developments in cognition and language.

Much of the research on the language development of mentally retarded children argues for these children being unable to acquire language in a normal manner because of their information processing disabilities. Different aspects of language processing have been measured in these children, and they have been found to be lacking and presumably different in some aspects of structural language knowledge. For example, Cromer (1972) examined these children's ability to comprehend subjectless sentences (such as, "The fish is good to eat"). He found that mentally retarded children in the process of acquiring knowledge of this structure do not make the generalizations about it that normally developing children do. He concluded that although mentally retarded children eventually acquire this structure, it is probably represented in terms of its surface form and in isolation from other related structures.

Naremore and Dever (1975) analyzed language samples of mentally retarded children at mental ages of six to ten years. They found that the retarded children did not begin to produce elaborations of basic clausal structures even at mental age ten, whereas normally developing children did so during the period from age six to ten. The findings of both studies indicate that educable retarded children have particular difficulty in processing complex structures rather than a general slowness in the acquisition of all structures.

Other retarded children have great difficulty in acquiring markers of tense and number in simple sentences; others have difficulty in acquiring simple sentence types; and still others have difficulty in acquiring any aspect of spoken language. The theory that differences in retarded children's process of development are caused by particular information processing difficulties makes good sense if one takes seriously the evidence of neurological studies of these children. Different underlying brain conditions have caused the retardation in individual children. These differing conditions could lead to different information processing outcomes and, therefore, to different language outcomes.

From a totally different point of view, researchers in the 1960s claimed that mentally retarded children acquired language in the same *manner* as children with normal I.Q. scores, but did so very slowly. In fact, the degree of retardation of a particular child would predict the rate at which that child would develop language (Lenneberg, Nichols, & Rosenberger, 1964). From this point of view, the innate ability to acquire language would be present in all mentally retarded children, but deficits in the nervous system would lead to a slowed — not different — development. Given the fact that the child's language acquisition was so slow, he or she would have passed through the "critical stage" (puberty) long before achieving adult competence. A reasonable conclusion of this position was that intellectual competence in general accounted for this delay and, therefore, that language development was dependent on innate cognitive competence but not particular cognitive products.

To test this hypothesis, a longitudinal study of language development in retarded children was carried out (Lackner, 1968). It was found that the pattern of acquisition of syntactic structures in the retarded children studied was quite similar to that found in normally developing children. Other more recent studies have found that when retarded children and children with normal I.Q. scores are matched for mental age, or when mean length of utterance and various aspects of language are measured, there are similarities in the patterns of language acquired, both in terms of vocabulary and in syntactic structures used (Ryan, 1975; Layton & Sharifi, 1979).

It appears from these studies that rate of language development, but not pattern of language development, is best predicted by I.Q. scores on standard tests of intelligence. Patterns of development are presumbably governed by the innate language acquisition device of the human child. Thus, these researchers appear to be arguing that all mentally retarded children will acquire language up to a certain level. They further argue that this level of development is dictated not by the cognitive competence of the child, but rather by the rate at which the child's cognitive competence allows the language acquisition device to do its job. Puberty marks the end of the period when the special competencies for language acquisition are remarkably modified. Once puberty is reached and the critical period thus over, the child will proceed at an even slower pace.

This position might appear to be a somewhat bewildering one in terms of its implications for determining the relation between cognition and language. However, there are two aspects of language development that it deals with, one quantitative and the other qualitative. Retardation can limit the quantity of language that is acquired but not the quality, since the latter is dependent on the innate language acquisition device of all human learners.

The two positions discussed thus far would argue in almost opposite directions about the relation between cognition and language. Clearly, research in the cognitive and linguistic development of retarded children has not clarified the relation between these two domains. Unfortunately, there is still a third position that has centered around mentally retarded children. This position, in the Piagetian school, holds that until retarded children achieve a certain stage in cognitive development, they will be unable to acquire language at all. Casby and Ruder (1983) argue that language development and symbolic play are both dependent on achievement of means–end and causality by mentally retarded and normal children. Bricker and Bricker (1974) suggest that mentally retarded children be given training in sensori-motor development as a support for language development. As we have already seen, much of the evidence on the relation between cognitive and linguistic products indicates that they are both dependent on the child's ability to deal with information in certain ways. Therefore, programs that are designed to teach the child to "means–ends" or "object permanence," in the hopes that this will lead to language acquisition, seem to be ill advised. Presenting language in a mode that is more accessible to some retarded children (for example, sign language) seems to be having more positive effects on language development than teaching them to achieve certain levels of cognitive development (Abrahamsen, Cavallo, & McCluer, 1985).

Bilingual Children

The bilingual child has often been the subject of argument about the relation between cognition and language. Having two languages has been viewed by one group as causing a cognitive deficit; by another as instilling a cognitive advantage. Comparing the bases for these two arguments and looking at research designed to determine the cognitive effect of having two languages does shed some light on the relation between the two domains of development.

At one time it was held that being bilingual somehow reduces the child's total language competence and, also, produces difficulties in the child's cognitive development. The notion was that the capacity for language acquisition is somehow limited. Therefore, having two languages instead of one meant a reduction in knowledge of either language. Further, if one considered that cognitive development was highly dependent on language knowledge, then this reduction in language would detrimentally affect cognitive development in bilingual children.

It was this position that first led a number of researchers to examine whether, in fact, bilingualism does have a detrimental effect on cognition. The results of these studies indicated that bilingual children are *not* cognitively disadvantaged. In fact, they showed an advantage in certain areas. For example, two studies (Feldman & Shen, 1971; Ianco-Worrall, 1972) found that bilingual children did better than their monolingual peers on a number of cognitive tasks. These tasks included observation of object constancy, switching names of known objects, learning nonsense names, and observing semantic relations among words. The findings of these studies made sense since bilingual children must learn at an early age that labels are arbitrary and that more than one label can have the same meaning. It seems that bilinguals have a specific cognitive advantage, rather than being cognitively ahead of their monolingual peers in all intellectual activities. They are certainly not behind cognitively.

One cognitive advantage of bilingual children that is in the process of being studied is in the area of metaprocessing. The hypothesis is that for the same reasons cited above — that is, knowledge of the arbitrariness of language labels and structural representations — bilingual children are able to "stand back" and think about language data (Bialystok & Ryan, 1985). Whether this metaprocessing ability extends beyond linguistic information has yet to be determined. Again, there is evidence of a bilingual advantage in areas that affect language, but no overall advantage.

What the data on these children indicate is that the state of knowledge of language that a child has can affect the way in which he or she processes language. These differences in language processing can, in turn, affect reading, for example. There is no evidence that an overall cognitive advantage exists for the bilingual child. Therefore, the relation between cognitive and language development is not clarified by studying bilingual children. Despite the fact that the results of such studies do not resolve the issue, they do provide important insights. They indicate that certain kinds of experiences in a domain (in this case, the language domain) lead to certain advantages in that domain. This would be true of other aspects of development as well. Further, findings about the linguistic and cognitive processing of bilingual children point to the fact that no simple decisions should be made about the education of children who come from different language backgrounds. Decisions, obviously, cannot be based on the disproven notion that having two languages results in a cognitive disadvantage.

Understanding Relations Between Language and Cognition

Very simple notions about the relation between cognitive and linguistic development have been held by some researchers and educators. Some of these notions are due to gross interpretations of the three giants of development — Piaget, Werner, and Vygotsky. Other notions are, apparently, due to intuitive prejudices about the relation. Unfortunately, these gross interpretations and prejudices have led to decisions concerning the education of "handicapped" children that have not benefited the children. For example, the view that mentally retarded children should have symbolic play training to help them learn language results from a misinterpretation of Piaget. The contradictory views that deaf children need to have oral language to develop cognitively and that they need no language to develop cognitively both seem to be gross interpretations of everything the developmental psychologists discussed. Finally, the view that bilingual children will be handicapped in both cognitive and linguistic development reflects a prejudiced misunderstanding of the nature of both cognitive and linguistic development.

Results of research on the relation between cognitive and linguistic development point to the fact that the two courses of development are both interdependent and dependent on developmental changes in information processing abilities and strategies. It seems clear that children need to categorize objects and events in the environment before they can learn the relation between these objects and events and the language that is used to represent them or predicate about them. It seems equally clear that after these early developments, language plays an important role in the development of meanings for these categories of objects and events, in the development of concepts, and in analytic and contemplative thinking about these categories and the relations among them.

Products of nonlinguistic and linguistic cognitive development appear to be the result of changes in the information processing abilities and strategies that are applied to particular domains in both areas of development. In some instances information processing changes appear to result in almost simultaneous changes in both areas. For example, certain levels of sensori-motor competence and the child's production of holophrastic utterances seem to be simultaneous developments. However, later cognitive and linguistic developments do not seem so closely related. This is probably due to differences in experience in the two areas. The more familiar the area, the more rapid is the developmental change that occurs in processing in that area.

In addition, two factors that play an important role in cognitive and linguistic development must be considered by educators: the factors of affect and of cultural experience. Werner and other psychologists (for example, Bruner, 1957) have shown that the threshold for attending and processing information can be shifted by the positive or negative affect of the information processor. This, in turn, can be a product not only of individual variation but also of cultural experience, since cultural experience will dictate the domains in which the information processing abilities of the child will be applied. The unfamiliar can generate negative feelings and the familiar, positive ones.

As can be seen, there are no simple answers to the question of the relations between cognition and language. However, the question is an important one for educational planning for children, both those who have developmental problems and those who are developing normally.

Chapter Four
Capacity to Acquire Language

The theories of language acquisition that were discussed in Chapter Two all suggest that the human infant has a unique capacity to acquire language. This was true of even the behaviorist S-R-R theories. Although these latter theories lay primary emphasis on the role of the environment in shaping language behavior, they also point to the special human ability to use speech as part of the response repertoire.

What this uniquely human capacity consists of has been a matter of much theorizing and research. One set of questions that has been addressed is: What, if anything, is different in:

1. Man's language compared to other animals' communication systems?
2. Man's use of language compared to other animals' use of their systems?
3. Man's acquisition of human language as compared to other animals' acquisition of their symbol systems?

Another set of questions is:

1. What are early, innate, or very quickly learned behaviors that might be prerequisite to language development?
2. Are these behaviors different in human infants compared to other animal infants?
3. What experiments of nature shed light on the nature of man's ability to acquire and use a language?

Answers to these questions not only contribute to a better theoretical understanding of the human infant's potential to acquire language, they also contribute to a better understanding of the language behavior of children with developmental disabilities. Furthermore, they provide insight into reasonable educational and therapeutic goals for children with developmental disabilities.

In this chapter the results of research comparing human language to other animals' communication systems are briefly discussed. A large portion of the chapter is devoted to the findings of research concerning the biological, social, and cognitive readiness of the human infant to acquire a human language system and examining whether these behaviors are unique to the human infant. The final section of the chapter will examine conclusions reached about the biological basis of language acquisition based on findings with brain-damaged children and adults and child and adult second language acquirers.

Language and Communication

Two of the questions cited in the introduction to this chapter bear on the issue of whether language is unique to man and, therefore, whether man is structurally and functionally different from other animals.

Language versus Communication and Language

The position that man's language is distinctly different from other animals' communication systems and the position that the animals' systems are primitive languages represent the different views of those who have examined the nature and use of communication interaction between members of nonhuman species and human groups. Some researchers consider that language is not comparable to other communication systems (Hockett, 1963) while others consider language to be a continuation of the behaviors observed in subhuman species (Campbell, 1970). These arguments appear difficult to reconcile since the evolutionary data needed are unavailable. One can only extrapolate from the evidence of the skulls of earlier stages of man that the ability to produce speech was not at first present in man and, therefore, that human oral language cannot be a product of the extension of subhuman primates' communication systems (Lieberman, 1974).

More crucial to deciding whether language is unique to man are discussions concerning possible differences in competence that are reflected by acquiring a language versus acquiring a communication system. That is, a feasible goal seems to be determining what one must know in order to fully use a language versus a communication system. Further, the product of this determination would shed more light on man's possible uniqueness than would resolution of whether or not man's language is an extension of other animals' communication systems. Resolution of what you have to know to acquire man's language is especially important for determining goals in therapeutic intervention with some populations of children. However, the two aspects, differences in systems and differences in use, must be related to each other since the content and structure of the system determine its use to some extent.

Some of the principal differences between human language and other animal communication systems that are frequently discussed (in, for example, Fromkin & Rodman, 1978) are arbitrariness, creativity, and discreteness of human languages. What these characteristics require from the language learner is the focus here.

Discreteness implies that the system is made up of separable units (that may exist at several levels) and requires that learners have the competence to determine what those units are. For example, words are made up of discrete sounds that can be rearranged in different ways ("top," "pot," and "opt"), and sentences are made up of discrete words that can be rearranged in different ways ("Mary kissed John," "John kissed Mary"). *Arbitrariness* implies that these units represent (but are not themselves) objects, events, and the relation between objects and events. The acquisition of language by a human requires the ability to represent by using symbols. *Creativity* implies that the separable units in the system can be combined in infinitely unique but constrained ways (as in the examples given above), and requires the ability of the language learner to determine what groups or sets of combinations are possible.

At one time it was suggested that no animal communication system, besides human language, had *all three* of these characteristics. For example, the dance of the bees to indicate the location of honey has two of the three characteristics. The dance is both arbitrary and creative. It is not, however, composed of discrete units embedded in each other. These differences suggest, at least, differences in the functioning of the human as compared to other animals.

There are abilities of the human language user that point very dramatically to differences in the structure and functioning of humans as compared to other animals. These are the traditional competencies pointed to by Chomsky (1965). They include the ability to detect *nongrammaticality* (judging that units are put together the wrong way), *anomaly* (judging that units are put together in meaningless ways), *paraphrase* (judging that units put together in different ways mean the same thing), and *ambiguity* (judging that units put together the same way can have different meanings). There is evidence that birds can detect that their recorded song is incorrect when it has been segmented and put together in the wrong order (Marler, 1963). Therefore, members of other species can judge nongrammaticality. But there is no evidence that they can analyze their system in terms of anomaly, paraphrase, and ambiguity. There is no evidence that animals other than humans are capable of using their communication systems in all these ways.

Given these differences in the characteristics of communication systems and in their use, one would expect to find differences in the structure and function of the nervous system of humans as compared to other animals. What these differences are is not easy to determine. One way to proceed is to examine the causes of the behavior of individuals who give evidence of differences in the structure and function of their language knowledge.

Differences in Language Acquired

The controversy between those who hold that apes and chimpanzees have shown they can acquire a sign language and those who say they have not revolves around whether the apes have acquired an organized grammatical system or, rather, simply a group of labels. Another crucial aspect of the argument is whether or not the behavior apes have acquired can be considered a stage in the development of an adult language, similar to the stage reached by two-year-old children. Those who argue for the ape as a language user say yes and those who argue against this notion say no.

Some theorists have held that the reasons for being concerned with the controversy are practical as well as theoretical. If humans are biologically different in structural and functional ways from the apes and chimpanzees, then determination of the nature of these differences is a feasible goal and one that would reveal the bases for language (and other special) abilities. If humans are not structurally and functionally different, but only more able than subhuman species, then the ways in which chimpanzees and apes learn should have bearing on how less able humans (for example, the retarded) should be taught.

The evidence of whether apes and chimpanzees have acquired a sign system similar to human sign language has been reviewed (Seidenberg & Petitto, 1979). This review suggests that the claim made for chimpanzees acquiring a language in a fashion similar to that of young children (Gardner & Gardner, 1975) is simply incorrect. In essence, the reviewers argue that there is little evidence provided by the researchers of chimpanzee sign acquisition that the animals use the same types of structure and combination of structures as young humans. Such behavior is either not evident in the continuous taped material of, for example, Terrace (1979), or there is insufficient material in other samples. Presumably there is only evidence of random concatenation of elements (for example, "me apple apple apple me") and a great deal of cueing on the part of the investigators.

In addition to no evidence in chimpanzees' signs of the structures used by children in the early stages of acquiring oral or manual language, there is also little evidence that what *is* acquired *is* acquired and used in the same way. That is, there is little evidence that chimpanzees attend to particular aspects of an "utterance" presented to them or make judgments of the grammaticality of utterances in the way that very young children do (Gleitman, Gleitman, & Shipley, 1972). These data suggest that there is no evidence to support the notion that chimpanzee sign acquisition reflects the beginning stages or foundation for the acquisition of more sophisticated language. Premack (1985) describes what he believes are the essential differences between humans' knowledge and use of language and other animals' use of sign and other man-made systems. He states that their language knowledge is asyntactic (as indicated by concatenated strings), they do not converse (as indicated by the fact that they do not engage in discourse on a topic), and they cannot induce rules from the data given them (their responses are conditioned, not rule-governed).

There is evidence of chimpanzees' and apes' ability to acquire a lexicon, a repertoire of signs to represent. This ability indicates that probably those structures and functions that are required for the acquisition of a lexicon are not unique to men. It is in the ability to use semantactic rules (rules for the combination of morphemes in meaningful ways) that there may be underlying differences in structure and function. Table 4-1 summarizes the differences and similarities in the language of humans as compared to other animals' communication systems, in the abilities of each to use their systems, and in the similarities and differences in chimpanzees' (and gorillas') and children's acquisition of natural languages.

As Table 4-1 indicates, there are differences in the language to be acquired and in the uses of that language between human language and other animal communication systems. These indicate differences of kind — not just of degree — and point to underlying differences in the structure and functioning of the human nervous system compared to that of other animals. This suggestion is further supported by evidence of differences in the acquisition and use of man-made language by chimpanzees and by young children. These differences

Table 4-1 Similarities and differences in human and subhuman primate systems, abilities, and aspects of acquisition of man-made systems.

	DIFFERENCES	SIMILARITIES
In system	Discreteness	Arbitrariness Creativity
In abilities	Judge anomaly, paraphrase, ambiguity	Detect grammaticality
In aspects of man-made systems	Semantax Pragmatics	Lexicon

need to be kept in mind when one attempts to evaluate the usefulness of approaches to teaching language to less able humans that are based on approaches used with chimpanzees and apes.

Readiness to Acquire Language

We have stated that there should be underlying structural and functional differences in the neurophysiology of humans and other animals to account for differences in the communication systems acquired. Evidence concerning human infants' *biological readiness* to acquire language will be discussed first. This biological readiness, the data indicate, includes early differences in information processing functions as well as neurological functions; this topic will be discussed under the heading of *cognitive readiness*. Since language is a communication system, involving social interaction among participants in its use, some form of *social readiness* may also be an important prerequisite for the development of language. This will be the final topic discussed.

The questions to be addressed in this section of the chapter are:

- □ Is there evidence of structural and functional uniqueness, specifically committed to language processing, in the central nervous system of man?
- □ Are there early behaviors that appear to be indications of innate or very quickly learned precursors to language development?
- □ Are these behaviors unique to the human infant?

Biological Readiness

Human infants are born with a structurally unique vocal mechanism, a uniquely functioning auditory system, and a structurally unique and uniquely functioning brain. These are the aspects of biological readiness that are said to be necessary precursors to the acquisition of human language. Each of these aspects of readiness, in turn, interacts with the other aspects. Various theoreticians and researchers have emphasized the different aspects, but, presumably, the biological preprogramming of the infant to acquire language consists of all aspects and their interaction.

The Vocal Mechanism. The infant's vocal mechanism is unique. Comparisons of the vocal mechanism of humans and subhuman primates indicate that there are several characteristics that are unique to man. These include the positioning of the larynx, the size and mobility of the tongue, the shape of the lips, and the relation between upper and lower jaw (Lieberman, 1974). The larynx of the chimpanzee is positioned much higher in the pharnyx and therefore the walls cannot be used to produce resonant sound. The tongue of the chimpanzee is much thinner than man's and much less mobile, precluding the possibility of much variation in the sounds produced. The much thinner lips and much further extending lower jaw of the chimpanzee also constrain the variation of sounds that can be produced. All of these unique vocal features make articulate speech a possibility for man — and an impossibility for members of subhuman species. This explains the total failure of researchers to teach chimpanzees to speak, despite heroic and long-term efforts (Hayes, 1952).

Examination of the vocal tract of the human infant indicates that the infant is not ready, at birth, to produce articulated sounds. Dramatic changes occur over the first six to twelve weeks of life in the sizes of and relation among the parts of the vocal tract. However, as early as twelve weeks, the potential for producing fully articulated sounds is present (Truby, Bosma, & Lind, 1965).

Clearly, the twelve-week-old infant does not produce a full repertoire of articulated sounds and, on the average, will not begin to do so until some five months later. This ability is dependent on the development of control of the vocal system and, therefore, on biological maturation. Readiness, then, consists of two parts. The first is the availability of certain kinds of structures, and the second is biological maturation along certain prescribed paths — the development of the units (pharynx, larynx, jaw, and tongue) of the vocal mechanism and their proportions. This should and does result in all infants following the same sequence of development in gaining control of the motor mechanism and, also, in individual variation in the rate at which motor control of the system develops.

There is no doubt that the vocal mechanism of man is unique and, therefore, that the normally developing human infant is biologically preprogrammed to acquire articulate speech. However, this unique aspect of man programs the infant to acquire *speech,* not *language,* and the evidence of the language competence that some cerebral-palsied individuals have indicates that they may have full understanding of language even though their speech is severely constrained.

The Auditory Mechanism. The auditory mechanism of man and, therefore, of the human infant, is not structurally unique. Guinea pigs, chinchillas, and certainly chimpanzees have auditory mechanisms that are structurally similar to that of man. Despite this similarity in structure, it has been suggested by some researchers that man's auditory system is functionally unique. This functional uniqueness resides in man's ability to perceive speech in special ways, which are based on man's ability to discriminate between speech sounds in a categorical way. Even though the actual production of a speech sound can vary from speaker to speaker and from time to time and can result in a partially different acoustic event each time, instances of a speech sound will be consistently identified. It has been suggested that this is based on the fact that different sounds have distinct articulatory gestures associated with them (Liberman, 1970). It has also been suggested that there are unique acoustic characteristics of different speech-sound sets that listeners are sensitive to (Blumstein, 1986).

If the first suggestion is correct, then human infants should process speech in special ways. Also, they should process it in ways that are different from other animals because human infants produce sounds that other animals cannot produce. If the second suggestion is correct, and infants can perceive acoustic differences between speech sounds in a categorical manner, then, also, infants should process speech in special ways. However, other animals should be able to make the same kind of discriminations because there are no differences between human infants' and other animals' hearing mechanisms. The question of whether infants perceive speech in special ways has been examined extensively over the past decade. Whether other animals can make the same kinds of discriminations has been examined more recently. (See Chapter Eleven for complete information.)

The question asked in many of the studies was: Do infants discriminate between speech sounds on an auditory (acoustic feature) basis or on a phonetic (speech-sound feature) basis? To answer this question, infants were exposed to computer-produced stimuli that contrasted either two speech-sound categories (such as /pa/ versus /ba/) or two speech sounds that came from the same category (for example, two /bas/) but varied in their acoustic characteristics. There were differences in voice onset time of the two /bas/. Given this task, adults would discriminate between the two speech-sound categories (/pa/ and /ba/) but not the two acoustically different stimuli within the same speech sound category (the two /bas/), unless specifically trained to do so. The same is true of infants. They also do not discriminate between the two /bas/, but only between /pa/ and /ba/.

A number of speech-sound contrasts have been examined in infants from one to twelve months of age. The overall finding of these studies has been that, regardless of the particular speech-sound contrast being examined, infants discriminate among speech sounds that come from different categories but not among those that are within a category and that differ only acoustically (Morse, 1978).

These findings might suggest that special speech-processing abilities are part of that innate biological preprogramming of the human infant that allows the acquisition of language. However, more recent findings indicate that discrimination of auditory stimuli in general, and not speech in particular, is categorical. Therefore, the ability to discriminate speech categorically may be necessary for language acquisition but is not a biologically preprogrammed special ability. It is only part of a larger ability to discriminate all types of sensory stimuli categorically (Aslin, Pisoni, & Jusczyk, 1983).

The second part of the question concerning the uniqueness of the human infants' auditory mechanism was: Do infants perceive in ways that are different from other animals? The answer appears to be no. Some studies of speech discrimination in the chinchilla (Kuhl & Miller, 1978) and in the rhesus monkey (Morse & Snowdon, 1975) indicate that with some training these animals can discriminate between speech sounds categorically.

These findings leave in some disarray the position that the auditory mechanism of the human infant is specifically and uniquely designed to process speech in special ways. What the infant can do in terms of processing sensory stimuli probably does play a very important role in language acquisition. It is clear, however, that the auditory processing of the human infant is not specifically but, rather, generally designed to perceive speech. Further, and very importantly, there is clear evidence from the sign-language acquisition of deaf infants that special auditory processing abilities are not necessary for the acquisition of language, only for the acquisition of oral language.

The Brain. The question of whether man's brain is structurally or functionally different from the brains of other animals has been self-consciously studied for many decades. Recently the results of this study produced new insights on the issue, but there is still a long way to go before there is real understanding of where the differences lie.

Some structural characteristics that distinguish man's brain from that of other animals would clearly be present at birth. In addition, there are structural changes that occur over maturation that could certainly affect the processing of information. For example, myelinization (forming a sheath about some nerve fibers), which results in more rapid transmission of information along nerve pathways, takes place largely over the first three years of life. This change in structure clearly affects information processing. There are, then, structural characteristics that might be unique at birth and others that develop over time, as was the case with the vocal mechanism. In addition to structural differences, there are functional differences. These differences will be discussed in terms of whether or not they are specifically related to the acquisition of language.

Structural Differences. Two special structural characteristics of the human brain that have been noted are (1) its size in relation to body weight and (2) its organization. The brain of the adult gorilla (the closest to man, intellectually) is less than one-half the size of the adult human brain. Size in proportion to body weight could affect the amount of information that could be processed. Grossly speaking, there is more cortex in the human brain, as compared to the gorilla's brain, that is dedicated to nerve pathways that associate visual, auditory, and tactile information (Geschwind, 1965). The result of this difference is the ability to make more rapid cross-modal associations (an object and its name, an object and what it feels like, and so on). In fact, it may be the case that the rate at which one can process information can have a profound effect on the kinds of information that are processed and the way in which information is stored.

Another structural difference between man's and other animals' brains is the degree to which the central nervous system is uncommitted to specific tasks. Another term for this is the greater degree of "plasticity" in the human nervous system as compared to other animals. This is said to be reflected in the much longer biological maturation period of the human nervous system (Lenneberg, 1967). The notion is that more can happen, given this greater potential for change.

None of these structural differences seems to be specifically dedicated to the acquisition of language. Rather, the differences may simply be the basis for man's greater ability to process certain kinds of information in certain ways.

The last structural difference is, in fact, the only one that seems specifically related to the acquisition of language, and it too might be the basis for a general ability. It has been found on postmortem examination of a number of infants that the left hemisphere is larger in a certain area than is this area in the right hemisphere of a large proportion of these infants (Wada, Clark, & Hamm, 1975). Since the left hemisphere is considered both the dominant hemisphere for most individuals and the area where speech resides, it has been suggested that this structural difference may be crucial for language acquisition. This does not seem totally correct, since only a large proportion of the infants showed this left hemisphere difference. One might assume that the others — with, perhaps, right dominance — would have acquired language as well.

The structural differences cited do not argue well for the brain being specifically designed to acquire language. Data concerning brain damage in adults certainly point to specific areas being specifically dedicated to language. Research results on the language processing of children with known or suspected damage indicate that areas of the brain might be specialized for certain tasks much earlier than suspected and, perhaps, point to the existence of underlying preformed structures not previously suspected. The possibility that areas of the brain are committed very early to engaging in specific tasks is also supported by findings that indicate left hemisphere commitment to speech processing. Molfese and Molfese (1979) report that even in neonates there is significantly greater left hemisphere electrical activity when speech is presented and significantly greater right hemisphere activity when music is presented.

Functional Differences. The functional differences being presently researched all deal with the types, amount of, and rate of information processing that the human system is capable of as compared to other animals. These differences, like the structural differences, do not point to a specific and unique capacity to acquire language. Even differences in left — as compared to right — hemisphere tasks can serve a general, not specifically linguistic, role in the different kinds of processing man engages in. Furthermore, man is not the only being that has a dominant hemisphere. However, man is the only animal that has specialized *functions* of the two hemispheres. Since many of the differences found between man and other animals are differences in information processing, they appear to have more to do with cognitive readiness than with biological readiness for language.

Cognitive Readiness

In a discussion of infant perception, Flavell (1985) summarizes what research has shown us about cognitive abilities of infants: "Infants' perceptual capabilities are a good deal more impressive than we used to assume they were" (p. 167). In fact, recent research indicates that the infant, from birth, processes information in ways that indicate preformed biological structures. These preformed structures act as filters on experience. To begin with, infants attend to only certain aspects of all sensory stimuli. The parameters of what they process change in time and these changes are a function of both biological and cognitive maturation as well as of experience.

There are two very early processing abilities that seem to be especially designed for language acquisition. One is the ability to relate auditory and visual information. The other is the ability to imitate. Developments of these processing abilities are, of course, dependent on changes in memory.

Research in intermodal perception concerned with the relation between seeing and hearing events and hearing and feeling events seems most germane to the process of language acquisition. In acquiring a lexicon, the child must relate a phonological sequence to an object or event. To acquire a productive speech-sound system, the child must relate what he says to what he feels.

Newborns can localize sound. This may indicate that they are searching for the source of the sound and have a predisposition to identify events intermodally. Such a possibility has been suggested by Gibson and Spelke (1983). They found, in examining the abilities of four-month-old infants, that the infants related the sight of an object with the sounds that accompanied the sight. Other research suggests that four- to five-month-old babies relate the articulation of a sound to what it looks like on the lips (Kuhl & Meltzoff, 1982), and that one-month-old infants can relate a previously experienced tactile stimulus to a sight (Meltzoff & Borton, 1979).

These findings do not have direct bearing on lexical and speech-sound acquisition, but do indicate that intermodal associations are possible for very young infants. The behaviors cited may be precursors to the sight- or feel-sound relations and speak-feel relations that are required in language acquisition.

Research on infant imitation — and, in particular, delayed imitation — not only addresses the issue of intermodal association but also seems to have a very direct bearing on language acquisition. Meltzoff (1986) found that two-to-three-week-old babies will imitate the facial expressions of adults, even after some delay. These data also indicate that even at a very young age the infant is capable of storing and retrieving information of certain kinds.

The development of memory in infants obviously plays a very important role in language development. That newborns can recognize seen or heard stimuli is shown by their ability to habituate. They grow tired of recognized stimuli and no longer display the interest they show to novel stimuli. Kail (1984) summarizes the research on memory development in infancy. He indicates that six-month-old infants can recognize stimuli seen and heard after about two weeks (they do not treat such stimuli as novel instances), and that two-to-three-month-old infants can exceed that retention time if the situation is cued; that is, when the experimenter sets up the situation to remind the infant of some aspect of a previous experience. At six to seven months, recall memory is observed. It is interesting to note that so-called true babbling, the motor repetition of consonant-vowel sequences, begins at approximately this time or shortly thereafter.

The newborn's attentional filter and the developing infant's ability to intermodally relate, recognize events, and, finally, to recall them seem very important precursors to the development of language. It is clear that without being given the experiences to remember, the infant would not develop these abilities. However, it also seems clear that these abilities are a function of the structures and functions of the human nervous system and of biological maturation.

Social Readiness

Social readiness, which might be presumed to be only a product of interaction, also seems to be dependent on either innate structures and functions or predispositions. The behavior of imitating facial expressions seems to be a very good candidate for indicating innate social readiness. The ability of the infant to imitate facial expressions might be an important precursor to the ability to recognize intent (as indicated by others' facial expressions) and, thus, to communicate appropriately. Sensitivity to paralinguistic cues (of which facial expressions is one) is a very important aspect of pragmatic competence.

Another aspect of pragmatic competence is the ability to use the suprasegmental aspects of speech: intonation and stress. These capabilities are summarized in Menyuk (1977). An early indication of the ability to do this is the three-month-old infant's ability to discriminate between male and female voices and between the voice of its mother and that of a female stranger. This is clearly the beginning of speaker identification, and is one aspect of identification and bonding with the mother.

Suprasegmental features, as well as facial expression, indicate the intent of the speaker. Without visual input, infants of three months and younger can discriminate between friendly and unfriendly voices. During the earliest months of life, infants can discriminate between falling versus steady and falling versus rising intonational contours on syllables, and during the six-to-eight-month period give evidence of being able to discriminate between question and statement sentences.

All of these data point to the infant's very early ability to use information that is crucial for comprehending the communication intent of others. In addition, there is apparently direct evidence of the infant's predisposition to communicate. The turn-taking behaviors of infants seem to indicate that they are very sensitive to certain fundamental aspects of conversation. They apparently recognize when they are or are not being addressed (Trevarthan, 1986), and they know when to take a turn (Bateson, 1969).

Conversational turn-taking, as represented by infants filling in the conversational slots their caregivers leave, has been observed at three months and even earlier. When infants are addressed by their caregivers, they will focus on their caregivers' faces and, given the cue of a pause, rising intonation, and facial expression, respond with vocalization. Even when the caregiver is facing the infant but the tone of voice is not appropriate (for example, the caregiver is addressing another adult), the infant will indicate understanding of the fact that she or he is not being addressed by looking away.

The signs of cognitive readiness are a product of both biology and experience. This is also the case with signs of social readiness. If the environment did not elicit responses and provide models to imitate and data to work on, the infant probably would not show signs of social readiness, or such signs might be quickly extinguished. The question of what comes first, the infant's or the environment's behavior, is not a trivial one. It certainly has important implications for education and intervention.

A well-known study by Bell and Ainsworth (1972) seems to have some bearing on the issue. These researchers studied the vocalization behavior of a group of infants over the first year of life to find out what effect parental response has on an infant's cry. They found that infants whose mothers responded promptly and frequently to their cries had lower amplitude and frequency of crying during the second quarter of the first year than did those whose mothers did not. They also began to use noncry vocalizations more rapidly, and used them more frequently during the third and fourth quarters of the first year. The researchers concluded that their data indicated an innate predisposition to communicate by vocalizing, regardless of environmental conditions. This is probably correct, given that all normally developing children do acquire language. Their data, however, also indicate that environmental response can affect the rate of development of vocalizations.

Summary of Readiness for Language

Data on the development of the infant during the first year of life give evidence of the infant's readiness in specific ways to acquire and use language. Table 4-2 lists the behaviors that are hypothesized to be related to language acquisition.

Table 4-2 Aspects of readiness for language acquisition at birth and in early infancy.

TYPE OF READINESS	ASPECTS OF READINESS	TIME OBSERVED
Biological	Vocal mechanism	At birth
	Categorical perception	At birth
	Brain maturation	At birth
	Proportional size	
	Structure	
	Specialization in function	
Cognitive	Cross-modal associations	At birth
	Imitation	2–3 weeks
	Recognition of stimuli	1 week
	Recall of stimuli	2 months
Social	Recognition of being addressed	2–3 weeks
	Imitation of facial expressions	2–3 weeks
	Turn-taking	3 months
	Recognition of affect of prosody	2–3 months

These behaviors appear to be a product of preprogrammed structures and functions of man's nervous system and the maturational path these structures and functions take. However, what these structures are, how they function, and how they develop in time has not been determined. Also, a close examination of the table indicates that some of the behaviors that are said to be innate structures or predispositions are within the repertoire of animals other than man. For example, recognition of affect in terms of facial expression and tone of voice is clearly not limited to human infants. Certainly, among subhuman primates, turn-taking is a common practice between infant and caregiver. However, the use of vocalization as the primary form of the interaction seems to be limited to human caregivers and infants.

Some of the other behaviors listed in the table also seem to be within the grasp of subhuman primates. They can imitate, discriminate on the basis of intermodal relations, and remember. Their attentional devices are probably somewhat different, as are their memory functions. Thus, while the behaviors listed may indeed be the product of innate structures, functions, and developments that lay the groundwork for language acquisition, it is not clear how these predispositions in themselves result in the acquisition of a *unique* communication system, human language.

The primary task in determining what leads to this unique acquisition appears to be a more precise definition of the structures, functions, and developments that make the acquisition possible. Some researchers have held that this more precise definition can be obtained by an examination of the language behaviors that result from experiments of nature.

Experiments of Nature

Only two types of experiments of nature will be discussed here. Excluded are those experiments of nature that result in blindness and deafness. Sight and hearing are not crucial to language acquisition in toto, only to some aspects of acquisition. Also excluded is mental retardation. The nervous system differences that are found with mental retardation clearly affect language, but it is also clear that these differences affect all aspects of information processing. Therefore, such a condition provides little information about mechanisms dedicated to language acquisition and use. The two types of experiments to be discussed are brain damage in children and adults and second language acquisition in children and adults. It has been held by a number of researchers that these conditions provide information about dedicated language acquisition and processing mechanisms. Whether or not this is the case will be become clearer as each area of research is discussed.

Brain Damage

Several questions have been asked about the effects of brain damage:

- □ What differential effect does later damage have on language behavior, as compared to early brain damage?
- □ Does site of lesion make a difference in the language-behavior consequences observed?
- □ Are particular language behaviors affected by particular types of lesion?

Answers to these questions should provide us with a clearer definition of the structures that may be dedicated to the acquisition of language. If damage at an early age has no effect on language behavior, then one might presume that there are no early preprogrammed mechanisms that are specifically designed to allow language acquisition. If the location of lesion makes a difference in behavior, then these preprogrammed mechanisms are locatable. Finally, if different types of lesion have differing effects on certain aspects of language, then one might be able to parcel out those aspects of language that are dependent on mechanisms especially designed for language acquisition and those that are not.

Early versus Late Damage. For a long time it was held that children who had initially lost — or were delayed in acquiring — some language behaviors after early brain damage eventually regained their total language competence. Adults who suffered language disabilities because of brain damage did not ever completely recover their language abilities. It was thought that this difference was due to two facts. Adults by virtue of development and experience have a committed nervous system that is organized to carry out linguistic tasks in certain ways and in certain places. Young children, however, have not achieved this organization, and, therefore, the undamaged tissues could take over the tasks of the damaged areas.

More recent research indicates that this is not correct. First, as has been noted, neonates give evidence of differences in at least the attention paid by the two hemispheres to different types of stimuli. The right hemisphere attends to music and the left to speech. Dichotic listening studies with younger and younger children indicate that lateralization of speech processing has occurred at a very young age (Kinsbourne, 1975). These data argue against the notion that the infant's nervous system is organizationally uncommitted and, therefore, that early damage can have no lasting effects.

Some researchers have questioned the validity of studies that made the claim that early damage has no lasting effects (Wittelson, 1977; Woods & Carey, 1979). These researchers have suggested that the subjects of the studies suffered varied types of damage and, therefore, that the persistence of the effects might be due to only certain types of damage. Another researcher (Robinson, 1981) reviewed such cases and stated that when the types of lesion are similar to those found in adults, then the difficulties encountered by the children are similar. Cooper (1982) found that children who had suffered lesions between three and twelve years of age showed a variety of impairments at ages ten to eighteen. There were those who had no or few difficulties and those with continued severe impairments. All these data suggest that the continued effect of early lesion depends on the site and extent of that early lesion.

Site of Lesion. Dennis (1980) has provided a great deal of data on the linguistic and nonlinguistic abilities of hemispherectomized (one hemisphere removed) children. She has found that those who have their left hemisphere removed have great difficulty with certain syntactic processing, reading, writing, and spelling.

Although all these studies do not directly address the question of the lasting effect of early lesion, they do indicate that location of lesion may be a crucial factor in determining whether there are or are not lasting effects on language behavior.

Pursuing the notion that only certain lesions have lasting effects, Aram, Ekelman, and Whitaker (1985) examined the effect of early lesion on two groups of youngsters, those with clearly documented left hemisphere lesions and those with documented right hemisphere lesions. The children with left hemisphere lesions suffered damage at one month to six years. Those with right lesions suffered damage at two months to three years. The left damaged children were tested at two to eight years and the right damaged at two to six years. Each child was matched on sex, age, SES, and race with a nonlesioned peer who suffered from a cardiac condition. The overall finding of the study was that children with left lesions performed significantly more poorly than their nonlesioned controls on a number of sentence-processing measures. The right-lesioned children performed somewhat poorer than their controls on a measure of morphology, but equal to them on other aspects of sentence processing. In particular, left-lesioned children differed from their peers in MLU (mean length of utterance), in their DDS score (a measure of the syntactic variety of the utterances produced), and in the percentage of sentences correctly produced. The differences between each lesioned group and their controls on these measures is shown in Figure 4-1.

As Aram, Ekelman, and Whitaker (1985) cautiously state, these children need to be followed to determine whether the differences persist. The results

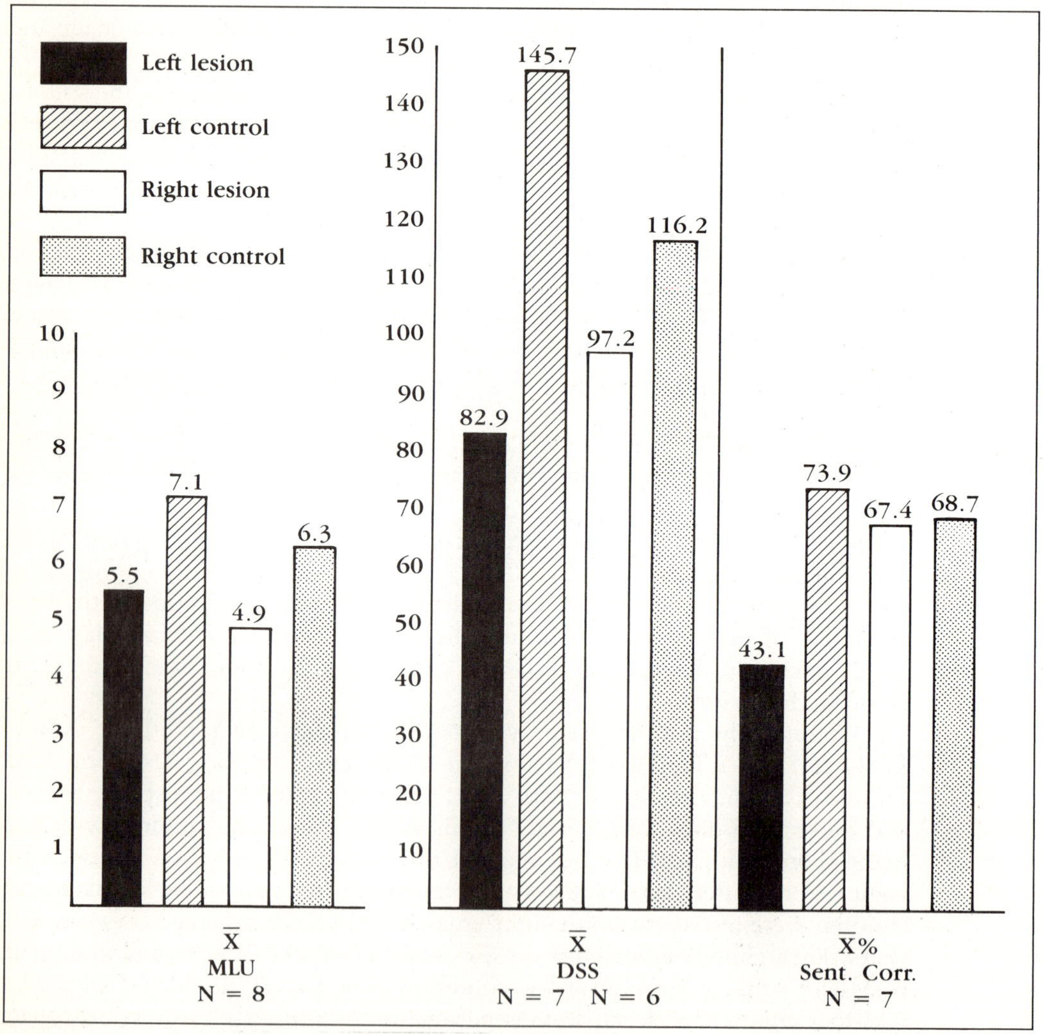

Figure 4-1 Performance of children with left- and right-hemisphere lesions and their controls on some measures of language.

of the study illustrated in Figure 4-1 indicate that early damage is not overcome after three to five years. Further, the study indicates that the left, or dominant, hemisphere is probably the site in which particular mechanisms for the processing of at least some aspects of language (production of sentences) reside. We can derive this information from the study because it is longitudinal and because the site of lesion has been carefully documented. What we do not know, because the question was not asked, is whether the particular type of lesion suffered by each child differentially affected different aspects of language.

Type of Lesions. Several researchers who have studied the language behavior of children with suspected but not frank lesion (there is no evidence that they have suffered a lesion) have suggested that there is evidence of differential behavior in these children that may be linked to different types of lesion. Aphasic adults exhibit different kinds of deficits, depending on the site and extent of the lesions that they have suffered. An analysis of the language behavior of children who have been labelled "dysphasic" led to the conclusion that differences among them were similar to some types of adult aphasia (Menyuk, 1978). The behavior of children labelled "learning disabled" also varies.

Children have been found to have several different types of learning disability (Knights & Bakker, 1976). Grossly speaking, there are some learning-disabled children whose deficits lie in the area of visual-spatial processing, and others with difficulties in auditory-verbal processing. One might logically hypothesize that the differences in behavior in linguistic and nonlinguistic processing among dysphasic and learning-disabled children are due to differences in site and nature of the lesion suffered by these children.

It appears likely that continued research with frankly lesioned children and those with suspected lesion will provide some information about the structures, functions, and developments that are especially committed to language processing. At the present moment, however, these structures, functions, and developments are not well defined. However, given the new techniques available for documenting site and nature of lesion, perhaps a greater definition of structure and function will be achieved.

Second-Language Acquisition

It was thought by some researchers that the study of the patterns of second-language acquisition would provide information about nervous system structures, functions, and developments that underlie first-language acquisition. This notion has developed from the work of Lenneberg (1967). Lenneberg hypothesized that there was a critical period of development for language acquisition that extended from birth until puberty. This critical period, he hypothesized, was similar to critical periods of learning in other animals. For example, it has been found that unless young birds acquire their song within a certain time period, they never acquire the exact song of their species (Marler, 1963).

Lenneberg based his hypothesis of a critical period for learning language on the following observations. He observed that children who become deaf after age two have much less difficulty in acquiring speech than do children who are deaf at birth. Thus, one could hypothesize that some exposure during the critical period was essential. Mentally retarded children were said to acquire language in much the same way as nonretarded children, although much more slowly, until they reached puberty. At this point their language development "plateaued" and very little further language development was observed. Therefore, one could hypothesize that the critical period lasted until puberty. Finally, prepubertal second-language acquirers were able to achieve native-like competence in the second language, whereas postpubertal learners were never able to do so — another example of the length of the critical period. These examples and others led Lenneberg to hypothesize that language developed in a fixed pattern within this critical period, and that this pattern was therefore dependent on neurological maturation.

For a long time the questions asked by researchers about the acquisition of a second language were based on these hypotheses. Two of the questions asked are similar to questions that have been asked about brain damage:

- Does the age at which a second language is acquired have an effect on the level of competence achieved in that language?
- What aspects of language are affected by the age at which this second language is acquired?

If prepubertal second-language acquirers are much more competent than postpubertal acquirers, then the notions of a critical period tied to neurological maturation might be substantiated. If some aspects of language are affected by the age at which these aspects are acquired, and not other aspects, then a clearer picture of the biologically based mechanisms for language acquisition might be obtained.

For some time the data obtained on patterns of second-language acquisition appeared to support the notion of a critical period. Krashen (1975) summarized the results of a number of studies. It appeared to be the case that early and later second-language acquirers differed from each other in the following ways:

1. Prepubertal acquirers were similar to first-language acquirers in the process by which acquisition took place, while postpubertal acquirers were not.
2. Prepubertal learners could acquire the second language without formal instruction, while postpubertal learners could not.
3. Postpubertal learners always had a foreign accent, whereas prepubertal learners did not.

4. Prepubertal learners acquired native competence in syntax and semantics, but postpubertal learners did not.

Despite these findings, Krashen suggested that the critical period hypothesis was incorrect. He argued that it must be incorrect since there are, presumably, lasting effects of early brain damage, and since lateralization for speech processing takes place long before puberty. The prepubertal-postpubertal differences that were found, therefore, must be due to some other, nonbiological factor. The alternative hypothesis presented was that a shift in cognitive functioning occurs between pre- and post-puberty. This is the shift from concrete operational to formal operational thinking. This shift, stated Krashen, results in a much greater awareness of language and self-consciousness on the part of the adolescent and adult learner, in contrast to the intuitive learning style of the prepubertal child.

Clearly the learning styles of children and adults are different. It is less clear that the learning style of the adult, as compared to that of the child, should inevitably lead to a lesser competence in any area of learning. These possibilities have prompted a more careful look at differences between child and adult language learners. These further studies have indicated that when the conditions under which the second language is acquired are kept constant across age groups, the advantage of the young child disappears.

One such study was carried out by Snow and Hoefnagel-Hohle (1978). These researchers compared the competence of different-aged second-language learners over time in different areas of language behavior. Their subjects ranged in age from three years to adulthood. They measured speech discrimination and production, vocabulary comprehension, various aspects of sentence production, and recall of stories. The overall finding of the study was that on practically all measures the older subjects did better than the younger subjects. The age group that did best on many of the measures was the twelve- to fifteen-year-old group. Interestingly, the one measure on which there was very little change over the age period was the pronunciation score. All the groups improved slightly in pronunciation. The youngest group improved the most, but none of the groups differed significantly from any other in their pronunciation score. Figure 4-2 indicates the scores achieved on last testing of each age group on three of the measures of language competence assessed — morphology, sentence repetition, and vocabulary comprehension.

It is clear that research in the area of second-language acquisition tells us very little about the structures, functions, and developments that may be specifically dedicated to language acquisition. Age is *not* the critical factor in successful language acquisition. There appears to be a multiplicity of factors that can account for degree of competence achieved in a second language and the potency of these factors appears to vary from individual to individual (Brown, 1980).

The answer to the question, "What aspects of second-language acquisition

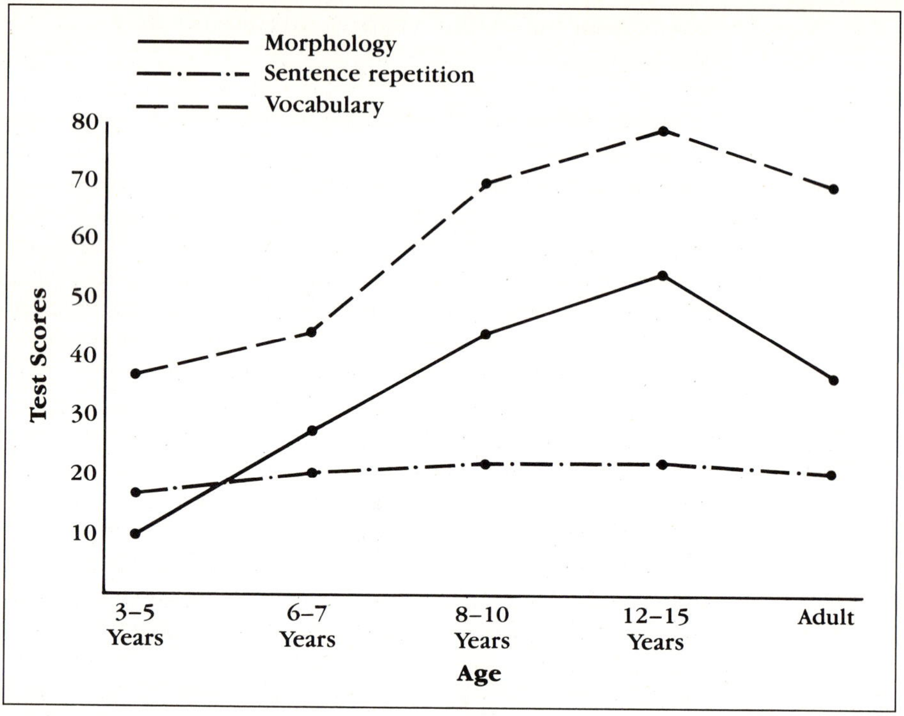

Figure 4-2 Performance of different-aged, second-language learners on various measures of language.

might be most affected by age of acquisition?" appears to be we don't know. In the Snow and Hoefnagel-Hohle study, the aspect of language behavior that seemed least affected by amount of exposure was pronunciation. There is a notion among second-language teachers that accent is more resistant to change when the language is learned at a later age. Unfortunately, this has not been carefully documented. Furthermore, it might be the case that this is the least well-taught aspect of a second language. If it were the case that speech production is that aspect of language behavior that is more resistant to change after some unknown age, an argument might be made that the predisposition to intermodally relate sound and articulation is based on some innate mechanism that is triggered very early in life. This makes sense, given the evidence that speech-sound dialects are acquired very early in life. Because these relations are established very early in life, they might be difficult to modify.

What Are the Capacities to Acquire Language?

We speculated above that pronunciation would cause the most difficulty in second-language acquisition because speech development takes place over a relatively short period of time and seems to be well established by the time a child enters middle childhood. A nonspeculative comment is that lesion to the left hemisphere leads to speech and syntax processing difficulties. One might continue to speculate and suggest that morphophonology and syntax are, therefore, the language behaviors that are supported by nervous system mechanisms that are specifically designed for language. However, the data from adult patients indicate that there are specific aspects of language that are processed in the right hemisphere (Levy, 1979). These aspects are, presumably, some lexical knowledge (perhaps imaginal representation) and some aspects of pragmatics (prosodics, facial expression, and gesture recognition). Given all the speculation, it is clear that many questions remain to be answered about the neurological structures and functions that are the bases for language acquisition, are innately programmed, and develop over time. Comparisons of other animals' communication systems and their ability to acquire man-made symbol systems do not provide answers to these questions. Answers may be forthcoming from new techniques that have been developed to scrutinize what is happening in the nervous system of normal and brain-damaged children and adults.

Obtaining information about underlying neurological mechanisms will not answer questions about whether these mechanisms are specifically committed to language or to processing information in general, nor about the special nature of information processing in human infants. Research concerned with the early cognitive and social functioning of infants has provided — and will continue to provide — answers to some of these questions. The data obtained on infant readiness seem to indicate that acquisition of some aspects of language (pragmatics and lexicon) is not special but, rather, the product of the ways in which the infant functions cognitively and socially. However, there are as yet few data that indicate how these general information processing abilities of the infant are specifically employed in acquiring these aspects of language. For example, although there is some information on the development of memory in infants, there are no data on the systematic changes that must occur in memorial representation in order to build a lexicon. It is just this kind of information that will give us a much clearer picture of the infant's capacity to acquire language.

Chapter Five
Input and Language Development

Regardless of the theoretical position held by any child development researcher, it is generally accepted by all that the language and communication environment of the child has an important effect on his or her language development. Disagreements arise, however, on the degree of importance of input on the child's language development and on just what aspects of language development are affected by input.

One of the reasons why all researchers attribute some importance to input is that all children acquire the language of their linguistic community. Another, and more important, reason is that it is obvious that exposure to language and interaction between the infant and other humans is necessary for the process of acquisition to take place. No one would hold that an infant could acquire language from a radio, television set, or other animals. Rudyard Kipling's character in the *Jungle Book* (Kipling, 1894), Mowgli, the wolf boy, is just a product of the author's imagination.

Other, nonfictional examples of feral children or children who have been almost completely isolated from other humans, such as the wild boy of Aveyron (Lane, 1976) and Genie (Curtiss, 1974), are said to provide evidence of the absolute need for human language input. However, in both instances, there is also evidence that biological factors may have played a role in their being isolated. Such biological factors certainly seem to have affected their patterns of language acquisition after they were exposed to communication and language. These cases, therefore, have not provided an in-depth understanding of the role that input plays in language development.

It is clearly important to identify the role of input in language acquisition. Although understanding the biological basis of this acquisition can help us to understand the structure and causes of language behavior in children with developmental problems, there is very little that can be done, at present, to alter the biology. However, if we were to understand the structure and function of language input, we could attempt to manipulate the input to children to enhance the development of all children and to help those with developmental problems.

Researchers who have been concerned with the role of input in language development have, with few exceptions, focussed on communication interaction between the child and others during the early years of life. In our culture this has meant, for the most part, mother-infant interaction during infancy and teacher-child interaction during the early school years. There are three questions that have been asked by these researchers:

- □ What form of language do caregivers/teachers use when talking to infants and children, and what effect does this have on their development of language?
- □ What patterns of communication interaction between adult and child have been observed, and what effect do differing patterns of communication have on language development?

- □ What effect do the form of language and the patterns of interaction used have on the language development of children with developmental disabilities?

The answers to the last question have both theoretical and practical implications. If input has a significant effect on the language development of language-impaired children, then the overall importance of input becomes more evident. A careful study of the input that results in any positive effects should lead to the development of educational programs that model such input.

Caregiver Talk to Infants

"Baby talk" is a behavior that has been observed in a number of cultures and over a long period of history (Snow & Ferguson, 1977). The definition of baby talk varies from talking like baby to talking to baby in special ways. In this section the characteristics of baby talk and the reasons for baby talk are discussed.

Characteristics of Baby Talk

Although it had been observed for some time by anthropologists and linguists that adults do not talk to young children in the same way as they talk to older children and adults, a full description of these differences was not provided until fairly recently. For this reason it seemed reasonable to claim that infants and children hear a large proportion of sloppily produced and nongrammatical sentences, as well as baby talk utterances, from which they then have to derive rules. To examine this claim a study of what adults say to young children as compared to older children was undertaken (Snow, 1972). The findings of this study were that speech to two-year-old and ten-year-old children was different and that the differences lay in the degree of complexity of the utterances to the younger and older children.

A number of subsequent studies have come up with similar results. This special way of talking to younger, as compared to older, children was labelled "motherese" (Newport, Gleitman, & Gleitman, 1977), and motherese has very special characteristics. The characteristics of this language are very similar to those found in speech to foreigners, the hard-of-hearing, and the very elderly — people who, the speaker assumes, might have some difficulty in understanding what was being said. Some of these characteristics are:

- □ Using simple sentences and vocabulary.
- □ Using clear articulation.
- □ Reducing the rate of speaking.
- □ Talking about the here and now.
- □ Ending sentences with rising intonation and using a great deal of contrastive stress.
- □ Repeating words, phrases, and sentences.

All of these characteristics, it was said, make the language acquisition task simpler for the child. First, the task of segmenting the stream of speech and determining what the units of the language are is made simple, since the adult indicates what the boundaries of units are. This is done primarily by repetition. For example, a sequence such as "See the giraffe, giraffe" makes clear that "giraffe" is a segment in the sequence. A sequence such as "Put the block in the box, in the box" makes clear that "in the box" is a segment in the sequence. Rising intonation at the end of an utterance makes clear that the utterance is a segment. Such segmentation is also made easier by slow and clear articulation.

In addition to help in segmentation, use of simple speech can make the task of determining basic relations in sentences clearer. For example, it is easier to observe the actor-action-object relation in a sentence like "The boy hit the ball," than in a sentence like "The ball that was hit by the boy broke the window." It is especially easier for the child if Mom talks about the boy hitting the ball while the boy is doing it and the child is watching him do it. Use of rising intonation at the end of sentences and use of gesture and facial expression can also help the child to attend to what is being said and to derive meaning from the utterances.

All of these observations, and conclusions about these observations, seem to make good sense. There are two questions that should be answered to increase the usefulness of these observations: (1) Why do caregivers modify their language in these ways? and (2) Do they modify in any principled, or rule-governed, way?

The Reasons for Motherese. Several reasons have been suggested to account for this special language to young children. One is that caregivers perceive themselves as being their children's language teacher; therefore, they are attempting to use good teaching techniques. Another reason posited is that caregivers have been taught by their culture to behave in certain ways to the young. A third reason is that they are being empathetic and trying to indicate their empathy by attempting to match the language behavior of the child. A fourth reason is that when caregivers interact with the child, they are observing some discourse rules, such as "be intelligible" and "let your addressee take a turn."

All of these reasons probably play some role in generating "motherese" behavior. However, the factor that apparently plays the most important role is the last — the desire to be understood so that conversation can take place. This conclusion is based on several types of findings. The first has come from studies of what appears to trigger the behavior. Phillips (1973) found that mothers began simplifying the structure of their language only after their infants were old enough to give some evidence of comprehension of language. Malsheen (1980) found that mothers began to clearly distinguish between their articulation of /t/ and /d/ only after their children began working on these sounds. What triggers the behavior is some evidence provided by the child that he or she is ready to participate in conversation and might benefit from particular aspects of motherese.

Another indication that the primary cause of motherese is the urge to be understood is the caregivers' acceptance of almost any response to keep the conversation going (Donahue, 1978). Until the child gives some indication that responses are based on the content and structure of the previous utterance, caregivers will accept very approximate phonological sequences, intoned babbling, an "uh huh" or "oh," or any filler. When the mobile infant does not attend to an utterance, the caregiver will go to extraordinary lengths to make the child attend (Watson, 1979). When these maneuvers do not succeed, the caregiver will shift the topic of the utterance to conform to the child's focus of attention. For example, when the caregiver states "See the ball," but the child is attending to the cup, the caregiver may try to point to the ball, hold it up, or roll it. If these moves do not succeed, he or she will shift the topic and state, "Yes, see the cup."

Caregivers' attempts to keep the conversation going can be observed in the early months of infants' lives and infants *do* take their turn. Caregivers' communication behaviors during the second year of infants' lives simply reflect this ongoing motivation. In addition, however, there is a gradual shift in what caregivers expect as a response over the first two years of life. Caregivers accept vocalizations until infants provide evidence that other responses are within their capacity. Then these more sophisticated responses become what is expected. What caregivers do as a response to these expectations can, in turn, provide the child with the data and motivation for firmly establishing their increased linguistic sophistication. Thus, motherese may play a subtle and indirect role in children's development of knowledge of the language.

These findings indicate that, although caregivers may perceive themselves as being teachers of language, they are in some sense being taught what to teach. That is, the child's behavior provides the cues that expectations about communication interaction can change. These expectations are far from being fine-tuned. As the examples of maternal responses to the infant's lack of attention indicate, the rule appears to be: Try anything that makes sense to keep the conversation going.

The Lack of Rules for Motherese. It may be said then that caregivers modify their language toward young children because they wish to be understood and to carry on a conversation with their young partners. Additionally, given the above findings, it appears that their behavior is not rule-governed. Rather it appears to be based on their intuition that trying a number of logical ways to be understood will, in fact, keep the conversation going. Also, caregivers seem to know intuitively what to expect as a response to these conversational moves as the child matures.

The characteristics of motherese that have been described thus far apply only to the behavior of middle-class caregivers in this society. Patterns of caregiver input in interaction with the infant and child can vary widely in different socioeconomic groups within a society and across societies. Given this fact, and given the fact that universally all normally developing children acquire language, one might search for universal aspects of motherese (DePaulo & Bonvillian, 1978). However, these facts also make us question the importance of *these particular motherese patterns* for language development. If such types of input are crucial to language development, then the educational implications are clear. If they are not, then recommendations to caregivers need to take this into account.

Effect of Motherese on Language Development

The effect of the form of input on language development has been examined in a number of studies. To date, the findings do not provide a clear picture of the effect of input on the language development of the recipients. This is the result both of conflicting findings and of the fact that some of the findings of a relation between input and development make sense but others do not. Discussion of some of the studies that have been carried out in this area make the problems clear.

Some researchers have looked at the role of particular aspects of motherese on particular aspects of structural language development (Cross, 1977). Others have examined wide aspects of motherese and their effect on wide aspects of language competence and use (Barnes, Gutfreund, Satterly, & Wells, 1983). And still others have looked at the effects of motherese on a number of basic semantactic acquisitions (Newport, Gleitman, & Gleitman, 1977; Furrow, Nelson, & Benedict, 1979). The role of motherese in children's development of patterns of interaction, conversation, and discourse will be discussed in the next section of this chapter.

The results of a study of the effect of mothers' limiting their reference to the here and now (Cross, 1977) indicated that mothers who more frequently do this have children who are more advanced lexically. Apparently, mothers talking about things that are present and actions that are ongoing help the child to relate words to objects and events and, as a result, to acquire lexical items. The Barnes et al. (1983) study examined both the effect of the form of input (structures used by caregivers) and interaction patterns on language development outcomes. Results pertaining to the effect of forms of motherese were that use of the auxiliary question form ("Is he going?") was significantly correlated with gains in overall syntactic complexity ($r = .45$, $P < .01$), that use of rising intonation to mark questions was significantly related to gain in pragmatic range ($r = .50$, $P < .01$), and in range of auxiliary meanings ($r = .42$, $P < .05$).

Some of these results make sense while others do not. For example, it makes sense that being clear in reference should have an effect on the rate of lexical acquisition. It should be noted, however, that this finding does not indicate a direct effect of caregivers' particular vocabulary on the child's acquisition of certain lexical items. Such a direct effect was also not observed in a study examining the frequency of use of lexical items, in a teaching situation, on children's acquisition of these items (Schwartz & Terrell, 1983). Providing the appropriate conditions for learning is the factor that seems crucial for lexical acquisition, rather than direct teaching or modelling of the behavior.

It also makes sense that frequent use of the auxiliary question form, which makes the auxiliary verb perceptually salient by putting it at the beginning of the sentence, should help in the development of early simple sentence structures. This, again, is a situation in which learning is made easier by the conditions provided. As Barnes et al. state, the meaning of the second two relations is unclear. It may be that the correlations found between caregivers' behaviors and infants' and young children's language development are, in fact, sometimes related, and at other times are simply the results of a statistical accident. Unless correlations make sense, one might assume that the latter has happened.

The findings of the two studies that examined the effect of motherese on sentence structure development led the two groups of investigators to come up with partially different conclusions. Both studies were carried out with small samples of middle-class mothers and their children. Furrow, Nelson, and Benedict (1979) examined the correlations between a number of maternal input measures at time 1 (when the seven children in the study were aged 1.5 years) and the language structures used by these children at time 2, some nine months later. Newport, Gleitman, and Gleitman (1977) measured the correlation between aspects of maternal input and the amount of gain over a six-month period in the language of fifteen children, who at the beginning of the study ranged in age from approximately one to two years.

Furrow, Nelson, and Benedict found a number of significant positive correlations between mothers' language at time 1 and the child's language at time 2. These were between:

1. Mothers' use of auxiliary questions (as in the Barnes et al. study) and the length of the children's utterances and their development of the verb phrase.
2. Mother's use of interjections and the frequency of verbs in the children's utterances.
3. The proportion of nouns to pronouns used, and the children's length of utterance and frequency of verb use.

A number of negative correlations were also found. These were between:

1. The length of mothers' utterances and child mean length of utterance (MLU) and use of verbs and nouns.
2. Her use of pronouns with child MLU and use of verbs.
3. Her use of verbs with child MLU and use of verbs.
4. Her use of copulas with child MLU and use of verbs and nouns.
5. Her use of contractions with the child's use of nouns.

A careful inspection of the above findings again indicates that some correlations, both positive and negative, make sense but others do not. For example, the first positive finding makes sense, the second does not (why should interjections be related to verbs?), and the third makes only partial sense (why should proportion of nouns used be related to frequency of verb use?). Although the negative correlations seem more sensible, there are problems there as well. These negative findings suggest that mothers' use of more complex utterances may cause delay in the development of some syntactic classes, but it isn't always clear how this works. For example, how can mother's use of verbs negatively affect the child's frequency of use of verbs and MLU?

The findings of the Newport, Gleitman, and Gleitman (1977) study were quite simple. Mothers' use of auxiliary questions significantly positively affected the development of the child's use of the auxiliary and verb phrase; her use of deictic terms positively affected the acquisition of plural markers; and her use of the imperative and repetition negatively affected the development of the auxiliary and verb phrase. The first positive finding seems clear, but the second, although not illogical, raises questions. The first negative finding, again, seems logical (imperatives never have expanded verb forms) but the second, again, raises questions.

The results of a reanalysis of the Newport, Gleitman, and Gleitman data (1984), dividing the sample into two age groups (eighteen to twenty-one months, and twenty-one to twenty-five months) indicated that there were different aspects of maternal input that played an influential role at different periods of development. For the older group of children, the only significant finding was the relation between mothers' use of auxiliary questions and the child's development of the verb phrase. For the younger age group, there was a significant correlation between mothers' use of the declarative and the frequency of the child's verb phrase use. There was a negative correlation between mothers' use of repetition and the child's development of the verb phrase.

What do these studies tell us about the effect of the form of maternal input on the child's language development? Very little. One important reason why this may be so is that the form of maternal input, or so-called motherese, may not play an important role in the acquisition of the structural aspects of language. Another possibility is that the effect is very indirect. The only universal finding in three of the studies discussed was that mothers' use of auxiliary questions has an effect on the rate at which children develop the verb phrase, not auxiliary questions. Therefore, mothers' input may provide data that children draw conclusions from, but not models that they copy. A final possibility is that the wrong aspects of input have been examined in studies that have limited themselves to the form of caregiver input. The possible causes of caregivers' special speech to children point to other aspects of input outside of form as having an effect. If the primary cause of modification of language on the part of the caregiver is to keep the conversation going, then effects of conversational or discourse maneuvers might be more crucial than simplification of language.

Effect of Patterns of Interaction

It is hard to keep separate the two aspects of input, *form* and *interaction*. For example, one of the types of motherese input categorized as form was repetition. When caregivers repeat, they repeat a category of language — a noun, a phrase, or a sentence. When they repeat, they are also engaging in a type of interaction. Use of imperatives is a form of input, but it is also a type of interaction, since imperatives are commands or directions. Some of the studies discussed in this section on patterns of interaction simply emphasize the interactional nature of the input, while others focus on interaction alone. Both types of studies are concerned with the effect of interaction on the child's development of both form and patterns of interaction.

The Barnes et al. (1983) study discussed previously examined the effect of various types of discourse functions (as well as forms) in caregiver language on gains in children's language development at two years. The researchers found that caregivers' use of directives was significantly positively related to gains in MLU ($r = .48$, $P < .01$) and, also, to gains in the semantic complexity ($r = .40$, $P < .05$) and syntactic complexity ($r = .40$, $P < .05$) of their utterances. Extension of the child's utterances (elaboration or addition) was significantly correlated to gains in MLU ($r = .38$, $P < .05$), and the amount of adult speech (perhaps, frequency of interaction) was related to gains in MLU and in semantic complexity.

These findings indicate that patterns of interaction can lead to gains in form; however, the cause for some of the relations observed is unclear. Why extensions and sheer amount of input might lead to syntactic and semantic progress seems clear. A greater amount of language and extensions provide the child with more data on alternative forms to express semantactic relations. Why directives (commands) should lead to growth in such relations is less clear. The researchers point to a possible explanation. They suggest that directives may be more congruent with the young child's language processing abilities than other types of discourse functions.

The positive effect of the language presented being congruent with the child's processing abilities is evident in some additional findings in the study. An additional type of discourse function was significantly related to gains in those children in the population who were more advanced linguistically. In this latter population caregiver use of the question-comment function was significantly related to gains in semantic range, semantic complexity, and pragmatic range. These findings indicate two things. The first is that different types of interactional patterns appear to be more effective at different stages of development. The second is that these different types of interactional patterns appear to affect different aspects of language.

These findings appear to lend further support to the conclusion that caregivers respond appropriately to the conversational competence of their young partners, and that the form and pattern of their input is motivated by their urge to keep the conversation going. These findings also suggest that providing the appropriate kinds of interaction more frequently has a positive effect on language gain. This positive effect may be due to the fact that appropriate interaction provides the best learning environment for the child, an environment that the child can take advantage of.

There are reasons outside of conversation that produce language from caregivers. McDonald and Pien (1982) found in their study of two-and-one-half to three-year-olds that caregivers had two types of intentions when communicating: one was to control the behavior of the child (as represented by commands); the other was to converse (as represented by questions). They suggested that this latter type of interaction pattern was the one that produced language growth. These data suggest an alternative hypothesis, which is that only certain types of interactional patterns are conducive to language growth. This is an important difference. If it is true that only certain types of interaction are conducive to growth, then certain specific recommendations could be made to caregivers and teachers. If the initial hypothesis is correct — that appropriateness is the factor that leads to growth — then very different recommendations might be made. The study to be discussed next sheds some light on this issue.

A longitudinal study of the language development of fifty-three infants ranging in age from one to thirty months and from ten months to thirty-six months was carried out (Liebergott, Schultz, & Menyuk, 1985). Data was collected on these children's language development and on the form and interactional patterns of input provided by their caregivers. Since the study was longitudinal, changes in these forms and patterns could be observed, and their effect on the children's achievement of certain language milestones (rate of development of word and sentence comprehension and production) and their performance on a battery of speech and language tests could be examined.

The first important finding is that there was great individual variation in the amount and type of interactional input observed in this population. For example, over the period of eight to twelve months, the smallest number of conversational turns between child and mother that was observed at one two-hour visit was 194 and the largest number was 582, approximately three times the smaller amount.

Analyses of the language gain scores of forty-three of the children in the study (Liebergott, Menyuk, Schultz, Chesnick, & Thomas, 1984) indicated that there were no significant relations between the form of mother input and the rate at which different language milestones were achieved. That is, mothers' simplification of the structure of their language input was not related to gains in language. The amount of speech to the child was also not related to gain scores. Only patterns of conversational interaction were related to gain

Table 5-1 Mothers' discourse and conversational characteristics in relation to children's residual gain scores.

Mothers' Characteristics at 12 Months	*Gains from 12 to 16 Months* F		Prob. > F
	15.74	Beta Val.	.0001
	F		Prob. > F
Complete model			
Absent ratio	2.68	–	.11
Conversational acknowledge	27.34	+	.0001
Request action	5.07	+	.03
Elicited imitation	5.94	–	.02
Mothers' Characteristics at 29 Months	*Gains from 29 to 35 Months* F		Prob. > F
	5.46		.005
	F		Prob. > F
Complete model			
Elicit imitation	6.8	+	.02
Paraphrase baby	5.74	+	.03
Request action	13.92	–	.002
Respond to baby	5.42	+	.03

scores between twelve and sixteen months, sixteen and twenty-two months, twenty-two and twenty-five months, twenty-five and twenty-nine months, and twenty-nine and thirty-five months. Thus, only interactional patterns predicted both early and later rates of growth in language. Table 5-1 indicates the results of a step-wise regression analysis to determine those variables of mother conversation that significantly accounted for rate of development between twelve and sixteen months and those that accounted for rate of development between twenty-nine and thirty-five months.

As Table 5-1 indicates, changes occur in which particular factors account for gain at different age periods. In the period from twelve to sixteen months, the proportion of utterances that referred to absent people or objects and elicited imitation resulted in negative gains, while acknowledgements and requests for action resulted in positive gains. Analysis of the videotape data indicated the requests for action at this stage were *protodirectives,* asking the children to carry out actions that they were in the midst of doing. At twenty-nine to thirty-five months, eliciting imitation, paraphrasing baby, and responding to babies' elicitations were all positively related to gain, whereas requests for action were negatively related to gain. Requests for information were positively related to gain at this age, although not significantly. These shifts in conversational moves led not only to more rapid gains in structural knowledge, but, also to more rapid true participation in conversation, responding to turns, and eliciting turns.

These data suggest that caregivers who (1) provide conversational situations that are within the processing abilities of their children, (2) provide opportunities for interaction that result in "successful" turns for their children, and (3) then switch to provide more challenging situations as their children mature, have children who achieve language and communication milestones more rapidly. Given that there is a great deal of variation in the rate at which children mature, there are obviously no formulae for interaction that one can suggest to caregivers of children of a certain age. The amount of variation in input observed in this study might be reflective of individual mothers responding to the rate of maturation of their individual children.

There are not only differences in the rate of maturation among children, but also individual differences in the styles of interaction they primarily engage in. Nelson (1973; 1981) found that there were some children who were primarily "expressers" (communicated to express needs and feelings) and others who were "referrers" (used language to state or label). These differences in style resulted in differences in the proportion of language forms produced by each group of children. These differences could lead to differences in the kinds of conversational and form responses that are produced by each group of caregivers. In a follow-up study on maternal input to expressers and referrers (Furrow & Nelson, 1984), it was found that mothers of expressers shifted in what they largely referred to in conversation with their children as their children's MLU grew. This shift was from reference to objects to reference to persons. This appeared to be related to expressive children using a higher proportion of pronouns as compared to nouns.

Differences in interactional styles are found not only in children but also in mothers. These styles are individualized and also stable across time. Olsen-Fulero (1982) found that mothers' conversational styles could be characterized as falling on a continuum of simple directive to conversation-eliciting. A second continuum (warmth, involvement, to desire to use social influence), when combined with the first continuum, described the purpose as well as form of the interaction of individual mothers. Some mothers appeared to be motivated to provide stimulation and training for independence, others were didactic, and still others used social influence to direct the behavior of the child, elicit conversation, or both.

Clearly, the very marked individual differences in caregivers' forms of input at different ages of the child and in caregivers' interactional styles should make interveners and caregivers cautious about formulaic recommendations for input and interaction. What seems to be important is to take cues from the child's behavior about what is or is not being processed and to provide the child with many opportunities to process language data and to participate in conversation. Table 5-2 summarizes what has been found thus far about caregiver language form and interaction input and the consequences of these types

Table 5-2 Caregiver input: Form and interaction effects on child's development of form and interaction.

CAREGIVER	CHILD
Form	
Use of auxiliary questions	Development of verb phrase
Interaction	
Appropriate speech acts for age	More rapid structural and pragmatic development
Reference to here and now	More rapid lexical development
Reference to person or object	Become primarily expresser or referrer
Providing turns	More rapid structural and pragmatic development
Acknowledging turns	More rapid structural and pragmatic development

of input on the child's language development. As can be seen in Table 5-2, there is very little direct relation between caregiver input and child output.

As stated previously, the meager evidence that has been obtained on the effect of input on child language growth may be the result of looking at the wrong aspects of input or trying to generalize too much about the effects of input. In a very thoughtful discussion of the relation between maternal input and child language development, it was concluded that "Some input is 'well adjusted' and 'important' to the child's acquisition of language and other input doesn't matter at all for language progress" (Nelson, Denninger, Bonvillian, Kaplan, & Baker, 1983, p. 51). The researchers summarize those input adjustments that appear to play a positive role: adjustment to the child's current level (above but not too far above), adjustment to the discourse situation, and adjustment to the individual child's approach to learning language. Rondal (1985) adds to this that there may be particular aspects of the maternal register that are most salient for the child at any given stage in the acquisition process. This addition points to the possible importance of changing aspects of motherese that provide clear conditions for learning at different periods of development. What these changing aspects are is, at present, unknown.

How Teachers Talk to Children

A great deal of interest exists in how teachers talk to children. This interest has, for the most part, not been focussed on the question of what effect teacher talk has on the child's acquisition of the basic categories and rules of the language. It is generally assumed that this knowledge is acquired by the time the normally developing child enters school. Rather, the interest in teacher talk lies in what is believed to be its effect on the child's ability to acquire more knowledge of language, to think about language, and to learn about the uses of language. Although so-called basic rules have been acquired by age five to six, there is still a great deal that the child has to learn about language to achieve awareness of language categories and relations. There is obviously a great deal that the child should learn about the uses of language. These are the two topics that are discussed in this section of the chapter.

In our discussion of caregiver-child interaction, it was suggested that the child cues the caregiver to the fact that different and more sophisticated responses should be *expected* from the child. The caregiver's responses to this expectation create both the motivation and the opportunity for the firm establishment of newly acquired structures and functions and the basis for extension of this knowledge. On the whole, the positive effect of this response can only be hypothesized about, but there is some evidence that mothers who adjust early to their children's advances in certain aspects of language stimulate the rate of growth of those aspects (Nelson & Bonvillian, 1978). Learning is possible under these conditions because children are only being extended within their "zone of proximal development."

Vygotsky (1978) defines the zone of proximal development as "the distance between the actual developmental level as determined by independent problem solving and the level of potential development as determined through problem solving under adult guidance or in collaboration with more capable peers" (p. 86). In his view, the role of education is to extend systematically the child's knowledge by engaging him in tasks that are within his zone of proximal development. One natural example, states Vygotsky, is the child's acquisition of language. The child comes to school knowing a great deal about language, and this knowledge can be extended in two ways. The first way is by engaging the child in linguistic tasks that add to this store of knowledge. The second way is by engaging the child in tasks that require the use of language to plan, remember, and learn (Vygotsky, 1962).

Although this seems to be logical, it is not always exactly clear how these two tasks are best accomplished. Since the caregiver-child interactions that were discussed in the previous section are largely successful in fostering language acquisition, one approach that has been suggested is that teachers should continue the task of language learning by continuing to interact with children in the way that caregivers do (Lindfors, 1980).

Wells (1983) compared the kinds of communication interaction children engage in at home and at school. His overall findings were that there were marked differences in many instances between home talk and school talk. Some of these differences related to the familiarity of topics of conversation, others were differences in terms of expectations of types of response, and still others, the inflexibility of the adult in the communication situation. At school there were certain directions in which the adult expected the talk to go, and these directions were the only ones that appeared to be acceptable. These expectations can place poorly understood demands on children who do not share the same expectations as the teacher about the form of conversation. This is particularly true of children who, because of a cultural background different from the teacher's, are accustomed to different forms of conversation.

Wells also found that a large proportion of the teachers' utterances were questions, and for the most part, questions for which the children knew that the teachers knew the answers. The finding that teacher conversation is primarily questions is a frequent one. Mishler (1975) found, in addition, that most of these questions were either yes-no questions or required only a single-word response. Wells argues that such interactions do not allow the kind of reciprocal conversation that occurs in the home. They also may place the interaction required outside the child's zone of proximal development and, therefore, may not lead to establishment and extension of existing knowledge.

Wells, however, argues that the school should not attempt to replicate the home in its style of communication interaction. He suggests that school must be a more formal setting that introduces the child to more formal ways of acquiring knowledge. Cazden (1974) also raised some questions about trying to replicate caregiver-child communication interactions in the school. She suggested that the kinds of communication tasks the child engages in in school are not commensurate with those in the home. Therefore, interactions that attempt to simply replicate the home interaction are not very effective in developing the child's knowledge of language use in these tasks.

One example of a marked difference between the home and school environments is that children spend an enormous amount of time simply listening to language in school. In distinction to the suggestion that teachers play the role of caregivers in their communication interaction, there is a long history of suggesting that the child be engaged in activities that train specific speaking and listening skills. In preschool and kindergarten, play is considered to be an activity conducive to development of language and language use. However, for the elementary grades it is generally held that children should be engaged in a variety of situations that call for varied speaking and listening skills. These would include such tasks as listening to tapes, taking dictation, following directions, telephoning, interviewing, giving formal and informal speeches, role playing, storytelling, improvisation, and so on (Flood & Salus, 1984). These activities are, in many instances, very different from home activities. The notion seems to be that engaging the child in a number of activities that involve the use of language will lead to positive results in both knowledge and use.

Although there has been little systematic research on the results of such programs on the development of competence in the appropriate use of language, the preceding activities seem right for young children and provide them with needed opportunities to think and talk about the use of language (Fox, 1980). Unfortunately, the frequency and duration of these activities, even in the primary grades, can be quite variable from school to school. If it is the case that children from grade one to three spend most of their time listening to the teacher and interacting with the teacher, then teacher-child talk can play a primary role in the child's language development. The observations of teacher-child talk that have been made suggest that there needs to be much greater opportunity provided in these interactions for acquisition of further knowledge of language.

There are particular activities in school that are ideally designed to further the child's knowledge of language. Children learn how to read and are taught grammar. Although the first activity, reading, is dependent on language knowledge, it, in turn, enhances language knowledge. The effects of the second activity, being taught grammar, have often been debated. It seems highly unlikely that teaching children how to parse sentences adds in any way to either their intuitive or conscious knowledge of language. However, some activities have been suggested that engage the child in thinking about and talking about the structure of language in varying contexts. These activities require that the child bring to conscious awareness what he or she knows about structures in the language. Bringing intuitive knowledge to conscious awareness helps the child to establish more firmly what he or she already knows and to extend this knowledge. Such activities take advantage of the zone of proximal development.

Vygotsky (1962) suggested such an activity. Although it was not specifically designed to enhance students' knowledge of language relations, it clearly could do so. He required children to complete sentences that contained conjunctions that described relations between events. Chomsky (1980) suggested that children be asked to think about creating sentences from words. Menyuk (1976) suggested that even very young children could be asked to judge the grammar of sentences. Mandler and DeForest (1979) asked children to passively judge the temporal organization of discourse. Hunt (1974) suggested that children could increase the sophistication of their writing by being asked to embed sentences into each other. Each of these activities requires that children think about categories and relations in sentences. Such metalinguistic activities take place spontaneously at an early age (Cazden, 1983) and can be elicited at a later age (Menyuk, 1976). Such activities enhance the development of language per se and, in addition, metalinguistic abilities. These latter abilities play a crucial role in the acquisition of written language.

Most studies of the style of teacher input have found that how teachers talk to children may not advance the childrens' knowledge of language structure and use. These studies also indicate that teachers can not and should not talk to children the way caregivers talk to young children. Some alternate suggestions about the structure of teacher talk have been made. These include talking *with* instead of *at* children, so that the child is a true participant in the exchange. This means providing flexible, rather than rigidly planned, interactions that can take different directions depending on the input of the children as well as the teacher (Wells, 1983). Activities that call for individual involvement in listening and speaking in situations that are directly applicable to school learning are also suggested. Finally, engaging the child in thinking about and talking about language is suggested as an activity that will lead to further growth in language knowledge and the use of language in various learning tasks. All of these suggestions presume that all children, regardless of their sociocultural background, should be able to take advantage of such activities.

Input and Language-Disordered Children

Input to language-impaired children seems especially crucial. Children who are developing normally seem to be able to develop competence in language knowledge and use, regardless of wide varieties in the language and interactional patterns they experience. Two questions about caregiver-child interaction are addressed in this brief review of the research on input to language-disordered children:

- Is caregiver input to language-disordered children similar to the input provided to normally developing children?
- What are the consequences of this input on the language development of the child?

It will be recalled that caregivers talk differently to young language learners than they do to older ones. They use a simplified form of language (motherese) and they use this form, primarily, to keep the conversation going. In addition, at the earliest stages of the child's development they take on primary responsibility for keeping the conversation going and accept as appropriate responses whatever their young conversational partners can provide. During the earliest months of life any vocalization is accepted; somewhat later, appropriate responses to requests for action are expected; and even later, appropriate responses to requests for information are expected. In essence, the caregivers' expectations are grossly in tune with the language developmental level of the child.

Children who are delayed or different in language development provide their caregivers with different kinds of cues than do their age peers. For example, a child who is four years old and approximately one year behind his or her age peers in language development is presumably displaying the language behavior of a three-year-old. If the child is more severely delayed (or different), the disparity between that child's language and a normally developing age peer becomes even more marked. If it is the case, as has been hypothesized, that caregivers' language input to their normally developing children is structurally and conversationally within their children's zone of proximal development, and that this may be one of the crucial factors for further development, the same pattern of input should be observed in caregivers of language-delayed children. A number of studies indicate that this is indeed the case.

Stein (1976) found that both mothers and fathers of language-handicapped and normally developing children, aged four to six years, adjusted their sentence length, sentence complexity, and conversational style to meet the linguistic levels of their children. Conti-Ramsden and Friel-Patti (1983) found that when language-impaired and normally developing children are grossly matched (mean length of utterance) for linguistic age, the two groups of mothers are similar in their discourse patterns. These findings indicate that caregivers of language-delayed children are providing them with input forms that appear to be within their zone of proximal development and encouraging them to participate in conversation.

When the language input provided by caregivers to age-matched language-impaired and normally developing children are compared, the differences in structural complexity and discourse characteristics of input of the two groups of caregivers becomes striking. For example, Buium, Rynders, and Turnure (1974) found that caregivers of mentally retarded children, when compared to caregivers of normally developing children of similar ages, produced a greater number of command and demand utterances, used a lower MLU, and produced more grammatically incomplete sentences and single word responses. This finding of a higher preponderance of imperative sentences to language-impaired children is a frequent finding. In a comparison of the input to language-impaired and normally developing children, aged approximately three to five years, Bondurant, Romeo, and Kretschmer (1983) found a number of significant differences. The use of directives to language-impaired children was almost twice as frequent as it was to normally developing children. Inversely, caregivers of linguistically normal children used significantly more questions, a significantly higher MLU, and significantly more frequently indicated acceptance ("That's right, yes, that's a ball").

The picture of caregiver language input to language-impaired children that many researchers seem to convey is that caregivers tend to be much more directive to language-impaired children and, therefore, do not give them the linguistic (and action) options that are available to normally developing children. These caregivers would fall on the left extreme of the continuum — simple directive to conversation-eliciting — found by Olsen-Fulero (1982). Thus far, however, all the data indicate is that caregivers of language-impaired children seem very similar to caregivers of younger, less competent, normally developing children. With these latter children, as with language-impaired children, there is much more frequent use of directives or requests for action.

It has also been found with normally developing children that caregivers shift their input and discourse patterns as the child gives evidence of increased sophistication in language development. The same appears to be true of caregivers of language-impaired children. For example, Siegel (1963) found that the input to higher-functioning retarded children was more complex. Rondal (1976) found that similar speech styles were used by mothers of normally developing and retarded children when the children were matched on MLU, and that the mothers of retarded as well as normally developing children changed their input appropriately as their child's MLU changed.

The results of studies of input by caregivers to the language-impaired child indicate that such input is very similar to the input the normally developing child receives. That is, it appears to be grossly in tune with the language development of their children. As in the case of normally developing children, the consequences of this input are unclear. It might be the case that the language development of the language-impaired child would be further impaired if caregivers were less sensitive to these children's levels of language development, but the direct benefit of such types of interaction are hard to determine.

The findings of a study by Sigel, McGillicuddy-Delisi, Flaugher, and Rock (1982) point to some interesting possibilities for parent-child interaction that might be of benefit to the development of language-impaired children. This study examined, among other questions, the relation between the teaching/managing behaviors of parents of language-impaired and nonimpaired children and the children's level of cognitive functioning and level of representational competence. Parents interacted with their children in a number of problem-solving tasks. The findings were somewhat similar to those already discussed. Parents of language-impaired children used more low-level demands and imperatives and appeared less sensitive to their children than parents of nonimpaired children. They also used more nonverbal task structuring, attention-getting devices, took longer to accomplish the task, and interacted longer in general. Overall, the intellectual level of the language-impaired child affected the parents' behavior.

In addition, however, the design of the study allowed the investigators to make the following observations. For the language-impaired children, parental use of "high-level cognitive demands" resulted in positive results on cognitive tasks. No such positive effects were observed with the nonimpaired children. The investigators hypothesized that no positive effect was observed in the nonimpaired group because they were already functioning at the higher competence level required by the tasks. This suggests that when language-impaired children are engaged in tasks that are within their zone of proximal development, but somewhat more demanding than the tasks they are usually confronted with, they respond by increasing their level of development. This might also be true of the kinds of language that could be used when parents are interacting with their children in these task situations. The sophistication of the language used might also be slightly increased when parents are interacting with these children in particular task situations.

Implications for Language Remediation

Language intervention programs are currently being designed to provide the language-impaired child with experiences that mirror, as much as possible, the natural discourse situations that all children engage in. The purpose of such programs is to develop communication skills in these children, rather than simply to develop knowledge of the structures of language (Schopler & Mesibov, 1985; Menyuk, 1986a). With severely language-impaired children, such programs are attempting to replicate the discourse situations that are natural to all young children and have as their goals achievement of at least some aspects of conversational competence: how to request, how to express needs and feelings, how to indicate, and so on. Despite the fact that these programs often use behavior modification techniques to keep the conversation going, they are small and carefully controlled replications of the types of input that caregivers provide their children and their reasons for providing such input. Caregivers also have as their primary motivation the need to keep the conversation going.

For less impaired children, the goals are achievement of near normal knowledge and use of language. With these children it is probably not sufficient to design learning situations that attempt to replicate early caregiver-child interactions. These children are beyond this level of development. The results of the study discussed earlier (Sigel et al., 1982) suggest that interventions need to be planned that allow the child to experience language that is within his or her zone of proximal development but, also, somewhat beyond his or her level of language development. This aspect of input may be particularly important for children who are delayed in language development.

Studies of the effect of caregiver and teacher input on children's development of language knowledge and use indicate that there are some generally appropriate conditions under which the child's learning of language is enhanced. One of them is for the caregiver or teacher, in interaction with the child, to use language that is congruent with the child's language knowledge and style and yet extends his or her present level of knowledge. The implication of this is that the best kind of language teaching or remedial program is one that is sensitive to an individual child's competence, something that has been known for some time. Another appropriate condition is providing opportunities for the child to take a turn. The implication of this is that any child is an active learner rather than merely an imitator, something that has also been known for some time. As more information is gathered about the details of successful interaction, perhaps the implications for intervention will become more definitive. In the meanwhile, research on the effect of input on language learning reaffirms the fact that children — including those who need remediation — are individual and active learners.

Chapter Six
Pragmatic Development

Structural knowledge of language is knowledge of how sounds and words are arranged to convey meaning. Pragmatic knowledge consists of knowing how to use structural knowledge in particular situations. When one examines any aspect of the development of language knowledge, it is important first to establish the domain of this aspect. Therefore, the first question we will address is: What is pragmatic knowledge?

After establishing what is generally held to be the kinds of knowledge that the child acquires in achieving pragmatic competence, we will look at results of research examining the development of this competence during infancy (birth to approximately three years), early childhood (from three to approximately seven years) and middle childhood and beginning adolescence (from seven to approximately fourteen years). The findings with adults are used for comparison purposes.

What the child learns during each period, how developments in this period are related to other aspects of language development, and the reasons why changes occur over each developmental period are discussed. Three questions, then, are addressed in the developmental portions of the chapter:

- □ What is the developmental course in the acquisition of pragmatic knowledge?
- □ How are these developments related to other aspects of language knowledge?
- □ Why do developmental changes occur in the acquisition of this knowledge?

In subsequent chapters those populations of children (and adults) who appear to have particular difficulties with pragmatic knowledge will be discussed. These populations are: autistic children, blind children, and children and adults with known right-hemisphere lesion. Children and adults from minority cultural communities and those acquiring American English as a second language do not have pragmatic difficulties in general but do have difficulties in acquiring the pragmatic knowledge of the nonminority group. The fact that these groups have particular difficulties with pragmatics provides a further understanding of the biological, cognitive, and social factors that lead to the acquisition of pragmatic knowledge.

What Is Pragmatic Knowledge?

Pragmatic knowledge has been described by Hymes (1964) as that aspect of language knowledge that is made up of the abilities and judgments that characterize peoples' performance as members of the linguistic community into which they have been born; that is, it is community-specific. To determine what pragmatic competence is, states Hymes, one needs to examine the actual speech behaviors of members of speech communities. These include (1) the totality of their communicative habits and (2) the foci of their communicative performance (the events, constituents of events, and functions that serve them). In other words, one needs to examine *what* speakers and listeners actually *do* in particular contexts and *why* they do it.

It is evident in Hymes's description and the descriptions of others who are concerned with ethnographies of communication that the social structure of the speech community constrains the communication behavior of members of that community just as the rules of the language constrain the way that sounds are encoded and interpreted in speech (Gumperz, 1975). This makes evident the fact that there must be variation across cultures in the repertoire of pragmatic behaviors that each speech community makes available to the child.

Despite the wide possible variety of communication behaviors that may be acquired by children from different speech communities, there do appear to be some general abilities that are needed to engage in communication. These include the abilities to produce and interpret behaviors that convey the intent of the communication within different settings. Different communication intents can be conveyed by various choices of what is said (the content of the utterance) and how it is said (its structure and the use of differing intonation, stress, facial expression, and gesture).

As an example, consider questions. The production and comprehension of questions occur in all speech communities. Questions are a type of speech act (representing requests for information or action) and also a type of semantic/syntactic structure. To generate a question successfully certain linguistic forms must be used, but to convey the specific intent of a particular question (for example, to accuse, as in "Why did you do that?") so-called paralinguistic signalling devices (facial expression, gesture, intonation, and stress) accompany the utterance.

In addition, what is said and how it is said are dependent on the settings in which utterances are produced. For example, questions of various kinds are generated in certain ways because of the setting of the conversation. This setting is made up of both physical and social characteristics. Physical characteristics include such things as the objects present, whereas social characteristics include such things as the relation between the participants in the conversation. An utterance such as "Why did you do that?" would probably be produced by someone who had either an equal or superordinate and close relation to the listener. It would probably be produced in the situation where some action had just been committed or where a previous action was known to both participants. A graphic description of the totality of parameters that might be involved in a conversational exchange was presented in Figure 1-2.

The abilities to convey communication intents, and to convey them appropriately, develop over the period from birth to 14 years. Over these years children convey more and more intents and they do so more and more successfully. It has been suggested that this increasing success in interaction is due to the child's increasing ability to keep certain conversational postulates in mind (Clark & Clark, 1977). A list of these postulates appears below.

1. Take your turn.
2. Be clear and nonredundant.
3. Be polite, truthful, and sincere.
4. Be appropriate.
5. Know how to back-channel.

Most of these postulates are held to a lot of the time by most adults. Clearly, they are not followed all the time by everybody. Some of them are overlapping. For example, to be appropriate one should be clear and nonredundant, but appropriateness also includes keeping in mind the social relations among participants. To be polite, one should back-channel (for example, nod one's head in agreement, say "uh-huh"), but being polite also means that one should be appropriate. For example, when a friend asks you if you would like to go to the movies, it would be inappropriate and impolite to say "I like vanilla ice cream." It would be inappropriate and impolite to simply reply "yes" to the request, "Could you close the door?"

Other aspects of discourse that are now receiving a great deal of attention have to do with the organization of discourse. Research has been carried out to examine how children organize their conversational exchanges and how they organize narrative discourse. It is of special interest to teachers of reading and writing how the child organizes narrative discourse, since the child's mental representations of the organization of narratives can have a profound effect on his or her reading and writing abilities. Two ways in which these organizations have been viewed are as scripts for conversation and story grammars for narratives.

What Is the Course of Development?

The kinds of developmental changes that will be discussed below are changes in what are held to be the universal aspects of the development of pragmatic competence: changes in speech acts, changes in styles of communication interaction, and changes in the organization of discourse. Although much of the research to be reviewed in this chapter deals with particular populations of children (those who live in the United States and are white and middle class) development in all three of these areas of abilities are found in all cultures.

The course of development is traced here through each period of growth by discussion of the speech acts conveyed, the ways in which they are conveyed, and the organization of discourse during each period. Comparing developments across periods sheds light on those factors that play a role in the development of pragmatic competence. One important factor that is discussed is the role of the acquisition of other aspects of language during the same period on the pragmatic developments of that period.

Infancy

The developmental period called infancy is usually described as the first and second year of life. We have extended the period to include three years because much of the research that has been done seems to cover this third year of life as well. The development of speech acts and conversational competence is discussed in this section. During the last year of this period developmental changes in the organization of discourse also occur.

Speech Acts. To convey intent, the speaker uses those linguistic and paralinguistic forms that will be understood by the listener as, in fact, conveying that intent. Obviously, the prelexical infant is very constrained in the use of linguistic forms but, at a remarkably early age, has paralinguistic means (intonation, stress, facial expression, and gesture) available to convey intent.

At approximately seven months of age, contrastive patterns of intonation appear in babbled utterances. These intonational patterns are similar to those used by the adults in the child's environment. The infant in the American-English environment uses a traditional statement pattern in some babbled utterances (a gradually rising and falling intonation contour), a command pattern on others (a shapely rising and falling intonation contour), and a request pattern on still others (a gradual rise in the contour at the end of the utterance). Figure 6-1 presents a stylized representation of the acoustic parameters of the three intonational patterns. There is also evidence, discussed previously, of the infant's ability, at around this same time, to differentiate between the contours of statement and question sentences (Menyuk, 1971).

Despite these findings, there is little evidence that the infant purposefully uses different intonation contours to convey communication intent. Rather than purposive use, these contour patterns might merely be expressions of internal state or imitations of adult patterns. Since the infant's patterns are often accompanied by appropriate facial expressions, there is support for the notion that such patterns are expressions of internal states. However, there is some evidence that a short time after this (at about ten months), the infant begins to use specific types of gestures to indicate intent. Bates, Camaioni, and Volterra (1975) found, in their study of three infants aged two to twelve months, that infants indicate intentions by their actions on objects. They show objects to adults (the declarative use of action) or they seek aid with objects from adults (imperative or request).

The sequence of development suggested by these researchers is that the infant first produces gestures and vocalizations, and this behavior has no intention but does have an effect on adults. Next, the infant has intentions and expresses them nonverbally. Finally, intentions are conveyed verbally. These researchers did not examine the intonation patterns used by the infants they

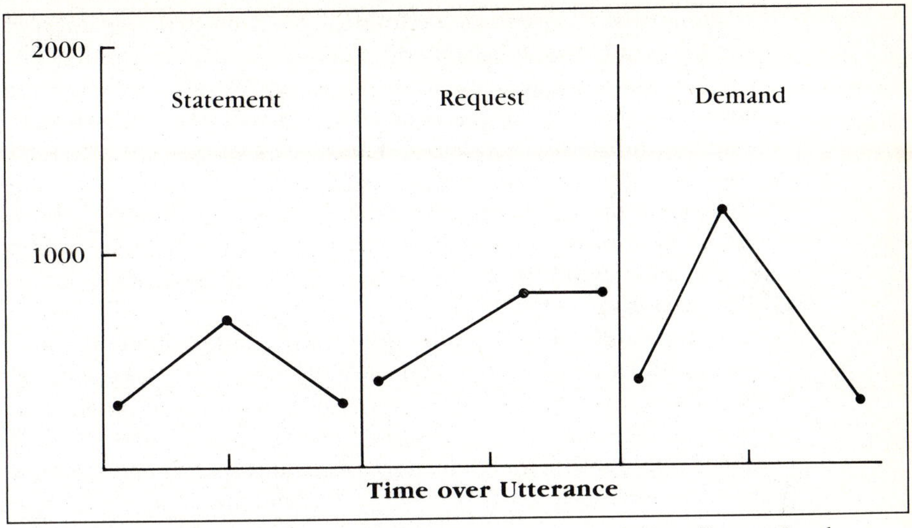

Figure 6-1 Stylized representations of the three basic patterns of intonational contour: statement, request, and demand.

studied. It is possible, given the findings on the use of intonation, that differential intonation contours accompany different gestures, and, therefore, that intentions are expressed vocally as well as motorically at the same time, although not lexically.

There is some evidence that older infants' particular gestures and particular vocalizations might be used to convey an array of intentions. Carter (1979) found in her intensive study of one infant, over the period when he was twelve to sixteen months, that there were several communication intents that could be identified in the communication behavior of her young subject. Three of the most frequent intents can roughly be characterized as declaratives, commands, and requests. In requesting an object, the infant would reach for the object and simultaneously produce an initial /m/. When drawing attention to an object, the infant would point or hold it out and simultaneously produce an initial /l/, /d/, or, less frequently, a /y/ (all alveolar sounds). When requesting the transfer of an object from self to other or from other to self, the infant would reach to the person and produce an initial /h/. No claim was made by the researcher that these were representative of semantic categories. Rather, suggests Carter, these vocalizations were only used to convey pragmatic intents.

The two studies cited seem to suggest that the sequence of behaviors that might describe the infants' use of verbal means to convey intent seems to be from gesture plus vocalization to gesture plus lexical item. These studies have not made clear how the development of intonation contours fits into the sequence. The results of an early study by Menyuk and Bernholtz (1969) suggest that during the holophrastic period, infants used differing intonation patterns on single words to convey intent. Acoustic analysis indicated that the words in one child's small lexicon were produced on different occasions with emphatic, statement, or request contours — those same contours that are used by the infant on babbled utterances. The specific intonation patterns used by this child were responded to by the mother as if they were either statements, demands, or requests. Even though there might be some question about the infant's intentions, the mother's consistent interpretation of these utterances in specific ways could bring the relation between intonation and intent to the child's attention.

Other studies have found early use of different intonation patterns on holophrastic utterances (Crystal, 1975; Dore, 1975; Halliday, 1975; Menn, 1976). Some of these studies have claimed that these intonational patterns are used to convey specific intents or rudimentary speech acts (Dore, 1975), while others have simply stated that, since adults interpret these utterances in specific ways, the infant, at least, *conveys* specific intents (Menn 1976), regardless of whether or not they are intentional.

Using gesture, vocalization at first and then word, and intonational contour, the infant communicates intentions to caregivers. Most of these intentions are concerned with manipulation of the environment, but some of them are comments on the environment. Halliday (1975) described these early utterances as falling into seven categories: instrumental, regulatory, interactional, personal, heuristic, imaginative, and representational. Dore et al. (1976) described them as expressing feelings, object want, and object indication. Carter (1979), in addition to the three most frequent categories of intention described previously — all concerned with either request or indication — found additional categories of intention related to affect. These included dislike, disappearance, and rejection (change the situation or take something away) and pleasure, surprise, and recognition. The categories that seem to capture all the varying intentions communicated by the infant are:

1. Demand
2. Request
3. Indication (showing or locating the presence of an object or event)
4. Statement
5. Negative affect
6. Positive affect

These categories of pragmatic intents represent a large proportion of the speech acts that we adults engage in. This indicates that at a very early age (from a year to two years) the infant has the ability to express (or convey) an important number of speech acts. However, these intents are conveyed by the surface structure aspects of the language; intonation and stress and, eventually, labelling with speech-sound production. Thus, these early abilities are based on the infant's ability to process and categorize, in some way, the speech signal.

Further, the success of these expressions relies heavily on the use of context and the cooperation of caregivers.

Much of what the infant conveys has to do with the here and now; take this object or event away, I like this object or event, give me this object or event, and can I have this object or event? A repeated finding, in studies of communication at an early age, is that a shift occurs from the here and now to what was or will be toward the end of the second year of life. The child requests absent objects and events and begins to report on objects and events that have or will appear or occur. Along with this shift, other marked changes in linguistic behavior occur. The rate of acquisition of lexical items increases dramatically, and two-word utterances begin to be frequently produced. The shift from communication about the here and now to the what was and will be, and the other linguistic changes that occur, probably reflect developmental shifts that occur in the organization and use of memory. The child at age two is remarkably different from the one-year-old in his or her ability to remember more, simultaneously, over a longer period of time and in the ways he or she stores and retrieves what is known.

With the production of two-word utterances, the child is able to convey intentions about specific objects and events and need not rely so heavily on the context of the communication and the cooperation of the caregiver. The range of speech acts, however, does not change. What does appear to change over the last year in this period of infancy is the child's participation in conversation.

Conversational Competence. In the discussion of the child's capacity to acquire language (Chapter Four), aspects of the child's early social readiness were examined. One of the important social behaviors observed in the infant was very early participation in conversation. Infants "take their turn" in conversation at about three months. This aspect of conversational competence is one that is acquired very early indeed.

Another conversational postulate was "Know how to back-channel." This, also, appears to be an early acquisition, although not so early as taking a turn. In a study of mother-child communication interaction (Donahue, 1978), it was found that during the second year of life four infants (two boys and two girls) gave back-channel responses to keep the conversation going. The boys used filler techniques such as "uh-huh" and "oh," and the girls attempted to repeat the mother's utterance and replicated the intonation pattern of that utterance. Not only does back-channeling keep the conversation going but it is also considered to be a form of politeness in conversation. Being polite in this and a few other ways is a form of conversational competence that is also acquired early. Certainly, mothers in our society request politeness from their infants at an early age by asking "What do you say?" or indicating by facial expression and body position that some modulation in a loud demand is required. Infants respond by saying "Peez" or speaking more softly when repeating the demand.

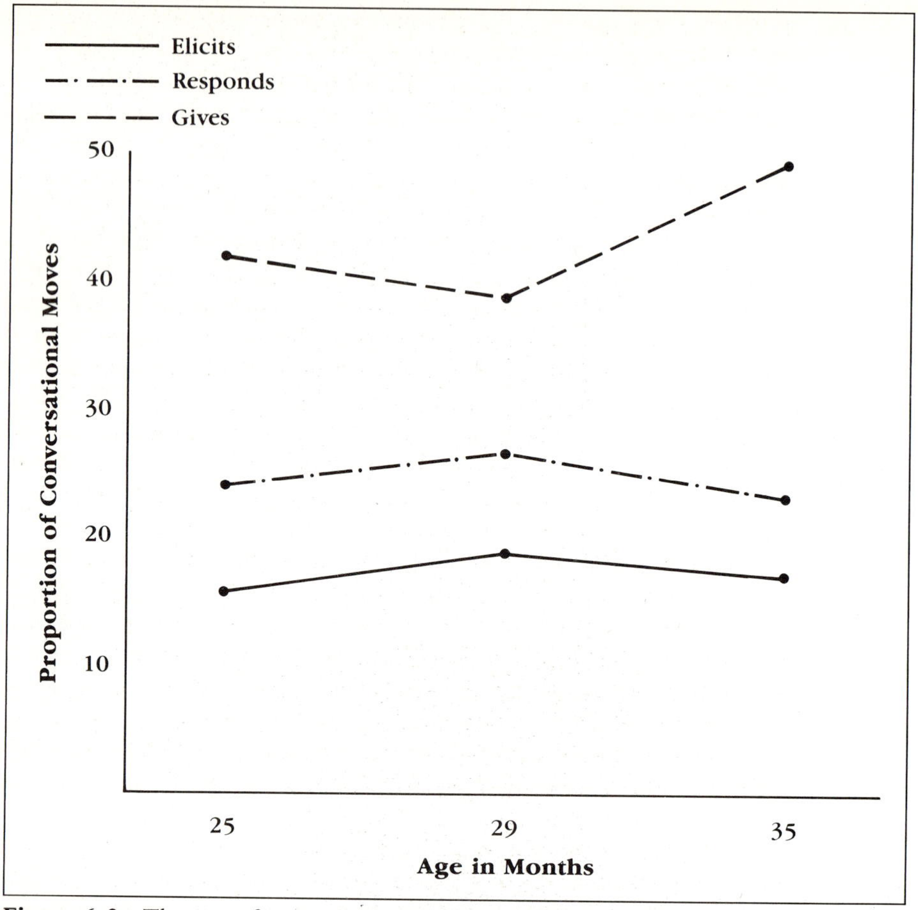

Figure 6-2 The most frequent conversational moves of children aged twenty-five to thirty-five months.

The very earliest conversational interactions that take place are primarily elicited and continued by the efforts of caregivers. By age two, however, the burden has shifted somewhat. In an analysis of the conversational roles of childrens' utterances at two to three years of age (Liebergott, Schultz, & Menyuk, 1985), it was found that, although a large proportion of the infants' utterances could be categorized as responses to Mom's elicitations, an even larger proportion of utterances were "Gives." These are utterances which contribute new information to the conversation. Figure 6-2 indicates the proportion of usage of the most frequently used conversational moves employed by children aged twenty-five to thirty-five months. As the figure indicates, there are no remarkable changes in conversational moves after twenty-five months.

Still another conversational postulate that is observed early is "Be appropriate." Observing this postulate is highly dependent on the child's ability to comprehend not only the pragmatic intent of caregivers' utterances but also their linguistic content, and to produce language that represents an appropriate response. As soon as children are capable of doing so, they respond appropriately.

In the Donahue (1978) study cited above, it was found that, with time, both the boys and the girls who were initially simply back-channeling eventually responded with meaningful lexical items rather than with fillers and repetitions. A study of seventeen- to twenty-four-month-old infants' responses to listener feedback (Wilcox & Webster, 1980) indicated that children's level of linguistic competence affected the frequency and type of their responses to requests for clarification. Children with larger lexicons and longer MLUs, as compared to their less sophisticated peers, responded more frequently and responded to requests for clarification with a higher proportion of recodings rather than repetitions. Thus, while the infant is clearly motivated to interact vocally with his caregiver, both lexical and semantactic development play important roles in the development of communication competence.

There is very little data on the organization of discourse during this period of development, probably because the infant does not engage in organized discourse. However, the infant's development of other aspects of pragmatic competence begins at a very early age. This makes sense, since the first use of vocalization is most certainly to interact with important others. In summary, by age two years the infant conveys a number of intentions by vocalization, gesture, facial expression, and intonation and stress. These so-called intentions appear to represent basic speech acts: demand, request, state, indicate, express positive and negative affect. These are the same speech acts that are used most commonly by adults. In addition to conveying intent, the infant participates very early in conversation with others. There is also evidence of early adherence to certain conversational postulates. These are to back-channel, to be as polite as you can, and to be as appropriate as you can. The degree to which the child can be polite and appropriate is dependent on her or his level of linguistic competence.

Early Childhood

Although the infant seems to have accomplished a great deal in the acquisition of pragmatic competence, there is still a great deal more that the child needs to accomplish. Developments in three areas of pragmatic competence during the early childhood period have been examined extensively.

Piaget (1926) concluded from his research that the communication abilities of the child would be hampered by the child's egocentric perspective. A great deal of research carried out with three- to seven-year-old children has been designed to assess the child's egocentricity in communication and the developmental changes that occur in this view. Much of the development that takes place over the early childhood period appears to reflect developments in the conversational postulates "Be clear and nonredundant" and "Be appropriate." In addition, there is acquisition of the abilities needed to engage in so-called indirect speech acts.

Egocentrism in Communication. The exploration of children's ability to take the other's perspective was examined by Piaget in a task that required that the child report on what another person, viewing a different perspective than that of the child, would see. The findings of the study indicated that early childhood subjects reported what they and not the other would see. Using these findings as background, a number of researchers (Flavell, 1966; Flavell, Botkin, Wright, & Jarvis, 1968) hypothesized that the young child's ability to communicate, keeping in mind the knowledge and experience of a conversational partner, would be limited.

Results of early studies indicated that children were egocentric in their communication behaviors when they were asked to tell another about an object in an array that the other could not see or about a series of events that the other had not witnessed. In the first instance, children would describe some objects in terms that were familiar only to them. For example, they might label an abstract geometrical form in an array as "Mommy's hat." They left out information crucial to understanding a sequence of events when telling about that sequence of events.

Subsequent to this initial research, there have been a number of studies that have come up with either conflicting findings or interpretations of findings that are in conflict with the egocentrism hypothesis (Garvey & Hogan, 1973; Shatz & Gelman, 1973; Maratsos, 1973). In essence, the results of these studies indicate that children aged three to four years *do* adjust their language, as do older speakers, to the age and state of their listeners. They will speak in simpler terms to younger listeners, and they will tell as much as they can about objects in an array or a sequence of events. Thus, four-year-olds very adequately describe an object such as "cat" in an array of animals but have difficulty in describing the object "the cat with one ear and no tail" in an array of cats.

The explanations for the differences in initial and subsequent findings also explain a great deal about the child's development of communication competence. The earlier findings were the result of placing young children in communication situations which were difficult for at least two reasons. In situations where children were asked to describe a sequence of events to a naive listener, the number and type of events in the situation caused a memory overload. In situations where children were asked to describe an item in an array, the nature of the object (for example, its abstractness or the types of features that distinguished it from others in the array) required that the child use descriptive terms that simply were not in the child's lexicon. When the communication conditions are made simpler, as they were in subsequent studies, the young child performs well.

These findings indicate that the developmental changes that occur in communication abilities are due to the child's increasing ability to hold in mind more information and more complicated information and to the child's increasing language knowledge. This is different from the assumption that the child needs to develop an understanding of the need to communicate. As is shown in the communication competence of the infant, that understanding appears to develop shortly after birth.

Many of the communication situations that were used in the earlier series of studies are very similar to the communication situations that children find in school; that is, children are often asked to recount a sequence of events or to distinguish an object or event from a series of similar objects and events. Understanding the conditions for success in these situations at various ages is important in terms of organization of classroom experiences. Further, a series of studies has indicated that the communication skills of children in these situations can be advanced somewhat if the children exhibit good skills to begin with. Shantz and Wilson (1972) found that second-grade subjects trained as listeners, speakers, and observers gave significantly greater information than their untrained peers. Coon, Lipscomb, and Copple (1982) found that comparison activities that narrow choice — such as providing specific verbal feedback or a chance to view the incorrect choice — helped kindergarten children to generate more adequate messages. Robinson and Robinson (1982) found that four- and five-year-olds improve their performance in referential communication tasks when they practice listening and speaking with a model, and do so even more markedly when they receive information about why and when listeners fail or succeed in a communication task.

Conversational Competence. The child exhibits increasing competence over the early childhood years in the ability to carry on clear, intelligible, and appropriate conversations. These developmental changes seem to be the product of developments in the acquisition of linguistic, cognitive, and social knowledge.

1. The effects of the development of *linguistic knowledge* are seen in the child's increasing ability to use linguistic cues to determine the meaning of conversational interactions.
2. The effects of the development of *cognitive competence* are seen in the child's increasing accuracy in referential communication situations.
3. The effects of the child's increasing *social competence* are seen in the child's increasing ability to engage in appropriate interactions in a wide range of communication situations.

Of course, developments in all three areas — linguistic, cognitive, and social knowledge — interact with each other and result in a high level of communication competence.

There are a number of linguistic cues that are crucial to the understanding of relations between objects and events in discourse. One example of the child's increasing ability to use linguistic cues to determine meaning in conversational interactions is the increase in the child's knowledge of *anaphoric relations* in discourse — knowledge of those devices that mark cross-reference within and across sentences. Tyler (1983) examined the development of the ability to interpret, in continuous discourse, anaphoric reference. The subjects in the study were five-, seven-, and ten-year-old children and adults. Three types of anaphora were examined; repeated noun phrases, general terms, and pronoun anaphors. The experimenter found that, by age five, anaphoric mapping had been mastered. However, all age groups found general terms most difficult to interpret, and the major development that occurred was in the lexical processing of anaphoric pronouns. With increasing age, the children were able to use all three types of cues — the lexical properties of pronouns, pragmatic inferences about the probability of relations, and the thematic structure of the discourse — to interpret anaphoric references.

The use of anaphoric reference is only one example of a number of linguistic devices that are used to tie elements of the discourse together. Another device is to indicate old and new information clearly. This can be done by the use of differential stress (stress the new information), by the use of certain semantactic structures (cleft sentences such as "It's John who kissed Mary"), and by the ordering of the use of specific and nonspecific articles (as in "I saw a boy. The boy sat on a bench"). These devices begin to be acquired at the beginning of the early childhood period and are usually mastered by the end of the period. However, such developments continue on into the middle childhood and adolescence periods. The principal change that seems to occur with development is in the number of cues that can be used simultaneously. Understanding of such cues is crucial in understanding written as well as spoken discourse.

The increase in the simultaneous use of cues seems to reflect developmental changes in memory, a cognitive development. Such changes can account for the increasing ability of children to present complete descriptions in referential communication situations. Older children can attend to more than one parameter at a time. It has been found in a number of studies (Whitehurst & Merkur, 1977; Whitehurst, Sonnenschein, & Ianfolla, 1981; Sonnenschein, 1982) that children aged five to six years have difficulties in comparing and contrasting (and keeping in mind) all those features that differentiate referents from nonreferents. Nine-year-olds are much better at it and actually benefit from more simultaneous information.

A similar kind of finding is that children of increasing age become increasingly better at using inferential cues to comprehend the meaning of messages. When we listen to messages or stories, we constantly make on-line inferences about what are the possible consequences of what has occurred or what might happen next. For example, when being told that "Kitty stole the cookies from the cookie jar," we might infer that what occurred was a punishable act and that, indeed, Kitty will be punished. We use both knowledge of the meaning of the message and world knowledge to make these inferences.

Schmidt and Paris (1983) studied the inferential abilities of children aged five to ten years as they listened to stories and answered verbatim and inferential questions. They found that the ability to answer inferential questions increased with age and with the *number of cues* provided. Children of all ages generated plausible inferences from the beginning, but older children generated more inferences and were more effective monitors. Older children used integrated cues for inference, whereas younger children treated cues as isolated sources of information. Again, the overall picture of development in this area is one of the child's being able to keep more in mind over longer periods of time and, simultaneously, to use a number of sources of information from real world and linguistic knowledge.

Thus far, it has been observed that children become increasingly good communicators over the early childhood years because of their growing linguistic and cognitive competence. They also become increasingly good communicators as they mature because they are exposed to more and different communication situations. One outstanding example of this development is the shift that occurs over the early childhood years from literal to nonliteral interpretation of the meaning of messages. This shift, although probably partially due to changes in linguistic and cognitive competence, is also due to changes in experience.

A number of studies (Singer & Flavell, 1981; Flavell, Speer, Green, & August, 1981; Bell & Flavell, 1984) found that there were developmental changes between the abilities of five- and seven-year-olds to detect whether a message was adequate in terms of quality, quantity, and type of information conveyed. It was suggested that younger children were less able than their older peers to evaluate messages because they were less aware of the question of the effectiveness of the message. They were more willing to solve the problem by making a guess, and they were unable to keep the demands of the task in mind. These difficulties, it was further suggested, were due to the cognitive limitations of the five-year-old as compared to the seven-year-old.

The findings of these studies were questioned in other studies (Ackerman, 1981; Ackerman, 1983). In these studies, the contents in which adequate and inadequate messages were produced were varied. The question being examined was whether the findings of the previous studies could be attributed to true inadequacies in young children's pragmatic abilities (inability to judge the adequacy of messages) or, rather, were the result of these children's good pragmatic assumptions (namely, the assumption that communicators, especially older ones, would produce adequate messages). When conditions of communication were altered so that inadequate communication became a possibility by providing a speaker who could produce inadequate messages, the younger as well as older subjects were able to judge the adequacy of the messages. Again, we have a finding that indicates that younger children perform as well as somewhat older children when the contexts that require that performance are simpler and clearer.

Practice in participating in a number of communication situations can, obviously, make clear to the child that the conversational postulate of "Be clear" can be violated in several ways. The child begins to learn that older as well as younger speakers are not always clear, intelligible, and nonredundant and, also, that speakers do not always mean what they say. This does not mean that the development of cognitive competence does not play a role in the development of the ability to evaluate the intelligibility and truth of a message or story, but only that social experience plays a role as well. The fact that a combination of linguistic, cognitive, and social factors plays a role in the development of communication competence has been made clear in a number of the reviewed studies. The interaction of factors is evident in the results of all of them. Indeed, a sign of developmental change is the increasing simultaneous use of all of these types of knowledge in increasingly different contexts.

Indirect Speech Acts. As was discussed earlier, during the third year of life all normally developing children develop the linguistic abilities needed to understand and produce a range of speech acts that directly convey their intents about specific objects and actions. They know how to question, state, demand, and negate. During the early childhood period the child also begins to produce some indirect speech acts. This occurs at approximately the same time that the child begins to understand that messages can be nonliteral.

Indirect speech acts are those that convey intents above and beyond the form and content of the utterance. Most messages that are conveyed to us and that we convey seem to fall into this category. A statement such as "I promise to wash the dishes" seems to be a direct speech act. It conveys the intent of the speaker to wash the dishes. Other speech acts seem less direct. For example, the statement "I'll wash the dishes if I can watch my favorite program" implies more than its content suggests. That is, the statement implies that bargaining is going on, although there is no explicit statement of this in the utterance itself.

One of the most frequently studied indirect speech acts is the request. It is also one of the earliest understood and used by children. Requests are formed by using the question structure: "Will you open the door?" "Can you pass the salt?" "Won't you stop doing that?" Even more indirect than the question is the statement that is a request. For example, the statement "I'm very cold," made in the context of an open window, might imply that the speaker is requesting that someone shut the window. In addition to requests being indirect speech acts, they are also polite forms for the imperative. Instead of making a demand by saying "Shut the window," we can be more polite and request by saying "Would you shut the window?"

Leonard, Wilcox, Fulmer, and Davis (1978) studied children's ability to understand three forms of request — positive and negative question forms and statements. They found that preschoolers could understand the first two types of request (negative and positive question forms) but that only six-year-olds could understand the statement kind of request. Statement forms of request require that the child take into account the context as well as what is said. Therefore, it makes sense that such requests are understood after question forms of request. Children not only use requests to get action or objects but, also, even during infancy, appear to select the request over the command for politeness reasons (Bates, 1976). These data indicate that cognitive and social factors lead to the early acquisition of this indirect speech act. It is completely acquired during the early childhood years.

Some of the data on input to children indicates that caregivers frequently use requests when interacting with their children (Holzman, 1974). These data may provide the reasons for requests being an early acquisition for children. The social pressure exerted by caregivers to be polite may lead to early acquisition of requests. However, there is little evidence that these young children have knowledge of the indirect nature of the act; that is, that such utterances have the sentence structure of questions even though they are used to convey requests. This appears to be true of the other indirect speech acts that are acquired during this period.

The other indirect speech acts that have been observed during the early childhood period are bargaining, insulting, praising, and lying (Woods, 1981). These indirect speech acts, together with the direct speech acts that have already been acquired, seem to represent the basic equipment needed for interaction with peers and adults during the early childhood period. They also appear to be learned rituals. That is, the steps needed to accomplish each one of these acts might be memorized and unanalyzed, just as greetings and farewells appear to be memorized ritualistic behaviors (Goffman, 1974). In this sense these early indirect speech acts may be similar to the early ritual interaction behaviors of the infant, such as patty-cake and bye-bye.

Scripts and Stories. By the time the child is three to four years of age there is marked evidence that internal representations of events can enhance conversational participation. These internal representations of sequences of events have been called *scripts*. Nelson and Gruendal (1979) found that, when talking about familiar sequences of events, four-year-olds were able to engage in a sustained dialogue. When the sequence of events was not familiar, children of this age might become egocentric in their conversation. Not only familiarity but also the overall structure of the sequence of events has an effect on their recall and, therefore, their ability to maintain conversational interaction about the script. Younger children are better able to sequence events that have a causal or enabling relation than they can those that form a sequence based on common occurrence (Nelson & Gruendal, 1981). This finding seems similar to those obtained in referential communication situations. When children are asked to communicate about familiar objects and events, which can be described in the language they have knowledge of, they are nonegocentric. When the situation becomes more difficult, they appear to be egocentric in their communication.

This finding about scripts and communication does not seem surprising in a common-sense way. Adults also can engage in better sustained dialogue on a topic they are familiar with as compared to one that they have little knowledge of. What is important about the finding, however, is that there is little evidence of sustained dialogue among peers at an earlier age. Any sustained dialogue that goes on before age three seems to be the result of sustained efforts on the part of caregivers. It appears that storage of mental representations of a sequence of events is necessary for such sustained dialogue. This, in itself, is an important finding.

Similar kinds of results have been obtained from children's telling and recall of stories. The research concerning the use of story structure in recall has been summarized by Mandler (1983). Familiarity with the topics covered in the story and knowledge of the structure of stories leads to better recall. Knowledge of the structure of stories is evident in preschool children. What changes with development is the amount of information that is recalled, but the patterns of recall remain the same.

The structure of stories has been described by various researchers as a grammar, a sequence of story constituents that follows a certain order from beginning to middle to end. Evidence that children use this structure to recall stories has been obtained from studies examining what happens to recall when this story grammar has been violated by changing the usual sequence of story constituents. Recall deteriorates and, in addition, both children and adults tend to correct the order of constituents in recall of these doctored stories.

Both story recall and story telling, as well as story reading, are very frequent activities in school. Having knowledge of story schemata is obviously important for carrying out these tasks. Some research indicates that there is cross-cultural stability in how stories are recalled (Mandler, Scribner, Cole, & DeForest, 1980). In this research it was found that patterns of recall were similar for both literate and nonliterate children and adults. However, there is some cultural variation in the patterns of oral stories in some societies that have a rich oral story-telling tradition (Watson, 1975). If children have different and, perhaps, conflicting schemata for stories, this can affect their performance in school. Such differences exist in the story telling of some black children (Michaels, 1981).

The child aged six or seven years is a highly accomplished communicator. This, of course, was true of the infant as well. However, much of the infant's good communication is the result of the willingness of caregivers to accommodate to the situation. The changes that occur over the early childhood period seem to be based on three developmental themes.

- There is a marked increase in the amount of information that is understood and conveyed in communications.

- □ There is also a marked increase in the number of differing contexts in which the child can communicate effectively.
- □ There is a marked decrease in the degree of literalness with which communications are understood and conveyed.

Despite the very dramatic changes that occur over the early childhood period, there are limitations in the pragmatic knowledge of children. During the next period of development dramatic changes also occur. Some of these changes appear to be a continuation of earlier developments, and others seem to be of a very different kind.

Middle Childhood and Adolescence

The dramatic changes that were referred to in the preceding paragraph occur in the conversational style of the seven-year-old as compared to the fourteen-year-old and in the topics of these conversations. Changes also occur in the types of speech acts that children understand and produce. Finally, there are changes that seem to mark the fact that children in middle childhood become aware of the communication behaviors they engage in.

Changes in Conversational Style. Children aged eight or nine years do much better as speakers and listeners in referential communication tasks than do four- and five-year-olds. They are much more complete and comparative in their descriptions of referents versus nonreferents in an array. These changes are a continuation of changes that have occurred over the early childhood period in the amount and type of information that can be conveyed in such communication situations. As pointed out earlier, increased ability in this area is useful in classroom situations and reflects developmental changes in linguistic and cognitive competence.

Other changes in conversational style seem to be a reflection of increasing social competence. Although children in the preschool and early school years show great conversational skill (Eisenberg & Garvey, 1981), developmental changes do occur in the organization of conversational interactions between and among children and between children and adults. These changes seem to reflect an increasing absorption of the conversational norms that exist in the child's culture (Boggs, 1978; Scollan & Scollan, 1979).

There have been very few studies of free conversational interaction among groups of older children and adolescents. Dorval and Eckerman (1984) carried out a very comprehensive study of developmental changes that occur in the conversation of children in a school setting in our society. Children's talk, in small peer groups in second, fifth, ninth, and twelfth grades, and adult talk were collected and analyzed after the members of each group became familiar with each other. The degree of topic maintenance as measured by the quality of the turns taken (unrelated, tangential, minimally related, factually related, and perspective related) and the proportion of focussed types of turns (agreement, disagreement, question, answer, and directive) were obtained from the

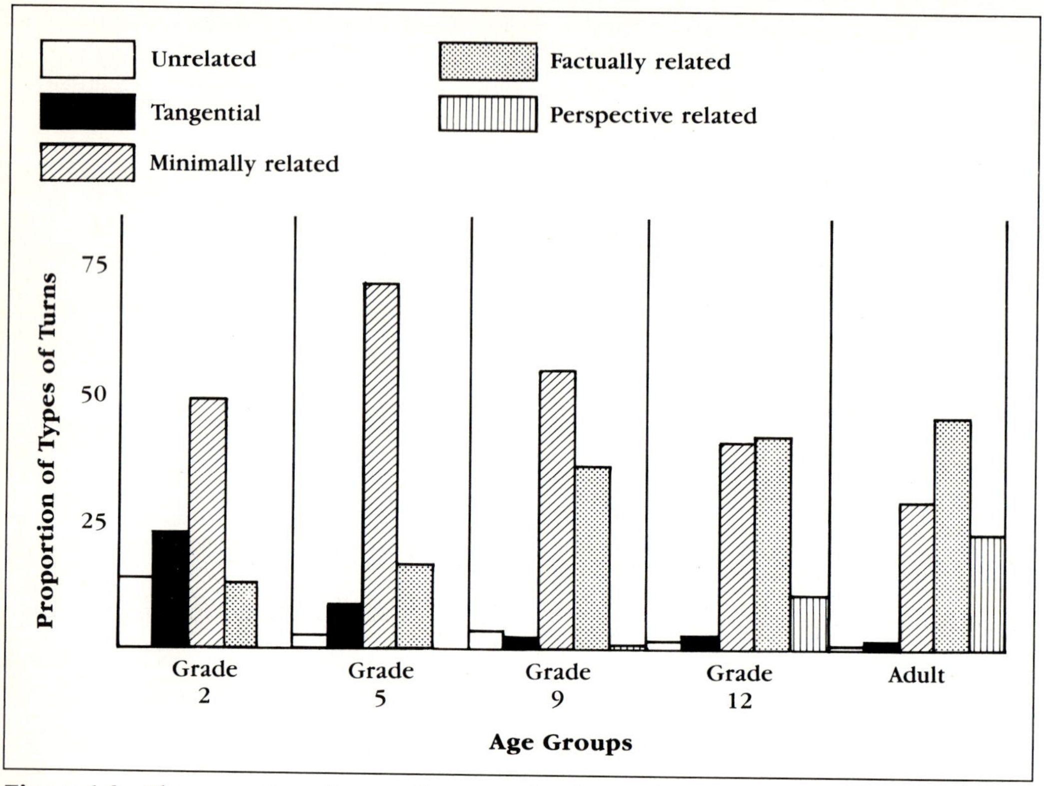

Figure 6-3 The proportion of types of conversational turn, from early childhood to adulthood.

conversations in each age group. The findings concerning the developmental changes in topic maintenance are presented in Figure 6-3.

As Figure 6-3 indicates, there are marked increases in the proportion of factually and perspective related turns taken over the age range, and a marked decrease in the unrelated and tangential turns taken. There are also increases in the proportion of agreements, questions, and answers used by older subjects in the study, and a decrease in the proportion of directives used. Overall, the proportion of focussed turns increases over time. The experimenters drew several conclusions from the results of the study. They observed that second graders are highly motivated to take a turn in conversation, that fifth graders show an increasing awareness of topic, and that ninth graders stay on the topic automatically and also psychologically evaluate others' contributions to a marked extent. Twelfth graders are more concerned with the perspectives of other participants and attempt to move from facts to perspectives in conversation, and adults are more able to maintain perspective-taking talk.

The results of this study indicate that children acquire different aspects of knowledge of how to participate in conversation over time, and that evaluations of what makes for a satisfying exchange in conversations change in time. A very early acquisition is knowledge of the fact that turn taking is required. A much later acquisition is the notion that perspective taking is required in such talk. Emphasis has been placed on the cognitive factors that bring about changes in perspective taking in conversation and in general (Selman, 1971). In fact, the term "social cognition" has been used to describe development in perspective-taking abilities. However, both cognitive and social factors appear to play an important role in these developmental changes. What a particular society expects of conversational participants at various ages and what participants are capable of doing are both reflected in these developmental changes. Although changes in conversational interaction occurred throughout the age range, the most marked changes occurred between ninth and twelfth grades and between children and adults.

Much more needs to be learned about the developmental changes that occur in the structure of conversations in different cultural groups. An aspect of change that might have a marked effect on the structure of conversation is change in the topics of conversation. In the study discussed above, second-grade children most frequently told stories and played games in their conversations, whereas twelfth graders and adults most frequently discussed social issues. Obvious effects on quality and types of turns could follow from these differences. Some applied questions concerning these findings might be: When are children ready to engage in topic-focussed and perspective-taking conversations? and What topics are needed to get them to do so? Answers to these questions have important implications for the planning of communicative interaction experiences in school.

Indirect Speech Acts. The early childhood period is the time when the child begins to acquire the ability to use indirect speech acts. During this period of development these abilities bloom. In addition, at about eight to ten years of age children begin to exhibit knowledge of the relations between the form and meaning of indirect speech acts. They act as if they were from another planet and playfully respond to requests such as "Can you open that door?" with "yes."

Three types of speech acts have been studied extensively, and these are the indirect speech acts that will be discussed as examples of developmental changes. These are lying, humor, and sarcasm. Lying and humor are certainly observed during early childhood, but there are marked differences in these speech acts when they are produced during early childhood and when they are produced in middle childhood and adolescence. The developmental changes that occur in the use of these speech acts seem to summarize all the changes in processing abilities that are required to achieve mature pragmatic competence.

What children find funny changes. A review of these changes (McGhee, 1979) indicates that the most marked change occurs between early childhood and later periods of development. In early childhood and before, children only find humor in comic situations or certain physical events. During this period of development children begin not only to produce puns, riddles, and jokes but also to understand them. The ability to appreciate riddles, puns, and jokes is highly dependent on our ability to process language. Understanding riddles (for example, "What has four wheels and flies?") is dependent on the knowledge that words can have double meanings. Understanding puns and jokes requires that we think about the meaning of words, or the relations among words in utterances, or the structure of narrative, to bring to conscious awareness what we know about language. Increasing linguistic competence plays an important role in these pragmatic developments.

During the early childhood period children lie, but they are not very efficient liars. They often lie without taking into account the entire context in which the lie is being produced. The example below illustrates this behavior.

> Mother and child leave the supermarket.
> Mother: Billy, where did you get that candy bar?
> Billy: You gave it to me.

As the example illustrates, in order to lie successfully one needs to take into account the attributes of the addressee, the relations between addressor and addressee, and the context. Past history and world knowledge also come in handy in successful lying. The amount of information that can be processed simultaneously plays an important role in the development of successful lying. Since older children can process more information simultaneously, they are better liars than younger children. Altruistic lying (lying to be kind to others) is also an accomplishment of older children. This type of lying is dependent on increasing social, as well as cognitive, competence.

The last type of speech act to be discussed is sarcasm. For correct interpretation of this speech act, the child needs to observe that the utterance is, in fact, a contradiction of what is being said. The bases for interpretation of sarcastic utterances are the context and the manner in which the utterance is produced, its prosodic features, and the facial expression and, perhaps, gestures of the speaker.

Some researchers have suggested that there are three stages in the development of knowledge of sarcasm (Demorest, Meyer, Phelps, Gardner, & Winner, 1984). At first, children interpret all remarks as sincere. At ages nine to thirteen they appreciate deliberate falsehood but see all false remarks as intending to deceive the listener. Only older children and adults recognize sarcasm. Ackerman (1982) came up with a different interpretation of developmental changes in children's understanding of sarcasm. He compared the abilities of first- and third-grade children with that of adults to detect sarcasm when only linguistic context was provided. Children and adults were read a number of paragraphs that contained sarcastic statements. In some of the paragraphs the context for interpretation came before the sarcastic utterance, in others it came after. Participants were asked questions about the paragraph and to recall information in the paragraph. The overall findings were that the position of the context information had an effect on performance, that third graders and adults did better than first graders in interpreting sarcasm, and that first graders comprehended the utterances in conditions that facilitate comprehension (that is, when the context for interpretation comes before the sarcastic utterance). The competence to process this speech act is evident at age six. However, the ability to do so under a variety of conditions increases as children enter middle childhood. This fact may account for the differences in the ages at which various experimenters have found knowledge of sarcasm.

Studies of the development of knowledge of these three types of speech acts indicate continuities and discontinuities between early and middle childhood and adolescence. There are marked changes in children's processing of certain kinds of indirect speech acts because there have been marked changes in their ability to bring to conscious awareness what they know about language. Understanding and production of humor fall into this category. There are marked changes in children's ability to lie successfully because the amount of information that the older child can process simultaneously has increased. In addition, the ability to lie under certain conditions (altruistic lying) increases because of increasing social awareness — the competence and willingness to take the perspective of the other. Finally, older children and adults can process certain speech acts more successfully because they have an increasing ability to process the information required under a variety of conditions.

Summary and Questions

Table 6.1 summarizes the developments in pragmatic knowledge that occur during different age periods. Many of these developments are due to children's increasing ability to simultaneously use a number of sources of information in conversation — information from their increasing real world knowledge and from their increasing linguistic knowledge. These developments are also due to the expanding social experiences of the child. An increasing number of different conversational partners and situations are encountered with age. A very important expansion of social experience occurs when the child enters school. Developmental changes in the ability to engage in perspective-related conversations on psychological and social issues are clearly a product of increasing cognitive/linguistic knowledge and social experience. The *willingness* to take the perspective of the other is present in the preschooler. Table 6-1 lists the remarkable developmental changes that occur in pragmatic knowledge over the three developmental periods.

The educational implications of the research results described in Table 6-1 are that they provide information that can be used in designing classroom communication situations that help rather than hinder linguistic growth in general, and pragmatic growth in particular. Understanding the general developmental changes that occur in children's ability to adequately participate

Table 6-1 Pragmatic acquisitions during different periods of development.

AGE PERIOD	CONVERSATION AND DISCOURSE	SPEECH ACTS
Infancy	Turn-taking Back-channeling Continue	Requests, demands, statements, indications (conveyed initially by intonation on vocalizations, gesture, facial expression)
Early childhood	Shift from literal to nonliteral Intelligible Appropriate in simple contexts Referring in simple contexts Script use Story grammar use	Most direct speech acts Bargaining, persuading, polite requests, insults
Middle childhood and adolescence	Referring in complex contexts Effective topic maintenance Development of psychological and social topics	Competent lying Appreciating and conveying sarcasm Appreciating and conveying humor

in conversation and to process connected discourse can, theoretically, help in the design of age-appropriate communication situations. However, the results of research studies of the development of pragmatic competence indicate that particular situations can very markedly affect the level of competence that different-aged children display. Therefore, to design appropriate communication situations for children, specific information about the dimensions (physical, social, and linguistic) that they can process need to be determined. The practical question is: What parameters of the communication situation can be manipulated to lead to appropriate and successful communication behavior on the part of children of different ages?

Age is not the only factor that produces differences in pragmatic competence among children. A second and related question is: What are the causes of marked individual variation in the rate at which various levels of pragmatic competence are achieved? Individual children can show marked variance from their age peers in pragmatic knowledge that is, apparently, not due to biological and social variations alone. In order to design effective communication situations in classrooms, not only should the variables of age and the dimensions of the communication situation be taken into account but, also, the abilities of individual children. In sum, since all these factors need to be taken into account for practical application of information about pragmatic development, more research that addresses the two questions posed above is needed.

Chapter Seven
Lexical Development

The acquisition of knowledge of word meaning and of the meaning relations among words are the topics of this chapter. Traditionally, a chapter on the topic of word meaning would be entitled "Semantic Development." However, semantic development includes more than acquisition of knowledge of the meaning of words and of the relations among the meaning of words. Semantic knowledge is knowledge of how meaning is represented in continuous discourse in particular contexts, not simply in words. Such meaning is represented both by words and by the structure of the utterances in which the words are embedded. For example, the meaning of the word "dog" in the utterance "His *dog* always fetched the evening paper for him" is somewhat different from its meaning in the utterance "It's a *dog*-eat-*dog* world."

This example makes it clear that interpretations of utterances are dependent on an interaction between the meanings of words and the context in which they are used. To try to disentangle this obvious interaction, the meaning of language is dealt with in two chapters; this one, Lexical Development, and the next one, Semantax Development. Despite the fact of the interaction, it also is clear that speakers of a language can provide definitions of words in their language and that speakers of the same language have similar definitions. Further, there is a great deal of evidence, primarily from those with suspected and known brain damage, that we, as users of a human language, have represented in our minds a lexicon or dictionary, and that we select words from this lexicon to produce and understand meaningful utterances. This is evident in the behavior that is called "word-finding problems" and is discussed at greater length in Chapter Eleven.

Certain specific questions about lexical development are addressed in this chapter. The first question is: What is the nature of lexical knowledge? A very important follow-up to this question is: How is the lexicon represented in our minds? Several different theories exist about how we represent lexical knowledge. Understanding the nature of the representation should help us understand the development of such knowledge and how this knowledge differs in people who have more than one language and in people with oral and written language problems.

The second key question to be addressed in the chapter is: What is the course of development in the acquisition of lexical knowledge? As in the previous chapter, and as in all subsequent chapters on acquisition of aspects of language, the developmental course is divided into infancy, early childhood, and middle childhood and adolescence. Patterns of acquisition within each period and the factors that appear to play a role in lexical developments within and across periods — including the effect of developments in other aspects of language — are discussed. The third and last question to be discussed is: How does lexical knowledge differ across different developmental periods? What has been written about how lexical knowledge is acquired, stored, and retrieved by children in one developmental period as compared to another is discussed to see if these changes shed further light on the bases for lexical acquisition.

What Is the Nature of Lexical Knowledge?

This question might be answered simply by stating that lexical knowledge is knowledge of the meanings of the words (or meaningful morphemes) in a language. Difficulties arise, however, when attempts are made to describe the nature of meaning. It will be assumed here that meaning has been defined and what will be described is some of the kinds of knowledge of meaning that a competent user of the language acquires.

One kind of knowledge that is acquired is knowledge that lexical items are either functional or categorical. There are lexical items that do not contribute to the meaning of the utterance but do contribute to its grammatical sense. These are called *functional lexical items*. Such a lexical item is the word "to" in the utterance "I want to go." There are parts of lexical items that do contribute to the meaning of the item. The last part of the word "played" (ed) has no meaning by itself but does contribute to the meaning of the verb "play." Lexical items and parts of lexical items of this kind are discussed in Chapters Eight and Nine. Those lexical items that represent categories of experience and conceptualization are discussed in this chapter.

The lexical items in a language represent experiences of objects and events and the attributes of objects and events. Although it is the case that societies and, therefore, languages differ from each other, to some extent, in the aspects that are represented, there is also universality in broad areas (Weinreich, 1966). For example, all languages have lexical items for foods, motion, location, affect, kinship, government, and the like. The competent user of the language not only acquires the notion of representation of a category but also acquires a sufficient number of lexical items so that effective communication with other users of the language can take place.

The acquisition of the *denotative* (a lexical item denotes a category) meanings of lexical items takes place in a number of semantic fields (the broad areas of experience referred to above). Lexical items are used to categorize not only objects but also objects of a certain kind (for example, food and clothing), events of a certain kind (for example, motion and state), attribution of objects (for example, color and size), and attribution of events (for example, place and manner). The competent lexicon user has notions of relations among lexical items as well as the lexical items themselves. That is, the competent lexicon user knows that the lexical items "object," "clothing," and "shoe" are in hierarchical relation to each other with "clothing" superordinate to "shoe" and subordinate to "object." Figure 7-1 provides some examples of the hierarchical relations among lexical items that children learn about.

There are additional kinds of relations among lexical items that the child learns about. The child learns that one word can have more than one meaning (a "pear" is something you eat, and a "pair" of shoes is something you wear) and that more than one word can categorize a similar experience or thing ("lady" and "woman," "shoes" and "footwear," "happy" and "joyful," "dead"

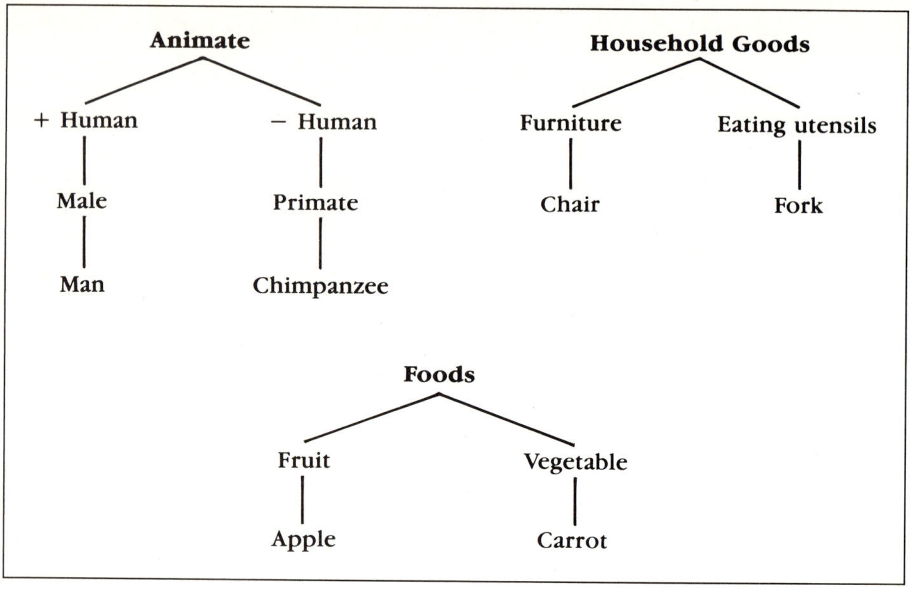

Figure 7-1 Some hierarchical relations among lexical items.

and "deceased"). The child also learns that some lexical items have opposite or contrastive meanings ("black" and "white," "cry" and "laugh").

There is a group of terms that describe relations between the propositions in sentences. These terms are conjunctive ("and"), causal ("because"), conditional ("if . . . then"), temporal ("before," "after," "then," "while," "when") and disjunctive ("but," "although," "despite"). The child learns how each term describes a relation between the actors, actions, and objects of the sentences that are joined by these terms.

In addition to acquiring denotative meanings of lexical items in the language, the child learns about connotative meanings, meanings that go beyond representation. For example, for polite communication the learner must acquire the distinctions between such terms as "stingy" and "thrifty," "fat" and "heavy," "cheap" and "inexpensive" that on the surface appear to be synonymous. The first term in each of these pairs connotes a negative aspect of the attribute categorized. Children learn that the same word can be interpreted in different ways depending on context. In the example given in the introduction to this chapter, the meaning of the word "dog" in one sentence represented or denoted an object category, but in the other the word connoted a category of persons with particular characteristics. Metaphors, similes, and idioms — so-called figurative language — are also forms of connotative meaning. For example, the idiom "break the ice" suggests, in general, to make interaction possible. A simile such as "She's as beautiful as a sunrise" suggests, in general, that her beauty is similar to that of a wonder of nature. A metaphor such as "The falling snowflakes were twirling ballerinas" suggests, in general, that the falling snowflakes were spinning in the manner in which ballerinas spin. It is obvious that "translations" of idioms, similes, and metaphors do not truly capture their meaning. Connotative lexical items and figurative language suggest a meaning that is different from the explicit meaning of the words used.

The types of knowledge that the competent language user acquires when acquiring a lexicon are:

1. Denotative meaning of lexical items.
2. Hierarchical relations of superordination and subordination among lexical items in a semantic field.
3. Parallel relations of homonymy, synonymy, and antonymy.
4. Relational meaning of terms that connect sentences.
5. Connotative meaning of lexical items.
6. Figurative language.

This list appears to cover many parameters of the child's acquisition of lexical knowledge. However, it has been suggested that developmental changes occur not only in lexical acquisitions but also in how this knowledge is represented in the mind and, therefore, in how this knowledge is stored and retrieved.

How Is the Lexicon Represented in the Mind?

How words are represented in the mind has been a matter of much philosophical discussion for a very long period of time. Recent notions of this representation have been the product of research in the area of semantic memory and of attempts to simulate lexical accessing by computer programs. Neither approach has left us with a completely satisfying model of how the lexicon is represented in our minds. Some of the models of lexical representation and arguments in support of these different models is presented here. How these models may be used in producing and understanding utterances and in recall is then discussed.

Models of Lexical Representation

Over the past ten years there have been many summaries of models of lexical representation, or the so-called "mental dictionary" (Glucksberg & Danks, 1975; Clark & Clark, 1977; Carroll, 1986). One difference that separates models is the distinction between referential and denotative meanings. Another difference is the distinction between componential and relational denotative meaning. Although there are further distinctions, these dichotomies catch the flavor of the primary differences between models.

Referential and Denotative Meanings. Those who support the notion of referential representation of the meanings of words suggest that each word in the lexicon has associated with it some mental image. For example, on hearing the word "dog," a listener would conjure up some mental image of a dog. Different words might call up different sensory images. Some words have high auditory imagery ("whistle") while others, such as "house," have high visual imagery (Paivio, 1971). It is clear that only some words might bring to mind a sensory image.

Studies that have attempted to test this model of lexical representation have frequently used paired-associate learning tasks (Paivio, 1968) and the effect of the imaginal properties of words (high or low) on subjects' ability to recall them (Paivio, 1969). The general finding has been that use of high imaginal words helps in associative learning, and that high imaginal words are easier to recall. There is, therefore, some support for the notion that, at least for some words, a mental image representing the word might be stored in the mental dictionary.

Objections that have been raised to this model of representation is that some words (for example, "think") cannot bring a mental image to mind, and that different words with different meanings could bring the same image to mind ("dog" and "terrier"). Despite these objections, it is clear that many words do conjure up images and that these images play an important role in one's ability to remember the meanings of these words. It is also possible that, in development, the *first kind of representation* of words is imaginal. It has been suggested, however, that these images apply to representatives of a word but not to its meaning. The meaning of a word, it is stated, is in its sense, not in its reference (Clark & Clark, 1977, p. 410).

It is not easy to determine what the sense of a word is. One way in which the sense of a word has been described is that it denotes or marks off a category. For example, the word "table" represents a category of objects that share certain properties. Further, there is agreement among speakers of the language that the word does denote the category. Such agreement among speakers is necessary for communication. Because words denote categories rather than refer to particular instances or to a perceptual (imaginal) representation of instances, it is possible for speakers of the language to share meaning even though their particular experiences might lead them to different instances and images.

The problem of how word meaning is represented in the lexicon, however, is not resolved. If referred instances and images are not stored, it is not clear *what* is stored. Although the word "table" might represent a category of objects that share certain properties, it is not clear what these properties are and how they are represented in the mind nor how such properties change in development.

Componential and Relational Meaning. There are three main models of the structure of the lexicon (Carroll, 1986): the hierarchical network model (Collins & Quillian, 1969), the semantic feature model (Smith, Shoben, & Rips, 1974) and the spreading activation model (Collins & Loftus, 1975). Although these models are not specific about the nature of the properties stored for each lexical item in the mental dictionary, they do suggest what these properties might be. Each model assumes that lexical items are stored in relation to each other but they differ in the nature of the relationship described.

The hierarchical network model relates words to each other in terms of superordinate and subordinate categories. For example, the word "animal" is superordinate to "bird" and "fish." "Bird" and "fish," in turn, are superordinate to "canary" and "ostrich" and "shark" and "salmon." Each superordinate term has properties that define all members of subordinate categories. In the example given, the properties of animal, the superordinate category, (has skin, can move around, eats and breathes) all apply to the subordinate categories.

The semantic features model represents words in the mental lexicon as a bundle of features rather than an entity. These features both define (are exclusive to the word) and are characteristic (usually are a part of the definition). For example, the defining features for the word "bird" are feathers and animacy. A characteristic feature is flying. Because the features of "bird" and "robin" are so similar, the relation between these two lexical items becomes evident. A great deal of research has been carried out to examine the relation between the posited semantic features of lexical items and the sequence of acquisition of these items.

The third model, the spreading activation model, suggests that the relations among words are not hierarchical. Rather, words are related to each other in multiple ways. Some of these ways are by degree of association (for example, "bread" and "butter"), others by categorical relations ("red" and "blue"), and still others by typicality (words that typify a category such as "robin" for bird and "apple" for fruit). Figure 7-2 presents examples of relations among words as described by these models.

All of the models in Figure 7-2 seem to capture parts of what people know about words. Given the fact that all competent users of the lexicon have knowledge of multiple relations among lexical items, the most correct of the models must be the model that suggests that there are multiple relations between each lexical item and other items, the spreading activation model. However, all the models, and especially the last one since it allows for all possibilities, tell us very little about how each lexical item is, in fact, represented in the mind.

None of these models, apparently, take into account the fact that lexical

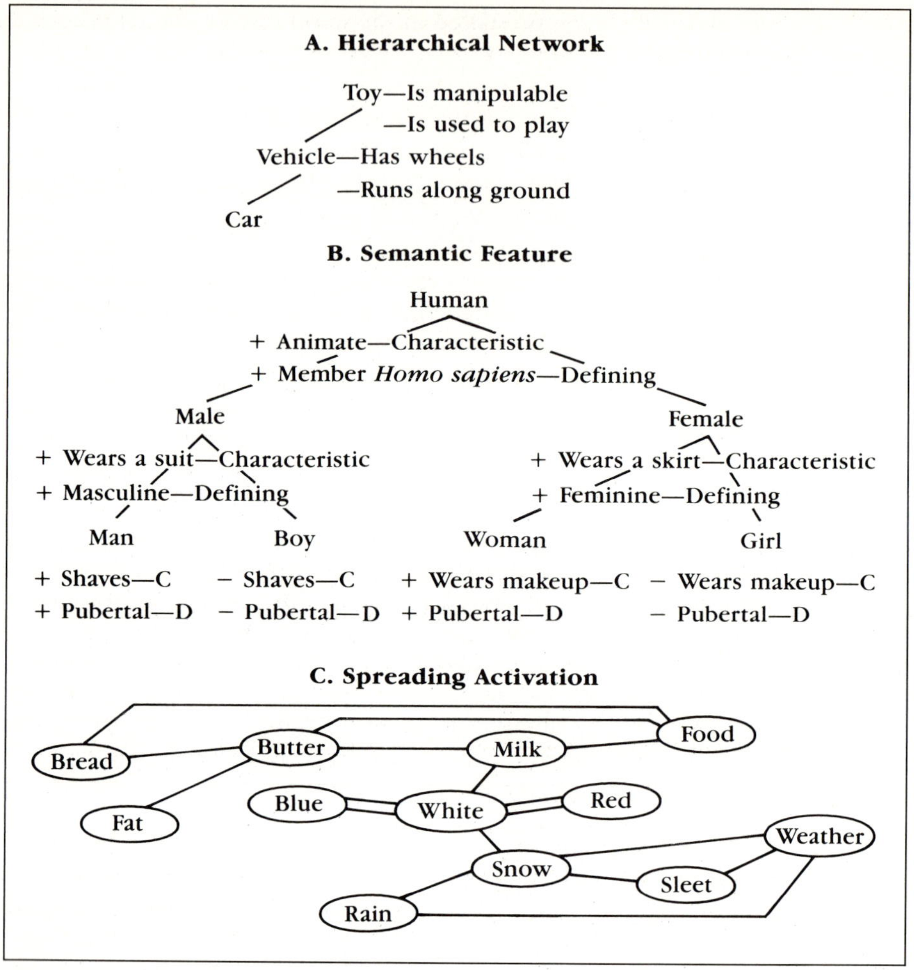

Figure 7-2 Models of lexical representation: (A) hierarchical network, (B) semantic feature, and (C) spreading activation.

items must be represented phonologically as well as semantically. After reading is acquired, lexical items are represented orthographically as well. It is possible that some items are represented imaginally, and it seems that all lexical items are represented syntactically as well. These models also shed little light on how these representations might be used to process the speech signal for meaning. The processing models discussed below attempt to do this.

Models of Lexical Processing

A variety of lexical processing models have been proposed. All of them attempt to take into account the fact that the linguistic context in which a lexical item is produced plays a role in its identification. Since this is a difficult enough task, none of them attempts to take into account the situational context also. The latter, of course, must play a role in the production and comprehension of lexical items. Of the many models proposed, three seem to capture the field and are, at least theoretically, useful.

The Logogen Model. The *logogen model* (Morton, 1982) proposes that words are recognized by a process of accumulating evidence. Words are represented as logogens in the logogen system. When enough evidence is accumulated, a particular logogen is excited. First, the acoustic evidence is used by the logogen system to decide whether a word has occurred. If the decision is made that a word has occurred, the word is sent to the cognitive system where computations relevant to the meaning are made. Acoustic and semantic evidence trigger the comprehension of a word. The model suggests that a word is represented in different ways, phonologically and semantically. It further suggests that the output logogens are separate from input logogens and that functional and categorical logogens are also separate from each other. This might be interpreted as meaning that different lexical representations are located in different places in the cortex. Certainly there is evidence from brain-damaged patients that this might be the case. For example, different sites of damage appear to be related to difficulties with content words such as "boy" or function words such as "for." The model might provide a partial explanation for word-finding problems. Individuals with these problems may not be able to rapidly collect sufficient evidence on a word to allow rapid excitation of a particular logogen.

The Cohort Model. The *cohort model* of lexical recognition (Marslen-Wilson & Tyler, 1980) proposes that words are comprehended on the basis of preliminary acoustic information in interaction with syntactic and interpretative information. There are, in this view, no levels of processing, from acoustic to semantic and structural to interpretative. The listener "recognizes" the meanings of words because all types of information are used simultaneously. A possible interpretation of this processing model might be that acoustic or phonological representations of a word are stored with semantic and syntactic representations. This model indicates that additional sources of difficulty may account for word-finding problems; that is, difficulty in on-line simultaneous processing of acoustic and linguistic information.

The Lexical Search Model. The final model to be discussed is the so-called *lexical search model* (for example, Forster, 1978). This model proposes that words are recognized by a process of elimination. Decisions are made on the basis of best fit. Words that are possible candidates — given the acoustic information and the context of the utterance — are reviewed, beginning with those candidates that have a high probability. This model suggests that semantically related words are stored close to each other in the lexicon. This model indicates yet another possible source of word-finding difficulty, the inability to use contextual information to home in on a semantic category.

Each of these three models has associated with it a large body of research studies. Naturally, each model proposer argues that the data fit his model best. A review of the three models, however, indicates that there is a great deal of similarity among them. All the models propose that on-line processing takes into account both the acoustic information and the contextual linguistic information. All three models propose that phonological, semantic, and syntactic information about lexical items is stored. They differ only in the sequence in which the three sources of information are accessed.

Those concerned with the development of lexical knowledge in children who are developing normally and those with developmental problems might question the value of theoretical models of lexical representation and lexical accessing in understanding the two patterns of development. As indicated in the examples given above the models might lay the groundwork for obtaining a much better understanding of the problems of children who have difficulty in acquiring and accessing the lexicon. These models may also give us a better understanding of lexical development in normally developing children.

Development of Lexical Knowledge

To parents and other relatives, the child's use of words is one of the most exciting events in the child's developmental history. Lexical acquisition, however, begins somewhat earlier than this event and continues throughout that child's lifetime. We are constantly acquiring new words. There are, however, marked differences in patterns of acquisition of word knowledge by infants and children and adolescents and adults. There are also similarities. There are both similarities and differences in the bases for these patterns of word acquisition and for developmental changes in these patterns.

Infancy

Patterns of Lexical Acquisition. The early words that children acquire are in semantic fields that they have most experience in. A number of studies have found that infants' first words represent specific people ("mommy" and "daddy"), specific objects ("shoe" and "cup"), general objects ("boy" and "toy"), action words ("up" and "on"), attributes ("dirty" and "nice"), personal and social words ("me" and "please"), negation ("no"), and question ("wuzzat" and "where"). In essence, most of the basic categories discussed at the beginning of the chapter seem to be represented in the early lexicons of infants. That is, they have terms for objects and events and for attributes of objects.

The quantitative findings concerning lexical comprehension and production during the first three years of life have been quite consistent across studies. Based on the diaries kept by mothers, infants comprehend the first 10 words at about twelve months, 50 words at about fourteen months and 100 words at about seventeen months. Infants produce 10 words at about fifteen months and 50 words at about nineteen months. Two things should be noted about these quantitative data. First, there is a lag between comprehension and production at these early ages. It is not a very wide lag to begin with, but gets somewhat wider with time. Second, the rate at which new words are comprehended increases with time from about 40 words per month at fourteen months to about 90 words per month at eighteen months. Rate increases for production as well as comprehension. The age at which 100 words are produced is not mentioned because once the child achieves 50 productive words, mothers find it impossible to keep track of all the new words acquired.

Children have been observed to start producing recognizable words at about nine to twelve months. In some very rare instances this parroting ability is observed even earlier. These early productions are probably simply that, parroted utterances (Nakazima, 1962). There is little evidence that these vocalizations are used to denote objects and events. On the other hand, as is the case with babbled utterances, they are used to convey pragmatic intent (Carter, 1979).

It has also been observed that children comprehend words at about eight to nine months, but this comprehension appears to be limited to certain contexts. For example, the mother may say "Daddy's coming" and the infant looks toward the door through which Daddy usually comes, or a favorite object such as "teddy" is named, and the child looks toward the named object. In these instances it is not even clear whether the child has learned to associate the name with an object in a certain context or if the mother has cued the child to look in a certain direction.

Some careful research on lexical comprehension indicates that infants aged approximately thirteen months can associate a small set of objects with their names, even when the context does not support the association (Thomas, Campos, Shucard, Ramsay, & Shucard, 1981). In this study, infants aged approximately eleven months and thirteen months were exposed to a visual array which contained a number of objects. The infants' mothers had provided the experimenters with the names of some objects known to the infants. During the experiment the mothers gave the names of known and unknown objects and some nonsense syllables to their infants with their backs turned to them. The thirteen-month-old infants, but not the eleven-month-old infants, looked significantly longer at those objects whose names they recognized than at objects with unfamiliar names, either real or nonsense. This study was one of the first to provide evidence of infants' comprehension of words without contextual support.

The production of words to denote objects and events takes somewhat longer. During the second year of life the infant shifts from initially labelling objects and events as specific entities to denoting objects and events as members of classes of entities. It is clear, however, that infants go through phases in the development of this knowledge. Vygotsky (1962) talked about the child's use of the same term to label different aspects of a situation. He observed a child first using the term "quak" to label a bird on a pond, then a bird on a coin, and then a bowl of water. This is one of the beginning stages of the use of terms to label. This might be called the "slippery" phase. The phase that may precede this is exemplified by a very small productive lexicon, perhaps ten words or less, and the use of terms for very specific objects or events. The word "cup" is applied only to the object that the child drinks from, the word "on" is only applied to the event of Mom turning the light on. This phase might be called *undergeneralization* or *overspecification*.

In word production, two phases follow this: *overgeneralization* and *differentiation*. The overgeneralization phase is the one that has received the most attention because it provides evidence that the infant is beginning to use words categorically. Although there are comparatively fewer studies of word comprehension, there is evidence that while the infant may be overgeneralizing in word production he or she is not doing this in word comprehension. Further, the infant gives evidence of understanding that words represent classes of objects or attributes. Oviatt (1982) found that infants aged fifteen to eighteen months could learn the name of a novel object (an unknown animal) and could recognize that the name designates instances of the object. Golinkoff, Hirsh-Pasek, Lavallee, and Baduini (1985) found that children in the third year of life were able to identify ambiguous objects with unknown names because they contrasted with the known names of known objects. They also found that these children were able to generalize the unfamiliar name in somewhat different instances (a change in color) of the ambiguous objects; a true instance of comprehending that words are used for categories of objects, not just for particular objects.

The data on overgeneralization in word production has been summarized several times, recently by Clark (1983). These data indicate that children apply a term to a number of objects that share some property or properties. For example, the word "doggie" may be applied to all four-legged animals with tails. These overgeneralizations occur on the basis of perceptual features that pertain in varying instances (shape, visual features, sound, and so on) and functional features. Such overgeneralizations appear in the language of children from one to two and a half years old. These data provide evidence that generalizations are being made about the use of words to denote categories of objects and events.

Children do not go through all the phases of word use for every word acquired, and these overgeneralizations do not occur for all categories. The types of generalizations seen seem to vary from child to child, indicating that particular experiences might lead to particular generalizations. The generalizations, also, begin to be replaced by differentiated use of words in previously generalized categories. For example, the child may very rapidly acquire the word "cat" to differentiate between short and tall four-legged animals. The further differentiation that occurs in word production was once explained by the acquisition of additional feature contrasts. However, there is little evidence to support this notion. A better explanation appears to lie in the child's increasing ability to observe what terms are being used by the adults in the child's environment to differentiate between items (Clark, 1983).

Like early word comprehension, early word production appears initially to be bound to particular contexts. After imitative and memorized routine behavior, children begin to use words to refer to objects and events in the here and now. During the second year of life infants begin to refer to absent objects and events. Some of their often used requests and statements indicate that this shift has occurred. Children begin to request absent objects ("more cookie") and to make statements about absent objects ("all gone cookie").

Summary and Explanations. Several very important lexical developments occur over the period of infancy. One of the most important is the shift from use of words to imitate and to engage in memorized routines to labels, and from labels to terms to denote. This is probably a shift that does not occur easily in subhuman primates. They are clearly capable of eventually accomplishing this, as indicated by their acquisition of symbol systems. Another shift that occurs over this period is the shift from comprehending and producing words only in the here and now to comprehending and producing words that are not tied to the particular context of their use.

The phases of lexical development that occur over this developmental period seem to be the following:

1. Overspecification: "cup" /=/ cup I drink from
2. Slipperiness: "quak" /=/ duck, then coin, then pond
3. Overgeneralization: "hat" /=/ whatever I wear on my head
4. Differentiation: "dog" /=/ dog, and "cat" /=/ cat

These developmental shifts interlace with the child's talking about the here and now and develop in the direction of categorical denotation. Parroting and routines occur before any of the phases. However, labelling occurs with overspecification and slipperiness, and denotation occurs with overgeneralization and differentiation.

Several explanations have been provided by varying theorists to account for these lexical behaviors and the developmental changes that occur in them. The basis for the child's acquisition of a lexicon is said to lie in the human infant's ability to learn a symbol system. Several particular cognitive abilities are said to account for lexical acquisition. The notion that lexical items denote or represent categories of experience implies that users of lexical items must have knowledge of the categories of experience that words represent before they acquire a word that represents a category (Clark & Clark, 1977). These categories or concepts are based on the perceptual and functional groupings that the infant has already developed, the natural groupings of objects and events that the infant has already observed. Words are mapped onto instances of these natural groups. The first lexicons develop, then, when the infant is able to observe the relation between the word and the natural category. Support for this position is experimental as well as theoretical. The work of Heider and Olivier (1972) indicated that people much more easily acquire new lexical items for natural perceptual categories than for those that cross these categories. For example, they can much more easily learn a new term for the primary color category "blue" than for the nonprimary color category "pink."

An alternative to this position is that of Vygotsky (1962). Vygotsky states that "The lines along which a complex (precursor to a concept) develops are predetermined by the meaning a given word already has in the language of adults" (p. 67), and "verbal intercourse with adults thus becomes a powerful factor in the development of the child's concepts" (p. 69). This position has already been discussed to some extent in Chapter Three, Cognition and Language. Here, Vygotsky's notion of concept development is expanded upon to present his position on the basis for the acquisition of a first lexicon. Vygotsky, in a series of experiments, observed children's acquisition of a concept when provided with a name for the concept. He observed several stages in the development of the concept. These stages represent changes in the bases for particular groupings of objects. Roughly, grouping changes as follows:

1. From grouping on the basis of contiguity or immediate perception to observing partial bonds between objects.
2. From forming various groups on the basis of differentiation of bonds to pseudo-concepts.
3. From pseudo-concepts to true concepts. Pseudo-concepts reflect grouping on the basis of a constant visible connection, whereas true concepts are abstract notions, ideas of categories.

These two positions may not, in fact, be so different. The infant may observe the relation between his or her groupings and the adult use of the word. Acquisition of the word may then lead to a redefining of the grouping and, therefore, to a different meaning attached to the word. The process becomes an interactive one in which psychological groupings and words act as catalysts to changes both in groupings and in the meanings of words. Such an interaction would lead to the developmental changes that have been observed in children's attribution of meanings to the words they understand and use.

If such an explanation is correct, then both the experiences and the language are needed to acquire the lexical meanings that are shared by all members of a linguistic community. Such an explanation would also account for the fact that there are particular semantic fields in which the "adult" meanings of words are acquired more rapidly than others. Differences in the developmental course of experience and the ways in which the language encodes the experience would affect the order of acquisition of the meaning of lexical items.

Early Childhood

Lexical development during early childhood takes place very rapidly and in all semantic fields. The term "fast mapping" (the ability to very quickly apply a new name to a new category) has been used to describe this very rapid acquisition (Carey, 1978). Because the changes that occur are so extensive, researchers have focussed upon certain aspects of these developments. There are, therefore, some areas that have been examined more than others. The child's notion of a category for object-word classification, the acquisition of *deictic terms,* (terms that describe the relation between self and others in space and time) and the child's knowledge of locative and attributive terms are some of the more researched areas. Although these types of terms are clearly not exhaustive of the semantic fields within which young children acquire lexical items, they do represent distinct semantic fields and are good illustrations of developmental trends in the acquisition of lexical knowledge.

Categorization and Lexical Representation. As was already discussed, what forms the category to which an object name applies changes in time over the infancy period. During this period of development, changes continue to occur in the child's notions about applicable categories. For example, Callanan and Markman (1982) found that children aged two to three years tended to organize objects as collections ("forest") rather than as classes ("trees"). They tended to distort natural language subordinate relations to superordinate hierarchical relations ("oak" in relation to "tree") into part-whole relations ("oak" in relation to "forest"). These results indicate that children of these ages have yet to acquire a true understanding of the hierarchical relations among categorical terms in the language, even though they may use superordinate and subordinate terms. This ability develops over the early childhood period as a product of further environmental and linguistic experience, but it is certainly not complete at the end of early childhood (Anglin, 1970).

Several experiments have been designed to examine what aspects of experience are attended to first to form a category. It has been suggested that perceptual experience is primary in forming the category to which a lexical item might be applied (Clark & Clark, 1977). Others have argued that generalization of functional experience is the basis for the first categorizations to which words are applied (Nelson, 1973). A number of studies were designed to examine the question of which attributes are first observed. The conclusion overall has been that different lexical items are coded in differing ways due to the nature of the item (Menyuk, 1977) and to the context in which it is used (Prawat & Wildfong, 1980). For many lexical items, the sequence of observation of the defining characteristics for its application appears to be from form to function (Tomikawa & Dodd, 1980).

The final aspect of the use of categorical terms that has been examined is the extension of the term to appropriate instances. Bernstein (1983) examined children's and adults' application of the term "chair" to a range of possible examples: first when the objects appeared alone and then when the objects appeared with persons sitting on them. It was found that three-, four- and five-year-old children were still in the process of developing the "concept" of chair. They were much less consistent than adults in decision making. Their criteria for inclusion of items to which the term might apply were all form criteria, although the rank ordering of items was affected by the function cue of a person sitting on an item. The developmental sequence in the application of a term seems to be first perceptual (possibly imaginal) representations of lexical items of this kind. Representation then shifts to the functional as well as perceptual attributes of the lexical items. Overall, the criteria for application of the term becomes more stable over time but is still inconsistent at age five.

Developmentally, the application of lexical items changes over time as a function of experience, of how this experience is encoded, and of how consistently the representations of the experience can be retrieved. This latter change is also probably due to the ways in which representations of the items are encoded. The more representations an individual has, the more swiftly may the lexical item be retrieved by a number of differing cues. Changes in both the logogen and cohort models of lexical interpretation might describe such developmental changes.

Deictic Terms. Deictic terms describe the relation in space and time between the speaker and the listener. Although there are other important ones, the terms most usually discussed are pronouns ("I" and "you"), demonstratives or determiners ("this" and "that"), verbs of motion ("give" and "take"), and adverbs of place ("here" and "there"). It is clear that the use of such terms, by both listener and speaker, are very important for effective communication.

A number of researchers have examined the acquisition of the meanings of these lexical items and have concluded that the child's acquisition of this knowledge is dependent on three factors: discourse experience, cognitive development, and further lexical development (Wales, 1979; Tfouni & Klatzky, 1983). Researchers have found that the development of knowledge of the meaning of such terms begins by participation in conversation and understanding of gesture.

Wales (1979) reviews his and others' research on the acquisition of a number of the contrastive deictic terms listed above. He suggests that infants begin to understand the general indicational functions of "this" and "that" and "here" and "there" as mothers use these terms, with appropriate gestures, in conversational interaction with them. Children acquire general notions of indication, or pointing, before they acquire knowledge of the contrastive meanings of the deictic terms themselves. Further, they initially relate the meaning of the terms to mothers' use of "this" and "here" to introduce the appearance of objects and "that" and "there" to talk about the disappearance of objects.

Thus, the beginning of the understanding of deictic terms occurs through conversational interaction and is limited to *specific* appearance and disappearance of objects.

The acquisition of the contrastive meanings of these terms was examined by Wales in a number of experiments. The overall finding was that children acquire knowledge of these terms in a gradual way. After the acquisition of the initial notions of indication and pointing and appearance and disappearance, they begin to realize that the contrast in the meaning of the terms is related to the spatial location of the speaker and the objects (or actions in the contexts of verbs of motion) that are in the physical situation. They learn that situations vary and, therefore, when and how the terms should be applied. Acquisition of adult knowledge of these terms, which is not totally accomplished by age seven, requires learning the conditions under which they apply. The ability to use the appropriate strategy for determining the meaning of the terms is the cognitive factor, states Wales, which plays the primary role in development of knowledge of these terms. The use of appropriate strategies, however, is dependent on the ability to take the entire situation into account, to process the entire situation.

Somewhat similar conclusions were reached by Tfouni and Klatzky (1983) in their study of three-and-a-half-year-old children, although the details of the findings and the questions asked varied to some extent. Wales found that acquisition of the particular terms "here" and "there" and "this" and "that" was not the function of the proximal or distal nature of the terms but, rather, of the situation in which they were used. These researchers found that "this" and "here" drew more inappropriate responses than "that" and "there." They attribute this to the greater proposed semantic complexity of "this" and "here." These latter terms are marked and therefore, have one more feature than the terms "that" and "there." This conclusion suggests that acquisition of additional lexical features plays an important role in the sequence of development of these terms. However, Tfouni and Klatzky and Wales agree that notions of the meaning of deictic terms are initially extracted from participation in discourse in which the pointing gesture plays an important role. It seems reasonable to add, along with Wales, that the meanings of these terms continue to develop on the basis of the observation of the many contexts in which they are used rather than on the basis of a hypothetical additional feature.

Attribution and Location of Objects. In the discussion of the semantic fields in which lexical items develop, it was stated that attribution of objects and of actions both develop. It may, therefore, seem unreasonable to discuss only location and attribution of objects and exclude discussion of location, manner, and time of action. The development of the verb phrase, as well as other topics concerned with the use of verbs, seems to fall more into the category of semantax rather than that of lexical development. The development of locative terms has been studied very extensively, and it has been suggested that developments of some spatial terms precede and exemplify the marking of time relations. Such terms as "in front of" and "behind" fall into this category.

Children's understandings of the meanings of terms that describe the perceptual and quantitative attributes of objects have been studied extensively. Children's acquisition of the meaning of the terms "big" and "little," "tall" and "short," "more" and "less," and so on, have been studied extensively. The overall findings of the studies of children's knowledge of the meanings of size and quantitative terms is that children acquire knowledge of the meanings of the so-called positive terms ("big," "tall," and "more") before they understand the meaning of their negative opposites ("little," "short," and "less"). It has been suggested that this is related to their perceptual/cognitive development. Negative terms are more complicated than positive terms because they mark an additional feature on a perceptual parameter. For example, the word "tall" may mark extension, the word "short" adds a feature, minus extension (Clark & Clark, 1977).

Similar findings were obtained in studies examining children's comprehension of the locative terms "behind" and "in front of." That is, children acquired the meaning of the latter term before the former, and this too signified the acquisition of the positive term before the negative. Extensive studies of children's acquisition of the terms "in," "on," and "under" indicated that children acquired knowledge of these terms in that order. This might be explained by the fact that unmarked location is exemplified by "in," whereas the location "on" is marked and therefore adds a feature and "under" is opposite to "on" and, thus, adds another feature.

A great deal of research has been carried out that has attempted to vary systematically the situations in which children have to identify objects in terms of these locational attributes or have to place objects in certain locations. Much of this research is reviewed by Clark (1983). The findings of these studies are that the child will try to use the strategy that is most appropriate to a particular situation. In some situations that do not provide too much information to process or too confusing information, the child successfully identifies the attributes of objects and locates objects in their appropriate place. This suggests that children's acquisition of knowledge of the meaning of these terms does not change in time in an absolute sense but, rather, that the particular applications of the term change in time due to cognitive and pragmatic development. The child gets better at processing all the information in a situation. He then discovers that it is pragmatically incorrect to assume that the most obvious answer is the correct one. Another interpretation is that knowledge of the meanings of these terms changes in time from knowledge of meaning in particular settings to knowledge of meaning regardless of setting (Carey, 1982). This also suggests that such lexical items would be represented in hierarchical and multiple ways to allow for interpretation in different contexts.

The terms used to denote size and many aspects of space have relational as well as absolute meaning. For example, the term "big" does not mean that something is big in an absolute sense but, rather, that it is bigger than another thing. Something may be "under" something else, not necessarily under everything. Children acquire the notion of the relative meanings of terms such as "big" and "under" over this developmental period — not just the contrasts between "big" and "little" and "on" and "under." Some Soviet psychologists found, for example, that children understood the term "under" in only an absolute sense and would not identify objects that were not absolutely under everything as being "under." Therefore, the children denied that a block that was under the table but on top of a box was, in fact, under the table (Slobin, 1966b). Another change in lexical knowledge that occurs over the early childhood period is acquisition of the understanding that these terms are indeed relative.

Summary and Explanations. It is obvious in the discussions of the studies cited that there are some disagreements among researchers about explanations for lexical development and, indeed, about what the child knows about the meanings of lexical items. All researchers would agree that lexical development and concept development are related. However, they disagree as to the nature of the relation. That is, some researchers suggest that concept development is necessary to lexical development, whereas others suggest an interactive relation such as the one described by Vygotsky. Some researchers emphasize the role of discourse experience in the acquisition of the meaning of lexical items, whereas others would place primary emphasis on concept development. Obviously, both concept development and experience in discourse must play an important role in lexical development. The discussion of the development of the understanding of deictic terms is just one example of this. This fact has implications for the teaching of language. Lexical knowledge does not derive from cognitive development alone but, rather, from learning to understand the meanings of words used in varying linguistic and situational contexts. The more complex these situations are, the later will the term be acquired.

What the child knows about the meanings of words changes over time. Children's acquisition of knowledge of the category to which a word applies changes in time. This change in time, it has been stated, is due to the child's ability to take into account simultaneously both the perceptual and functional parameters that make up the category to which the word applies *and* to be consistent about the representation of the category. This implies that what marks developmental change is the nature of the representation and the consistent use of the representation.

The ability to interpret the meaning of deictic lexical items changes in time, and this change is apparently due to an increasing ability to use contextual information in appropriate ways. The acquisition of knowledge of the meaning of words that describe location and attribution of objects is also a matter of being able to take into account the situation in which these words are being used. All that these statements imply is that the child's meanings for words change as a function of the context in which they are used. This increasing flexibility in interpretation of meaning is an indication of growth in lexical knowledge. Thus far, discussions have centered on physical contexts but, clearly, linguistic context plays a role as well. To incorporate such information for each lexical item, lexical representations would have to be very elaborate.

Representation of meaning from the point of view of several researchers is initially perceptual (perhaps imaginal, for some words), and then functional representations are added. The child must also learn how to interpret the meanings of these words in differing contexts, both situational and linguistic. This may mean that what the child must learn are the multiple representations of these words and that development is simply an increase in these representations in time. This does not seem to be an efficient way of storing information about meanings. However, the spreading activation model of lexical representation suggests just this sort of representation, and certainly the nervous system could accommodate such multiple representations.

By the end of the early childhood period the child has learned a great many words and a great deal about word meaning. However, it is clear that there is a great deal more to be learned. Earlier in this chapter, it was stated that the child must learn the denotative meanings of lexical items. All aspects of the denotative meanings of some lexical items and some aspects of the connotative meanings of some lexical items have been acquired by the end of early childhood. Some parallel relational meaning has been acquired as well. Children acquire knowledge of the parallel relation between antonyms during the preschool period (Clark, 1972) and the relation between homonyms at about six to seven years (Shultz & Pilon, 1973). Children have yet to acquire:

1. The adult denotative meanings of all the lexical items they are using.
2. Understanding of the relations between propositions marked by different connectives.
3. The connotative meanings of lexical items.
4. Understanding of hierarchical relations.
5. The understanding of figurative language.

Middle Childhood and Adolescence

Only certain aspects of each of the areas of development can be dealt with here. Further development of denotative meanings is discussed as the development of definitions of words. Acquisition of knowledge of causal, temporal, and disjunctive terms to mark relations between sentences is also discussed here. Connotative meanings are covered as the acquisition of knowledge of the relation between the denotative and connotative meanings of adjectives. Figurative language is discussed as the acquisition of knowledge of simile and metaphor.

Definition of Words. The discussion of the changing meaning of words for children at three to seven years indicated that researchers suggest that during this time there is a shift in the meaning of words for objects. Meaning being represented as percepts changes to meaning being represented as functions. However, some research indicates that when children in grades two, four, and six and adults are asked to provide definitions for common nouns, their definitions change with their ages from mentioning only functional attributes to combining functional and perceptual attributes (Wehren, DeLisi, & Arnold, 1981). Definitions for words, then, might differ from the way these words are represented in the mental lexicon. This seems unsatisfactory. Children's meanings for words should somehow be reflected in the definitions they supply.

Another approach was taken to examine children's definitions of words (Keil & Batterman, 1984). Children of approximately five to ten years old were asked which of two stories best defined a word. In each of these two stories either the defining properties of the word or the characteristic properties of the word were described. For example, in one story the word "twins" was described as two girls who look alike, dress alike, and so on (characteristic features) but are two years apart in age. In the second story "twins" were described as two girls born at the same time and from the same mommy (defining features) but who lived in different parts of the country. The overall finding of the study was that there was a shift from a preference for characteristic features to a preference for defining features for almost all of the words used in the study.

In the discussion of models of lexical representation, the semantic feature model regards words as being represented as bundles of defining and characteristic features. However, the results of this study led the researchers to conclude that representation of words is not made on the basis of features — either characteristic or defining — but, initially, as *example-based* representations and then, in a transitional phase, by both examples and some defining features. Finally, words are represented in terms of analytic defining components — just those components that differentiate words from each other. This shift occurs for different words at different times because familiarity with the concept that the word represents has an effect on how rapidly the shift from representation by example to representation by defining parameters occurs. This increasing familiarity occurs because of the increasing experiences the child has with the use of words in discourse (Watson, 1985).

Words differ not only in terms of their familiarity but also in terms of their nature. Therefore, some terms that are used to describe biological entities (such as "fish") and physical entities (such as "wave") need to be understood in much deeper ways before their complete meanings are acquired. These deeper ways are, in fact, a product of not only experience but also formal education (Carey, 1986). Continued development of the meaning of words can take place over a lifetime, since meanings change as a function of a wide range of experiences.

Causal, Temporal, and Disjunctive Terms. There is a sequence in the development of the understanding of causal, temporal, and disjunctive terms that connect sentences. Well within the early childhood period, knowledge of the meanings of the conjunctive term "and" is evident. Children understand very early both the simultaneous ("Bill and Jeff ran the race") and sequential ("Bill ran home and got his lunch") meanings of the term. They also exhibit knowledge of the cause-effect relation between sentences when the relation described is a familiar social situation ("He shouldn't play ball in the house because he could break a window"). More complete understanding of the causal relation between physical events comes much later because, like true understanding of terms that denote biological and physical entities, such understanding is dependent on formal education. This, however, does not imply that there is no understanding of the meaning of "because."

Understanding of the meaning of temporal ("when" and "while") and disjunctive ("but" and "although") terms seems to follow the understanding of conjunctive and causal terms (Katz & Brent, 1968). The cognitive complexity of the latter terms has been cited as the reason for later acquisition of the understanding of temporal terms (Werner & Kaplan, 1964) and disjunctive terms (Bruner, Goodnow, & Austin, 1956; Vygotsky, 1962). However, much of the research that examined the use of these terms indicates that they are produced early in middle childhood but, apparently, are only truly understood later. Such results may indicate that, like the "cause" connective, these terms are first understood and produced in contexts where the relation between the sentences is understood. Application of the understanding of these terms would increase over time as the contexts of the relations described become understood. Eventually some abstract knowledge of the meaning of the term is acquired, which can then be applied to all contexts. In this way, the development of the meanings of these terms mirrors the sequence of development of other words.

Connotative Meanings of Adjectives. A classic study was carried out by Asch and Nerlove (1960) to examine children's understanding of the possible double meanings of such adjectival terms as "sweet," "hard," "cold," and "crooked." Such terms can apply to both objects and people. The researchers found that it was not until age seven or eight that children were able to apply the connotative as well as the denotative meaning of these terms to people. Initially, people who were described as cold and hard were considered to be physically cold and hard. It was not until age ten to twelve that children were able to talk about the dual function of these terms and how they are related to each other.

These findings suggest that the course of development of the connotative meanings of words is, first, understanding of the contexts in which these words are applied; then, some understanding of the double meanings of these terms; and finally, the ability to talk about these terms. The ability to talk about the relations between denotative and connotative meanings indicates an awareness of the relation. This shift from use and comprehension of lexical items to an awareness of the relations among lexical items also probably marks developmental changes in the ability to see hierarchical relations (superordinate and subordinate) and the parallel relation of synonymy among lexical items. The age at which these developmental changes begin to occur and the age at which the shift from syntagmatic to paradigmatic word associations occurs appears to be similar to the age at which awareness of connotative meanings appears — that is, in middle childhood (Anglin, 1970; Clark, 1983; Jenkins & Palermo, 1964).

Figurative Language. A great deal of research has been carried out examining children's acquisition of knowledge of the meanings and the use of metaphors and similes. All of this research indicates that the roots of understanding such figurative language begin during the early childhood period, but that an awareness of the meanings of such language is not accomplished until the end of middle childhood or adolescence.

Gardner (1974) found that preschool children were able to apply adjectives from one domain to another domain. They were able to talk about "hard" and "soft" colors and "red" and "blue" sounds. The ability to make these cross-modal associations increased with age, and nineteen-year-old subjects made these associations significantly more easily than did preschool children. However, the most remarkable developmental change that occurred was in the ability to *talk* about the matching across domains, to explain why such matches were possible. Preschool children could not provide explanations for their performance, and seven-year-olds answered concretely. It was not until age eleven that creative and insightful answers were provided. Again, there is evidence that the most dramatic changes that occur in the use and understanding of double-meaning words and phrases is in an awareness of the meanings and an ability to talk about them.

In addition to achieving the ability to talk about the meaning of figurative language during middle childhood and adolescence, the ability to interpret simile and metaphor increases with age (Green, 1985). Various reasons have been proposed to account for these developmental changes. Some researchers have suggested that the particular form of the figurative language (simile versus metaphor) and the complexity of the language used in a metaphor will have an effect on the age at which such figurative language will be understood (Reynolds & Ortony, 1980; Vosniadou, Ortony, & Reynolds, 1982).

Others have suggested that achievement of levels of thinking according to Piaget's classifications (concrete and formal operational) should affect the child's ability to interpret metaphor. Billow (1975) found that the type of metaphor children were asked to interpret and explain had an effect on the age at which they could do so. Even five-year-olds could interpret some simple metaphors ("A butterfly is a flying rainbow") and seven-year-olds were able to explain such metaphors. However, only older children could interpret proportional metaphors, those that entail an analogy ("His life was a ship constantly battling a storm;" "My stomach was the Atlantic Ocean without water"). Their performance with proportional metaphors and proverbs was, presumably, related to their formal operational abilities. Even the thirteen-year-olds were still unable to explain the complete set of proverbs that they were presented with.

The sequence of abilities that has been observed in comprehension of metaphors is the ability first to interpret the metaphor or paraphrase it and then to explain it. The question is: Are these abilities dependent on levels of thinking or on other factors, such as the ability to process the language of the metaphor or the familiarity with the references made in the metaphor (for example, butterfly, rainbow, ships battling storms) or on reading competence (Malgady, 1977)? There is a reciprocal relation between reading competence and the understanding of figurative language. Comita and Eson (1978) found that children who could paraphrase were at the concrete operational level of thinking, whereas only children at the intersectional stage and the formal operation stage could explain their interpretations. Similar conclusions were reached by others (Winner, Rosensteil, & Gardner, 1976).

It is possible, given the above findings, that the increasing abilities of children in middle childhood and adolescents to interpret more "complex" figurative language is a product of both increasing linguistic competence (lexical and semantactic) and increased experience with the situations in which similes and metaphors are used. The kinds of materials that these older children might read, and the writing activities they engage in, is clearly a very important source of this increased experience. Thus, formal education can play a vital role in these developments.

It has been suggested by many of the researchers cited that the ability to explain figurative language is due to the metacognitive or metalinguistic abilities of children in the middle years and adolescents, and that this is related to formal operational thinking. The problem with this conclusion is that metalinguizing about other aspects of language occurs long before children interpret and explain figurative language (Menyuk, 1983). Therefore, the ability to metalinguize cannot be the product of formal operational thinking. The other factors cited, increasing linguistic competence and familiarity with the situations in which such language is used, seem to be better explanations of this development.

Summary and Explanations. These are the three developments that take place over the middle-childhood and adolescent period and that appear to be marked changes in the mental lexicon and its organization:

1. A change in the representation of lexical items from characteristic representation to defining representation.
2. The representation of such entities as being hierarchically related to other entities.
3. The understanding of the connotative meanings of words.

Other changes that have been noted to occur during this period — such as understanding causal, temporal, and disjunctive connecting terms and understanding figurative language — do not seem to be the result of marked changes in the lexicon. These changes seem to be the product of the extension of previously acquired knowledge to further contexts and the ability to talk about this knowledge, rather than marked changes in the meanings of lexical terms and phrases and their organization in the lexicon.

Research on the shift from characteristic to defining meanings of lexical items indicates that familiarity with the category that a lexical item represents determines the age at which this shift occurs. The shift itself, however, seems to indicate a marked difference in how an item is represented in the lexicon and may indicate that the lexical choice model represents lexical processing by this period of development. This representation allows interpretation of the word in comparison to others and frees this interpretation from particular physical contexts. Understanding the connotative meanings of words also seems to indicate a shift in lexical representation. Words are represented in terms of defining features and then, also, in more than one defining way. Research on children's ability to group words hierarchically, to respond paradigmatically, and to observe synonymy indicates that the meanings of words are now stored in connection with other words that share some defining characteristics.

All of the developments of this period appear to be the result of (1) further experience with the use of words in multiple contexts, and (2) the acquisition of further knowledge of categories and relations in the real world. One product of this further experience is the child's awareness of word and relational meaning and the ability to talk about it. Another is the child's ability to understand the use of connecting terms — such as "but," "because," "and not," and "if . . . then" — that describe complex physical relations among events. Two developments in the meaning of language during this period seem to be particularly dependent on education. These are acquisition of knowledge of the meaning of terms that categorize biological and physical entities and acquisition of knowledge of the meanings of figurative language. Acquisition of written language knowledge and school experiences seem particularly to affect the understanding and use of more complex figurative language.

Differences Across Developmental Periods

It is obvious that acquisition of knowledge of the meaning of words takes place over a lifetime. However, the developments in this knowledge that have been described by various researchers seem to indicate marked differences in the developments of each period. Table 7-1 lists some of the differences within and across each period.

The lexical acquisition in the infancy period is marked by two developmental changes. The first is the shift from labelling items and events by lexical

Table 7-1 Changes in lexical knowledge within and across developmental periods.

PERIOD	LEXICAL KNOWLEDGE
Infancy	From imitation and memorized routines to Labels for specific instances to Denotative slipperiness to Denotative generalization in here and now to Denotative differentiation in there and then
Early childhood	Addition in semantic fields denoted Further differentiation of semantic fields Flexible interpretation due to context for some terms Consistency of application of meaning for some terms Addition to situations for word application
Middle childhood and adolescence	From characteristic to defining features representation Addition of societal and educationally defined meanings From denotative to connotative meaning From description of relations within sentences to description of relations among sentences From literal to figurative use of language Awareness of categorical and relational meaning

items to denoting items and events with the use of lexical items. This developmental change appears to mark the beginning of changes in concept development. The other change that occurs is a shift from talking about the here and now to talking about the there and then. This change appears to mark a change in the way in which lexical items are stored and can be retrieved.

Developmental changes that occur over the early childhood period indicate that there is a rapid accretion of lexical items that mark different semantic fields. The child appears to be breaking down the world of objects, events, and modification of objects and events into more detailed categories. The child is also acquiring knowledge of which lexical terms are the appropriate ones for particular linguistic and physical contexts. Semantic syntactic development and semantic lexical development take place rapidly during the early childhood years. It is not clear how lexical items are stored during this period. It has been suggested that they may be stored as entities with characteristic properties and also indications of the contexts in which they can be appropriately used.

The developments that occur in middle childhood and adolescence seem to be different from the developments that have already occurred, and, probably, they represent the way in which lexical acquisitions occur thereafter.

These developments are: representation of lexical items in terms of defining features and organization of the lexicon to account for double (or more) meanings, and parallel and hierarchical relations among words.

The models of the mental lexicon and of lexical processing described at the beginning of this chapter were designed to apply to adult representation and processing. However, the middle-childhood-to-adolescent child seems to have already organized the lexicon in very adult ways and also to process lexical items in adult ways. The child represents lexical items in multiple ways that may be best described by the spreading activation model. As we shall see in the next chapter, she or he is able to use not only physical context to interpret words, but also linguistic context. This may be best described by the cohort model of lexical processing.

There are many questions — both theoretical and applied — about lexical development that still have to be answered. The theoretical questions have to do with how words *are* represented in the child's mental dictionary during various periods of development and with how lexical items *are* processed in connected discourse during these periods. The applied questions have to do with how lexical knowledge *can be increased* and with how lexical processing *can be improved* for some children. Some research findings indicate that use of words in different physical and linguistic contexts, both spoken and written, increases knowledge of the definitions of words. Research also suggests that practice in developing associations among words, in using on-line contextual information, and in categorizing lexically may all help in processing lexical information. These research suggestions need to be carefully explored in studies that examine which factors are most conducive to increased lexical development.

Chapter Eight
Semantax Development

The previous chapter described the child's acquisition of the knowledge of the meaning of words. In this chapter what the child knows during different periods of development about how to *select* and *combine* words to convey particular intents about specific categories and relations among categories is discussed. This is *semantax knowledge*. Such knowledge has been termed *semantactic* because both selection from the lexicon and construction of a sequence of such selections are involved.

The semantax of the utterances produced by speakers are structural realizations of what speakers wish to convey. They are understood by listeners in this way. For example, to realize a statement about a particular relation that will take place between Mary and John, the speaker would select certain lexical items (Mary, marry, and John; or , Mary, John, and tell) and order them in a certain way ("John will marry Mary" or "Mary will tell John"). Simply uttering the list of words (John marry will Mary or tell will Mary John) would obviously not convey any meaning. Along with the paralinguistic features of facial expression, gesture, intonation and stress, the force of the utterance, the relations among the categories in the utterance, and the categories themselves are all conveyed with semantactic structures. Acquisition of such knowledge, as well as pragmatic knowledge, is necessary for adequate communication.

There have been various theoretical descriptions of the semantax of languages. A revolutionary one was *transformational* or *generative grammar,* now called the *traditional generative grammar* (Chomsky, 1966). This theory suggested that syntax was the basis for semantic interpretation. A more current theory of generative grammar, *government and binding* (Chomsky, 1980), attempts to describe the notion that certain structures predict others in sentences, and, therefore, that there are constraints on the types of structures that can appear in sentences. Children would first acquire what is known as the "core," knowledge of how to express basic relations in the language. They then would acquire the "periphery," the particular constraints that exist in their native language. Other current theories, such as *lexical grammar* theory (Bresnan, 1978), place much greater emphasis on the role of the lexicon in shaping the structure of an utterance. These theories have affected researchers' descriptions of the kinds of knowledge children have as they develop from producing holophrastic one-word utterances to simple word combinations, from these to simple sentences, and from these to complex sentences.

As theoretical descriptions of language have changed, so have descriptions of children's linguistic knowledge changed — especially children's very early knowledge (Bowerman, 1973; Menyuk, 1977). As stated, the current dominant theoretical positions suggest that either basic lexical and syntactic knowledge are acquired simultaneously (Pinker, 1981) or that semantic categories are precursors to syntactic development (Maratsos, 1983). The term *semantactic development* is used here to describe the changes in structural knowledge that occur over time and that appear to be the product of both lexical and syntactic development.

Descriptions of the kind of knowledge that the child must acquire in order to understand and produce semantactic structures have been less variable than descriptions of what they know about these structures. What the child must learn has been neatly summed up by Slobin (1979) in his description of grammar. The child must learn "All these things together — order and various forms of markers — [that] make up grammar and convert a disconnected string of words into a sentence" (p. 8). What must the child learn about semantax? That is the first question addressed in this chapter. The second is: What is the course of semantax development? As the developments of each period are described, the explanations for these developments are also presented. The final question in the chapter is: What are the bases for individual variation in semantactic knowledge? Knowledge of the bases for individual differences can shed further light on the causes of semantax development.

What the Child Learns About Semantax

The description of grammar given above indicates that there are two categories of knowledge that the child acquires when achieving semantactic competence. The first category is *order* of elements in a "string" (or sentence); the second is various *markers* of relations in a string. In generating and understanding utterances, order rules and marker rules are employed simultaneously. Under each category of knowledge — order and markers — there are subcategories that have to be acquired.

A final type of knowledge that the child has to acquire is not included in the above description of grammar. This knowledge consists of rules of permissible combinations of elements in a string that take into account the meanings of the lexical items that are to be combined — not just word order. For example, the sentences, "The crayon kissed the girl" and "I'm putting fire here" follow the rules of word order in the language but do not follow the rules for combination of types of subjects and verbs (crayons are inanimate and do not kiss) and verbs and objects (fire is not an object that can be put somewhere).

Rules of Order of Elements In and Across Utterances

Since language is used to communicate with others (and with oneself), one of the first aspects of semantax that a child will learn is how to convey varying intents with whatever means available — how to demand, request, state, indicate, question, negate, and express affect. The child will then learn how to convey these intents in a manner that conforms with the language of the community. It is this latter aspect of semantax acquisition that is discussed here. As part of conveying intent, the child learns how basic semantic relations are realized as subject-verb-object and are ordered in his or her language. The semantic relation actor (or agent)-action-object (or patient) ("The boy hit the ball") and instrument-action-object ("The ball broke the window") both contain the semantic categories subject-verb-object (SVO). There are two aspects of semantax that must be acquired in order to convey basic intents — how to express SVO relations and how to structure the different basic speech acts.

English is one of the languages that uses word order to convey basic relations, and it employs the order SVO. Other languages are not primarily word-order languages. They are so-called *case languages,* and, although subject, verb, and object are ordered in utterances, their order is not fixed. Russian is such a language. Subjects and objects have endings that mark their case (whether they are, for example, subject or object in a sentence), and SVO and SOV are both used. Since English is a word-order language in which the most usual order is SVO, this is what the child learning English must learn.

The child also learns how to convey basic intents; for example, to state, command, negate, question, and request according to the forms used in a particular language. The following sentences are examples of different intents conveyed using the same subject, verb, and object.

1. Statement: The boy is eating the apple.
2. Command: You (boy) will eat the apple.
3. Negate: The boy is not (or isn't) eating the apple.
4. Question: Is the boy eating the apple?
5. Request: Would you (boy) eat the apple?

In all of these examples, the subject, verb, and object are in the SVO order. In examples 2 and 5, the subject is understood to be the addressee. The addition of items ("not," in sentence 3) and the order in which items appear (in addition to the paralinguistic aspects of their production) change the intent of the utterances. The auxiliary verb "is" in sentence 4 is moved to the beginning, and the auxiliary verb "would" in sentence 5 is moved to the beginning. Every language provides ways in which these intents can be realized, just as each language has ways of indicating subject, verb, and object relations.

Some other and more advanced ordering rules are those that involve passive, conjoined, relative clause, and complement constructions. Some examples of these sentence types are:

1. Passive: The apple was eaten by the boy.
2. Conjunction: The boy and girl are playing.
3. Relative clause: I see a boy who is wearing a red hat.
4. Relative clause: The boy who is wearing a red hat is in the garden.
5. Complement: I believe that Mary will win the prize.
6. Complement: I want him to play with me.

The passive sentence, number 1, reverses the SVO order usually followed in sentences. Sentences 2 through 6 all involve relations between two sentences. In Figure 8-1, simplified diagrams of the structure of sentences 2, 3, 4, and 5 are presented.

The ordering of elements within sentences (or utterances) and the ordering

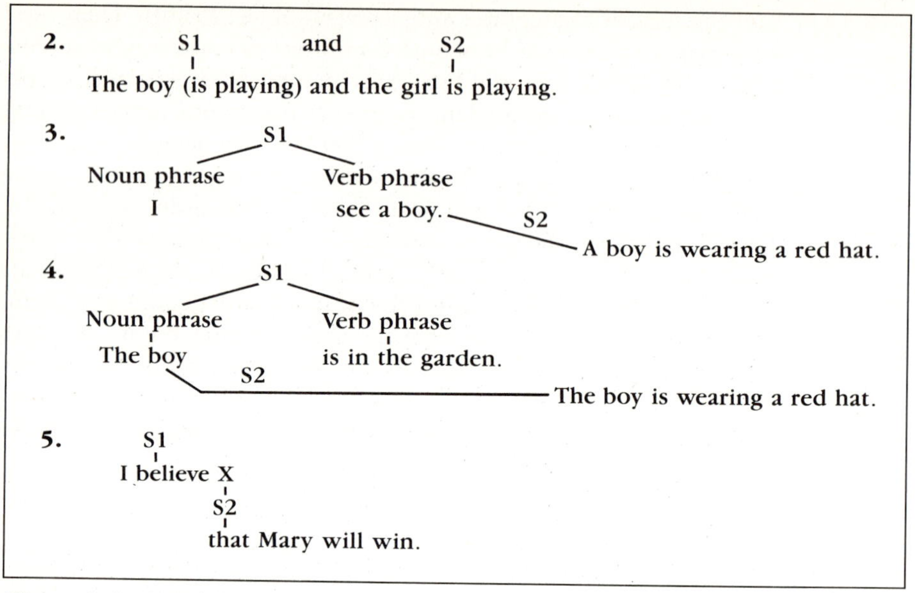

Figure 8-1 Simplified diagrams of conjoined and embedded sentences.

of elements among sentences when sentences are combined are only two aspects of ordering. A third aspect of ordering that the child learns is ordering of elements within longer stretches of discourse. For example, in our culture when we tell a story, we begin with the beginning, move to the middle, and finish with the end. There are other styles of narrative in other cultures, but each culture has a narrative style. As has been shown, knowing how to convey intents involves both pragmatic and semantactic knowledge. So does knowing how to tell stories. The semantactic knowledge involved in knowing how to tell stories is comprised of so-called "cohesion devices" — devices that relate pieces of the story to each other. One of the most important of these is *anaphora,* referring backward to indicate the relations among subjects, verbs, and objects in the discourse. This topic was discussed briefly in Chapter Six, Pragmatic Development. In that discussion, the focus was on organization of discourse. Here we focus on the semantactic rules of anaphora. Some examples of this device follow:

> Jack liked Jill, and *he* wanted *her* to come up the hill with *him* to fetch a pail of water. *She* didn't want to do *this* because she thought *doing so* would be dangerous. Furthermore, *she* thought *it* was a silly reason for going up the hill. Unfortunately, Jack persuaded *her* to do *it. They* both went up the hill and *they* both were injured.

In this paragraph, the italicized words indicate those places in the story where reference is made to previously mentioned subjects, objects, and verb phrases. Use of this device makes understanding the story easier. However, knowing when and how to use it is a semantactic as well as a discourse accomplishment. The child must know the rules for substitution of such elements as nouns, verbs, and phrases. These rules fall under the heading of *rules of markers*.

Rules of Markers

In each of the sentences given as examples of ordering, there were also examples of rules of marking. In the example of anaphora as a cohesion device, all the pronoun substitutions had to follow rules of number, gender, and case. That is, "he," a singular masculine pronoun, had to be substituted for Jack, whereas "she" was substituted for Jill, and "they" became "him," "her," and "they," under the appropriate conditions.

Markers can be *free morphemes* — such as articles or pronouns — or *bound morphemes* (those that have no meaning by themselves and may be attached to words) — such as those that mark aspect, tense, and number. They modify the relation between main categories of the sentence, SVO. Thus, markers of place, time, and manner modify action; and markers of definiteness, number, and gender modify subject and object. Both free and bound morphemes also modify relations across sentences. The two sentences that follow contain examples of different types of markers that are used to modify subjects and verbs in and across sentences. To indicate all the markers that modify subject verb and object categories in these sentences, morpheme boundaries are indicated by #.

1. A# little# boy# want# ed# to# play# in# his# friend#'s# garden.
2. The# boy# ran# very# quick#ly# to# his# friend#'s# house.

In sentence 1, the indefinite article "a" is used to modify the subject, "boy"; the past tense marker "ed" is used to indicate that the action took place in the past; and the possessive marker "s" is used to mark the possessor and to modify the object, "garden," in the prepositional phrase. In sentence 2, the definite article "the" is used to indicate that we are talking about a specific boy that has been mentioned; the tense of the verb — since "to run" is an irregular verb — is incorporated, changing "run" to "ran"; the verb is modified by the adverb "quickly" (which is marked as an adverb by the suffix "ly"); and, again, a possessive marker "s" is used to mark the possessor and to modify "house." Figure 8-2 schematically represents those categories in single utterances that mark relations among categories and modify the categories themselves.

Combinatory Rules

The rules for combining elements in a string must take into account the meaning of the elements combined. If we did not have this knowledge and knew only rules of order and rules of markers, we would produce meaningless utterances. The following list contains some examples of how only the application of order rules and marker rules could lead to unacceptable sentences.

1. The apple ate the boy.
2. Round thoughts jumped out of the table.
3. He believed into the box.

These sentences are considered unacceptable because in each instance some combinatory rule has been violated. In the first sentence, "apple" cannot be the subject of this SVO sentence, because "apple" is inanimate and cannot carry out the action of eating. In the second sentence there are two violations. "Thoughts" are never modified by shape terms, and, because "table" represents a flat surface, something cannot jump "out" of it. In the third sentence the verb "believe" represents a state of mind, not an action. State-of-mind verbs cannot be modified by prepositional phrases of location.

A close examination of these sentences indicates that they refer to actions and states that could not exist in the real world. In each instance, expected relations between actors, objects, actions, and modifiers of these are violated. This is true even though a schematic representation of these sentences would fit in well with those presented in Figure 8-2.

The Course of Semantax Development

The rules of order, the rules of markers, and the combinatory rules described above form the body of semantactic knowledge that the child acquires. Some researchers have stated that the child achieves basic semantax competence at an early age, perhaps by five or six years (McNeill, 1970). Others have argued that this competence may not be achieved by all adults (Geer, Gleitman, & Gleitman, 1972). The problem may be that it is difficult to clearly define what is basic or adult semantax competence (Menyuk, 1977). In this section on development, what researchers have said children know about semantax during different periods of development and whether or not adult competence is achieved during middle childhood and adolescence is discussed.

Infancy

The traditional age period of birth to two years is used here in describing the infant's acquisition of semantactic knowledge. There appear to be quite remarkable differences between two- and three-year-olds in this knowledge. The explanations given for these dramatic differences will also be discussed. Since from birth to two years old, the child usually acquires little knowledge of markers, only the child's acquisition of semantic and syntactic categories, relations among categories, and rules of ordering are discussed.

Acquisition of Semantic/Syntactic Categories. There have been many studies of the infant's budding word-combination abilities (Bloom, 1970; Bowerman, 1973; Brown, 1973; Menyuk, 1969). All of these studies indicate that word combinations usually begin toward the end of the second year of life (eighteen months plus). There is a growing body of evidence, however, that indicates that the infant is able to comprehend action-object and even actor-action-object relations before he or she can consistently produce two-word utterances. Sachs and Truswell (1978) found that children in the latter part of the holophrastic stage of development (primarily one-word producers) can act out commands that describe a relation between action and object (for example, "roll ball") and can do so even when the relation is an unusual one (for example, "tickle car").

These researchers claimed that the child's ability to carry out the actions described is due to their comprehension of the meaning of the lexical items and the semantic relation of self acting upon object. Some other data, however, indicate that children who are holophrastic can understand a word-order rule as well as semantic relations. Hirsh-Pasek, Golinkoff, Beaubien, Fletcher, and Cauley (1985) found that sixteen- to nineteen-month-old children appear to comprehend word-order rules in three-word sentences (for example, "Big bird kiss cookie monster" and "Cookie monster kiss big bird"). The paradigm used to assess infants' comprehension of word-order rules was to depict actors acting on objects displayed on a split video screen. It was found that infants looked significantly more at the one of the two video screens that depicted the order in the sentences presented to them. The position of actor and patient (left or right in the picture) was varied. Verbs were varied, and left-right presentation of correct depiction was alternated. These data suggest that before infants produce two-word utterances, they comprehend three-word sentences and do so on the basis of word order. Comprehension of some semantax relations, therefore, appears to preceed production by several months.

Mean length of utterance is a frequently used measure of semantax productive development during this early period. It has been found that as children mature the number of words in their sentences increases (Brown, 1973). It has also been found in a number of studies that there is a great deal of individual variation in the age at which children begin to combine two words and, then, three words. However, the average age at which two-word combinations occur is twenty-five months, and the average age at which three- to four-word combinations occur is thirty-five months (Liebergott, Schultz, & Menyuk, 1985; Miller & Chapman, 1981). The gap between comprehension and production of semantactic relations appears to be very wide indeed.

The types of semantic relations that are expressed in early two-word combinations appear to be both universal and individual. That is, a number of these relations appear in the language samples of children who are learning a wide variety of languages. However, there is an effect both of individual learning styles (Braine, 1976) and of individual languages (Schlesinger, 1977; Slobin, 1982) on the particular patterns that are acquired first and used most frequently. There is some effect of the particular language the child is acquiring on the order in which she or he will express semantic relations. Relations that are encoded in complex ways will be acquired after those that are encoded simply. It has been found that children acquiring two languages will encode a relation in one language before they do so in the other because the first language encodes it more simply than the other (Slobin, 1973). The factors that universally affect the order of acquisition and frequency of use of certain relations are not unexpected. In summary, they are the pragmatic intents that infants wish to convey, the order in which they understand semantic relations, and the sequential order of complexity of the encoding of relations in the language being acquired.

What all researchers appear to agree upon is that the relations expressed do *not* represent the syntactic categories of subject, verb, and object, and, therefore, that infants do *not* have knowledge of these categories during this period of development. In the chapter on lexical development it was stated that syntactic properties as well as other meaning properties of words must be stored in the mental lexicon. The belief is that during infancy such properties are not yet represented. As an alternative, it has been suggested that the infant observes how elements appear as sequences in the language being acquired and, therefore, acquires knowledge of the distributional characteristics of categories in the language (Maratsos, 1983). For example, in English, the infant would learn that words for modifiers of objects usually appear before words representing objects ("big boy" not "boy big") except in certain conditions ("boy is big").

There is some suggestion that certain relations (such as the "big boy" and "boy-big" ones) may be acquired in terms of their distributional characteristics, and that knowledge of them is stored in this way. Others may be acquired in terms of their generative characteristics; that is, their ability to generate a large number of possible semantic relations. Examples of such generative relations are agent + action or action + location ("daddy go" and "go there"). This distinction between types of relations acquired is said to mark differences in the learning styles of children during this period (Braine, 1976). That is, there are some children who first acquire associational patterns and then generative patterns, whereas other children learn in the inverse sequence. Table 8-1 lists the semantic relations that have been found in the language samples of a number of children acquiring English.

Explanations. As Table 8-1 indicates, all the pieces of sentences that are needed to generate SVO sentences are present in the two-word combinations of infants. The pieces for generating SVO sentences containing modifiers of objects and actions are there as well. All the pieces are, also, in the order appropriate to the English language. Long before the child is producing these pieces of utterances the child is able to comprehend SVO relations in sentences based on word-order rules in the language.

The accomplishments of this period are said to be due to infants' abilities to observe how the pragmatic intents they wish to convey and how relations between objects and events in the real world are encoded in the language that

Table 8-1 Semantic relations in two-part utterances.

SEMANTIC RELATION	EXAMPLE
Agent + action	Daddy sit
Action + object	Push truck
Agent + object	Baby car
Possessor + possessed	Baby car
Demonstrative + noun	That fish
Attribution + noun	Nice boy
Location + object	Here truck
Action + location	Fall here

the infant is acquiring. However, the acquisitions of this period cannot be the result of simple translations of real-world events. The infant must be able to analyze the language in the environment to determine what the translations are. This middle step has to be explained.

One of the explanations that has been provided for the child taking this middle step is that the child forms semantic categories such as actor, action, modifier, location, and the like, based on the ability to form a concept (similar to the concept-formation ability used to explain lexical acquisition). In addition, the child is able to observe the distributional characteristics of the combination of these categories. The information processing abilities of infants, if this were the case, would be quite impressive. Other explanations, calling upon the infant's innate ability to determine SVO categories in language, are clearly open to question as well. Motherese, as we have seen, plays some role in early acquisitions of semantax but, apparently (as indicated in the 1977 study by Newport, Gleitman, and Gleitman) is not related to the acquisition of basic semantactic relations. At present there appear to be no fully satisfying explanations for these important first steps in semantax development. Research on the processing abilities of infants is a blossoming field. Further research on the information processing abilities of infants in relation to the kinds of language information provided by caregivers may provide us with the needed insights to satisfactorily explain these early developments.

Early Childhood

The accomplishments of the early childhood period of development are quite formidable. For this reason, the claim was made that basic semantax competence had been achieved by the end of this period. Although more recent research indicates that further acquisitions take place in the middle-childhood-and-adolescence period, much of the kinds of knowledge described in the first section of this chapter are acquired by the end of the early childhood period. It has been suggested that the primary reason for these dramatic developments are due to the "learnability" of language (Pinker, 1984). That is, the structure

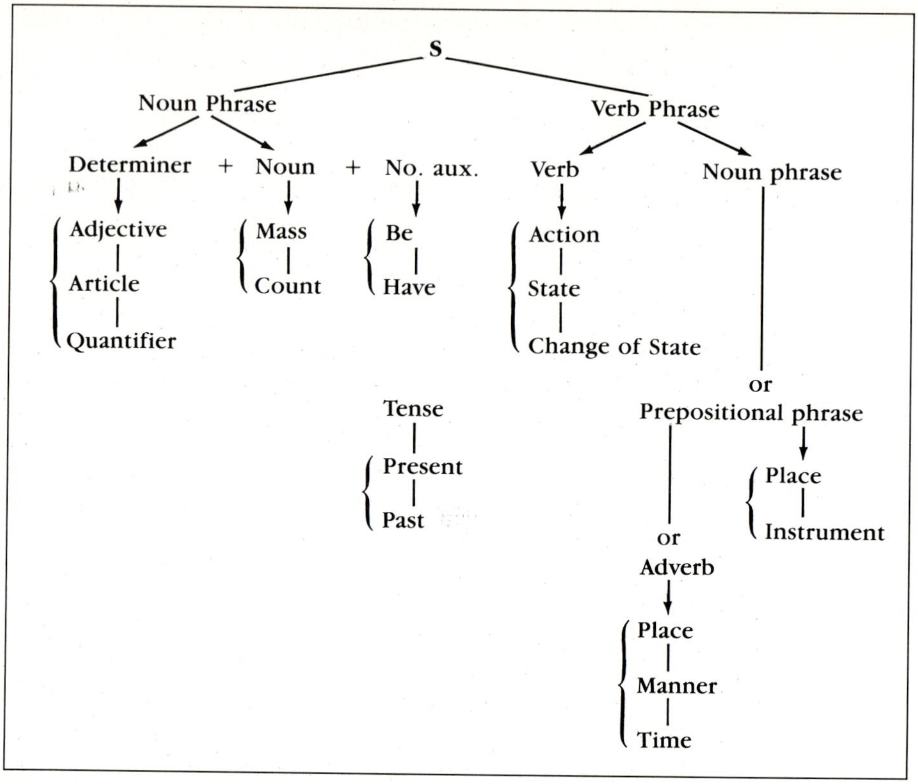

Figure 8-2 Categories in simple sentences.

of human language is, presumably, designed to make its acquisition an easy task for humans. Since human language is the product of the assets and liabilities of humans, this makes some sense. If this is the case, then determination of what makes language "easily" learnable is a matter of great theoretical and practical interest. Each of the types of knowledge that the child is said to acquire is discussed in the following paragraphs; then the theory of the learnability of language and other explanatory theories are discussed.

Markers. Another way of describing the acquisition of markers in sentences during this period of development is as *expansion* of the subject, verb, and object. Subjects are expanded into determiners + nouns, those nouns are modified by number, verbs are expanded into auxiliary verb + verb or tense + verb, and object is expanded into determiner + noun or prepositional phrase or adverb. (See Figure 8-2.)

Evidence has been obtained in a number of studies that these expansions begin during the period of two to two and a half years and are structurally complete by three years of age. Even markers that appear on the surface to be quite complex, such as markers of gender on pronouns and inflected verb forms (Levy, 1983) and articles (Maratsos, 1979), are in the process of being acquired during this period. There appears to be a giant leap in structural development from two to three years. The results of some of the studies examining early sentence structure production beyond SVO are summarized in Garman, 1979. What has *not* been acquired by age three are rules that prohibit combinations of certain members of the categories that have been expanded. The rules of combination of specific Ss, Vs, and Os that were discussed in the introductory section of this chapter take much longer to acquire than do the categories themselves. That is, children order the syntactic classes in appropriate ways before they learn that only certain combinations of these classes are permissible.

Each category of expansion has been studied in great detail by a number of researchers. The overall findings have been that two factors play a role in the sequence of acquisition of these categories — *meaningfulness* and *perceptual saliency*. Children will acquire markers that are meaningful before acquiring those that are arbitrary. Meaningful markers are those that represent categorizations of objects and events that are known by the child. Children will acquire markers that are clearly indicated before they will acquire those that are less clearly indicated (Slobin, 1986). For example, Brown (1973) found that children acquired the plural marker /s/ for nouns before they acquired the third person singular marker /s/ for verbs. The former is an important marker of meaning difference (singular versus plural), while the latter is an arbitrary and redundant marker in that third person singular is indicated by the subject of the verb. Some markers are acquired later, not simply because they are arbitrary and redundant, but also because they are encoded in a complex way *phonologically*. For example, markers of plural in irregular nouns (children) and past tense in irregular verbs (sang) are not as clearly marked and, therefore, not as perceptually salient as markers for regular nouns and verbs.

In general, the child's acquisition of markers of tense seems to be a good example of these general trends. Children represent known before unknown categories; they mark meaningful before meaningless categories; and they mark the perceptually salient before the less salient. A number of researchers have found that present ongoing action, as marked by /ing/, is acquired before general markers of past, /ed/. This is the case, presumably, because of the child's ability to mark what is known before marking what is unknown. Other than memorized forms, regular past tense forms are acquired before irregular past tense forms, presumably because of the saliency of regular markers (for example, "played" versus "brought").

Some researchers have indicated that certain aspects of verbs (to denote, among other things, durative or complete actions) are apparently understood before markers of tense (present, past, and future) (Bronckart & Sinclair, 1973; Fletcher, 1979). Apparently children take this into account when marking verbs and mark past tense only on verbs that are change-of-state verbs (Antinucci & Miller, 1976). The markers acquired appear to be based on the lexical characteristics of the verbs (Bloom, Lifter, & Tanouye, 1980). This suggests that there is one other factor that affects the order of acquisition of marking of temporal aspects — the lexical features of the verbs to which the markers are attached. There are some verbs that appear to mark ongoing activities ("sleep") while others seem to mark completed activity ("fall"). Different verbs have inherent temporal characteristics, and this is reflected in early markers of time. This seems to be another example of semantactic development, (simultaneous acquisition of semantic and syntactic rules) and, also, an example of children's observation of combinatory rules; that is, markers of present progressive and past tense are combined only with some verbs.

Combinatory Rules. Children appear never to violate certain syntactic class boundaries; that is, they do not use auxiliary verbs as adjectives (for example, "the has boy") or prepositions as articles (for example, "under boy ran"). One violation that does occur are so-called class extensions, in which nouns are used as verbs, verbs as nouns, and adjectives as verbs (Bowerman, 1974; Clark, 1982). Another occurrence is the novel use of causative verbs (Braine, 1971; Bowerman, 1979). Finally, selections from syntactic categories that do not take into account some constraints on selection are made (Menyuk, 1971). Some of these constraints are rule governed and others are arbitrary. The following examples of each of these occurrences have been taken from the cited studies:

1. The dog is flagging his tail. (Noun as verb)
2. I like the sleep. (Verb as noun)
3. Why don't you nice me. (Adjective as verb)
4. Grapes cough me. (Novel use of causative verb)
5. I see a blue leaves. (Article number)
6. He'll be six on June. (Preposition in time phrase)

Two reasons have been given for the occurrence of the violations of combinatory rules in these sentences. One is that the child may not have the vocabulary needed to express what is intended (Clark, 1981). Sentences 1 and 3 may be examples of this. Another reason is that children make generalizations based on regular occurrences in sentences without analyzing the specific contexts in which certain nouns, verbs, and adjectives are used (Bowerman, 1979) and do not make explicit judgments about the syntactic class of items in a string (Menyuk, 1963). Sentences 2, 4 and 5 may be examples of this. However, the violations illustrated in all six sentences disappear by about five or six years of age.

The fact that these violations of combinatory rules occur indicates that children first observe the surface structure of utterances and try to produce strings that contain all the necessary elements needed to convey their intents. They next analyze the properties of elements to determine the constraints that exist because of the meanings of these elements. Thus they become aware of the syntactic categories of elements. Finally, they observe the arbitrary rules for combination that exist in a particular language. Just such a sequence of development was found in a study examining the ability of two-, five-, and seven-year-old children and adults to comprehend, judge, and produce class extension sentences (Bushnell & Maratsos, 1984). The sentences given contained nouns as verbs ("mommy me"), verbs as nouns ("a real fast chase"), and adjectives as verbs ("big this boy"). Although five-year-old children were quite good at producing class extensions, only the seven-year-olds were able to consistently judge that these extensions were deviant. The researchers suggest that only children aged seven are able to "inhibit" the generation of these class extensions because they have knowledge of exceptions to the general rule.

Rules of Ordering. There is some evidence that children who are two years of age make judgments about the goodness of sentences, based on ordering rules (Gleitman, Gleitman, & Shipley, 1972). They state that sentences such as "ball the roll" are funny. Although they do not pinpoint the source of error — word order — in their corrections, they do indicate in their judgments that they have intuitive knowledge of what is correct word order. At about twenty-seven months they carry out tasks that require "big doll (to) push truck" and "doll (to) push big truck" (Liebergott, Schultz, & Menyuk, 1985), indicating that they are able to process modifiers as well as SVO relations in utterances.

From two to three years, the child begins to put together the pieces of utterances that were present in two-word combinations. The child takes pieces, such as actor + action and action + object, and puts them together in actor + action + object utterances. There are limitations on these three-word combinations. Modifications of subjects or objects cannot be produced simultaneously with SVO productions. This would result in four-word combinations. Since children can, at an earlier age, correctly interpret the difference between modifiers of subjects and objects in sentences, as in the example given above, we again have evidence that comprehension precedes production. Table 8-2 lists the kinds of relations that are expressed in three-word combinations.

Table 8-2 Semantic relations in three-part utterances.

SEMANTIC RELATION	EXAMPLE
Agent + action + participle	Donny running
Agent + action + object	Mommy push truck
Demonstrative + possession + possession	That my hat
Location + attribute + object	Here big ball
Action + object + location	Put truck here
Action + location + time	Fall down right now
Demonstrative + agent + action	That boy run
Possession + possession + state	My foot hurt

In the discussion of developments during the infancy period, it was stated that there is evidence of the child having knowledge of the semantic categories of actor, action, and acted upon — but not of the syntactic categories of subject, verb, and object. There is, however, evidence of the development of this knowledge during early childhood. Children at about age three and a half show an awareness of the significance of word order in determination of the actor or agent category (Bridges, 1984). In a series of studies (Braine & Wells, 1978; Hardy & Braine, 1981; Braine & Hardy, 1982), the ability of children aged approximately five years to identify agent, instrument acted upon, recipient, and location, and to associate these semantic categories with the syntactic categories of subject, direct and indirect object, and prepositional phrases was examined. It was found that children of five years did make these associations. The researchers suggest that this knowledge is acquired by observation of the range of sentence structures in which semantic categories play a role. The relation between syntactic and semantic categories becomes clear through these observations. For example, the child could acquire the knowledge that an inanimate object could serve the role of instrument — and, therefore, serve as sentence subject — by observing sentences of the following kind; "The boy broke the window with his ball" and "The ball broke the window," in which the inanimate object "ball" plays the roles of, first, instrument and then, agent.

From the period of about three to four years the child begins to acquire the specific rules of the language for generating speech acts. Although, as we have seen, negative and question utterances appear during the holophrastic stage, the development of negative and question sentences as they are represented in the language takes place in gradual steps over this age range (Menyuk, 1971). These steps seem to reflect an increasing ability to program out all the pieces in a single utterance and then to interrupt the canonical SVO form. Examples of these developmental changes for negatives and questions are:

1. He no go; 2. He no can go; 3. He can not go.
1. Where he go? 2. Where he do go? 3. Where do he go?

During this developmental period children begin to generate passive sentences and conjoined, relative clause, and complement sentences. One type of developmental change that applied to the development of negation and question sentences applies to the generation of these types of sentences as well. It has been found that children tend to try to keep the order of SVO undisturbed in negative and question sentences, as indicated in the examples above. They also do this in generating conjoined sentences. For this reason, the earliest conjoined sentences are full sentences that are conjoined ("John played ball and Mary played ball") and then conjoined predicates ("He likes ice cream and cake") (Menyuk, 1969; Lust & Mervis, 1980). The earliest relative clause sentences have the relative clause at the end of the sentence ("I like the book that my daddy got me") (Menyuk, 1969). In all of these instances, SVO order is maintained.

The comprehension of conjoined structure seems to take a somewhat different course than the production of such forms. Ardery (1980) examined comprehension of conjunction in four- to six-year-old children and found that conjoined verb phrases in the context of intransitive verbs ("The frog ran and fell"), then conjoined objects ("The giraffe kissed the tiger and the cat"), and then conjoined sentences ("The dog ran and the cat fell") were best understood by the youngest children in the group. Only 10 percent of the almost-six-year-olds understood conjoined sentences with the verb missing ("The giraffe kissed the horse and the frog the cat").

Comprehension of passive sentences has received a great deal of attention because subject and object are permuted in this structure. This results in the usual order of events (SVO order) being violated. In this case, interpretation of meaning must wait until the end of the sentence. Therefore, children's abilities to process passives give evidence of how closely knowledge of passives is tied to the natural order of events and of how much information about the sentence the children can keep in mind.

There is evidence that both factors play a role in the comprehension of passives. Bever (1971) found that children under three years tend to use an NVN (noun-verb-noun) strategy (interpret the first noun in the sentence as the subject) to interpret passives. Comprehension of passives is initially based on expected order of natural events (Slobin, 1966; DeVilliers & DeVilliers, 1974), since children understand nonreversible passives ("The ball was kicked by the boy") before they understand reversible passives ("The boy was kicked by the girl"). These data indicate that a number of factors can play a role in the comprehension of structures. Therefore, comprehension of structures should be viewed not simply as comprehension of a structure but, rather, as comprehension of a structure within a particular context, both situational and linguistic. It will be recalled that this was also true of the comprehension of lexical items.

The order of production of passives does not seem to be in keeping with the general findings about the comprehension of passives. In a study of the spontaneous production of passive structures by children ages two to fourteen, Horgan (1978) found that semantically reversible and nonreversible passives were used with equal frequency by two- to four-year-old children. However, they would, for example, produce the sentence "The cat was chased by the girl" when describing a picture of a cat chasing a girl. This response indicates they did not understand the relations depicted. In this instance, production appears to precede comprehension. However, the differences observed in the order of comprehension and production of various types of passives may simply be a product of the fact that children *know* what they want to say when they produce sentences. Therefore, they are not confused by the task of interpreting pictures as well as sentences.

The development of complement types and the acquisition of different types of verbs seem to go hand in hand, a true example of semantax development. Limber (1973) found that some two-year-old children were able to generate sentences with complement structures such as "I want to go" but only produced complement structures with objects when they acquired verbs such as "need," as in "I need him to go." Bloom, Tackeff, and Lahey (1984) also found that complements were used by two- to three-year old children with a small class of verbs. Sentences with complement structures often contain thought verbs such as "know," "believe," and "think," or state verbs such as "expect" and "desire," as well as "want" and "need," as in the following examples:

1. I know that John likes me.
2. I believe that John likes me.
3. I think that John likes me.
4. I expected John to like me.
5. I desired John to like me.

Overall, the production of complex sentence types does not simply follow the comprehension of these sentence types. In relative clause and complement comprehension, as was the case for comprehension of conjunctions and passive voice, there is evidence that children produce structures that they appear to have difficulty understanding. A number of studies have examined children's ability to comprehend different types of relative clause and complement structures and have found that children show difficulty with particular types of these structures (Chomsky, 1969; Sheldon, 1974). Following is a list of the types of sentences that five- to six-year-old children still have difficulty in comprehending:

1. The boy who kissed the girl ran away.
2. The dog the horse bit chased the cat.
3. Joe promised Bill to go.
4. John asked the teacher to leave the room.

In sentence 1, the difficulty lies in determining who ran away, since boys and girls could run away and "girl" is nearer the verb "ran." In sentence 2, the difficulty lies in the fact that the "dog" is both the subject of the underlying sentence "The dog chased the cat" and the object of the underlying sentence "The horse bit the dog." The problem in sentence 3 is, presumably, similar to the problem in sentence 1; that is, both Joe and Bill can go, and Bill is nearer the verb "go." Sentence 4 is ambiguous. It is not clear who will leave the room.

The overall difficulty that children have with these sentence types appears to lie in a combination of semantic and syntactic factors, a semantactic difficulty. Children attempt to interpret these sentences in ways that are congruent with their expectations of the meanings of sentences in terms of actor-action-object relations, while ignoring those aspects of the sentence which interfere with this interpretation. When they are generating passive, conjoined, relative clause, and complement sentences, children obviously know what they want to say and have no problems with interpretation. The difficulties that children have with comprehension of all of the structures listed above may arise from the fact that the *conditions* of comprehension tasks require metalinguistic processing — conscious awareness of linguistic categories and relations. Such awareness is also required when reading sentences that contain passive, relative clause and complement structures. Children are always, initially, in the position of having to bring knowledge of these relations to conscious awareness. However, awareness of complex categories and relations seems to be the product of developments in middle childhood and adolescence.

Explanations. The child at the beginning of early childhood is primarily producing two- or three-word utterances and understanding the basic relations of SVO ("Boy kiss girl") and modifier plus S, V and modifier plus O ("little boy kiss little girl"). By the end of this developmental period the child is producing complex utterances that contain all the markers that are needed to modify subjects, verbs, and objects and has intuitive knowledge of the rules of a particular language for combining elements in utterances. The reasons proposed for these dramatic changes in language knowledge appear to fall into three categories:

1. The innate abilities of the child.
2. The learning strategies of the child.
3. The learnability of the language.

Innate abilities. As might be suspected, all three factors must play some role in semantax acquisition. It is possible that different factors affect the acquisition of different aspects of semantax. The child's innate ability to determine the canonical form of a sentence in his or her language apparently brings about the acquisition of knowledge of the rules of SVO. This innate ability has been described as a cognitive ability to determine the categories of actor (or agent), action, and object or as a specific linguistic ability to determine these categories. It has been found in a number of studies that children very quickly acquire knowledge of these types of rules and respond only to those sequences that are congruent with the canonical sentence form of their language (Slobin & Bever, 1982; Bates, MacWhinney, Caselli, Devescovi, & Venza, 1984). Thus, children exposed to English, Serbo-Croation, Turkish, and Italian rely on order or inflection or lexical meanings to interpret such relations in sentences, depending on how their particular language marks these relations. However, all children, regardless of the language they are exposed to, derive this knowledge very early on.

Learning strategies. Particular learning strategies have been pointed to to account for the child's acquisition of the markers of the language. These strategies include searching for those elements that encode meaningful distinctions in the language and those elements that are clearly and unambiguously marked. The learning strategy of looking for meaningful elements is a very general one and can be observed in the acquisition of all aspects of language. The strategy of observing those elements that are clearly marked is also quite general and is reflected not only in the child's acquisition of markers but also in the child's acquisition of complex sentence types. Children first acquire those forms of complex sentence types that do not interrupt SVO relations in sentences. Children's sentence processing strategies, due to the limitations of their immediate memory, are said to account for the first types of simple and complex sentences that they produce and comprehend. That is, they first comprehend and produce those sentence types that do not require keeping the whole sentence in mind before they can be interpreted. Certain embedded relative clause and complement sentences fall into this category. However, the measure of a child's comprehension of semantax forms is also a measure of the child's comprehension of particular situational and linguistic conditions, not just of the form itself. The child may have uttered sentences containing these forms on previous occasions but not be able to comprehend their meaning in experimental situations.

In comprehension, the learning strategy of looking for the way in which language expresses natural events is the most used strategy for obvious reasons (MacNamara, 1972). This has been called the *event probability strategy*. Many of the studies discussed above have found that children's first successes and failures are due to this strategy. For this reason passive sentences that describe irreversible relations are understood before those that do not ("The flowers are watered by the girl" before "The boy is chased by the girl"), embedded relative clauses that describe irreversible relations are understood before those that do not ("The boy who finished his homework ran away" before "The boy who kissed the girl ran away"), and sentences with missing subjects that describe irreversible relations are understood before those that do not ("The book is easy to read" before "The doll is easy to see"). One other suggestion has been made about the strategies for comprehension and production of complex sentences. An analysis was carried out of the structure of complex sentences comprehended and produced by children from age three to age eight (Hsu, Cairns, & Fiengo, 1985). It was concluded that children used four different types of "grammars" over this age range; a subject-oriented, an object-oriented, a mixed-oriented, and an adult-like grammar. Although children of all ages used all the strategies, there was a tendency for older children to use the mixed-oriented and adult-like grammars. These findings suggest that focus on parts of sentences (beginnings, endings, and middles) change as the child matures.

Another learning strategy that has been discussed is one of learning from one's own errors. It has been suggested that since children are not usually corrected when they make semantactic errors, then language acquisition cannot be a product of learning from mistakes. However, a recent discussion suggests that children do, in fact, work on their own errors and could, possibly, develop further knowledge of language in this way (Platt & MacWhinney, 1983).

Clearly, children are sensitive to errors that reflect their own mistakes in sentence production and, eventually, achieve an awareness of the nature of the mistakes (Menyuk, 1963). However, this awareness usually occurs after they have acquired knowledge of the "correct" form of the structures.

Learnability of the Language. One other reason that has been suggested for the dramatic changes that occur during this period is the essential learnability of language. The language the child hears is said to provide essential cues for the acquisition of certain structures. These cues are in the surface of the utterance so that the child's ability to search for those elements that carry meaning can lead to successful results. There are a number of surface structure cues to the structure of utterances. For example, one such cue is stress on particular words in an utterance or pauses between groups of words in an utterance. Other types of cues are markers of the relative clause by any WH-relative word (for example, "who" or "what") and markers on verb forms. Finally, it appears to be the case that there is simultaneous acquisition of verb classes and syntactic structures, such as the acquisition of stative verbs and "that" complements ("I know, believe, think, that she is coming"). Although these cues seem to be quite different from each other, they all provide information about the structure of the utterance.

Children and adults rely on the surface structure cue of pause in production to comprehend potentially ambiguous forms, such as "She sent her kids' books" or "She sent her kids books." The surface structure markers of passive are the form of the verb in passive constructions and the "by" clause. Children are better able to comprehend passive constructions with marked verb forms (such as "washed") than passives with unmarked forms (such as "hit"). Children also understand embedded relatives with marked WH forms ("I see the bird which is sitting in the tree") earlier and better than they understand those without them ("I see the bird sitting in the tree"). There have been a number of studies — referred to earlier — that indicate that complement structures and certain verbs are acquired simultaneously. In fact, particular types of complement structure, those that have the subject of the main sentence as subject of the embedded sentence ("The turtle promises the skunk to push the car") and those that have the object of the main sentence as subject of the embedded sentence ("The turtle tells the monkey to drop the penny"), have been shown to be initially understood in relation to the *particular* verbs used in the complement structure (Sherman, 1984).

The explanations provided for the child's acquisition of semantax can be useful to language teachers. They indicate what might be appropriate sequences in the presentation of language materials and the approaches that can be taken in getting students to understand the language materials. Children in the early childhood period are still going to have some difficulty in understanding semantactic relations in complex structures that are not clearly marked. However, at the end of this period they are beginning to have intuitive knowledge of possible exceptions to the general rules they have acquired. The next period of development seems to represent a leap from intuitive knowledge to conscious knowledge by some children and adolescents.

Middle Childhood and Adolescence

We have already referred to some of the semantax developments that take place during this period. That is, all those types of sentence structure that children still have difficulty with in early childhood are processed successfully by children in middle childhood and by adolescents. During this period difficulties with sentences that embed and reverse relations disappear. Although this change in what types of sentence structure children have difficulty with seems to represent simply a continuum in growth of semantax knowledge, these acquisitions may be the results of two types of developments: one in representation of knowledge and the other in the processing of language. These developments have been termed *reorganization of knowledge* and *metalinguistic processing*.

It has been suggested by a number of researchers that the semantactic developments that take place before age seven are universal. Those markers, combinatory rules, and rules of ordering elements within and across sentences — discussed above — are presumably acquired by all normally developing children. A question has arisen about the universality of the developments that take place during the middle childhood and adolescence periods. What these developments are is discussed first.

Reorganization of Knowledge. The organization of semantax knowledge is said to change during this period. The findings of research on class extensions, discussed in the section on combinatory rules, indicated that children at about age seven were acquiring knowledge of exceptions to a generative rule. In general, reorganizations occur during middle childhood in categorization of rules that generally apply and those that are exceptions to general rules (Karmiloff-Smith, 1978). What the child must learn in order to do this is the particular contexts in which general or specific rules apply. This seems to be an across-the-board phenomenon affecting acquisition of all aspects of language. For example, in lexical development, connotative and figurative use of words might be considered an exception to the general use of lexical items. In morphophonological development, markers of tense and number for irregular verbs and nouns are an exception.

To account for the reorganization of knowledge in the semantax domain, it has been suggested that lexical items are marked in terms of the syntactic roles they may play. Just such an explanation was presented to account for the changes that occur in knowledge of relations in complement structures. As different verbs are acquired, the child simultaneously acquires knowledge of the meanings of SVO relations in sentences in which the verbs appear. Another explanation of such developmental changes is changes in knowledge of the underlying structure of subject-complement and object-complement sentences (Chomsky, 1969). Still another explanation is that changes in knowledge occur concerning the implications of surface markings for interpretation of the relations in these types of sentences (Chomsky & Lasnick, 1977). Such changes in knowledge would take into account the fact that even when the verb remains the same, different relations can be expressed in complement sentences. In the following sentences 1 and 3, the case of the pronoun indicates the subject of the complement structure. Sentence 2 is ambiguous.

1. Bill believes him to be sick.
2. Bill believes that he is sick.
3. Bill believes himself to be sick.

Each of these explanations of the child's changing knowledge of semantax relations in complex sentences implies something different about what the child learns about language in middle childhood and adolescence. The first explanation implies a lexical reorganization; the second, acquisition of new structural knowledge; and the third, changes in the child's knowledge of how to use surface structure cues to understand underlying relations. What the best explanation of these developmental changes is has yet to be determined. It is possible that some combination of all of these factors is most explanatory. Much more information about children's processing of these sentences under varying linguistic and situational contexts needs to be obtained. Knowing what the explanation is would be helpful to language teachers of middle childhood and adolescent learners.

Metalinguistic Processing. The change in semantax development during this period that is considered to be most dramatic is the shift from intuitive knowledge to conscious knowledge of the relations marked in the language. Earlier, it was stated that many of the problems in comprehension of semantax structures that have been found in studies of young children's comprehension of complex structures might be attributed to their inability to metaprocess in particular situational contexts. This shift in the processing of complex structures has been attributed to a shift in the child's ability to process the linguistic information in utterances per se without relying on extralinguistic factors (Karmiloff-Smith, 1979). However, this ability to use intralinguistic information seems to be just an example of the maturing child's ability to think about relations described by the structure of the sentence, not just the meaning of its lexical items and the situation in which the sentence is produced.

The development of awareness of categories and relations in language occurs for all aspects of language, just as reorganization of knowledge occurs for all aspects of language. For example, children become aware of the double meanings of words, an advance in lexical knowledge. Children become aware of the meaning of markers of tense as an entity separate from the verb itself, an advance in morphophonological knowledge. This awareness of different categories and relations in the language develops at different times for different aspects of language (Menyuk, 1976; Menyuk, 1985a). It also takes place in gradual steps. For example, children may be aware of markers of plurality in a language before they are aware of the relations described in center-embedded relatives. They may be aware of the relations described in center-embedded relatives before they are aware of relations in certain complement structures with the verb "promise." As they become aware, they appear to go through the steps of: first, unconscious appropriate use of a structure; then, the ability to judge correct or incorrect instances of a structure; and, finally, the ability to correct and talk about the category or relation being examined (Menyuk, 1983).

Given these facts, it is not the case that metalinguistic abilities suddenly appear at age eight to ten years. Rather, what does oçcur during middle childhood and adolescence is an awareness of the relations described in complex structures *and* the ability to talk about the relations. Karmiloff-Smith (1979) suggests that the results of studies examining children's comprehension of these complex structures under more simple and clearer circumstances does not indicate an awareness of how the language codes these relations, but only the child's ability to use extralinguistic information. This is a reasonable suggestion. The question then is: What leads to conscious awareness of these complex relations?

A possibility arises from studies that have examined a phenomenon called alternation of rules (Menyuk, 1964; Maratsos, 1983). These studies indicate that children may go through a period of development during which their new knowledge of a particular category or relation is still tentative. They alternate between old and new representations of this aspect of language. This alternation disappears in time and the new knowledge becomes firmly established. It is possible that the child can bring new knowledge that is firmly established to conscious awareness. In the case of complex structures, knowledge of exceptional rules (those that violate the expected order of elements in an utterance) would not be firmly established until middle childhood and adolescence, depending on the child's rate of development. Other aspects of semantax knowledge, however, would be firmly established during the early childhood years. This is a speculation supported by interpretation of studies of semantax development. A full exploration of what the child is aware of during middle childhood and adolescence and the previous period of development has yet to be carried out. Metalinguistic awareness and reading ability appear to be related to each other and, therefore, it is important to determine what aspects of language children are aware of or can be made aware of during different periods of development.

Anaphoric Knowledge. Anaphoric knowledge is knowledge of only one of the types of cohesion devices (devices that pull the whole together) that are used in connected discourse. Another kind of cohesion device, the organization of a narrative (story grammar), was discussed in the chapter on pragmatics. Because cohesion devices in spoken discourse cover many developmental areas, they cannot be discussed in detail here.

The development of anaphoric knowledge seems to be particularly appropriate to a discussion of semantax because anaphoric devices clearly require semantactic knowledge. Thus far, semantax knowledge of only the structures of utterances has been discussed; in the studies cited, the child was required to produce or comprehend various semantax structures within the narrow domain of a sentence. Processing of anaphora requires keeping in mind the relation between initial references and substitutions for them across sentences — sometimes across several sentences. Thus, the problem is not only one of semantax, but also one of memory. In addition, appropriate use of anaphora requires knowledge of when original references must be reasserted. There are, then, three processing requirements in anaphoric knowledge. The first is the knowledge of appropriate semantax substitutions. The second is the ability to keep in mind the relation between the reference and the substitution over a number of sentences. The third is the ability to judge when reiteration of the initial reference is required. Development of anaphoric knowledge takes place along each of these dimensions.

Although pronominal development continues throughout early childhood, the use of pronouns appears early in children's utterances, and children appear to understand some pronominal references within sentences at ages two to five (Chomsky, 1969; Maratsos, 1979). The most common anaphoric device used is pronominalization. That is, pronouns are used to substitute for subjects and objects ("Mary wanted the ring. She wanted it very much"). In the story telling of kindergarten and second-grade children, Salus (1982) found age differences in the use of anaphora. Some kindergarten children used anaphoric pronouns very little in their story telling, and others used them more frequently — but always to refer back to characters in the story, to subjects of sentences. There was no substitution for verbs or phrases. Children from five to six years of age sometimes began narratives with an unreferenced pronoun, and they also used them ambiguously within the story. An example makes this clear.

> "So the boy ran away and the owl knew where he went. And then he saw where he went, so he just went where he went" (Salus, 1982, p. 107).

Children who were slightly older (age seven) used anaphoric pronouns to a greater extent in their stories, and they were less ambiguous in their use. These older children appeared to be more sensitive to the fact that the initial reference should be reintroduced after a certain lapse of time. This may very well be a product of the story-telling activities that go on in school and of the beginning of their literacy. They still, however, only referred back to the characters in the story using the pronouns "he" and "they" and were ambiguous in their reference. It appears that at the end of early childhood anaphoric pronouns are beginning to be under control. However, there is very little evidence of the use of other anaphoric devices or of sensitivity to the domains in which anaphora can be used. These developments take place over a long period of time.

Several studies have examined older children's and adults' comprehension of anaphora in written material. Since poor readers have overall comprehension difficulties compared to good readers, it is difficult to determine the cause-effect relation in the frequent finding that good readers do better in comprehension of anaphora than poor readers. Aside from this finding, results of these several studies indicate that older subjects do better than younger ones in comprehending anaphoric reference. For example, Chai (1976) studied the ability of fifth-grade to adult subjects to relate pronouns to ambiguous antecedents. It was found that only eighth-grade and older subjects were able to resolve the ambiguity. Type of anaphora and distance from referent can play a role in the reader's being able to do this. The results of another study (DeTore, 1978) indicated this. In DeTore's study it was found that as the inferences required to resolve the antecedents of anaphoric references grew more complex, the age at which they could be resolved also grew. Finally, it has been found that the type of anaphora, not just what it refers to, affects the age at which it can be comprehended (Kubilius, 1979). In this study, students in grades four, seven, and ten were asked not just to understand the anaphoric devices in the sentence that refer back to antedecedent categories but to comprehend ellipses. These are empty slots in sentences that refer back to antecedent categories. The ellipses were of the following kind:

1. Sheila bought some flowers and Julie bought some too.
2. Sheila bought some roses and Julie some asters.
3. The soup was cooked by Sheila and the roast by John.

In sentence 1 the deleted item refers to flowers, a noun. In sentence 2 the deleted item refers back to the verb, and in sentence 3 to the verb phrase. It was found that nominal ellipses were easier to understand than verbal ellipses. These were easier to understand than phrasal ellipses.

The findings of studies of the development of anaphora knowledge indicate the close relation between the development of such knowledge and the development of semantax knowledge. That is, as children acquire knowledge of relations within and across sentences, they appear to be better able to deal with different kinds of anaphora. In a very real sense, use of anaphoric devices is an application of semantax knowledge in continuous discourse. There is, however, something beyond semantax knowledge that is required in the use of anaphoric devices, and that is the ability to determine when and how they may be used without introducing ambiguity. This ability seems to reflect knowledge of the others' (listeners or readers) perspective. This ability is particularly crucial in writing, where the producer of anaphora gets no on-line feedback that the material is becoming ambiguous. It seems likely that this kind of knowledge is the product of literacy experience, reading a wide variety of materials. This suggests that the development of anaphoric knowledge is the result of relations among semantax knowledge, pragmatic knowledge, and reading experience.

Individual Differences in Semantax Development

All who have studied semantax development agree that there are individual differences in the rate of this development. So far as is known, regardless of rate, all children who are developing normally achieve the types of knowledge discussed in preceding sections of this chapter. The differences discussed here are differences in early patterns of development and in strange gaps in development and the reasons given for these differences.

Several studies of early semantax development have been carried out that indicate differences in the content of the actor or agent category in two-word combinations (Bloom, Lightbown, & Hood, 1975; Nelson, 1981). These studies have found that some children fill the category of agent or actor with pronouns frequently, whereas others fill it frequently with nouns. This is, thus far, the most consistent finding of individual differences at an early age. All of the children studied begin to use both pronouns and nouns at an early age. The reasons given for this difference are individual variation in childrens' style of language use or particular input from caregivers. Nelson (1981) found in her study of early language development that children who were "expressers" used pronouns frequently, whereas those who were "referrers" used nouns frequently at an early word-combination period. At a later word-combination period, referrers shifted to more pronominal use. In a recent study (Furrow & Nelson, 1984) these data were reanalyzed, and it was found that when the children were at a low MLU level, mothers of referential children made proportionately more object references, whereas mothers of expressive children made proportionately more person references. The referential children's shift to pronoun use was accompanied by their mothers' more frequent use of person reference. Thus, mothers' references are affected by the children's language as well as the children's language use being affected by the mothers'. The researchers conclude that discourse patterns affect early patterns of difference. This seems a reasonable conclusion, given the data. However, there is no evidence that these early differences are reflected in later patterns of development of any aspect of language.

At the other end of the continuum, several studies have found marked differences between groups of older children and adults in semantax development. Carroll (1979) suggests that mental abilities, including language abilities, are the product of specific kinds of environmental and educational experiences. Specifically, states Carroll, vocabulary development (lexical development) and the ability to comprehend connected discourse containing difficult or abstract concepts (semantax development, pragmatic development, word knowledge development) are affected by these individual differences. Carroll further suggests that such differences are more or less amenable to change through learning and various kinds of intervention.

The results of studies of strange gaps in older subjects' knowledge of semantax suggest that differences in the kind of knowledge Carroll talks about, and of semantax knowledge in general, are the product of experience and, therefore, *are* amenable to change. One study examined older children's and adults' ability to process certain complement sentences (Kramer, Koff, & Luria, 1972). The results of this study of complement structures was that all the subjects could process some complement structures (those with the verb "tell"), but some older children and adults could not process other structures (those with the verb "ask"). Another study examined adults' ability to paraphrase nominal compounds (Geer, Gleitman, & Gleitman, 1972). The results of this study were that all the adults could process nominal compounds with three words ("black bird house" or "blackbird house") but only some could paraphrase nominal compounds with four words ("black bird tree house").

The results of these studies indicate strange gaps in the acquisition of semantax knowledge by older children and adults. These gaps were apparently caused by differences in measured intelligence and education in the first study and education in the second study. The first study was a longitudinal study; subjects' semantax knowledge was measured during two times in their development. During the first time, measured intelligence was the factor that differentiated between those who could or could not process certain complement structures. During the second time, education was the factor that differentiated among the subjects.

It appears from the results of these studies that not all middle childhood and adolescent children achieve reorganization of knowledge into general and exceptional rules and conscious awareness of all categories and relations in the language. However, given the causes for these differences, these studies also indicate that it is theoretically possible to fill these strange gaps for all children if they are given the appropriate educational experiences.

Summary and Questions

Table 8-3 presents a summary of some of the marked changes in semantax knowledge that occur across developmental periods. The shift between infancy and early childhood is a shift from comprehension and use of actor-action-object relations to comprehension and use of the syntactic relations of SVO. A further and very marked development occurs in the expansion of SVO. This expansion takes place within sentences and in the use of coordinated and embedded sentences. The dramatic change that occurs between early childhood and middle childhood and adolescence is in the reorganization of semantax knowledge and conscious awareness of such knowledge. However, these latter developmental changes are not universal.

Table 8-3 Semantax knowledge during periods of development.

PERIOD	KNOWLEDGE
Infancy	Basic semantic relations Some linguistic context rules Word order rules
Early childhood	Syntactic relations of SVO Expansion of sentence categories Sentence coordination and embedding in certain contexts Conscious knowledge of well-learned rules
Middle childhood and adolescence	Reorganization of semantax rules Conscious knowledge of complex rules Exceptions to rules and surface cues Sentence coordination and embedding in all contexts

Much of early semantax development does appear to be universal. The exceptions to this finding of universality are those that indicate differences in children's development of the actor category. Some children fill this category with nouns, and others with pronouns. These differences also, apparently, reflect differences in the use of language — to express and to refer. Although no long-term effect of these early differences on language development has been found, the first question is: Do these early differences result in differences in the use of language that, in turn, affect how language is used to learn? It has been hypothesized that expressers use language primarily to communicate and referrers use language to learn. This would be an interesting hypothesis to explore in follow-up studies of expressers and referrers.

A second, and perhaps more urgent, question is: How can the differences in middle childhood and adolescence that have been observed in semantax knowledge be prevented? Those experiences that lead to reorganization of knowledge and metaprocessing of this knowledge need to be determined. These experiences, then, could be replicated early for those children who appear not to be getting them in the natural course of events.

Chapter Nine

Development of Morphophonology

Morphophonology is the fourth and last aspect of language development that will be discussed. Its being last does not by any means make it least. As has been said in previous chapters, the surface structure of an utterance (the sounds made in a sequence) plays a very important role in the comprehension of that utterance. It provides cues for lexical recognition and for understanding the semantax relations in the utterance. Some older models of language processing suggested that in language production the sequence in generation is from the intent (speech act) to the categories and relations (lexicon and semantax) to the realization (morphophonology) of speech acts, categories, and relations. Language comprehension might take the opposite path. Current models suggest that the process is not sequential but parallel. That is, in generating an utterance we select appropriately in sequence from all aspects of the language and, at the same time, keep the context in mind. The same is true of comprehending language. We refer to all aspects of our knowledge, including the context, to understand what is being said. Representations of top-down, bottom-up, and parallel models of processing utterances were presented in Chapter One.

In addition to its important role in comprehending and producing language, the morphophonology of the language, as it is produced in certain contexts, is the first aspect of language that the child has access to. It is only with time that the child acquires knowledge of the relation between the speech signal and the intents, categories, and relations — or the meaning — in this speech signal. Descriptions of how the child acquires this knowledge or breaks the code are descriptions of the child's acquisition of morphophonology.

The questions to be addressed in this chapter are:

- □ What knowledge does the child acquire when acquiring morphophonological knowledge?
- □ What is the course of morphophonological development?
- □ Is speech input essential for morphophonological development?

To examine this final question, research on the sign-language acquisition of deaf children is discussed. Such research allows us to examine further man's assumptions about the factors that play a role in morphophonological acquisition.

What Is Acquired?

The child acquires three kinds of morphophonological knowledge. One kind is knowledge of how speech sounds are combined into meaningful units, or morphemes, in the language and of how such units are produced. The nature of this kind of knowledge, the one most intimately related to lexical processing, is discussed first. The second kind is the ability to perceive and produce the speech-sound segments in the language — phonological knowledge. The third kind of knowledge is knowledge of the meaning of intonation and stress — suprasegmental knowledge.

Knowledge of Morphemes

A morpheme is considered to be the smallest meaningful unit in the language. That smallest meaningful unit is made up of the speech sounds of the language or its phonology. Morphophonological knowledge is knowledge of how to comprehend and produce morphemes by combining speech sounds in particular ways. As stated in Chapter One, speech sounds in themselves have no meaning, although single sounds can be used in morphemes. For example, morphemes such as "a" or "I" are composed of a single vowel sound or diphthong (combination of two vowels into one). In general, it is only when speech sounds are combined into a morpheme that they convey meaning. Therefore, the child's task is not simply to acquire the pronunciation of the sounds in his or her language but also to learn how to understand and produce speech sounds in a meaningful unit. There is, then, interaction between morphophonological and lexical and semantactic knowledge.

In Chapter Seven the child's acquisition of a lexicon was described as a process in which the child develops changing representations of words. Several models of how the meanings of words are accessed were discussed. All these models described the important role of the phonology of the word in accessing meaning. Further, just as the child's meaning representation for a word changes in time, so does her or his phonological representation.

Conflicting developmental theories exist about the discrimination and identification of the phonological sequences that compose morphemes and about their production. Some researchers have suggested that perception of words by infants is similar to adults' perception (Smith, 1973). Others have theorized that there is a sequence of development of perceptual distinctions that is later reflected in the sequence of development of productive distinctions (Shvachkin, 1973). There is a great deal of data on the infant's ability to discriminate between the syllabic units of the language (for example, between /ba/ and /pa/ or /ba/ and /da/) but very little data on the transition from being able to discriminate speech-sound differences to discriminating between meaningful morphemes.

There have also been different accounts of the development of the production of morphemes. One of the pioneers in the study of the phonologies of the world's languages described the process of achieving native-like speech production as a process of increasing differentiation among the speech-sound features that distinguish one sound from the others in the language (Jakobson, 1968). Another theoretician called the process "natural" and described it as a process of suppressing natural, biologically given speech movements to achieve the speech-sound productions of a given language (Stampe, 1969).

Finally, there are controversies about the relation between the development of speech perception and production of meaningful units. There are those who claim that the sequence of speech perception and production are closely matched, with perception preceding production (Shvachkin, 1973). There are others who claim the two processes are totally distinct from each other, with different representations of speech-sound sequences for each process (Straight, 1980). The underlying bases for speech perception and production have also been argued about. For example, claims have been made that we make distinctions among sounds on the basis of the distinct articulatory gestures that are used to produce the sounds (Liberman, Cooper, Shankweiler, & Studdert-Kennedy, 1967). Others suggest that these distinctions are based on certain acoustic characteristics of sets of speech-sound contrasts (Stevens, 1972). All of these controversies have not been completely resolved. However, the evidence from language acquisition studies provides support for certain positions.

There are, in addition to meaningful morphemes, morphemes that are only meaningful when attached to another morpheme. These are called "bound" morphemes. These fall into two categories; morphemes that form new words with different meanings, and morphemes that add meaning to another morpheme. The former are morphemes that change both the reference of the word and — sometimes — the syntactic class of a morpheme. They are called derivational markers. The latter — which were discussed in Chapter Eight — are markers of tense, plural, and possession and are called *inflectional markers*. Some examples of both types of bound morphemes are presented below.

Morphemes That Add Meaning. Morphemes that add meaning have different sounds, depending on the sound that ends the morpheme to which they are added.

1. Plural: boy/z/, book/s/, ros/iz/
2. Possession: boy'/z/, book'/s/, ros'/iz/
3. Third person singular present: goe/z/, walk/s/, kiss/iz/
4. Past tense: play/d/, walk/t/, paint/id/

Across examples, there are similar rules. If the word ends in a + voice sound, such as a vowel (/oy/, /ay/ and /o/), the added morpheme is also + voice (/z/ and /d/). If it ends with a − voice sound, such as /k/, the added morpheme is also − voice (/s/ and /t/). If the word ends in the kind of sound that is going to be added, an additional sound is introduced to avoid confusion. In "painted" the /t/ and /d/ are separated with /i/, in "kisses" the /s/ and /z/ are separated with /i/. In acquiring such morphemes, then, the child has to acquire two kinds of knowledge; knowledge of the meanings of these morphemes, and knowledge of how they are realized morphophonologically.

Morphemes That Change Meaning. When the syntactic class of a morpheme is changed, it is obvious that the meaning of the morpheme has changed.

1. Noun to different noun: farm + er, allergy + ist
2. Adjective to adverb: wild + ly

3. Adjective to noun: sane + ity
4. Verb to noun: discuss + ion
5. Noun to adjective: history + ical

In the first example, where there is no syntactic class change, meaning or reference has, nevertheless, changed. In the other examples, syntactic class and meaning are changed. It should be noticed that although in each instance referents are changed, there is a relation between the meanings of the two words. For example, the definition of "farmer" is one who carries out the activity of farming and does it on a place called a "farm." The stem morpheme that is repeated in each of the pairs of words above carries the information that the words are related.

Phonological Knowledge

The language that a child acquires is composed of a specific speech-sound set. Languages differ from each other, to some extent, in terms of the members of this set. For example, American-English speakers do not have as part of their speech-sound set the "click" sounds that are used in some African languages. Japanese speakers do not have the distinction between /r/ and /l/ used by American-English speakers. Part of the child's morphophonological task is to acquire the ability both to perceptually and productively distinguish between members of the language's speech-sound set. The child must do this in order to perceive the meanings of words that differ from each other only minimally and to produce distinctions between these minimally different words. In English there is a very large number of these minimally distinctive words. Some differ only in terms of the medial vowel sounds ("bit, bat, boot, but, bait"); some in terms of the word initial sound ("date, late, Kate, gate, fate"); and some in terms of final sounds ("bag, bat, back, bad, bass").

The basis for perceiving differences in these minimal pairs must be in the speech signal heard; the productive distinctions must be in the articulation movements made. Beyond these simple statements there is very little consensus about the basis for these perceptual and productive distinctions. Different suggestions have been made concerning the basic units of speech-sound perception and production. Some researchers have suggested that syllables or word-form features are basic, at least at the beginning stages of speech development (Menyuk, Menn, & Silber, 1986). Others have suggested that distinctions among types of speech-sound segments are basic (Stevens, 1972), and still others have suggested that distinctive features among sounds are used to distinguish among sounds (Jakobson, Fant, & Halle, 1963). Table 9-1 is a graphic representation of the levels of analysis that have been suggested for perceiving distinctions between minimal-pair words and planning for the articulation of words.

In addition to these suggestions, it has also been theorized that perception of the speech-sound differences among the words in the language is not based

Table 9-1 Possible bases for distinctions between minimal-pair words.

BASIS FOR DISTINCTION	EXAMPLE OF DISTINCTION	
Morpheme distinction	Kate	Gate
Syllable distinction	/kei/	/gei/
Segment distinction	/k/	/g/
Feature set distinction	+stop +back −voice	+stop +back +voice

on the speech signal itself but, rather, on contextual information in a sentence and in the situation in which the sentence is produced. For example, the knowledge that the final word in the following sentence is "bill" and not "pill," without perceiving the speech sound /b/, could come from the meaning of the entire sentence "I want to pay the ?ill." It could also come from the situation (the speaker is in a restaurant) when the sentence itself provides no cues, as in "I want the ?ill." However, it is clear that such information is not available to the two-year-old child. This theory, as well as those presented briefly above, will be discussed in greater detail when the child's acquisition of this knowledge is discussed.

The child acquires one other aspect of the phonology of the language: knowledge of permissible and impermissible sequences of consonants. Each language has different rules about such sequences, and a child learns what the rules are for a particular language. Sometimes there are strange gaps in such sequences, but very often the sequences have developed because they allow for ease of articulation. Some examples of initial and final sequences follow. Although an American-English speaker would have great difficulty in producing some of the forbidden combinations and less difficulty with others, all would cause some difficulty. The reader might like to try some of them.

1. s+ p, t, k, pr, tr, kr, m, n, l, w *but not* b, d, g, or r: for example, spit, stand, skip, spring, string, small, snail, slip, and swim, *but not* sbit, sdand, sgip, or srail.
2. p+ r, l *but not* w; for example, prim and plum, *but not* pwit.
3. t+ r, w *but not* l; for example, trim and twin, *but not* tlick.
4. n+d, t *but not* + b; for example, stand and tent, *but not* stanb.
5. m+ p, *but not* k; for example, bump, *but not* bumk.

This list is not exhaustive. All speaker-listeners of the language have such knowledge and, therefore, are capable of making judgments about what is or is not a permissible sequence in the language, regardless of whether a phonological sequence is, in fact, a word in the language. For example, an American-English speaker would probably decide that a "swip" is a permissible sequence, but that "srip" is not. All children must, of course, be equipped to produce all possible sequences so that they can acquire the speech sound sequences in their particular language. In addition, American-English speakers borrow words from other languages that allow sequences that don't exist in American-English (for example, "tsar" — usually pronounced "zar").

Suprasegmental Knowledge

Knowledge of the meaning of intonation and stress patterns is termed suprasegmental knowledge. Just as each language has its own repertoire of speech sounds, so does each language have its own intonational patterns. For example, the intonation patterns (the rises and falls and emphases on syllables) in Swedish and American-English are very different, as anyone familiar with speakers of both languages would know. The Swedish speech has more sharp rises and declinations than does American-English speech. The child acquires the intonation pattern of his or her language as well as the speech-sound distinctions and morphemes of that language.

As we have seen in previous chapters, intonation carries information about the intent of the utterance and the affect of the utterance. There are different intonation patterns for statements, questions, requests, and commands, and different intonation and stress patterns are used when the speaker is, for example, friendly or unfriendly, angry or happy, sad or ironic. In addition, the speaker can convey by his intonation what items should be "chunked" in the sentence (sometimes the clauses), when the utterance is over, and whether the speaker wishes to continue. Thus, intonation can mark the end of a turn. Intonation is a powerful pragmatic tool.

Contrastive stress is also a powerful tool. The use of contrastive stress can indicate what is old information and what is new and, therefore, play an important role in conveying the intent of the utterance. Use of such stress can emphasize just those aspects of the utterance that the speaker wishes the listener to focus on. The use of such stress can also play a role in categorizing the meaning of lexical items. Some examples of these uses of stress are:

1. He put the book in *Mary*'s room. (Stress on new information.)
2. I like *warm* colors but I hate *red*. (Emphasis to focus listener's attention on contrastive elements in sentence.)
3. I want to sign a new *con*tract so I won't have to con*tract* my budget. (Contrastive stress to mark a difference in the meaning of words with the same sound sequences.)

The Course of Morphophonological Development

In discussion of this aspect, the course of development is again divided into infancy, early childhood, and middle childhood and adolescence. The aspects of morphophonological knowledge, both perceptual and productive, that research indicates are acquired during each period are presented.

Infancy

It is clear that during the first nine months of life an infant has little knowledge of the morphological structure of the language. That is, there is little evidence that the infant is producing or comprehending morpheme-length utterances. There is evidence, however, that the infant is capable of distinguishing between syllables that are minimally different from each other in terms of speech-sound segments and in terms of intonation contours. There is also evidence that the child is producing vocalizations that change in structure over the period of the first nine months. From approximately nine months on, the structure of the infants' vocalizations are dramatically different.

From twelve months to two years a dramatic shift appears to occur in the comprehension and production of speech-sound sequences in the language. It will be recalled that over this period of time the infant's comprehension of different words increases from approximately ten words to approximately five hundred words, and production of different words increases from approximately ten words to two hundred fifty words. Given these data, it seems reasonable to suggest that the bases for the infant's perception and production of syllables or speech-sound sequences changes dramatically over the second year of life, from distinguishing between speech-sound sequences on the basis of their acoustic characteristics to distinguishing between them on the basis of their meaning. Because the morphophonological developments of the first and second year of life appear, on the surface, to be so different in kind, they are discussed separately.

The First Year of Life. There is now a very large body of literature concerning the infant's ability to discriminate between syllables and sequences of syllables over the first year of life. Much of this research has been periodically summarized (Morse, 1978; Aslin, Pisoni, & Jusczyk, 1983; Jusczyk, 1986). Theories about infant speech perception have changed quite radically since the first experiments were carried out with computer-generated speech stimuli (Eimas, Siqueland, Jusczyk, & Vigorito, 1971). These changes in thinking are reviewed as the research results are discussed.

Before computer-generated speech stimuli were used in experiments on infant speech-sound perception, a number of studies had found that infants could discriminate between human voice-produced syllables such as /pa/ and /ba/ and /ba/ and /ga/ at about six to eight months of life. This was an interesting finding because it indicated that infants were perceiving speech-sound differences long before they gave evidence of perceiving differences between words and of producing these differences in words. One might argue that the later development of word comprehension was based on differentiation of speech sounds and, therefore, that there was a direct relation between early speech discrimination and later word comprehension. This, in turn, might imply that infants might be in the process of acquiring a specific language at a very early age.

This early interest in the relation between early and later developments shifted to the question of whether the infant was preprogrammed to differentiate between speech-sound segments due to innate feature detectors. Initial findings that infants could only discriminate between speech-sound segments that were across but not within a speech sound category, similar to the behavior of adults, had led to the conclusion that they were preprogrammed for human speech-sound discrimination. Research with other animals has indicated that these animals can be taught to discriminate in a manner similar to the way in which humans do, and, therefore, that this ability is not unique to the human infant.

Recent research on infant sound discrimination indicates that, initially, infants may partition the speech signal on the basis of certain psychophysical (acoustic) properties and only later shift to discrimination on the basis of phonetic categories (Jusczyk, 1982). This shift may not occur until about ten months of age, or when the infant begins to observe those speech-sound differences that mark differences in the meaning of speech-sound sequences (Strange, 1986). However, there is some evidence that in infants as young as six and eight months there are specific language effects on speech-sound discrimination (Eilers, Gavin, & Oller, 1982). The bulk of the evidence indicates that the early ability to discriminate between syllables that contrast in their initial segment is based on acoustic differences, whereas later discrimination is due to phonetic differences that are specific to a particular language. It is possible that shortly after that the infant's perception of speech-sound differences is related to semantic differences (Menyuk, 1974). When this proposed shift from acoustic to phonetic distinctions occurs, the infant begins the process of acquiring the speech-sound differentiations of a specific language. Before that period one would assume that infants from many linguistic communities are capable of making the same acoustic distinctions. Such distinctions depend on the functioning of the auditory system, not on experience. That is, one might argue that when the infant is making acoustic — but not phonetic — distinctions between speech-sound segments, the acoustic features of segments (duration, amplitude, and frequency characteristics) are used initially to discriminate between speech-sound events.

When the shift occurs, this question arises: What is the basis for the phonetic distinctions made? Is it syllable, segment, or features of segments? Some researchers have found that young infants are unable to observe that syllables that have the same initial segments (for example, /da/, /di/, /du/) have something in common. This suggests that segmental discrimination does not occur even at an early age (Katz & Jusczyk, 1980). Other data, however, suggest that they *are* able to observe similarities in syllables that begin with the same sound (for example, /si/, /sa/, and /su/) (Kuhl, 1985).

Contradictory findings do not resolve the issue of the basis for discrimination. However, an explanation for the conflicting results cited above may be the nature of particular speech-sound sequences examined by the different researchers. That is, when the syllables contain segments that are *longer in duration* (/s/ + vowel), analysis in terms of segment or features can take place. Sequences of *short duration* (/d/ + vowel) need to be analyzed in terms of overall characteristics, since each segment remarkably affects the other in such short sequences. From these data one could argue that the syllable is the basis for discrimination when the consonant is short in duration in a syllable, and that the segment or feature is the basis when the syllable starts with a sound that is longer in duration.

Some other data shed further light on the issue. The speech-sound discrimination behavior of older infants and children indicates that the basis for their discrimination is the characteristics of a meaningful syllable or word (Menyuk & Menn, 1979) and that syllabic segmentation of words is much more accessible than speech-sound segmentation until the child begins to read (Liberman, Shankweiler, Fischer, & Carter, 1974). Although these data on older infants and children do not exclude the possibility of discrimination of syllables on the basis of some specific features of the syllable as well as overall characteristics, they do point to the syllable rather than the segment or feature as being the basis for discrimination among meaningful phonological sequences.

One other aspect of early speech-sound sequence discrimination that is beginning to receive attention is the question of how much of the speech-sound sequence the infant can remember, and for how long. Most of the speech-sound discrimination studies that have been carried out in the past only examined the infant's immediate memory for a syllable or a group of syllables. Since one might assume that lexical acquisition is a process of relating phonological sequences to representations of the meaning of words and remembering the relation, the infant's ability to remember sequences for periods of time must play a crucial role in this acquisition.

Research in this area has just begun, and there are largely theoretical notions about how the infant stores information about speech events and about how this storage might change in time. In a number of studies, using a conditioned head-turning response, Kuhl (1986) has examined the infant's ability to build a speech-sound category and what makes for a "good" category, that is, one that is easily learned. Thus, there are easily learnable syllables, and these may be the first type of "words" stored. Jusczyk (1986), following from this, has theorized that the infant establishes a prototype for a word (perhaps an easily learned syllable) and then changes this prototype in time to accommodate the distinctions in a particular language. A study of young infants' storage of syllabic information (Cowan, Suomi, & Morse, 1982) indicated that infants store such information for a longer period of time than do adults. One can hypothesize from these results not only that infants are capable of keeping such information in echoic store, but also that their keeping such information for a longer time than adults indicates that they process such information at a slower rate.

These are very small beginnings to the very important topic of how infants' memories for speech events are developed and how they may change in time due to changes in the nature and amount of information that can be processed. As we have seen in the discussion of lexical acquisition, the infant at twelve months appears to have already acquired a small recognition vocabulary, which indicates long-term storage of speech-sound sequences that represent lexical items. The steps in this transition still have to be plotted, but it will probably turn out to be a critical area of study in the determination of the relation between early speech discrimination and lexical development.

There is a long history of the study of speech-sound production by infants. Studies were carried out largely by researchers listening to infants and attempting to phonetically transcribe the sounds that the infants made. The results of such studies led to widely differing hypotheses about the relation between early productions of sounds and later productions of words. Some theorists held there was no relation between early speech-sound production and later word production; others that there was a step-by-step acquisition of the speech-sound production of the sounds of a particular language (a shaping of the production of the words of the language). Still others held that there were universal steps in the production of speech sounds that were dictated by the constraints of the infants' vocal mechanisms, that infants produced sounds in an order that reflected the maturation of the vocal mechanism (Menyuk & Menn, 1979). Recent research has been carried out using the modern tools of acoustic analysis — speech-sound spectrographs and computers. This change in analysis, however, has not led to completely definitive answers about the relation between early sound and word production.

Two studies were carried out using a combination of listener transcription of infant vocalization and acoustic analyses to determine the developmental changes that occur in these vocalizations. One study emphasizes the gradual shift from cry and noncry vocalization to speech-sound production (Stark, 1979), and the other emphasizes some of the dramatic changes that occur in this vocalization (Oller, 1986). Both studies concur that at about seven to ten months of age the infant begins to produce "true" babbling, or the production of syllables. Before this time the infant engages in numerous types of vocalizations, none of which have the characteristics of a syllable. These studies, and some others that have not used acoustic analysis, suggest that at seven to ten months the infant begins to produce variegated babbling. Within this babbling are repetitions of syllables that contain various combinations of consonants and vowels. The order in which these consonants are produced seems to reflect the degree of difficulty of articulation of these sounds; that is, the easier-to-produce sounds are produced first, the more difficult later. Both kinds of findings — the beginning of syllable production at about eight months and the order of appearance of consistent production of different sounds — suggest that early patterns of speech-sound production are the result of the infant's increasing control over the vocal mechanism (Menyuk, 1971; 1985). Similarities in the sequence of speech-sound productions by infants in the different linguistic environments that have been studied lends further support to this explanation.

The Second Year of Life. There have been many studies of what happens in speech-sound production during the second year of life but few of what happens in speech-sound perception. Most researchers have hypothesized about perception from the production data. It is not clear that this is a valid thing to do, since there is evidence that speech-sound production and speech-sound perception may take different paths, each being dependent on somewhat different abilities and input factors. Given that there is much more data about speech production than speech perception, the discussion of the infant's phonological development in this period begins with that dimension.

There appears to be evidence from a number of studies that several factors play a role in the speech-sound production of children's first words. The first of these factors is the constraints of articulating sounds that vary in the demands they place on the child's motor abilities. There is some evidence that this affects the order in which speech sounds are mapped onto syllables and words and, therefore, that there is a continuity between production during the latter half of the first year and the second year of life (Locke, 1983; Menyuk, 1971; 1984; Kent & Bauer, 1985). These findings indicate that theoretical notions about "natural" phonological development (overcoming natural constraints on the vocal mechanism) are supported by some evidence.

The factors that appear to play a role in the child's realization of speech sounds in words have been summarized by Menn (1981). She states that the child's task in phonetic realization is one of problem solving. There are physiological factors that "load the dice" in certain directions. There are contextual or coarticulation factors that are given by the particular words the child selects to produce first. There are all-important motivational or social factors that may lead the child to make extraordinary and creative efforts in its word productions. Children may give a particular word an almost-adult pronunciation, even though they have difficulties with some of the sounds in the word when they appear in other words. For example, Chao (1973) found that his granddaughter would produce the sound /s/ correctly in the Chinese word for water but not in any other words. Children also will try to preserve distinctions between words by sometimes introducing sounds that do not exist in the phonology of their language. For example, Leopold (1947) found that his multilingual daughter introduced vowel lengthening to distinguish between two English words although vowel lengthening was not used in any of her own languages to differentiate between words. The motivation to communicate about important topics leads to multiple attempts to realize words, an awareness and avoidance of certain words that cause difficulties, and pleasure (indicated by word-play) in success. All these factors, in combination, lead to word-by-word acquisition of some speech-sound contrasts and to acquisition of others by a general rule (Mack & Lieberman, 1985). Some of the general rules that appear to govern first word production are:

1. Repetition of syllables (as in "baba" for "baby").
2. Weak syllable deletion (as in "bella" for "umbrella").
3. Consonant cluster reduction (as in "pitty" for "pretty").
4. Forward and backward assimilation (as in "pop" for "pot" and "pop" for "top").

It is clear that the operation of all these listed factors could lead to large individual variation in the development of early speech-sound production, and such variation has been found (Ferguson, 1986) despite early claims of universality (Jakobson, 1968). In the discussion of early speech-sound discrimination, it was suggested that infants do not discriminate between words on the basis of the particular contrasts in their language until about eight to ten months. The productive distinctions of a particular language — for example, the way in which the language contrasts +/− voice sounds such as /t/ and /d/ — do not appear to be made until later; some suggest not until two years or later for some distinctions (Eilers, Oller, & Benito-Garcia, 1984). There has been some research, however, that indicates that the timing and intonational characteristics of an infant's particular language are acquired at least a year earlier (De Boysson-Bardies, 1986). Thus the suprasegmental aspects of the language are realized much earlier than its segments.

There have been few studies of speech-sound discrimination during the second year of life, primarily because the experimental paradigms used at an earlier age are not feasible with older infants. Two studies of these older infants' speech-sound perception are often referred to. The results of these studies suggest either a wholly ordered sequence of development of speech-sound distinctions that is related to the supposed universal order of speech sound production (Shvachkin, 1973), or a partially ordered sequence with the proposed order grossly represented and with a large degree of individual variation (Garnica, 1973). However, the results of these studies have been questioned. The paradigm used in these studies requires that infants discriminate between nonsense syllables that vary in their initial sounds (for example, /fa/ versus /ra/) and relate them to novel objects. This behavior seems to be very dissimilar from the task of speech-sound discrimination of words.

Some researchers have theorized about speech-sound perception during the second year of life, based on observations about speech-sound production. For example, Ingram (1974) suggests that infants discriminate between some of the segments of the language but probably have difficulty in discriminating between some complex sequences that involve consonant cluster (CC) discrimination (for example, /st/ versus /sp/). This suggests that infants may have difficulty discriminating between phonological sequences that they have difficulty producing, since the accurate production of CC sequences comes at a much later age. In some children, accurate production of these sequences does not appear until three or four years, and then not for all of these sequences. Other research, however, indicates that infants do not necessarily have difficulty in discriminating between segments that they have difficulty in producing (Eilers & Oller, 1976).

Given the results of studies with somewhat older children, which indicate that children discriminate between words on the basis of their meaning (Barton, 1976) or on their whole-syllable composition and only can be *taught* to attend to the initial segments of words, it has been suggested that early discrimination is based on whole-word discrimination. However, this shift in the basis for speech-sound perception, which has been observed in a number of studies, may only indicate what children do first, not what they are capable of doing. It is possible that they are capable of making segmental discriminations during this period — since they appear to be able to discriminate between segments earlier — but have little reason to do so because they are seldom confronted with the task of having to make minimal-pair distinctions. As can be seen, the full answer to the question of the child's knowledge about distinctions between speech-sound sequences has not been completely answered by the research carried out so far. The answer to the question would add to our understanding of the relation between developments in the first and second year of life and of the process of morphophonological development. A better understanding would be useful in early detection of children who may have difficulty in using the speech signal to process information and, therefore, are delayed in other aspects of language development (Menyuk, 1986b).

Early Childhood

There is no evidence of the child having knowledge of the markers in the language (such as plural and past tense) during the first two years of life. However, as was discussed in the previous chapter, by age three there seems to be a great deal of evidence that the child has acquired knowledge of an array of such markers. It also appears to be the case that by age three to four the child has little difficulty in distinguishing between the speech sounds of the language when they appear in utterances whose meaning is known in connected discourse. This includes consonant cluster distinctions as well as single consonant distinctions. Thus, there appears to be little development of speech-sound perception that occurs over this period. However, experimental evidence indicates that children may continue to have difficulty in distinguishing between certain minimal pairs that contrast certain speech sounds because such tasks require that the child become aware of segmental differences. The most marked changes that occur over this period are in phonological and morphophonological production.

Phonological Production and Perception. Four important questions have been asked about speech-sound perception and production during early childhood:

- □ What is the sequence of development of speech-sound production distinctions?
- □ What is the sequence of development of speech-sound perceptual distinctions?
- □ What is the relation between the development of speech-sound perceptual distinctions and the development of speech-sound productive distinctions?
- □ When does the child achieve adult-like competence in perception and production of speech sounds?

As we will see, the answers to questions about production seem much more clear than the answers to questions about perception.

At a surprisingly early age (three to four years) children seem to be aware of what are permissible and impermissible sequences in their language (Menyuk, 1968), which may be related to their production of sequences in the language. However, there is evidence that the child does not achieve adult-like phonological productions of the vowel sounds of the language until into the teen years (Kent, 1981). The differences that are observed are due, almost entirely, to the differences between children and adults in their source of sound making, their vocal mechanisms. Boys don't sound like men nor girls like women until after puberty. There are speech-sound productions of single sounds and clusters that continue to cause some children difficulty. Again, these are speech sounds and sequences that are difficult to execute because of their articulation and coarticulation requirements. Others are difficult because of their timing characteristics. A number of researchers have examined children's development of mastery of the consonant sounds and consonant clusters of the language. These two factors, articulatory difficulty and timing, appear to explain the sequence of development of such mastery.

The role of articulation ease in the mastery of production can be seen in the fact that sounds that have clear anchor points in their production are acquired before those that do not. This means that stop sounds such as /b/ and /d/, which are produced by lip closing and tongue tip against the alveolar ridge, are acquired before continuant sounds such as /z/ and /th/ (as in "that"). Frequently, the child substitutes these more difficult sounds with sounds that are easier to produce and similar to each other in terms of distinctive features (for example, /t/ for /s/). By the time the child enters school there is accurate production of both stops and continuants, but the child is very much in the process of mastering these sounds over the ages of two to five years. The role of articulation ease can also be seen in children's later acquisition of consonant clusters. In this instance the child must move quickly through the production of two consonants and must produce, as part of the cluster, more difficult sounds, such as /s/ (as in "step") and /r/ (as in "break"). Consonant cluster production is complicated both by articulatory gesture and by timing constraints (Gilbert & Johnson, 1977). Accurate production of clusters occurs much later than accurate production of single simple elements. For many children these sounds are not produced accurately until the child is approximately seven to eight years of age.

Research on the acquisition of the +voice/−voice distinction of the cognates (sounds that are similar in every other way; for example, /b/ and /p/, /s/ and /z/) indicates that +voice sounds are acquired before their −voice cognates. In fact, children appear to realize +voice and −voice sounds as all +voice before age two. They then begin to make distinctions between the two types of sounds, but they make very broad distinctions. The distinctions they *do* make are inconsistent and vary within each category of sound (ages two to four). The +voice sounds approximate adult timing at age four. Children acquire adult-like timing release for + and −voice sounds at ages four to eight (Macken & Barton, 1980; Banker, 1985). As can be seen, the course of development of the production distinctions that involve timing is a long one.

The production of speech sounds begins when the child begins to babble and evolves over a long period of time. However, long before the child has achieved adult-like mastery of the production of speech sounds — before age eight or the teen years — the child is understood by listeners. Certainly by age four to five most children are intelligible to most listeners. There seem to be a number of reasons for this. First, although the child may still be substituting some sounds for others, these substitutions are not markedly different in terms of distinctive features from the target sounds, and the child is by this time much more consistent about the substitutions used. During infancy, the child makes multiple attempts at a target and is very inconsistent about the use of types of attempts. Second, the child now is speaking in sentences and in connected discourse as well as in a particular situation. The linguistic context helps the listener. This is obviously not the case in infancy. Finally, the child is observing some distinctions in his or her production of speech sounds that allows the listener to make good guesses. For example, although the child only makes broad distinctions between + and −voice sounds at approximately two and a half years, a distinction is made and this helps the listener. This is true of vowel productions and consonant cluster productions as well (Menyuk, 1967; Menyuk & Klatt, 1968). The infant will use any device to introduce distinctions that help convey meaning. The child in this period has well-established categories of speech sounds and is simply in the process of refining them.

As indicated before, a great deal of transitional data are missing on the development of speech-sound perception in the older infant and young child (age twelve months to twenty-four months). The assumption has been that speech-sound differentiation must take place perceptually before the child can acquire a distinction productively. This seems to be a reasonable assumption, but there are little longitudinal data on the relation between speech-sound production and perception in children aged two to three years, a critical time for the development of speech-sound distinctions in both domains. In one such study (Edwards, 1974), children's perception and production of contrasts among stops and fricatives — /s/–/z/, /f/–/v/, /sh/–/˘Z/ (as in gara˘Z), /ch/–/J/, and /th/ (as in "thin" and "that"), both + and −voice — were examined when the children were aged one year eight months to over three years six months. The older (two years six months to three years six months) children's perception and production of glides (/w/, /r/, /l/, /y/) were examined as well. Speech-sound production was sampled in spontaneous language, perception (using the paradigm discussed earlier of getting children to learn to associate nonsense syllables to novel objects), and tests of their ability to identify the objects. It was found that even children aged three were having some difficulty in perceiving differences between some of the sounds examined. For the most part, perception of differences preceded production of differences. There were some instances in which this was not the case. Perception of distinctions was found to develop gradually over the age period tested and although there was general uniformity in the sequence of speech-spound distinctions made perceptually and productively (stops before fricatives, fricatives before glides), there was great individual variation in the details of this development.

The data of this study indicated that, for the most part, perception precedes production, but there were instances in which this was not the case. It was also found that children were still having perceptual difficulties as well as productive difficulties in distinguishing between some sounds. This finding might be due to the perceptual paradigm used, which, as stated earlier, might inaccurately measure children's perceptual abilities. The study lends support to the notion that the child must perceive the difference between certain speech sounds before he or she can produce this difference, but leaves questions about why the inverse occurs in some instances. Also, this study did not address the question of whether children perceived distinctions in the same sequence as they produced them. That is, it might be the case that the child uses different kinds of abilities when making perceptual and productive distinctions, and therefore the sequence of acquisition for particular distinctions within each task is different, although, overall, perception precedes production. The findings of another study (Menyuk, 1972) indicated that there was a difference in the ease with which children made perceptual or productive distinctions with the same speech sounds. When three- to four-year-old children were asked to differentiate among three members of sets of +voice and −voice stops, glides, and fricatives, both productively and perceptually, it was found that the order of difficulty was different for the perception and production tasks. For example, the distinctions among the −voice stops were most difficult to perceive but among the easiest to produce. It is possible, however, that the task requirements produced the results obtained, rather than that an accurate picture was obtained of the sequence of development of either perceptual or productive distinctions. It is possible that both studies cited examined childrens' abilities to solve experimenter-generated tasks rather than provided information about the relations between perception and production of speech-sound distinctions.

There have been many studies of infant speech-sound discrimination using computer-generated stimuli. Also, there have been many studies of adult speech-sound perception that indicate that this perception is categorical (Liberman, Cooper, Shankweiler, & Studdert-Kennedy, 1967). The experiments used to determine that this is the case with infants and adults have used computer-generated speech-sound continua (for example, the speech sound /b/ is changed gradually to a /p/ by gradually changing, step by step, the timing of the beginning of voicing in the syllable). These studies have found that adults hear all examples within a certain range of steps as one sound and all examples within another range of steps as another sound, hence categorical perception. There have been a few studies of children's perception of steps on these continua. One such study (Strange & Broen, 1980) examined children's behavior with three continua, /w/–/r/, /r/–/l/, and /w/–/b/. The finding of this study was that three-year-old children carved up the continua in a categorical manner similar to the way that adults did. Figure 9-1 presents an idealized example of

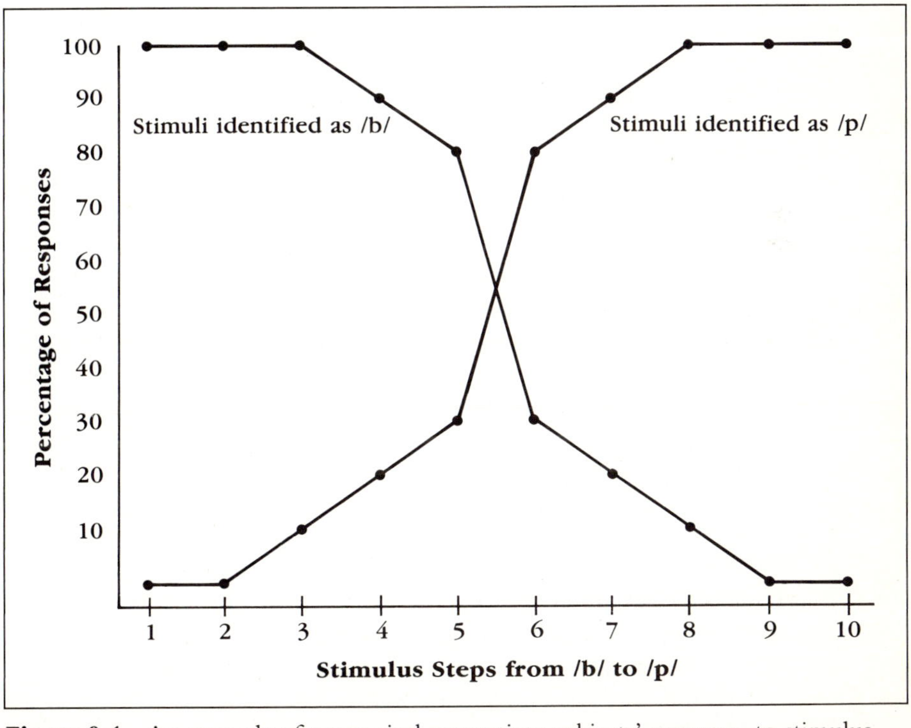

Figure 9-1 An example of categorical perception: subjects' responses to stimulus steps in the continuum from /b/ to /p/.

categorical perception of a speech-sound continuum from /b/ to /p/. Steps in the continuum are identified as one sound or another by both children and adults.

The data from the study just cited seem to indicate that even when three-year-old children are asked to perceive distinctions between speech sounds that are late productive acquisitions (the /r/ – /l/ distinction), they perform as adults do. It may be that the ability to perceive all the phonetic differences that are crucial to acquiring the lexicon, pragmatics, and semantax of a language are present in the infant. As a result, the task may not be one of perceiving speech-sound differences, but one of relating the differences perceived to meaningful sequences in the language. Such has been proposed by a number of researchers (for example, Lieberman, 1986; Miller & Eimas, 1983). As can be seen, there are varying opinions about when the child achieves adult competence in speech-sound differentiation. In fact, it may be inappropriate to examine speech-sound discrimination in isolation from connected discourse. Speech-sound differentiation takes place while perceiving the intent and meaning of utterances heard and, therefore, is never employed as a separate ability after some higher-order categories of language knowledge have been acquired. The child's ability to segment and categorize the speech sounds in words, rather than perceiving the differences in speech-sound sequences on the basis of lexical knowledge, is apparently not used until the child begins to learn to read. In teaching the child to read, it is important to know that such segmentation and categorization are not easily available to the child.

Morphophonology. The acquisition of morphophonological knowledge is dependent on the child's lexical and semantax knowledge. It is also dependent on his or her ability to perceive the difference between a word stem and an addition (for example, stems and endings such as "friend/z/," "bat/s/," and "roz/iz/"). The combination of lexical knowledge in speech-sound discrimination and morphophonological knowledge allows the child to segment the stream of speech into morphemes and to observe the phonological rules that hold for the combination of these morphemes. The acquisition of the semantactic and phonological aspects of American-English morphophonology begins to take place during the early childhood years. The task for children acquiring English is, presumably, easier than the acquisition of the morphophonology of a case language such as Russian, which marks basic relations with endings and has a much richer system. Despite the suggested comparative simplicity of the task, the acquisition of morphophonological rules takes place over the entire period of early childhood and continues on into middle childhood and adolescence. It has been suggested that the length of time it takes to acquire some aspects of the system may be due to the fact that English morphophonology is comparatively impoverished (Hyams, 1986). For example, English-speaking children may have no expectation that third person singular, present tense is marked (want/s) since all other persons (I, you, we, they) are unmarked (want). Therefore, they must learn an exception, not a rule. Below, we discuss the general developmental trends in the acquisition of this system and the explanations provided for these trends.

The order in which morphological markers are acquired is affected by a number of factors, only one of which is the phonology of the markers. There have been numerous studies of the acquisition of this aspect of the language. These studies have examined the development of the system in differing ways. For example, some studies have examined the use of morphological markers in the spontaneous speech of children (Brown, 1973), others have examined the child's ability to freely generate morphological markers on nonsense stems in an experimental situation (Berko-Gleason, 1958), and still others have examined the child's comprehension of morphological markers when applied to nonsense stems (Anisfeld & Tucker, 1967; Derwing, 1979). All these studies have found the same general order of acquisition of markers that add to the meaning of a morpheme, markers of plural, possession, and tense.

The child initially has no markers for any of these categories. Later, the child uses separate words to indicate these categories. Some examples of this are:

1. Plural: "two (or any number) shoe"
2. Possession: "*daddy* hat" (stress on the possessor)
3. Tense: "fall down now," "come yesterday"

These behaviors indicate that the child has acquired the notions of each of the categories, but has not, as yet, learned how the language marks them. The child then begins to use, in an imitative fashion, some irregular forms that are very frequently used by adults in the environment and, therefore, frequently heard by the child (for example, "that's," "came," "feet"). The next step is acquisition of the markers themselves. The markers of these categories are acquired in an order that seems to reflect the degree to which the marker can be generally applied. That is, markers that are applied most generally are acquired first, then the next most general, and so on until the most specific markers are acquired. The order of acquisition of markers of tense involves sequential acquisition of knowledge of aspects of time, not simply a concept of tense. This knowledge, as we have seen, is also partially related to children's understanding of categories of verbs (for example, durative and punctual verbs). In addition, the order of acquisition of past tense markers reflects the acquisition of most general to least general phonological representations.

1. Plural: "boy/z/," "hat/s/," "rose/iz," and "feet"
2. Possession: "Mary/z/," "Nat/s/," and "miss/iz/"
3. Tense: "play/d/," "walk/t/," "paint/id," "went"

Some steps in the acquisition of the plural of irregular nouns and the past of irregular verbs ("feet" and "went") are overgeneralizations in the application of regular rules. For example, children have been observed to produce "goed" or even "goed/id/" on the way to learning "went," and "foots," "feets," and even "feets/iz/," on the way to "feet." There are other, more specific markers that are acquired by some children and not by others. For example, some children acquire the marker "roo/vz/" as the plural of "roof," while for others the plural of "roof" is "roof/s/." This marker, and others, varies from dialect to dialect.

In addition to acquiring markers of plural, possession, and tense, the youngster in early childhood is able to change the syntactic class of words. For example, the child can mark adverbs appropriately ("quick/ly/") and knows how to derive words that mark "one who" ("farm/er").

All of these markers are ones that are added to the end of a word to modify or change its meaning. The first type of markers acquired, then, are those that are added at the end. Slobin (1973) has suggested that children attend to the ends of words because of the perceptual saliency of word endings and, therefore, acquire markers at the ends of words before those that appear in the beginning (for example, "dislike," "unkind," "precede") or those that bring about a change in the stem of the word (for example, /s/ to /sh/ in "discussion" or /y/ to /i/ in "historical"). Slobin (1979; 1981; 1985)) has attempted to describe a number of strategies that children may use in the acquisition of the morphophonology of a language in addition to paying attention to the ends of words. Some of these are "avoid ambiguity," "avoid exceptions," and, most important, "grammatical markers should make semantic sense." These strategies are reflected in the order in which various markers are acquired. These strategies, however, do not explain the process by which morphophonological information is stored in memory.

MacWhinney (1978) attempts such an explanation by describing three learning devices that may be used to acquire these and other markers. The first device is learning by rote. The child simply memorizes the whole word and has no knowledge of its separable parts. Some examples of such behavior, at the beginning stages of marker acquisition, were correct use of "went" and "feet." It has been suggested that children who are acquiring French acquire the correct gender of articles for words ("la guerre," "le mot") because they store the whole sequence in memory.

Another device is analogy. The child learns by comparing memorized forms (such as "rug" and "rug/z/") to another comparable form ("bug") and comes up with the appropriate plural form ("bug/z/"). It is possible that the markers of plural for regular nouns and of past tense for regular verbs are learned by analogy, and irregular plural and past tense forms are learned by rote.

The final device is combination. The child learns to combine the morphemes in the language. Those who view morphophonological development as being the acquisition of a set of rules suggest that all of morphophonology is acquired by learning the rules of combination. It might be the case that acquisition of markers that change syntactic class and word meaning fall into this category.

Using a computer analogy, MacWhinney suggests that learning takes place by application of all three learning devices in an economical way. That is, the devices are ordered. Combination is applied only when rote fails, and analogy is applied only when rote and combination fail. Therefore, the first device applied is rote. Changes occur in storage of knowledge about markers by a process of correction. The child hears his own errors and matches these to other forms heard or intended. There have been many arguments against rote learning of any aspect of language. This, presumably, would be too taxing on the memorial abilities of humans. There have also been arguments against the possibility that developmental changes could occur by self-correction, given negative evidence (or correction by others). It has been held that unless the child has already acquired some knowledge of the "new" form, he or she could not determine that the form produced is an error.

A full explanation for acquisition of morphophonological knowledge during early childhood and middle childhood is still not available. However, the theorizing and research carried out thus far have provided information about the sequence of development of such knowledge. They have also led to interesting hypotheses that can be further explored. A full understanding of the processes employed in acquisition of such knowledge would be enormously helpful in devising techniques and materials for teaching second-language acquirers and those language-learning-disabled children who have particular difficulties with this aspect of language.

Middle Childhood and Adolescence

By the time the child is six to eight years old, most of the morphological markers of plural, possession, and past tense have been acquired, with some few exceptions (Menyuk, 1971). On the surface it appears to be the case that children's knowledge of the information conveyed by sentential intonation and contrastive stress on words in sentences is also complete. However, the results of a study of ten-year-olds' ability to comprehend the meaning of different intonational and stress patterns in complex sentences indicates that even at ten years (and in some cases even in adulthood) knowledge of the meaning of different patterns of tone, primary stress placement, and "chunking" are still in the process of being acquired (Cruttendon, 1985). These results, however, may have more to do with the comprehension of complex sentences than with the ability to use suprasegmental cues.

Much of the research on morphophonological development during middle childhood and adolescence has been concerned, primarily, with the acquisition of knowledge about derivational morphological markers. One of these markers is contrastive stress within words. In the Geer, Gleitman, and Gleitman study (1972), adults' ability to understand the meaning of artificial "nominal compounds" (nonsense words derived by combining nominals and applying stress) was examined. Some nonartificial examples of such compounding are words such as "telephone operator" and "lighthouse keeper." In this study not only semantax knowledge but also morphophonological knowledge (how words with new meaning are devised by combining words and applying stress) was examined.

Morphophonology of Derived Words. There appears to be acquisition of knowledge of some aspects of the morphophonology of derived words during the early childhood period. Children appear to have knowledge of the marker of "one who" (er) and knowledge of markers of adverbs (ly), at least as indicated by their use in spontaneous speech. However, when conscious knowledge of how to derive words by using these endings is tested by asking children to add the appropriate ending to a variety of words, it is not until the middle or late years of school that children can consciously apply such knowledge to nonsense stems (Derwing & Baker, 1979). This is true of some other forms of derived words — instrument ("ruler") and adjective ("funny"). The percentage of items within a set of six nonsense stems that were successfully completed by children of varying school ages are presented in Figure 9-2. As can be seen in this figure, it is not until the late school years that almost all the endings are applied appropriately to over 50 percent of the nonsense stems. Frequency of use does not seem to be the factor that accounts for differences in the ages at which children have conscious knowledge of different types of endings.

Previous studies as well as the study illustrated in Figure 9-2 indicate that children seem to have conscious knowledge of the stems used to indicate plural, past tense, and possession by the end of the preschool years. They seem to have no conscious knowledge of how derived forms are generated until the high school years or beyond. Other studies of development of this kind of knowledge indicate that children have conscious knowledge of different categories of derived forms at different ages, and that different children acquire such knowledge at different ages.

In a study of the ability of children to perceive and produce the difference between noun + adjective ("green *house*" and "hot *dog*") and nominal compounds ("*green*house" and "*hot*dog") it was found that at age six some children could perceive and produce most of the distinctions, while at age thirteen some children were still having a few problems with items in the task (Atkinson-King, 1973). The researcher suggests that there are differences in how the two types given as examples are acquired and in how different children approached the task. She suggests that items like "*hot* dog" are acquired as whole lexical items and not related to the noun-adjective pair "hot *dog*," while others such as "*green*house" (green *house*) are. She further suggests that some children approach the acquisition of the items analytically and observe the relation, while

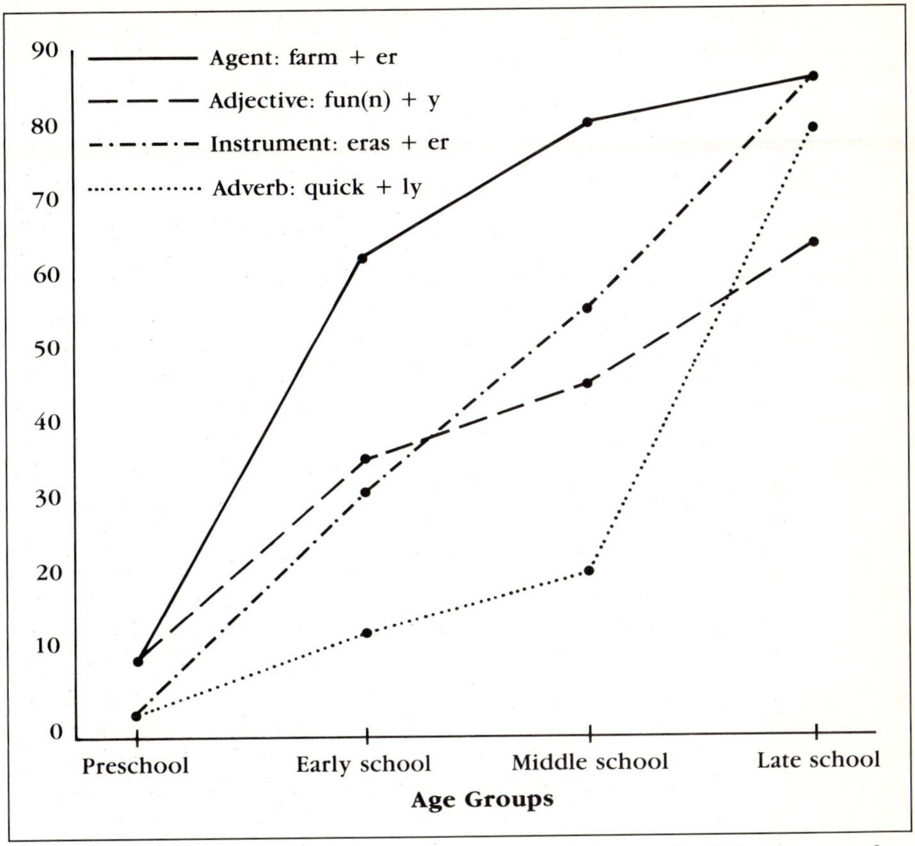

Figure 9-2 Percentage of children at varying ages able to apply different types of derivational markers to nonsense syllables.

others simply learn each nominal compound as another lexical item. The question then arises as to why there are differences among the children.

Some clues to the bases for these differences can be found in two other studies of children's conscious knowledge of complex derivational rules. The ability of children aged eight to seventeen years to apply their knowledge of relations between words such as "relate" and "relation," "sane" and "sanity," "meter" and "metrical," "moral" and "morality," and "history" and "historical" to nonsense stems was examined (Myerson, 1976). It was found that children had conscious knowledge of the different relations at different ages. Children first understood the relations between "relate" and "relation"; second, between "sane" and "sanity"; third, between "moral" and "morality"; fourth, between "history" and "historical"; and, last, between "meter" and "metrical." It was also found that there was a significant relation between children's conscious knowledge of these forms and their reading ability at all the age periods examined. In another study (Loritz, 1981), the ability of children to use the cues at the end of a word to decode complex words was examined. The relation of this ability to their reading and spelling performance and to the extent of their vocabulary was also tested. To test use of word-ending cues, fifth-grade children were asked to read real and nonsense polysyllabic words that represented some of the forms listed above as well as others. The children were selected from three communities; two that were suburban middle class and one that was urban low socioeconomic status (SES). Second-grade children from the communities were asked to listen to the list of words and to indicate which ones they recognized. It was found that there was a significant relation between use of cues and reading, spelling, and vocabulary. There was also a significant difference among the groups on the performance measures and their accuracy in the experimental task. The urban low-SES group performed more poorly than the other groups. The second-grade results indicated that prereading vocabulary might be related to later performance, but the results were weak.

It is impossible to parcel out from the above findings the relation among the abilities in terms of cause and effect. Certainly, though, the level of vocabulary available has been found to affect reading (Loban, 1976). There is also evidence that vocabulary is increased by reading. Children from poorer communities may, therefore, be behind their richer peers in reading on two grounds, the smaller vocabulary of complex derivational words they bring to the reading task and the slower development of their reading skills because of this different vocabulary. A smaller vocabulary of complex derived words will, in turn, reduce the number of complex derivational words that will be acquired. Oral and written language experience are the two factors that affect level of development of complex derivational morphophonological rules. Frequent use of such words in listening and speaking and in reading and writing leads to conscious knowledge of their derivation. Like the more advanced levels of lexical and semantax development, which were also affected by these factors, experience in general and educational experience in particular can play an important role in the development of this conscious knowledge.

The Morphophonology of Deaf Children

In hearing children, the acquisition of morphophonological knowledge has been attributed to perceptual strategies in combination with innate language learning devices. A presumed requirement for morphophonological development, then, is that the child be exposed to the mature use of the system by speakers of the language. Results of research with deaf children acquiring the morphophonology of sign both support and question this assumption and shed further light on the factors that affect acquisition of the morphophonology of a language.

Although deaf children, obviously, have a great deal of difficulty in acquiring the speech-sound system of the language they are exposed to, they can acquire a sign language in a natural manner. That is, sign language is the native language of deaf persons. There have been, by this time, many studies of the structure of sign and many studies of deaf children's acquisition of sign. Studies of the structure of the language indicate that it has a highly complex morphophonology, a rich system (Wilbur, 1979). Signs are generated by a combination of features of hand movements in space (similar to combinations of speech-sound distinctive features combined to form words), and signs are combined into sequences that reflect the relation among elements in the sequence (similar to the semantax and morphophonology of utterances). American Sign Language (ASL), unlike American-English, has a very rich morphophonology.

Acquisition of sign language by deaf children of deaf parents indicates that they develop this rich morphophonology of their language in an order that is consistent with the factors that seem to affect the order of acquisition of morphophonology by children acquiring a spoken language. That is, their order of acquisition appears to reflect those strategies and those learning devices discussed previously, although there are obvious differences in the nature of the task (Kantor, 1980). Further, some studies of the language development of deaf children of hearing parents indicate that there is a difference, overall, in their patterns of development as compared to deaf children of deaf parents (Goodhart, 1984). This makes sense since one might assume that the language input that these former children receive does not provide them with the language data that they would need to develop complex morphophonological rules. Even if hearing parents of deaf children use sign with them, it is probably recently learned and nonfluent.

A study that examined the course of development of two deaf children of hearing parents indicates that despite the fact that they were not being exposed to native sign language they were, nevertheless, developing knowledge of all aspects of the language, including its rich morphophonology (Mounty, 1986). The results of the study were compared to the observations of Bickerton (1981) that children exposed to a Pidgin language (a language without a rich morphophonology) nevertheless developed a Creole (a language with a rich morphophonology). It was suggested that children do this on the basis of their "bioprogram," which leads them in certain directions in development despite impoverished input. This explanation has been questioned, and alternative explanations have been provided for Creoles (Aitchison, 1983). The changes introduced in Creoles are the result of changes that language learners might introduce naturally and have been found in studies of historical change. Another possible explanation is that children who are exposed to Pidgin speakers are also exposed to native speakers and can acquire from them as well. However, it is not clear how much exposure to native signers deaf children of hearing parents have. Although research on the morphophonological acquisition of deaf children of hearing parents acquiring sign does not provide the full explanation desired, further research may possibly do so. This population could provide important insights into the causes and processes of language development in general and of morphophonological development in particular.

Summary and Questions

Table 9-2 lists the principal morphophonological accomplishments during each period. The infant starts out by processing the speech signal in terms of its acoustic parameters and ends up discriminating among meaningful morphemes. The transition period is one in which the child is identifying the characteristics of syllables in the language and eventually relating them to objects and events in the world. Production appears to take the same path in infancy. That is, the child begins by vocalizing (making vocalic sounds) and ends up producing recognizable word approximations. In the transition period the infant babbles (produces strings of syllables) with different intonation patterns, then produces word-length syllables, and, finally, real word approximations.

During early childhood the child begins by discriminating among words on the basis of their meanings and treats each word as a whole. The child then is able to observe segmental differences between words and can reconstruct words from segments (identify "cat" from /k/ pause /a/ pause /t/). Morphophonological suffixes on regular stems are identified, and then plural and tense

Table 9-2 Morphophonological developments during different age periods.

	DEVELOPMENTS	
AGE PERIOD	PERCEPTION	PRODUCTION
Infancy	Differentiation of acoustic categories Differentiation of phonetic categories Semantic differentiation among syllables	Vocalization Babbling Intonation pattern on babbling Word approximation
Early childhood	Semantic differentiation among words Phonological differentiation among words Differentiation of regular stems Awareness of sound segments Awareness of regular stems	Consistent sound production Mastery of articulation of sounds Production of regular stems Production of derived words
Middle childhood and adolescence	Further knowledge of intonation and stress Awareness of derivations	Production of all forms of derived words

markers on strong nouns and verbs are understood. In production, the child's word approximations become more consistent. All of the singleton speech sounds and clusters are produced in identifiable ways. Affixes on regular nouns and verbs are produced accurately. Some generalizations still occur on some strong nouns and verbs. A big advance in this period is the development of awareness of speech-sound segments and of suffixes. This takes place because the child decodes words in order to read.

In middle childhood and beyond, the child increases knowledge of the role of intonation and stress in changing the meaning of utterances (for example, he uses intonation and stress in conveying sarcasm). There is also development of knowledge of complex derivational rules, those that prefix, change stress, modify the sounds in the stem (for example, "sane/sanity," "discuss/discussion"). These changes are probably also influenced by exposure to written language.

Many puzzles still remain about the process of morphophonological development. One of the most challenging is to determine the relation between early speech-sound discrimination and lexical development. The data suggest that at some point the child is able to segment the stream of speech into morphemes, remember the phonological sequences that are morphemes, and also remember their relation to objects and events in the world.

Some of the controversies about this morphophonological development appear to have been resolved and others have not. Whether the basis of speech-sound perception is the feature, the segment, or the syllable seems to have been resolved in favor of the syllable. Less clear is the relation between perceptual development and productive development. There must be some perceptual basis for the word approximations that appear early, but they are clearly also a product of the child's developing speech mechanism. Given the fact that individual children appear to take somewhat different paths in their development of speech-sound production, it is probably going to be impossible to determine a universal developmental process. A better understanding, however, would help in determining possible paths that might be followed by children who have difficulty in speech-sound discrimination and production.

Some questions remain about how children learn morphophonological markers, although the topic is rich in theory and data. Presumably they learn the system by looking in the right place in the stream of speech and by imitation, analogy, and rule generation. However, how each aspect is acquired has yet to be fully explained. Answers to such questions have immediate practical uses. There are a large number of children with language problems who have particular difficulty in acquiring the system. There are many learners of English as a second language who also have problems with the system, usually with the complex derivational rules. Understanding how this knowledge develops can provide clues to the way in which the system can be taught.

Chapter Ten
Language Disorders

The special population of children that this chapter is concerned with is children who have difficulty in acquiring their native language (the language of their sociocultural community) because of known or suspected biological insult. Although the number of children who have these problems represents a minority in the schools (estimates range from 5 to 15 percent, depending on the problem), they are either in special settings within the school or in regular classrooms. Further, the results of studies that have examined these children's language shed light on the factors that must play an important role in the language development of children without problems.

Three questions have concerned clinicians and researchers who work with language-disordered children. The first is: What is a language disorder? This question is not as simple-minded as it sounds. There is still a great deal of controversy about what the contrast is between normal and disordered language. Resolution of this controversy can help in understanding the problems of language-disordered children and in devising appropriate interventions. A second question, and a more theoretical one, is: What are the causes of language disorder? It is a more theoretical question because, even if the biological cause is known or suspected, there are limits to what can be done to overcome the cause. However, having knowledge of possible causes enhances the understanding of particular children's problems and leads to informed planning of educational intervention. The third question is: What are the language development manifestations of particular causes of difficulty in language acquisition? Answers to this question also can lead to better programs of language intervention, those designed to deal with those specific aspects of language knowledge and language use that particular children are having difficulty with. In presenting the answers to this last question, the differing aspects of language development, pragmatics, lexicon, semantax, and morphophonology that seem to be affected by different causes will be discussed.

The way in which studies of language-disordered children can help us understand the factors that affect language development is in the findings of these studies on the relations between causes and specific language behaviors.

In the final section of the chapter there will be a brief mention of some new approaches in intervention. Some of the new proposals that have been made for clinical intervention with children with language disorders are based on the findings of research with normally developing children. However, the successes that have been achieved with these interventions begin to reveal the nature of various language disorders.

What Is a Language Disorder?

There are a number of children who, at birth, can be identified as having a condition that, in all likelihood, will affect their language development. These are children who are born blind or retarded or with obvious severe central nervous system involvement; for example, cerebral palsied children. Despite the fact that one can predict that these children's language development will be affected in some way, no confident prediction can be made about the degree or even the nature of the language impairment that these children will suffer. There is, also, an even larger number of children with no obvious birth defects who will, over the course of infancy and early childhood, show some behavior that will be labelled as a language problem. These children are regarded as specifically language impaired. There are still others whose language problem may be overlooked until the later elementary school — or even high school — years because it only becomes evident when the child has difficulty in acquiring written language. These children have been labelled as language learning disabled.

The fact that a child's language behavior is labelled "problematic" is part of the nature of the problem. Children are usually labelled as having a problem because their language behavior differs in some way from that of their age peers. They are first detected as having a problem because either they are later than their age peers in producing vocalizations (or in producing language) or they appear to have difficulty in understanding what is said to them. They may simply sound different from their age peers. Whether the child has or does not have a problem is usually substantiated by using checklists of behavior for the very young child (for example, Hedrick, Prather, & Tobin, 1975) and tests of language processing for children three years and above. If the child has a problem, his or her behavior, according to the checklist or the test, will be substantially different from that of a child of a similar age from the same sociocultural environment. In essence, the decision as to whether a child has a language problem or not is based on age norms. Children labelled as having a problem are said to be performing (if they are performing at all) the way a younger child would.

This standard way of determining a language problem suggests that such problems can be characterized as a *language delay*. It has been suggested by a number of researchers that all children with language problems are language delayed. Other researchers suggest that these children have a problem because they take *deviant* (different from normal) paths to language acquisition. Still a third position is that at least some children with language problems will be neither delayed nor deviant but will simply *level off* when they reach the utmost that they can achieve in language development. These three positions suggest three different things about the nature of a language disorder. The first suggests that language-disordered children are slower than their age peers in acquiring language but go about the language acquisition task in much the same way as do normally developing children. The second position implies that they do not go about acquiring language in the same way as normally developing children but, rather, use somewhat different means and thus acquire different types of knowledge. The third position states that they go about acquiring language in much the same way as normally developing children and at the same rate, but that they stop after having acquired a certain amount

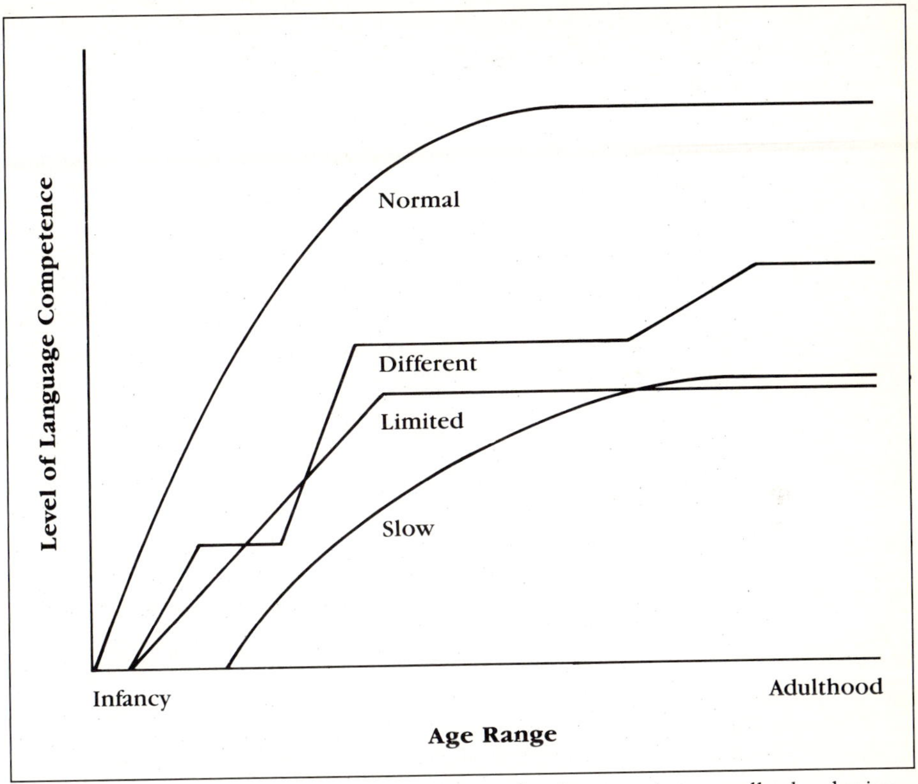

Figure 10-1 Theoretical patterns of language development in normally developing children and those with language disorders.

of language because they do not have the neurophysiological basis for going any further. Figure 10-1 presents the curve of language development for language-impaired as compared to that for normally developing children, according to the three positions.

The position that language development in language-disordered children follows a normal but delayed developmental course in, at least, mentally retarded children was proposed by Lenneberg (1964). In support of this position, a number of researchers have found similar patterns of sentence development in normally developing and retarded children (for example, Graham & Gulliford, 1968; Lackner, 1968). This position was discussed at some length in Chapter Four and is based on the notion that language development is a function of an individual's neurophysiological endowment and maturation of the system. This results in an orderly and universal sequence of development until some critical period is ended.

The second position, that language development follows a different developmental path in mentally retarded and other language-disordered children without obvious cognitive impairment (so-called specifically language impaired or SLI children), was proposed by a number of researchers. Menyuk (1964) found that SLI children developed more slowly and remained at a level of development for longer periods of time than did their normally developing peers. For example, they would produce sentences such as "Me no go" and "That not chair" at age five. A number of researchers have found differences in the language behavior of these SLI children when they are engaged in speech processing tasks (Tallal & Piercy, 1978; Weiner, 1972). It was found that these children take longer to process speech sound units than do non-SLI children.

A number of researchers have found differences in the patterns of language development of children with cognitive impairment (for example, Naremore & Dever, 1975; Cromer, 1972). These researchers have found that children with such impairment do not make the same generalizations as do normally developing children (for example, "comed" for "came" or interpreting "The fish is good to eat" as the fish doing the eating). They either never acquire a mature understanding and production of some aspects of the language, or they get some structures eventually, but this knowledge is not a result of their development of the rules for those structures. Rather, it represents rote knowledge of these structures. However, there have also been studies that suggest that differences between SLI children and those without language disorder are a matter of degree, not kind (Leonard, 1972; Schwartz, Leonard, Folger, & Wilcox, 1980). Those who have found differences in patterns of language development and processing suggest that the cause of language disorder or delay in these children is the language processing deficits that these children have. Those who have found similarities in sequences of development seem to support the notion of a universal pattern of development based on underlying maturation of the nervous system — even if that nervous system is not completely intact. Such a position also suggests that language development is highly resistant to minor perturbations in the central nervous system (CNS).

The third position is that some children who seem to be delayed in language acquisition (such as Down's syndrome children) are not simply delayed in language development (Fowler, Gelman, & Gleitman, 1980). These researchers suggest that these children develop language at the same rate as their normally developing peers. Therefore, their pattern of language development is not similar to their cognitive development where general delay in all aspects is observed. These children follow the same path in language acquisition as do normally developing children, up to the limits of their nervous system's potential. This usually means acquisition of basic categories and relations but not of the further developments that occur in middle childhood and adolescence. Since these children do suffer a delayed and slow but continuous development in all other areas, their nervous system limits are concerned with language learning alone. However, much of the data obtained in studies on the language development of developmentally delayed children points to both late onset of language and slow acquisition up to a point rather than to normal onset and rate of acquisition up to a point.

Any position on the question of the nature of a language disorder is based on a very rich interpretation of the available data. Different researchers have looked at different populations of children who have language disorders and at different stages of development. In addition, they have asked questions about different aspects of language knowledge in examining their data for similarities and differences between normally developing and language-impaired children. Some researchers have examined the spontaneous language produced by these children, others have examined their processing of specific aspects of language.

Despite this variability — and even contradiction — in findings, two generalizations can be made about the data obtained in studies comparing language-disordered children with their normally developing age peers. The first is that at some stage of language development the language-disordered children are behind their age peers in their spontaneous production of language. They sound like younger children, and they have particular difficulty in going beyond simple sentences. The second is that they do not process language in specific tasks in the way their age peers do. They have difficulty in segmenting and organizing linguistic information, or they take longer to do the same segmentation and organization. The best definition of a language disorder, then, appears to be *delay* (or reaching asymptote too early, given the third position) in acquisition of productive patterns of language and *difference* in language processing. It is very tempting to assume that the delay, or the plateaus reached, in acquisition is due to the differences in language processing. Results of research on the next topic, causes of language disorder, suggest that this might be the case.

Causes of Language Disorder

The causes of language disorder are ordinarily thought of as being the array of diagnostic categories that label the developmental problems of children. For example, mentally retarded children are thought of as having a language disorder because they are retarded, blind children because they are blind, cerebral-palsied children because they are cerebral palsied, and so on. The situation is much more complicated than that because of at least one outstanding factor. There can be enormous variation among children within a particular diagnostic category in language knowledge and use. This wide variation may be due to differences in the particular underlying causes of the language behavior observed and the particular intervention history that a child may have experienced. A diagnostic label does not explain the cause of a language disorder suffered by a particular child nor his or her experiential history.

Researchers have focussed on three causes of language disorder. They are:

(1) general cognitive impairment, (2) specific language processing difficulties, and (3) brain lesion or brain maturation differences. These are, obviously, not mutually exclusive categories of cause. That is, brain damage could cause both specific processing difficulties and cognitive impairment. Differences in the maturation of the nervous system could also cause such differences. These categories of cause, however, have been frequently referred to as the basis for the delay and differences in the language behavior of language-disordered children. Within each category of cause, distinctions are made as well. Different types of brain lesion, processing difficulties, and cognitive impairments have been discussed. These differences, in turn, lead to differences in language knowledge and use.

Cognitive Impairments

Measured intelligence has been the yardstick that has been frequently used to discuss cause of language problems. Children who are severely retarded suffer more severe impairment of language than do children who are moderately or mildly retarded. However, outside of these gross characterizations, there appears to be little relation between measured intelligence and specific language knowledge and use. There are large differences in the language performance of children who are moderately retarded, and these differences are not significantly related to measured intelligence. In fact, retarded children of similar measured intelligence perform differently on certain measures of language knowledge (Yoder & Miller, 1972). Similarly, although autistic children who are called "higher functioning" (some with performance I.Q.s of 120) may do much better in certain cognitive tasks than their severely retarded peers, they nevertheless can have a great deal of difficulty in comprehending and producing language.

Other measures of cognitive functioning outside of measured intelligence appear to be better related to language behavior. For example, Moorehead and Moorehead (1974) discuss a possible relation between sensorimotor development and the development of a productive lexicon. Bricker and Bricker (1974) point to the fact that retarded children who are provided with the experiences necessary for sensorimotor development are successful in acquiring a first lexicon. It is not at all clear, however, what the relation is between the development of an early spoken lexicon and certain stages of development of sensory motor intelligence. It is possible that both types of development are independent from each other but dependent on advances in information processing. Recent research on the question of possible cognitive causes for language problems has been more concerned with specific aspects of cognition and language, the possible relations between certain cognitive functioning and certain linguistic functioning.

Curtiss, Fromkin, and Yamada (1978) examined the relation between six language-disordered children's cognitive processing abilities and their language behavior. According to standard tests, the subjects in this study were intellectually functioning from nine months to eight years below age norms. In addition to measuring intelligence, the researchers collected and analyzed language samples for syntactic, morphophonological, and semantic structures. They also tested language comprehension with a picture-pointing task and measured the subjects'

1. short term memory
2. visual sequencing and recall
3. copying and drawing figures
4. classification of objects and faces
5. disembedding hidden figures
6. conservation ability
7. spatial location ability
8. conceptual sequencing ability

These listed behaviors were selected because they are ones that various researchers had claimed were related to language behavior. Some significant correlations were found between linguistic and nonlinguistic behaviors. They were:

1. Expressive syntax and morphophonology and auditory short-term memory
2. Expressive semantics and conservation
3. Expressive semantics and conceptual sequencing
4. Expressive semantics and drawing
5. Expressive semantics and spatial relations
6. Receptive language and conceptual sequencing

These data, the investigators conclude, indicate a strong relation between semantic ability and cognitive ability but no relation between general cognitive abilities and syntax and morphophonology. From an information processing point of view, the researchers appear to be incorrect on both grounds. That is, there does not appear to be a relation between general semantic expression and general cognitive abilities but, rather, between aspects of semantic expression and specific cognitive abilities (for example, between lexical representations and concept development). Further, there does appear to be a relation between syntax, morphophonology, and short-term memory and, therefore, between a certain aspect of language behavior and a very important aspect of information processing.

In another study of the possible relation between language disorder and cognition (Johnston & Weismer, 1983) twelve first- and third-grade SLI children and twelve normally developing children in each of these grades were matched on measured intelligence and sex. They were engaged in a mental rotation task and asked to decide whether two geometric arrays were similarly ordered when the match was parallel or rotated a number of degrees. The results indicated that there was no difference between the two groups of children in their accuracy of response or the amount of training that was required to teach the task. There was, however, a significant difference between the groups in the amount of time taken to respond. The language-disordered children were significantly longer in their response time. This study and the Curtiss, Fromkin, and Yamada study (1978) indicate that language-disordered children, both those who are retarded and those who are not, have specific processing difficulties (a short-term memory problem and/or a delayed rate of processing) which may affect specific aspects of their language development.

Specific Processing Difficulties

Before the results of studies of information processing in language-impaired children are discussed, some of the findings of studies of word, sentence, and passage recall in normally developing children and adults will be briefly summarized. The results of studies undertaken to examine the recall of meaningful material indicate that categorization of words on semantic grounds helps retrieval and that such categorization is imposed on verbal material that is not organized in this way. Organization strategies (such as chunking and observation of surface markers) are used across words to recognize and recall sentences. "Gist" extraction strategies, which reduce sentence information into basic SVO relations (or propositions), and inferencing are used across sentences to recall passages. All of these data indicate that storage and retrieval of linguistic information takes place at a level higher than the speech-sound segment, although it seems clear that words are stored in memory phonologically as well as semantically (these findings are reviewed in Carroll, 1986). As was observed in the chapters on acquisition of aspects of language, normally developing children engage in the acquisition process by segmenting and categorizing the stream of speech into *meaningful* units and observing the relations among these units. Indicated in Table 10-1 are the types of processing that are said to take place at every level of language.

The Johnston and Weismer (1983) study discussed suggests that language-

Table 10-1 Extraction of meaning at various levels of language.

LEVEL OF LANGUAGE	MEANING EXTRACTED EXAMPLES
Words	Semantic characterization boy (male, human, young)
Sentence	Chunking to determine relation (The boy)((chased)(the ball))
Connected discourse	Gist extraction Boy chase ball Ball break window Inferencing Boy wants to get man out Boy gets punished

impaired children who are not cognitively impaired, as indicated by a test of measured intelligence, nevertheless have difficulties in the rate at which they can make judgments about the orientations of visual stimuli. A number of studies have indicated that these children have difficulty in the rate at which they can discriminate between and identify auditory stimuli. Tallal and Piercy (1978) described a number of studies in which they compared the ability of dysphasic children (or SLI children) and normally developing children to identify patterns of tones (high and low pitch) and speech sounds (vowels and stop consonants) at varying rates of presentation. In the studies of tone pattern recognition, the duration of each stimulus was varied as well as the rate of interstimulus interval. In the speech-sound studies, the duration of the stimuli varied as a function of the type of speech stimulus since vowels are intrinsically longer in duration than stop consonants. The overall findings of these studies were that both the length of the interstimulus interval and the duration of the stimuli had an effect on the accuracy of the performance of the dysphasic children. They were similar to their normally developing peers when the interval between tones and the duration of the tones was long enough. They did as well as their controls when discriminating between vowels. There were, however, limits on the number of stimuli in a sequence that they could recall, regardless of length of interstimulus interval or duration of the stimuli.

These data indicate that these children have a problem in the rate at which they can identify speech-sound segments. Given these results, the researchers suggest that these children suffer from an auditory perceptual deficit that may be the cause of their specific language problem. That is, they either do not hear as accurately or discriminate between important units as well as their normally developing peers. However, the researchers also point to the possibility that these children have difficulties in recalling a sequence of auditory or linguistic events. One example of this problem is that these children appear to have great difficulty in following commands that contain multiple expansions of the noun phrase into adjective plus noun (for example, "the big red plastic circle") because such structures place too heavy a load on their short-term memory. This, it will be remembered, was the information processing behavior that was significantly related to expressive syntax performance in retarded children. In short, it is possible that all these children's language processing problems stem from difficulties in storing and retrieving appropriate information in working memory rather than a specific auditory perceptual deficit.

Several questions arise from these combinations of findings concerning the auditory and linguistic processing of children who are language disordered and who are or are not cognitively impaired as well:

- □ How are memory problems related to particular problems in aspects of language?
- □ Do language-impaired children have difficulty in encoding acoustic and lexical information, or in retrieving such information, or in both storage and retrieval problems?

□ Do language-disordered children have difficulty in encoding and/or retrieving only acoustic information?

The results of the studies discussed thus far seem to suggest that the answer to the first question is that the primary problem lies in an inability to discriminate between and categorize speech sound segments. The answer to the second question is that children without cognitive impairment have a retrieval — not a storage — problem, whereas children who are cognitively impaired have both. The results of other studies suggest other answers to these questions.

In answer to question one, how are memory problems related to particular aspects of language, it seems to be the case that children with severe cognitive impairments, those who have difficulty in acquiring any aspect of spoken language, are unable to segment and categorize the stream of speech into meaningful units and to relate these units to objects and events in the environment. Therefore, these children do not acquire a lexicon (Mackworth, Grandstaff, & Pribram, 1972). Other children with cognitive impairments may have enormous difficulty in segmentation and appear to categorize meaningful units in very shallow ways (Wing & Gould, 1979). That is, lexical items may be stored and remain stored in terms of simple visual associations or as memorized acoustic events rather than in terms of the multiple representations that are acquired by normally developing children over time (phonological, semantic, syntactic, relational, hierarchical, imaginal, in association, and so on). These children may be limited to lexical acquisition or simple word combinations because they are unable to retain complete sentences in working memory. Because of this they are unable to determine the ways in which relations among words are expressed in sentences or to develop knowledge of relations expressed by word order and surface markers (Curtiss, 1981). Children who do acquire knowledge of basic relations in sentences because of sufficient working memory may still have difficulty in acquisition of the meaning of sentence markers (for example, markers of number, tense, and location) because they cannot keep in mind both basic relations and surface markers (Menyuk & Looney, 1972). Although this knowledge may be eventually acquired by some, they may still have great difficulty in processing coordinate and embedded sentences because they are unable to keep in mind how relations among sentences are encoded in the language (Levy, 1977).

In sum, language-disordered children with severe cognitive impairments have great difficulty in developing lexical knowledge. Those without such severe impairment develop both lexical knowledge and knowledge of basic relations in sentences. They develop both kinds of knowledge up to the level of early childhood knowledge. There are others without such impairments who may, throughout life, have some difficulty in auditory and speech discrimination tasks but who have developed knowledge of basic relations. They also have a great deal of difficulty in acquiring knowledge about how relations within sentences are marked by bound morphemes. Those who achieve this knowledge may still have difficulty in acquiring knowledge of how relations among sentences are stored. Because of the limitations in the storage of information there probably is, for each aspect of development, a comparatively shallow or poorly established representation of knowledge (as compared to that of normally developing children). This shallow representation would lead to reduced accuracy and increased rate of retrieval of such information.

In answer to the question, Do language-impaired children have a storage or retrieval problem or both?, the lexical and semantactic difficulties of language-disordered children appear to lie in limitations in the storage of linguistic information, not in retrieval per se. However, because of limitations in storage there are difficulties in retrieval. If these difficulties and differences in storage of information actually describe the difficulties of language-impaired children, then there are intervention techniques that can be used to overcome some of these difficulties. There is now a great deal of information on the development of memory strategies in children and the conditions under which recall can be advanced by the use of various storage and retrieval devices (for example, categorization for storage and use of cues for recall) (Kail & Hagen, 1977; Kail, 1979). These devices can be taught to language-impaired children to help them in their recall of linguistic material (Brown, Campione, & Barclay, 1979).

Some studies of the use of covert and overt organization strategies for word recall by language-impaired and nonimpaired children shed some light on the nature of the storage deficit that these children have. Strand (1982) compared language-impaired and nonimpaired children's use of metamemory skills for word recall. The impaired children's ages were five to eleven, and those of the unimpaired, three to nine. Children were asked to do anything they wanted to do to recall twenty-four pictures. The experimenter asked some questions to determine the child's awareness of the strategy used. A week later the children were asked to freely recall the pictures by naming them. They were then asked to use their own cues or experimenter cues for recall. The language-impaired children showed a delay in the kinds of organizational strategies they used for recall (how they stored the information) and in the persistence with which they used these strategies for recall (how they retrieved the information). This resulted in fewer words being recalled and in less accuracy in the recall of words.

Oken (1984) examined the naming accuracy and speed of four- to nine-year-old, language-impaired and unimpaired children. It was found that language-impaired children took longer to name items and also produced more errors in naming. In addition, the unimpaired group most frequently made semantic/perceptual errors, whereas the impaired group produced more circumlocutory and noninformative errors. This latter result indicates a possible difference between the groups in how they represented words in long-term store, and a clear difference in how they retrieved these representations. Kuder (1984) compared the organizational strategies used and the recall of pictures and written words by mildly retarded, reading-disabled, and normally developing children. The retarded children were approximately fifteen years of age and the children in the other two groups were approximately eleven years of age. The children were asked to recall the words and pictures after no organization, after their own organization, and after experimenter organization. The results indicated that the disabled children were slower and recalled less than the normal children. These differences were attributed to the nonuse of organizational strategies by the mentally retarded children in the recall of both pictures and words and the nonuse of these strategies for word recall by the reading-disabled children. The nonuse of organizational strategies by these children indicates that their representations for the words were not organized and elaborated in their mental lexicon. All these studies suggest that there are developmental differences in how lexical items are organized in the mental lexicon of language-impaired children and, therefore, in how organization is used in recall.

The answer to the third question posed, Are the storage and retrieval problems of language-impaired children limited to auditory and linguistic events?, appears to be no. A study cited previously (Johnston & Weismer, 1983) points to a problem in rate of processing of visual information by language-impaired children. Another study (Kamhi, Catts, Koenig, & Lewis, 1984) found that language-impaired children, aged approximately six years, had more difficulty in a haptic (tactual) recognition and discrimination task than did their nonimpaired age peers. In a study (Tallal, Stark, Kallman, & Mellets, 1981) examining and comparing the auditory, visual, and cross-modal processing of language-impaired and nonimpaired children aged five to nine years, it was found that the language-impaired children had both visual and auditory processing problems. However, the younger children in this group made an equal number of errors on visual and auditory processing tasks, whereas the older children made twice as many errors on the auditory as on the visual tasks. This finding that language-impaired children have problems in the nonlinguistic as well as linguistic domains of information processing supports the notion that they have an information processing problem. The last study cited may indicate that the complexity and fast-fading nature of linguistic and acoustic information may be especially problematic for language-impaired children and become more so as the language acquisition task becomes more complicated.

One of the causes of language impairment that has been discussed thus far is a general information processing problem that limits the amount and complexity of the representations that are stored in memory. Processing of spoken information is particularly problematic because such information is highly encoded (many levels are represented simultaneously) and because the information fades rapidly. For children who are cognitively delayed as well as being linguistically impaired, the problem is one of developing categories as well as processing increasing amounts and types of information. These difficulties do not fully explain the cause of language impairment. Such explanations still leave the question of why these deficits exist in some children and not in others. With these children the answer may lie in the organization of information and in the structure of their nervous systems.

Brain Lesion and Retardation in Maturation

Varying statements have been made about the underlying neurophysiological causes of various types of language impairments. Some statements have been based on hard evidence of central nervous system (CNS) impairment, and others are merely speculation. Retardation in maturation of the central nervous system has generally been noted as one cause of mental retardation and subsequent language problems. However, other forms of language impairment have been attributed to such retardation in brain development. As far as lesion is concerned, most statements about a relation between brain lesion and language impairment indicate that site, size, and time of lesion are all related to the kind of language impairment, as well as other impairments, that the child may suffer.

Site of lesion is deemed important primarily because of what has been learned about the language functions of the left and right hemispheres of the brain. Size of lesion is obviously important because of the possible involvement of larger and larger areas of the brain. Time of lesion is said to be important because of the presumed plasticity of the nervous system, but, as was indicated in Chapter Four, how plastic the nervous system is during the early years of life has been questioned, given findings concerning the long-term effects of lesions suffered during the very early years of life. The types of language disorders that are said to be the result of variations in site of lesion indicate that we still have a great deal to learn about the underlying neurophysiology of language impairment. To clarify the notion of site of lesion as an important factor, Figure 10-2 is a representation of the left hemisphere of the brain and the areas that are said to be dedicated to the different functions of language.

In a survey of the types of language impairments that might result from lesion or maturational delay in the development of the nervous system, Rapin and Wilson (1978) found four distinct types of impairment. They are:

- Disorders in the processing of acoustic input.
- Linguistic processing disorders.
- General disorders of brain function.
- Disorders of speech.

Specific language problems may result from each of these impairments and each of these specific types of problems are attributed to different underlying neurophysiological causes.

Difficulties in acoustic processing may be due to anomalies in the auditory system and may cause deafness or hearing impairment. This, in turn, results

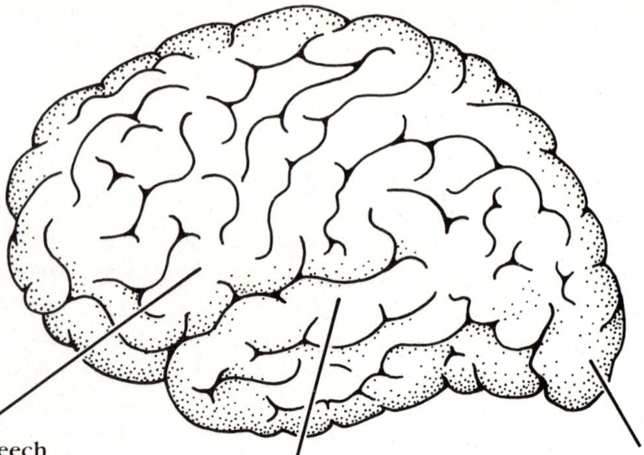

Figure 10-2 The left hemisphere of the brain. Different sites, said to be dedicated to different aspects of language processing, are indicated.

in particular types of speech processing difficulties. Deaf individuals are capable of acquiring a language, sign language. However, moderately hearing-impaired individuals do acquire spoken language and have difficulties in processing the speech signal. Auditory imperception, due to a brain-stem lesion, results in difficulties in temporally integrating and resolving on-line auditory information. This condition may be similar to the one described as the difficulty that SLI (dysphasic) children have when perceiving speech. Another example of difficulty in processing acoustic input is verbal auditory agnosia — word deafness — similar to the condition observed in adult aphasics and due to the same underlying lesion.

Linguistic processing disorders are said to be due to hemispheric asymmetry, or, as in the case of adult asphasics, left hemisphere damage. Along with linguistic processing difficulties, the child has motor problems and auditory memory problems. General disorders of brain function, which are in some instances due to retardation in the development of the CNS, result in such disorders as hyperactivity, mental retardation, and autism; language problems accompany at least the two latter conditions. Disorders of speech may be due to the kind of left hemisphere damage that is similar to that observed with adult Broca's aphasics and apraxics.

The relations between certain types of disorder and brain anomalies have only been grossly described. Since this survey was carried out, there have been many more studies of the possible underlying neurophysiological bases for differing types of language disorder in children and some changes in theorizing about what the possible causes could be. Some of these changes have come about because new evidence has been found and others because of better-informed hypothesizing about the site of lesion. As an example, it was once thought that developmental dyslexia was caused by a lag in the functional development of the brain (Satz, Rardin, & Ross, 1971). However, research on the brain of a dyslexic individual indicated that dyslexics are probably born with a lesion in a certain area of the left hemisphere (Galburda & Kemper, 1979).

As another example of new evidence, it was once hypothesized that autism was the result of a left hemisphere lesion, since the language development of autistic children was profoundly involved. It was then hypothesized that the right hemisphere must be involved as well, because of these children's nonuse of facial expression, gesture, and intonation and stress — aspects of communication that are presumably the product of right hemisphere functions. A more recent suggestion is that lesion of the brain stem may be involved, given the nature of the behaviors that are observed in some autistic children (for example, echolalia) (Fein, Skoff, & Mirsky, 1981). It seems highly likely, given the differences among autistic children as well as their similarities, that the particular neurophysiological (and possibly neurochemical) causes of autistic behaviors vary among the children (Ornitz, 1978).

Clearly, variation in underlying causes applies to all children who fall into the diagnostic categories of mental retardation, autism, dysphasia (or SLI) and learning disabilities. Their language problems, then, are probably due to a variety of underlying CNS conditions and to their particular experiences. This variation in underlying causes becomes evident when the wide variety of language behaviors that occur within a diagnostic population is observed (Menyuk, 1975; 1978). This leaves us with a fairly murky understanding of the neurophysiological differences between children with language problems and children without such problems.

Since there is probably a wide variety of causes for the wide variety of language behaviors of children within these populations, the question arises as to why researchers pursue the very difficult task of trying to determine relations between particular language behaviors and brain functions. This pursuit is particularly questionable since even if underlying causes are determined, there would be very little that could be done to correct neurophysiological faults. One of the answers appears to be that understanding the neurophysiological causes of the behaviors observed in children provides better insight into the relations among these behaviors. That is, one can determine which behaviors are linked, in what way they are linked, and which are independent. For example, if a right hemisphere lesion is the neurophysiological cause of problems, then a number of language problems that are related to each other (in this case the paralinguistic behaviors of use of intonation, stress, facial expression, and gesture) could be predicted. Difficulty with semantic features of words, also said to be a right hemisphere operation, would be independent from paralinguistic problems. Intervention could be designed to address these relations among behaviors. A second, and most important, answer is that, given the recent advances in understanding the structure and functioning of the CNS, further research could lead to "cures" for the underlying causes.

Language Behaviors of Language-Disordered Children

In our discussion of causes of language problems, mention was made of the possible products of such causes. Terms such as "speech perception difficulties," "difficulties in forming categories," and "shallow representation of lexical and semantactic knowledge leading to retrieval problems" were used. The difficulties that particular groups of children have in acquiring particular aspects of language because of these processing difficulties is discussed next.

Difficulties in Achieving Pragmatic Competence

There are some populations who appear to have particular difficulty in acquiring pragmatic competence. The reasons for their difficulty shed additional light on the bases for acquisition of pragmatic competence and on possible neurophysiological bases for this acquisition.

Blind children are slower than their sighted peers in achieving early turn-taking behaviors (Fraiberg & Adelson, 1973). Some cues to turn-taking are in eye gaze, facial expression, and gesture. Early vocal dyadic interaction and the sustaining of this interaction is even more a product of parent effort with this population than with sighted children. A much greater proportion of monologue on the part of blind as compared to sighted children has been observed (Urwin, 1978). Blind children continue to have some difficulties later in life because of their inability to process some addressee and contextual cues that not only signal a turn but also signal some of the implications of what is said (Anderson & Kekelis, 1982). It is also clear, however, that visual cues are not absolutely vital to the development of communication interaction, since blind persons eventually do well in conversation.

Another population that is said to have pragmatic difficulties is certain learning-disabled children and adults. They appear to have difficulty in referential communication situations because of limitations in their knowledge of appropriate language use (Wiig & Semel, 1980; Donahue, Pearl, & Bryan, 1983; Wiig, 1984). In evaluation of the communicative intent of indirect speech acts (for example, sarcasm), they have difficulty because of their literalness. They are unable to integrate visual (facial expression and gesture), auditory (intonation and stress), and verbal cues (Greene, 1982). These communication difficulties cause some of the academic problems of these children but, more importantly, they appear to be the basis for these children's social problems. Because of their difficulties in communicating appropriately, they have difficulties in making and keeping friends. Their difficulties in communication can also be affected by limitations in their knowledge of the structures of language (Donahue, Pearl, & Bryan, 1982). Modeling communicative interaction for these children is a technique that is being currently used with some success (Donahue & Bryan, 1983).

Some language-learning disabled children have difficulty in conversation because they have difficulty in comprehending the structure of what is being said and, simultaneously, processing the conversational situation. For these reasons some studies have found that these children have difficulty in referential communication (Donahue, 1985). Both language-learning disabled children (Donahue, 1985) and SLI children (Graybeal,1981; Johnston, 1982) have been found to have difficulty in the production and recall of narrative. The basic finding of studies that have examined these children's narrative abilities is that there is coherence in their narrative production and recall. However, they make temporal inversions in their production and sometimes in their recall, and in comparison to children without language-learning problems, they do not recall as *much* of the narrative. Techniques such as getting them to answer inferential questions about small chunks of the story appear to improve the amount of information that they recall (Graybeal, 1981).

The autistic population has been noted as being particularly deficient in pragmatic competence, even though recent research suggests that they may be using unique ways in which to communicate (Prizant & Duchan, 1981). Even high-functioning autistic children do not take their turn appropriately. Some autistic persons never establish eye contact with their conversational partners and do not use prosody, facial expressions, and gestures to convey the particular intent of their utterances (Ricks & Wing, 1975). Mentally retarded individuals, with whom the autistic are frequently compared, do not have the same pragmatic difficulties. Their conversational difficulties appear to stem from their lack of opportunity to communicate, due to preconceived attitudes about their conversational abilities (Calculator, 1985). The pragmatic deficits of autistic persons, therefore, cannot be attributed merely to retardation. Because of their particular problems in the paralinguistic aspects of communication, it has been suggested that part of their problem may be due to difficulties with getting information processed in the right hemisphere. This suggestion has been made because adults with right hemisphere lesion also display difficulties in processing prosody, facial expressions, and gestures (Levy, 1979).

The differences between the conversational interactions of the children (and adults) with pragmatic difficulties and those of normally developing children seem to indicate that there are probably different processing and neurophysiological bases for different aspects of pragmatics. Conversational turn-taking and the use of paralinguistics to understand and convey intent appear to be based on the ability to process and integrate audio and visual cues that are suprasegmental aspects of the speech signal. Apparently, this is a right hemisphere function. Other aspects of pragmatics — such as referential communication, the comprehension and production of direct and indirect speech acts, maintenance of topic in conversation, and the structure of conversation — all appear to be dependent on simultaneous processing of contextual, linguistic, and social cues. This must involve both left and right hemispheres, the whole brain.

Difficulties in Achieving Lexical Competence

All of the groups of children that have been discussed thus far have difficulty, in varying degrees, in acquiring lexical knowledge. At one end of the continuum of difficulty, severely retarded individuals (with and without autistic behaviors) have great difficulty in developing the categories or concepts that are represented by words. At the opposite end of the continuum, some learning-disabled children can develop *some* of the aspects of representation of lexical items (phonological, semantic, syntactic, orthographic, hierarchical, multiply-associated, and defining). However, they have difficulty in developing *all* of them. Because of this difficulty, they are unable to rapidly retrieve a word from their mental lexicon as they read. In the middle of the continuum are higher-functioning mentally retarded and autistic children, who have less difficulty in establishing a category than the more severely mentally retarded or their more severely retarded peers but, nevertheless, have difficulty. Closer to the learning-disabled children on the continuum are SLI (dysphasic) children. They have difficulty in relating a category to a phonological sequence and, like learning-disabled children, probably have limited representations of a lexical item in their mental lexicon. However, SLI children have little difficulty in establishing a category. Children outside the continuum are deaf and blind children. They represent lexical items in terms of features that are different from those of sighted and hearing children, but they have no difficulty in developing categories and relating these categories to symbolic representations. Figure 10-3 indicates which groups of children have which types of lexical problems.

In a series of studies (Tager-Flusberg, 1985a; 1985b), the ability of autistic and mental-age-matched mentally retarded and normally developing children to categorize lexical items and to indicate exemplars of categories was examined. After training, all three groups of children performed approximately the same on a number of tasks. One task required them to select from two pictures an example of a given category (for example, chair or dog), and a second task required selection of examples of prototypical (bird) and nonprototypical (tool) categories. The third task required naming of prototypical and nonprototypical examples. The experimenter concluded that these higher-functioning autistic and retarded children develop categories in much the same way as normally developing mental-age-matched children. She also suggested, given these results, that higher-functioning retarded and autistic children have a retrieval, not an encoding, problem because they, like normally developing children, are helped in recall of a list of words by semantic cues. However, these children take a much longer time than normally developing children to *establish* categories. This suggests that the retarded and autistic children have a storage as well as retrieval problem and would continue to have such a problem with new lexical items.

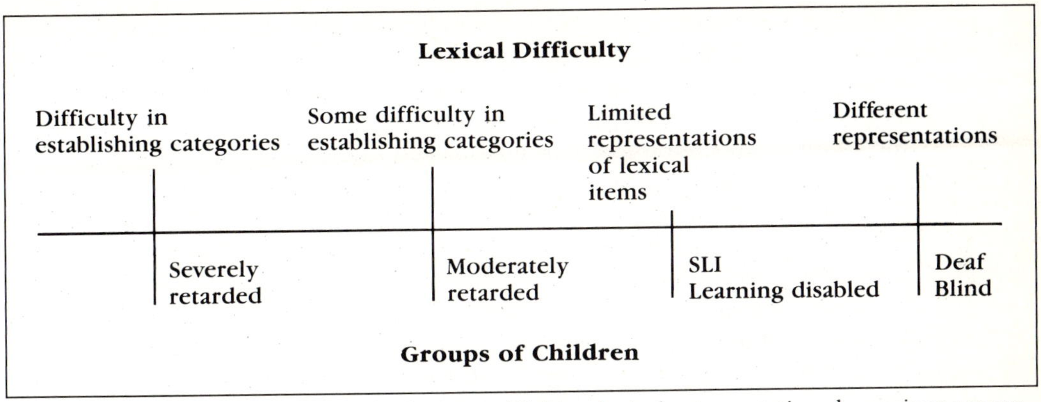

Figure 10-3 A continuum of difficulty in establishing lexical representations by various groups of children.

SLI and learning-disabled children apparently have difficulty in developing representations of lexical items that include all the features that are acquired by normally developing children. These children develop lexical categorizations for denotative words with some difficulty. It seems likely that they would have even greater difficulty with connotative words. Their ability to deal with the connotative aspects of lexical items has not been studied to any great extent. The results of one of the few such studies indicate that children with early histories of language disorder do have difficulty with figurative language (Nippold & Fey, 1983). This study also indicates that these children continue to have lexical difficulties into adolescence.

The lexical problems of SLI and learning-disabled children may be a result of particular difficulties in information processing (for example, auditory or visual) or the amount of information that must be kept in mind to increase the number of representations. All the SLI children have particular difficulty in phonological representation and some of the learning-disabled children in orthographic representation as well. As SLI children listen and speak (or, in some instances of dysphasia, only when they speak), they have difficulty in retrieving the lexical item and its representations. Because of their difficulties they are delayed in acquiring lexical items (Leonard, 1979) and have difficulty in producing words (Menyuk, 1978; Schwartz & Solot, 1980). Dyslexic and reading-disabled children have difficulty in rapid naming of (or retrieval of words for) objects, colors, numbers and letters, and written words (Denckla & Rudel, 1971; Wolf, 1983). The neurophysiological explanations for these difficulties are not clear. Presumably, phonological representations are in the left hemisphere of the brain, but semantic representations may be in the right hemisphere. It probably is the case that both hemispheres are involved in storage of lexical representations. In retrieval of lexical items, perhaps only the left hemisphere is involved. Some of the data on the development of lexical knowledge in normally developing children indicate that increased experience with lexical items in contexts causes a shift in the representation of words from characteristic to defining. These language-learning-disabled children not only need increased experience with words (in linguistic and nonlinguistic contexts) but also strategies for organizing and representing linguistic items. Exercise in the use of categorization of lexical items and in the use of cues in on-line processing of lexical items can help these children build up such representations.

The lexical development of blind children indicates that most acquire words and word combinations at approximately the same time as sighted children. However, some researchers suggest that these children's early knowledge of the meanings of the words they use is different from that of sighted children. Urwin (1978) called these early words *formulas* or *labels*. She found little generalization or overextension in the use of these words. Similar conclusions were reached by Anderson, Dunlea, and Kekelis (1984). They also found that early words were labels and that the children had difficulty, in particular, with deictic terms which require being able to assume a shifting perspective. Both studies suggest, however, that at a later stage of development these children develop lexical representations which have similar, if not the same, characteristics as do those of sighted children. Contrary to these findings about early development, other researchers suggest that blind children can develop concepts based on quite abstract evidence and have representations of lexical items, not simply labels, from the beginning (Landau & Gleitman, 1985).

It is assumed by most researchers that lexical acquisition by the deaf — unlike that of blind children — is quite similar to that of the hearing. In fact, there appears to be some evidence that deaf children may begin to produce lexical items somewhat earlier than hearing children, presumably because it is somewhat easier to produce words with fingers than with the articulatory mechanism (Bonvillian, Orlansky, & Novack, 1983). Of course, the representations of the words acquired are stored in deaf children's lexicons as manual sequences, not phonological sequences. Given the fact that deaf persons' lexical representations are stored in a different modality, some questions about the underlying neurophysiology of this representation have arisen. In one study (Neville, 1980) it was found that the event-related potentials, in response to line drawings, of deaf children who used sign showed a cerebral asymmetry, but in the opposite direction to that of hearing children. Deaf children processed this information in the left hemisphere, and the hearing children in the right. Since sign language incorporates features of space and location, one might conclude that such features are processed in the left hemisphere, as are the structural aspects of sign language by a signing deaf child.

Semantax Problems

Just as with lexical development, all children with language disorders have problems with semantax development. Also, as with the other aspects of language discussed, the degree of difficulty that particular children have can vary. There are dependencies between lexical acquisitions and syntactic acquisitions.

Therefore, children with severe lexical problems, due to severe difficulties in categorization, will acquire little or no semantactic knowledge. Other children with minimal lexical problems will acquire a great deal of semantactic knowledge but will have difficulty in acquiring the more advanced aspects of this knowledge, developments that occur after five to seven years. In addition to the effect of limited lexical development on semantax development, there is the effect of difficulties with the particular processing requirements of semantax development. That is, children with problems in the amount of information they can store in short-term memory will have problems in this aspect of language. For example, they will have problems in comprehending and producing elaborated noun phrases ("the big round red apple"), and coordinated ("John and Mary liked ice cream") and embedded sentences ("I saw the boy wearing a red hat") because of their length. Children who have difficulty in analyzing information in sentences that contain structures that move SVO around (for example, in passive sentences such as "Joe was hit by Bill") or that move one sentence into the middle of another (for example, embedded relatives such as "The boy who was wearing a red hat was in the garden") will have problems, even though they can keep the entire sentence in short-term memory.

Like lexical development, the development of semantax knowledge by various language-disordered children falls along a continuum, to some extent. Children who suffer from severe retardation have severe lexical problems, and therefore, have severe problems in the acquisition of semantax. They represent one end of the continuum. Children who are moderately retarded (as well as some autistic children) develop comprehension of basic semantax structures (subject, verb, and object). They are able to learn how to categorize items in a string as being subjects and objects both in simple sentences ("The boy hit the ball") and in those with locative phrases ("The boy is sleeping in the bed") (Quill, 1985). Some children who comprehend these basic relations appear to do so on the basis of word-order rules alone rather than the semantax relations among the lexical items in the sequence. That is, they do not find sentences such as "The mother fed the baby" (a probable event) easier to process than "The boy kissed the girl." Some high-functioning autistic children do not differentiate among these simple sentences on the basis of event probability (real-world knowledge) but only on the basis of order (Tager-Flusberg, 1981). Some children who do acquire an understanding of the relations of SVO can still have difficulty in acquiring markers of place, time, and manner that indicate relations among basic categories beyond that of SVO. This limitation may in some instances be due to short-term memory constraints, in other instances to difficulty in acquiring the concepts of time, place, and manner. For example, the difficulty of some dysphasic children in acquiring these markers seems to be due to short-term memory constraints. This is indicated by their inability to repeat sentences containing these structures despite their apparent understanding of these relations (Menyuk & Looney, 1972). For some retarded children the difficulty lies in concept development as indicated by their inability to comprehend structures containing these relations. They have a representational deficit (Miller, Chapman, & MacKenzie, 1981).

Dysphasic children spend a great deal of time, in comparison to normally developing children, in the acquisition of knowledge of how relations are described within sentences. They spend an even greater time on acquisition of knowledge of how relations are described across sentences (Menyuk, 1978). Children who are language-learning-disabled appear to have the same difficulty, but to a lesser extent. They have difficulty in processing sentences that describe embedded relations of a certain kind ("The boy who kissed the girl ran away") but not in processing sentences with conjoined relations ("The boy kissed the girl and ran away") (Goldsmith, 1977). Dysphasic children have difficulty in acquiring knowledge of conjoined as well as embedded relations.

The behavior of children with semantax problems indicates that the process of acquisition of such knowledge takes place as a series of accomplishments of tasks that increase in complexity. The levels of tasks become increasingly complex because of a number of factors. One of these factors is the need to keep in mind a certain amount of information in a fast-fading sequence of acoustic events while simultaneously analyzing the situation in which the events occur. Another factors is the nature of the relation between the events and the situation. That is, the relation is sometimes clear because it occurs without interruption in an expected sequence, or it is unclear because it occurs with interruptions and with events that are represented in an unexpected sequence. Because of varying degrees of processing difficulties, children apparently stop at a certain level of development or spend much more time at a level of development than do children who do not have these processing difficulties. Those children who do not exhibit overt semantax problems nevertheless continue to have difficulties in semantax processing. Their difficulties are manifested in their poor reading abilities and in their inability to metaprocess complex semantax structures. Techniques to develop their metaprocessing skills in chunking and analyzing sentences by asking them to make judgments and corrections of various types of linguistic material can have a positive effect on their oral and written language knowledge (Menyuk & Flood, 1981; Flood & Menyuk, 1983). When listening to or reading connected discourse, these children do not make inferences about the sentences heard and have greater difficulty in recalling the content of this discourse. Getting them to infer as they listen can have a positive effect on their recall of stories and passages (Graybeal, 1981).

Children who have semantax difficulties are said to suffer from a left hemisphere lesion because syntax processing is thought to take place in the left hemisphere. There is certainly a great deal of evidence that supports this notion from adult aphasics and, as discussed in Chapter Four, from children with known lesion in the left hemisphere. That semantax development is affected by left hemisphere lesion has also been said of morphophonological development, the next aspect of language knowledge that is affected in children with language disorders.

Morphophonological Problems

Morphophonological development entails two processes, perception and production. This becomes very evident in the case of children with problems in this aspect of language. There are children who have problems in both perception and production and those who, apparently, have problems in production only. There are children who appear to be delayed in development in this area, and others who appear be taking very different paths, as compared to normally developing children. Finally, there are children who appear to be affected in all aspects of development, and children who appear to be affected in only this aspect of development.

At the less severe end of the continuum of severity of problem are mildly hearing-impaired children whose speech-sound processing is affected by the loss but whose language development seems unaffected, although they may have difficulties in certain settings (Jaffe, 1977). Children with fluctuating hearing losses due to chronic middle ear infection (*otitis media*) have been found either to suffer no effects on their language development or to have difficulties in speech-sound processing that lead to problems in morphophonological and lexical development (Menyuk, 1986a). Whether these children will have problems depends on the amount of hearing loss they suffer due to the number of episodes of otitis they have during the first three years of life.

At the severe end of the continuum are children within the severely retarded population, both autistic and retarded, who have enormous difficulties in, at least, the generation of phonological sequences. There are cerebral palsied children who also are incapable of producing speech-sound sequences but who apparently can understand such sequences. With these children, alternate systems — nonspeech symbol systems, such as Rebus, Blissymbols, and signs — are being used with some success (for example, Clark, 1981; Bristow & Fristoe, 1984; Menyuk, 1986b). There are varying factors that play a role in the success achieved with such systems, among them the iconicity of the system and the nonfading nature of the symbol. Since sign, on the whole, is both noniconic and fading in time, the acquisition of such a nonspeech system has special requirements. Not all these children can acquire sign language. They can, nevertheless, acquire a symbol system for communication purposes.

There are moderately retarded individuals who do acquire the morphophonology of the language. They can, for example, slowly learn how to mark number and tense. Some of them have particular difficulty in the realization of speech sounds, however, because of physiological anomalies in their vocal mechanisms. Others appear to be quite inconsistent in their realization of speech sounds. It seems reasonable to suggest that these children are inconsistent in their realizations because they have difficulty in establishing phonological categories as well as semantic categories and relating the two. The difficulty, however, does not appear to lie in the development of their vocal mechanisms. Data on the early vocalizations of Down's syndrome infants indicate that they are quite similar in overall structure and sequence to that of normally developing infants (Smith & Oller, 1981). It is possible, given these two different sets of data, that some mentally retarded children do have vocal mechanism difficulties and others do not, but that all have some difficulty in mapping phonology onto morpheme categories. An example of children who have vocal mechanism problems are children with cleft palates. However, these children may also have difficulties in speech-sound realizations because of hearing loss, which frequently occurs in this population.

The data on the morphophonological development of two populations indicate that there may be both dependencies and independence between the perception and production of morphophonological structures and between knowledge of morphophonology and other aspects of language. Some studies of the speech discrimination of SLI children have found that there are marked differences in the order of difficulty of discrimination of sounds by some of these children and their normally developing peers. Other children in this population show delayed but normal patterns of discrimination (Menyuk, 1980; Tallal & Stark, 1980). There are also differences among children in the number of sound discriminations that they have difficulty with. There are, therefore, differences among these children in the degree of difficulty they have and in the patterns of difficulty they have in speech-sound discrimination.

It has also been found in some studies that examined the phonological development of young language-delayed children that these children use the same strategies in their phonological realizations as do normally developing children (Leonard, Miller, & Brown, 1980; Schwartz, Leonard, Folger, & Wilcox, 1983). Similar results have been obtained in studies of somewhat older children. One such study observed that the speech of such children, aged four to almost seven years, showed a normal but delayed phonological development (Magnusson, 1983), and another showed that there was similarity in the phonological development of the language-disordered child and the young normally developing child (Nettelbladt, 1983). The results of these studies would indicate that in some SLI children one can observe a slowed-down pattern of phonological production. Other studies of phonological production in language-disordered children indicate that they may produce phonological realizations that are markedly different from that of their normally developing peers (Menyuk, 1980). These data, taken together, suggest that there are at least two groups of children within this population: those who have slowed patterns of morphophonological development and those with somewhat different patterns of morphophonological development. It is possible that slowed but normal perceptual discriminations lead to slowed but normal productions, whereas different perceptions also lead to different productions. There is still another population of children within this population, children who only have production difficulties.

There are some children within this population who have problems in other aspects of language processing and some who do not. Some studies have found a significant relation between the articulation difficulties of only some of these children and their ability to accurately reproduce and produce sentences of varying syntactic structure and the morphological markers in these sentences (Menyuk & Looney, 1972; Smit & Bernthal, 1983). It seems very likely that those children who have difficulty in accurately perceiving the phonological events in sentences are those who have difficulty in other aspects of language as well as markedly different patterns of phonological production. Children with only production difficulties are probably unimpaired perceptually.

A relation has been found between the phonological perception abilities of children and their reading (Shankweiler & Liberman, 1976) and between their memory for word strings and sentences (Mann, Liberman, & Shankweiler, 1980). These researchers suggest that the degree to which the child has developed his or her phonological system and the subsequent phonological encoding of lexical items will play a very important role in how reading is acquired initially and how reading progresses. Thus, children with reading problems are unable to decode the words they read because they have not learned their phonological system well enough and cannot bring it to conscious awareness. Presumably, they cannot then progress to automatic word recognition in reading. Learning-disabled children appear to have a developmental delay in their acquisition of morphophonological knowledge, not a difference in their development. They do not have any difficulty in producing the speech-sound segments and sequences in their language. Most of the recent techniques being employed to help these children entail engaging them in metaprocessing of the speech signal and, as indicated previously, of other aspects of language (Menyuk & Flood, 1981).

Some Educational Implications

Table 10-2 lists some of the intervention suggestions that have been made to help children deal with problems in the various aspects of language. There has been great emphasis recently on what has been known for some time: Use of *any* technique of intervention should take place in settings that are motivating, in the sense that learning the language being taught is immediately useful, either for communication or for using language to learn. Indeed, the emphasis is on learning to communicate more effectively or learning to learn more effectively, rather than simply learning language.

What Language Disorders Tell Us About Language Development

Data on the language development of language-disordered children provide us with further insights about the process and the relations among aspects of development. Much of the data that has been collected on the morphophonological development of normally developing children suggests that perception and segmentation of the stream of speech into meaningful units is a necessary

Table 10-2 Some suggestions for intervention for varying language problems.

PROBLEM	SUGGESTED INTERVENTION
Pragmatics	
Conversation	Modelling
Connected discourse	Organization schema Gist extraction Inferencing
Lexicon	Sign or nonspeech symbols Experience in contexts Strategies for organization
Semantax	Sign or nonspeech symbols Chunking and analysis Metaprocessing
Morphophonology	Analogies Recombination Segmentation

prerequisite to the acquisition of higher-order (lexical and semantax) categories. However, once those categories are established, they begin to play an important role in how speech-sound events are perceived. In the discussion of on-line lexical processing, it became clear that the semantactic structure of the utterance (as well as the situation) plays a crucial role in the comprehension of sentences and discourse. Studies of the development of language-disordered children lend further support to this description of development. Children who have some difficulty in perceiving and categorizing speech-sound events are initially delayed in the development of higher-order categories. Those with more serious perceptual difficulties are more seriously delayed and may develop somewhat different categories in all aspects of language. This will further delay their development. Under the latter conditions, there should be an observable relation between phonological difficulties and the acquisition of other aspects of language. Children who only have difficulties in producing speech-sound events can be unaffected in other aspects of language. It can be an isolated disability.

Some Questions

At the outset of this chapter, it was stated that the children to be discussed were those with known or suspected biological insult. Thus, the position taken throughout has been that the cause of the language behavior observed was due to some underlying structural lesion and that differences within and across populations was due to variation in this underlying lesion in terms of place and extent. However, these causes of problems do not determine the educational fates of these children. Some of the children discussed, those on the severe end of the continuum, are usually in self-contained classrooms in regular schools or in different settings. Children at the less severe end of the continuum, however, (the moderately or mildly retarded and the language-learning-disabled) have been mainstreamed and spend at least part if not all of their time in regular classrooms. Thus, their language-learning problems are dealt with by the teacher and clinician in the school system.

The categorization of these children as mildly or moderately retarded or language-learning-disabled is usually based on standard intelligence tests. Those labelled as retarded are children who usually test as being equally competent on the language and performance scales of such tests. Those labelled as language-learning-disabled are children whose language scores are surprisingly below their performance scores. The former children use language commensurate with their mental age peers, whereas the latter do not. In addition, the mentally retarded children have difficulties in adaptive and motivational behaviors (Kahmi & Johnston, 1982). The latter have a long-term history of academic problems (Aram, Ekelman, & Nation, 1984).

The diagnostic classifications and observations do not define the nature of the problem that these children have nor provide information about how their language problems can be alleviated. In this chapter it has been suggested that all children with a language disorder have specific problems in processing their native language in specific communication situations. Their problems lie in how they organize, store, and retrieve information. If this is the case, then a very important question to be answered is: What is the nature of specific children's processing problems? Some attempts have been made to answer this question with groups of children, but much more research needs to be done to obtain more complete answers to the question. Having determined what some of their processing problems are, intervention techniques in specific contexts can be designed to present information to these children in ways that are more congruent with their processing abilities.

Another very large question that arises is: How does one discriminate between children who have specific processing problems with their native language because of biological insult and children who have difficulties in learning their nonnative language and in using this language to learn? It is clear that such a question has been a matter of great concern to educators and clinicians for some time. Children have been labelled as language-delayed and -disordered (implying biological insult) when they are, in fact, language-different.

Chapter Eleven Language Differences

There is a group of children who may encounter language development problems because their native language knowledge and use is *different* from that of the majority group in the community in which they live. They have no problem in acquiring their native language because, unlike the children discussed in Chapter Ten, they have no processing problems or underlying neurological deficits. However, these children are a matter of some concern to educators for a number of reasons. One reason is the presumption that because their language knowledge and use is different from that of their age peers in the mainstream group, they will encounter difficulties in school. Another is the presumption that the cultural background of children from the varying linguistic communities will be incongruent with the culture of the school environment. Because both these presumptions often turn out to be correct, these children *often do* encounter difficulties in school. Clinicians are also concerned with these children because some of them will, indeed, have language disorders. The task of the clinicians is to determine the presence and nature of the language problems they have and to distinguish between difference and disorder.

A group of children who were not discussed in the previous chapter are children whose knowledge and use of their native language would be considered normal in some communities, but who are labelled as having a problem in their own community. Children who have these language problems are usually those who live in middle- or upper-middle-class communities and who are not keeping up with their peers. These children are often placed in remedial situations, as a way to try to help them "catch up" to their age peers. Community standards, then, are often used to determine the normalcy of children who are acquiring the language of the majority group and have cultural backgrounds that are similar to that of the group. In like fashion, the standards of the majority group have also often been applied when determining whether a child from a different linguistic and cultural background has a developmental or educational problem. The normalcy of these children, then, is also often determined by community standards — this time, the standards of the community at large.

Children whose native language is different from that of the majority group in their environment face two problems. They may encounter a school situation that is not congruent with their linguistic and cultural background, and their behavior may be labelled as disordered because it varies from that of the majority group. An ever-growing number of children who enter school in this country — and in many other countries of the world — are children with different linguistic and cultural backgrounds. The problems of these children, therefore, are the problems of educators and clinicians.

The answer to the question Who is considered to be language different? is addressed in this chapter. What researchers have found to be the nature of these children's language differences is presented. This research provides at least partial answers to the questions: How is language processed by these children?

and What is different about their language development? A final question that has been of great concern is, How do language differences affect nonlinguistic processing? The final section of the chapter is concerned with the assessment and educational implications of research on language difference.

Who Is Language-Different?

There are three groups of children who are usually considered to be language different. These groups are:

- Children who have as their native language a nonmajority dialect of the language community.
- Children who are bilingual (perhaps multilingual).
- Children who are acquiring the language of the community as a second language.

There are varying degrees of language difference between each of these groups of children and age peers acquiring the majority language. As we shall see, the degree of difference in language knowledge is not necessarily correlated with the degree of difficulty a child may encounter in school. Language use and other factors play a more important role.

Dialect Variation

All of us speak a dialect of our native language. Our dialects are a product of our geographical region, socioeconomic status, cultural background, and historical change. Theoretically, speakers of dialects should have no problems in understanding each other because dialects are supposed to be different from each other in minor ways. There are, however, regions of the world where speakers of different dialects have great difficulty in understanding each other. Cockney speakers in London, England, speak a dialect so different from the "standard" English of other Londoners that English subtitles were required in a film in which Cockney was spoken. Some of the variation among dialects in this country and other countries is due to phonetic differences in the pronunciation of words, that is, surface-structure differences (Somerfelt, 1968; Labov, 1986). However, there is a great deal of variation among speakers of a particular dialect in how they produce some sounds and how they produce them on different occasions. Also, except for ambiguous situations and ambiguous linguistic contexts, we do not use phonetic information to resolve the meaning of discourse but, rather, higher-order categories. It is when there is marked variation in the lexicon and semantax of the utterances of different dialects that problems in understanding the content of utterances among dialects should become difficult. Differences in the pragmatics of various dialects create marked problems as well, since our pragmatic knowledge is used to understand the intent of utterances and the social and physical situation in which the utterance is produced.

One of the dialects in the United States that has received very marked attention is Black English. Varieties of this dialect are spoken by black people in various parts of the United States. Because this dialect has been extensively studied, it will be used as the example for the discussion of children who acquire a nonmainstream dialect. There have been many linguistic analyses of the structure and use of Black English (for example, Labov & Cohen, 1967; Fasold, 1969). These analyses were designed to reveal the fact that Black English, like any dialect of any language, has structure, is rule governed, and can convey all the intents that the community wishes to convey. While proving this, these analyses also uncovered the important generalizations that could be made about the structure of the dialect and users of the dialect. One important generalization was that speakers of Black English have knowledge of the rules of standard English because they understood sentences containing standard English structures. Another generalization was that Black English speakers, in some parts of the country, can code-switch; that is, they can speak their native dialect or the dialect of the mainstream group and can comprehend both dialects. A final generalization was that differences occur in all aspects of language, pragmatics, lexicon, semantax, and morphophonology. Of particular interest of late are discourse differences.

Certain dialects spoken by minority groups throughout the United States have been linguistically analyzed. Some American Indian, Appalachian Mountain, and Wisconsin dialects are examples of those that have received attention. Some examples of variations of the majority dialect (usually labelled "standard English") that are just beginning to be carefully analyzed are the "Tex-Mex" spoken by some people who have emigrated to the United States from Mexico and the "Spanglish" spoken by some people who have emigrated to the mainland from Puerto Rico. These forms may be representations of a dialect that has developed as a result of one language influencing another. In the cases cited above, Mexican or Puerto Rican Spanish has influenced the English spoken. Alternatively, a Creole, a separate language made up of a combination of Spanish and English rules, may have been developed by the peoples of these communities as their knowledge of English changed in time. Speakers of such Creoles may be bilingual. They speak Mexican Spanish and a Creole of English, or Puerto Rican Spanish and a Creole of English. It may also be the case that some children within these communities have knowledge of a language that is somewhat different from either Spanish or English, at least at some points in their development. Clearly this factor needs to be taken into account when assessing the language knowledge of these children.

Examples of structural differences between Black English and standard English from each aspect of language follow. (The pragmatic differences cannot be neatly delineated and will be discussed in the section on development of language and educational implications.) Lexical differences appear and disappear. The mainstream dialect often borrows from Black English (for example, "bread" for "money"). Although the examples are given in isolation, it should be clear that the differences should not create major problems in understanding.

1. Phonology — Consonant cluster reduction
   "tol" for "told"
2. Morphophonology — Tense marking
   "be watching" for "is watching"
3. Semantax — Negative, relative clause
   "nobody can't" for "nobody can"
   "the sister, she" for "the sister, who"

Bilingualism and Second-Language Acquisition

In the introduction to this chapter, children who are bilingual and those who are second-language acquirers were placed into two distinct groups. However, the children who fall into these groups really fall along a continuum from bilingual to monolingual with some limited knowledge of another language. The description of two types of bilingualism used by Lambert (1972) makes clear that it is difficult to separate bilinguals from second-language acquirers. The description provided is that bilinguals who acquire two (or more) languages simultaneously from birth on are *compound bilinguals*. Those who acquire another language on entrance to school are *coordinate bilinguals*. Time of acquisition of a second language is being used by Lambert to discriminate between classes of bilinguals, but the same time distinction has been used to differentiate between bilinguals and second-language acquirers. Still other factors appear to distinguish children and adults who fall along this continuum from bilingualism to second-language acquisition.

One of these other factors is communication competence, the ability to comprehend and produce the two languages with equal facility. Bilinguals who achieve equal competence, knowledge of structure and use, in two languages are considered to be very rare. But there clearly are those in this country who do achieve native knowledge and communication competence in one language and native-like knowledge and communication competence in the other language. They are able to converse in either language in most situations and to read and write in both languages. At one time it was thought that only exposure at a very early age could lead to the level of communication competence described above but, as discussed in Chapter Four, there have been serious doubts raised about the absolute necessity of acquiring a second language before puberty for this level of achievement.

More and more data have been collected on the bases for successful learning of a second language. These data indicate that there are multiple factors that play a role at any age. These factors include attitude toward the second language and affectual factors in learning (Shumann, 1975), language learning facility (Caroll, 1979), and the conditions under which the second language is presented and learned (Long, 1981). The interaction of these factors will lead to variable outcomes in levels of knowledge of each language's structures and uses. As we shall see in the discussion of educational implications, those learning environments that attempt to replicate the conditions of first language learning by immersing children in the second language on entrance to school do not foster successful learning in all children. The age of the learner has an important impact on the effect of strategies of teaching. The outcomes can be varied, with the learner achieving communicative competence in listening — but not speaking — in the second language to both listening and speaking with limited or very limited success, and in reading and writing with similar variations — again a continuum. Figure 11-1 is a graphic representation of what the continuum would mean in terms of levels of knowledge of how to communicate in a first and a second language.

In all of these descriptions of bilinguals and second-language acquirers, it has been assumed that the first language will be acquired to the extent that "native" competence will be achieved in all aspects of language knowledge and use and that such knowledge will be maintained throughout life. More and more evidence is being collected to support what has been termed the "interdependence" hypothesis (Cummins, 1979). This hypothesis suggests that because some children's first-language acquisition has been interrupted by imposing a second language on them, the usual positive effect of first-language

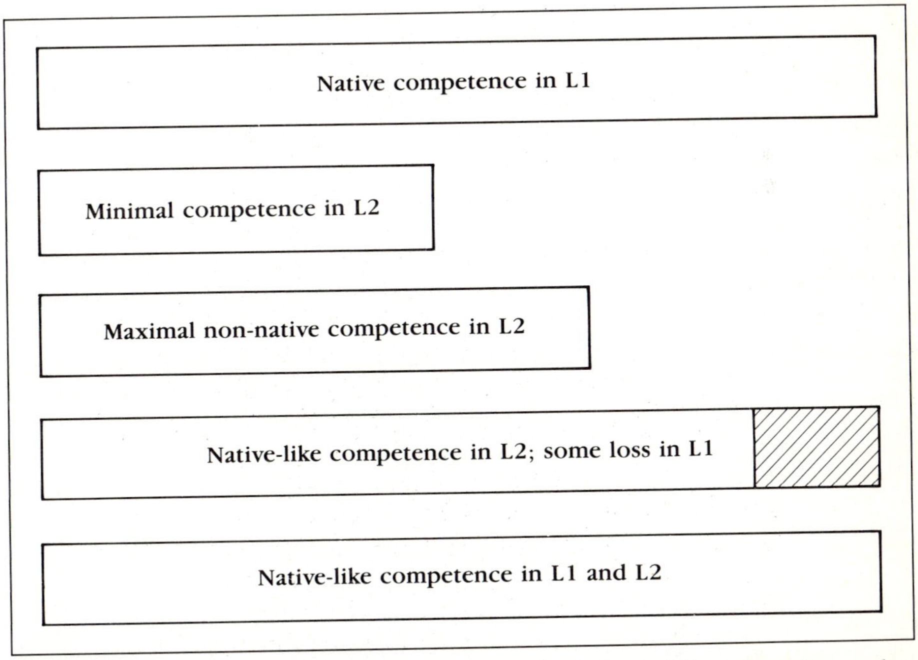

Figure 11-1 Theoretical continuum of L1/L2 knowledge in bilinguals and second-language acquirers.

knowledge on second-language acquisition is not achieved. In addition, when first-language acquisition is interrupted, a pattern of first-language loss has been observed in a number of instances. That is, some children (and adults) who are in the process of successfully acquiring a second language begin to lose knowledge of their first language and do so to varying degrees (Hamp, 1978; Merino, 1983). Just as there are a number of factors that lead to success in second-language acquisition, there are a number of factors that lead to loss of first language. One argument made to account for the academic failure of children who have had a second language imposed on them is that these children have not acquired their first language to the extent needed for use of this language in academic settings. This fragile language knowledge is further undermined by requiring that these children learn a second language, and that they use this language, which they have not mastered to any great extent, to learn to read. A very different argument that has been presented is that these children are simply not as ready for school as are majority group children, and that their school experiences reinforce rather than eliminate these differences.

What Is Different in Language Processing?

At least two questions have been asked about the processing of language information by children and adults who have two or more languages:

- □ Are the lexicons of the two (or more) languages independent or related?
- □ What cues indicate entry into one language system or another?

Studies have been designed to obtain answers to these questions, but, as is the case with all such questions about internal processing, they are difficult to answer.

Bilinguals, second-language acquirers, and nonmajority dialect users all store information about their two languages or dialects. They have to access this information when they speak or listen to speech in particular contexts. Much of the research that has examined the language processing of bilinguals has been concerned with lexical processing only. Although research has been limited to only this aspect of language, the question of the accessibility of the lexicon of L1 and L2 (first language and second language) for bilinguals and second-language acquirers is an important one.

One of the questions asked in some of the studies examining lexical processing is whether there are differences between the lexical processing of those who are and those who are not exposed to two languages in infancy. Segalowitz and Lambert (1969) and Lambert and Rawlings (1969) studied the processing of lexical items from both languages by adult coordinate and compound bilinguals. In the first of these studies it was found that both types of bilinguals show semantic generalization to the same and different language synonyms of the target words presented. There were, however, differences between the groups. Coordinate bilinguals depended more on the semantic content of the words than did compound bilinguals. The latter were better able to differentiate the particular language (French or English) that was used for a word. This difference may represent the history of language learning in the two groups of bilinguals. Compound bilinguals initially mix lexical items and then differentiate them at about two to three years. Thus, mixing may pose a greater problem for compounds than coordinates and lead them to develop techniques for keeping the two languages apart. Presumably, bilinguals have the ability to "switch off" and "switch on" their two languages. Compound bilinguals are, apparently, able to do this with greater ease than coordinates. The results of the Lambert and Rawlings study support this theory. Compound bilinguals had more skill than coordinates in a task requiring that they process mixed-language lexical lists (for example, *chaise,* food, desk, *bois, manger*) to get at a core concept (for example, table). These studies point to the fact that compound bilinguals can more easily access the lexicons of their two languages than can coordinate bilinguals and, therefore, more easily than second-language acquirers.

The data from these studies suggest two further things. First, they point to a switching mechanism that bilinguals use to access each of their two languages. However, this switching mechanism, perhaps cued by the orthographic and phonological representations of lexical items, may only operate most effectively for compound bilinguals. One would assume that these differences in effective switching would be even more marked in the lexical processing of individuals who are not bilingual but, rather, second-language acquirers. The second thing these data suggest is that the semantic properties of lexical items from both languages form one system. Obviously the phonological and orthographic properties of these items must be represented separately. How access to a common semantic pool takes place under these circumstances is the important question.

There is a great deal of data to support the notion of one semantic lexical system. Guttentag, Haith, Goodman, and Hauch (1984) found that bilinguals' responses in a word recognition task were affected by the meaning of the "to be ignored" words that flanked the target word. This occurred when these "flanker" words were in the same or a different language. Although these data suggest a single lexical system, they do not support the notion of a switch which operates to put the bilingual in one language mode or another. The same types of results were obtained in a similar study of child bilinguals (Goodman, Haith, Guttentag, & Rao, 1985). A study examining latency of response to pseudowords as compared to nonwords when words were presented in written and spoken form led the researcher to conclude that orthographic, phonological, and semantic representations form a common lexical store for the bilingual's two languages (Nas, 1983). However, there is also evidence that the bilingual's two lexical systems may not be one. In a series of studies (Kirsner, Smith, Lockhart, & King, 1984) found that the effect of repetition on the decision that a lexical item was seen before was much greater

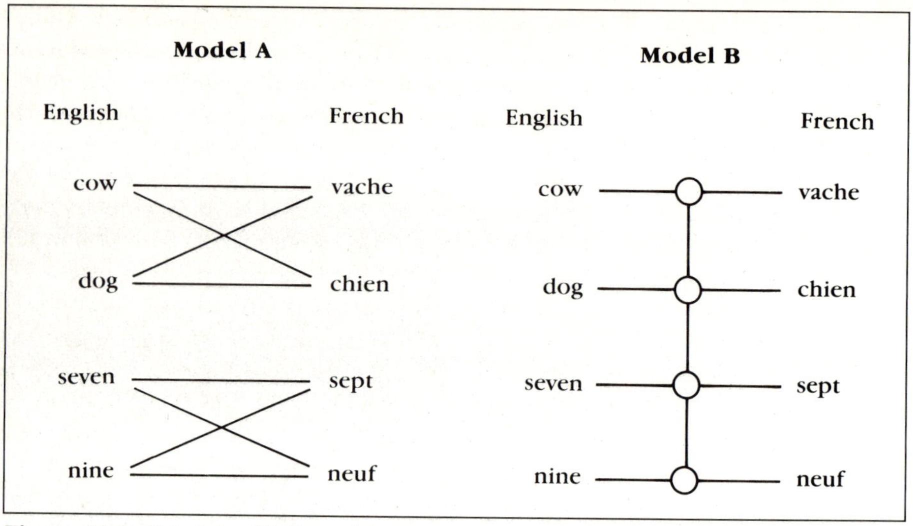

Figure 11-2 Models of bilinguals' representations of their two lexicons.

within one of the languages of a bilingual than across the languages. What model of lexical organization could best explain these results was examined by the researchers. These models range from those that propose no connection between each language system to one which suggests the single system of representation discussed above. The two models that appeared to best account for the results obtained are represented in Figure 11-2.

Model A represents each lexical system as being unique, but with connections between words in each language and among words that are categorically related. Model B (based on the work of Potter, So, VonEckardt, & Feldman, 1984) represents the two systems as separate and related to each other only through a common conceptual node. As can be seen, even when processing of language by the bilingual is limited to a discussion of only lexical representation, there are still many conflicting views about it. It is possible that part of this conflict in views may be due to variations in the degree of bilingualism among the various subjects used in these studies and to variation in the tasks that subjects are engaged in.

Taking a somewhat different position, Grosjean and Soares (1986) suggest that there are two modes in which the bilingual functions: the monolingual mode (either one of the two languages) when interacting with monolingual speakers, and the bilingual mode when interacting with fellow bilinguals. They suggest that even in the monolingual mode the bilingual does not deactivate the other language totally, and in the bilingual mode both languages are activated. A number of the studies cited above provide evidence of the residual activation of the other language when processing lexical items. Grosjean and Soares examined the bilingual mode of processing in their subjects as indicated by code switching ("*On n'est pas assez* quick") and switches ("*Il faut* switcher *les places*") in connected speech. They found evidence of on-line rapid and rule-governed changes, from one language to the other, in the phonology, lexicon, and semantax of the utterances produced. They also found evidence of rapid and automatic processing and comprehension of the language mixes.

Much of the discussion of language organization and language processing was concerned with bilinguals, only one group of language-different children. However, answers to questions about how language is processed in different modes by different groups of bilinguals can help us to begin to understand some of the processes employed by second-language acquirers when they attempt to comprehend and produce their nonnative language in either spoken or written form. We may also understand the difficulties that they encounter when trying to process language in the classroom and when trying to learn to read and write. The difficulties that are encountered by nonmajority dialect speakers are less explainable by reference to differences in representations of the two dialects. There is evidence that these dialect users *can* comprehend — if not speak — the other dialect. There is also evidence that they can read text that more closely represents the majority dialect rather than their own (Labov & Cohen, 1967). Their difficulties seem best explained by pragmatic differences and, more importantly, by educational factors.

What Is Different in Language Development?

By definition, children who are becoming bilingual or who are second-language acquirers are in the process of developing knowledge of two languages. In this sense their language development is different from that of children acquiring one language. There is evidence that children — at least in urban areas — who are acquiring a nonmajority dialect are acquiring two dialects, their own and the majority dialect. Thus, their language development is also different from that of children acquiring one dialect. The questions that arise about the language acquisition process in these instances are:

- □ What is these children's knowledge of the uses of both language one and two (or dialect one and two) during different periods of development?
- □ What is their knowledge of the structures of language one and two (or dialect one and two) during differing periods of development?

Given the observation that there are many different patterns of dialect acquisition, bilingualism, and second-language acquisition, it is clear that there can be no conclusive answers to these two questions. We will, however, discuss some general findings about aspects of language knowledge in bilinguals, second-language acquirers, and dialect speakers.

Knowledge of the Use of Language

Children from different cultures acquire different sets of pragmatic competences. Children from one culture encounter difficulties when they are required to interact with others from another culture. This does not mean that they — like autistic children, for example — have difficulty in acquiring pragmatic competence. The culture's rules for communication begin to be absorbed by the child during infancy and are very well entrenched by the time the child reaches middle childhood and adolescence. This means that children begin very early to develop cultural rules for how to generate speech acts and how to participate in conversation. Given these facts, it is very understandable why children from one culture encounter difficulties in all aspects of communication in schools where another culture's rules for communication interaction are practiced.

There have been many studies of the communication patterns of children who are speakers of one of the dialects of Black English. Many of these studies indicate that there are distinct differences in these patterns and those of children acquiring a mainstream dialect. These differences exist in the topics of discourse and the nature of the discourse (Erwin-Tripp, 1971; Wolfram, 1973). There is also evidence of the particular difficulties that these children may encounter in school settings. For example, Labov (1973) describes the differences in the sheer verbosity, permissible topics, and style of interaction of an inner-city black adolescent in school and in conversation with a friend outside the school setting. This description makes clear the constraints on communication that this child experiences in school. Other researchers have found differences between black and white speakers in the paralinguistic cues of turn-taking behavior (LaFrance & Mayo, 1973). One of these differences involves eye contact during conversation. Black listeners look away from speakers, while white listeners keep their gaze on the speaker. This difference could lead to problems in the classroom. This behavior on the part of the black child can be (and sometimes is) labelled as being sullen or discourteous. The behavior of repeating the final phrase of an utterance (for example, a speaker says, "I'm going to do that," and the listener repeats and says "Yeah! Do that") also can lead to problems in the classroom. Such behavior can (and sometimes is) considered to be speaking out of turn or speaking when silence has been called for.

Although many of the studies referred to above were carried out in the late 1960s and early 1970s, the differences in the pragmatic knowledge of Black-English-speaking children and children who speak a majority dialect have not disappeared. At present, a great deal of attention has been placed on Black-English-speaking children's organization of narrative and how this may affect their interactions in the classroom and their acquisition of literacy (Michaels, 1981; Heath, 1982). In the chapter on pragmatics, the child's organization of information into "scripts" and how these scripts were used to converse on a topic and to recall events were discussed. Script organization also plays an important role in reading. Without such an internalized organization, prediction and inference in reading becomes more difficult because much of the literature the child must read is also organized by such scripts.

Research results indicate that not only black children but also children from Hispanic backgrounds (Iglesias, 1985), some American Indian children (Greenbaum, 1985), and Hawaiian children (Au and Jordan, 1981) confront discourse situations that are foreign to them in the classroom. The so-called "switch-board" form of teacher-child interaction of the majority group (teacher asks questions and children answer) is different from the "talk-story" interaction they are accustomed to. The specific differences in expected style of interaction led children from a Mississippi Choctaw community to use shorter utterances in their interactions and to interrupt the teacher more than did majority children in the school. The Choctaw children tended to gaze at peers while the teacher was talking. This, in turn, led the teachers to take longer turn-take pauses, ask more questions, and use shorter utterances in asking questions when speaking to these children.

Children who are bilingual presumably are bicultural as well. Therefore, they should have no difficulty in communicating with others in either culture or language. Those who are second-language acquirers, however, will have difficulty in acquiring knowledge of the pragmatic rules used by speakers of that second language, and they will encounter some of the same problems as children who use a nonmainstream dialect. Indirect speech acts seem to create particular difficulties. Some studies examined the ability of adult and child second-language acquirers to vary the politeness of their requests as a function of the situation and addressee variables in the second language. It was found that both children and adults had difficulties in this task (Zimin, 1978; Walters, 1978; Rintell, 1980). In both age groups there was a tendency to evaluate these situations in terms of the rules of the native culture and language and to impose these evaluations on the form of the speech act in the second language. Specifically, children and adults used different degrees of deference in communication situations than native English speakers did. Interference occurs not only in the structural aspects of language, but also in the pragmatic aspects.

Differences in direct speech acts and in referential communication have been observed in children who speak American English, Japanese, and British English. In one study, four- and five-year-old children were asked to respond to false statements (Akiyama, 1985). The American-English-speaking children produced semantic denials frequently ("ship is small" when told "ship is large"), whereas Japanese-speaking children produced negatives ("ship is not large"). In another study (Foorman & Kinoshita, 1983), it was found that American-English-, Japanese-, and British-English-speaking five- to seven-year-old children varied in their decoding and encoding accuracy as a function of the adjective-ordering rules of their language and stylistic variables. These data suggest that the pragmatic competence a child can achieve in a second language might be affected by the way in which structural relations are expressed in the first language, as well as by its rules of discourse. These differences might lead to misunderstandings, by teachers and monolingual peers, of the communicative intent and quality of second-language acquirers' communication interactions.

Knowledge of the Structures of the Language

Dialect speakers obviously have knowledge of the structures of their dialect. In addition, speakers of Black English have knowledge, to varying degrees, of the majority dialect. This knowledge appears to be primarily receptive. Some code-switching has been found in speakers in large urban areas. They appear to have a "home" language and a "school" language, which indicates productive use of at least some aspects of the mainstream dialect (Labov, 1966). However, most studies have found primarily receptive ability in the mainstream dialect. This receptive ability is indicated by the repetition performance of these children. They reproduce mainstream dialect sentences in the form of their own dialect (Labov & Cohen, 1967; Baratz, 1969). For example, they repeat sentences such as "My aunt, who lives in Baltimore, came to visit me" as "My aunt, she live in Baltimore, come to visit." Or they repeat the sentence "She was the girl who didn't go to school because she had no clothes to wear" as "That girl she ain go ta school cause she ain got no clothes to wear." Some children simply show increasing knowledge of how to produce the structures of standard English by accurately repeating these structures (Hall & Freedle, 1973). There are developmental changes in these children's knowledge of the other dialect which indicate, not surprisingly, that the amount of time that the child is exposed to the other dialect has an effect on his or her degree of knowledge of that dialect. Interestingly, the Baratz study (1969) found that there was increasing usage of Black English forms such as tense marking ("He be goin") when the children reached ten to eleven years. This finding may indicate an increasing awareness of the dialect differences by adolescents and a purposeful use of the differences to indicate group loyalty and affiliation.

Structural knowledge of the two languages of a bilingual begins as the child is exposed to two languages. Some patterns in the development of these two languages have been observed. A majority of the researchers who have examined language development in a bilingual context suggest that the acquisition process is similar to that of a monolingual child. That is, the child treats the two systems as one and acquires aspects of the two languages simultaneously (Leopold, 1939; Redlinger & Park, 1980; Swain, 1977; Vihman, 1985; Volterra & Taeschner, 1978). Each of the researchers cited has found that language mixing occurs during the early stages of the bilingual child's language development. For example, a child learning Spanish and English might say something like "I want eso" rather than "I want that" because "eso" is easier to say than "that." Such mixing is primarily lexical. Children in the various studies have been found to mix functional words most frequently. Nouns are the most frequently mixed contentive words. After some level of language sophistication is reached, mixing rates decrease (Redlinger & Park, 1980).

It has been observed that children learning Spanish and English show awareness of the phonological differences in the languages that mark lexical differences at about two years (Oller & Eilers, 1983). A child acquiring these two languages marked voicing distinctions in the phonology of the two languages at about age two and a half (Mazeika, 1971). A child acquiring Estonian and English used syntactic structures from both languages initially to express negation; then acquired the appropriate negative form for Estonian, the more dominant language; and then the negative form in English (Vihman, 1985). A somewhat different pattern was observed in children's acquisition of word-order rules in Quechua and Spanish (Lujon, Minaya, & Sankoff, 1984). The children first applied the word-order rules of Quechua (the dominant language) to Spanish, and then acquired the word-order rules of Spanish. Bilingual proficiency was found to be weighted toward English in bilingual children acquiring Spanish and English because there was differential use of Spanish and English in the home (Garcia, 1983). Thus, initially, the language which the child uses most frequently affects all aspects of the less frequently used language.

The data on word and structure mixing, phonological differentiation, and application of dominant language structures on the less dominant language all make sense, given the fact that the exact conditions, both linguistic and nonlinguistic, in the environment probably vary from child to child. It seems to be that all bilingual children mix words initially and mix function words more than contentive words. Awareness of the phonological differences between the languages and an increasing knowledge of all aspects of language leads to differentiation between the two languages at some time between two and three years of age, the beginning of early childhood and a period of dramatic growth in language knowledge and use. However, the two languages of the bilingual are never separate. The adult bilingual and the child in becoming an adult bilingual is ". . . not the sum of two complete or incomplete monolinguals; rather, he or she has a unique and specific linguistic configuration (Grosjean, 1985, p. 5). This unique representation of language knowledge may be the product of how language is organized for storage and retrieval by the bilingual.

Development of structural knowledge of either the first or second language can vary enormously in the second-language acquirer. Despite the possibility of this great variation, it was held at one time that the second-language acquisition process was like the first (Dulay & Burt, 1975). It was suggested that children acquiring a second language would acquire the structures of the language in the same order as first-language acquirers of this language. The data obtained by these researchers and others who held this position indicated that, in a gross sense, the position was correct. That is, for example, second-language acquirers of English, regardless of their native language, acquired knowledge of the English morphemes described by Brown (1973) in approximately the same order as native speakers of English. This led some researchers to assume that, just as in first-language acquisition, exposure alone could lead to acquisition of a second language by, at least, young children. However, more detailed longitudinal studies of second-language acquirers provided evidence of differences, as well as similarities, in their process of acquisition (for example, Hakuta, 1978; Hoh & Hatch, 1978). These differences are due to a number of factors, some of which have already been mentioned. They include age, experience, education, socioeconomic status, learning environment, language background, and personality.

Understanding those factors that lead to differences in second-language acquisition and the use of this second language to learn is of great importance to educators. Saville-Troike (1984) did a retrospective study of nineteen elementary school children — aged six years and eleven months to twelve years — who came from diverse language backgrounds. At the beginning of the school year they had equal proficiency in English, and at the end of the year they reached different levels of achievement in academic subjects taught in English. At the end of the school year the students were given the Comprehensive Test of Basic Skills in English. The test assesses reading, language, social studies, science, and mathematics. The question asked in the study was: What factors account for differences in performance on this test? The variables looked at were proficiency in oral English, home language influence (transfer from native language and out-of-school language and educational experience), and personality and attitudinal factors. The conclusion reached by the experimenter was that there were wide individual differences among the students in those factors that best accounted for achievement. These differences existed even among students who shared the same language and cultural background. The few generalizations included:

1. Vocabulary knowledge in English was the most important aspect of English proficiency for achievement.
2. Emphasis on interpersonal communication may *inhibit* academic achievement in the second language.
3. Knowledge of English morphology does *not* contribute to academic achievement.
4. Most of the children who achieved best in content areas of English had the opportunity to discuss the concepts they were learning in their *native* language.

Thus, hypothesized the researcher, bilingual education provides the best context for academic achievement in English. It is clear from this study that to determine factors that will lead to academic achievement for all students is a difficult task.

Many of the earliest studies of patterns of second-language acquisition focussed on the effect of language 1 on language 2 in terms of the types of interference that might occur. Later studies examined the learning strategies that might be employed (Tarone, Cohen, & Dumas, 1976). Still more recent research has been concerned with the effect of the individual's learning style on learning a second language (Fillmore, 1979) and the effect of the environment

Table 11-1 Some strategies for second-language acquisition and their products.

STRATEGIES	PRODUCTS
Transfer from L1	The book of Jack
Overgeneralize	He is pretty
Memorize	I don't know
Overelaborate	I would not have gone
Avoid	
Topic	
Word or words	
Appeal to authority	How do you say?
Code switch	I want a livre

on learning (Cummins, 1979; Skutnabb-Kangas, 1979). Some of the language-learning strategies and personality effects on acquisition of aspects of language are listed in Table 11-1.

As you can see in Table 11-1, the second-language acquirer's first language can interfere with his or her acquisition of all structural aspects of the second language after some competence in the first language has been achieved. Knowledge of a language can also help the second-language acquirer. This is shown by the second-language development of children who are labelled as coordinate bilinguals, even when they acquire a second language after age five. In fact, there is evidence to suggest that second-language learning is better for adolescent than for younger children (Snow & Hoefnagel-Hohle, 1978). This may be due to the fact that having knowledge of categories and relations in one language can help the acquisition of a second language. Most of the learning strategies listed in Table 11-1 are the same language learning strategies that first-language acquirers use. The pattern of language development used by first- and second-language learners may not be the same, but the learning strategies apparently are. Finally, those factors that are listed as being a product of the learner's personality probably play a role in the style of first-language learning, if not in the end product. It is these types of factors, in combination with each other, plus the environment of learning, which lead to the individual patterns in the acquisition of a second language that have been described (Brown, 1978).

What Is Different in Cognitive Development?

The theory that bilingual children have crowded heads has faded away (Diaz, 1985). The theory that bilingual children are cognitively deprived has received serious blows. In the minds of educators, both theories were related. The notion was that bilingual children would be delayed in language development and, therefore, would be cognitively delayed also. Because of this theoretical position, one could argue that a monolingual environment is best suited for cognitive growth. The research that has been reviewed thus far on bilinguals' language development certainly argues against delay in that development. Some of the studies reviewed in Chapter Two also argue against the cognitive delay theory. And there continues to be evidence disputing a cognitive delay. The situation in the case of second-language acquirers and nonmainstream dialect speakers is much less clear because of a number of factors. Two of the most important of these factors are cultural differences and SES (socioeconomic status). These factors affect performance on standard measures of intelligence and, therefore, on views concerning the relation between second-language acquisition, nonmajority dialect use, and cognitive development.

Bilingualism and Cognitive Development

Studies of the cognitive development of bilinguals compared to monolinguals all have found a cognitive advantage in being bilingual. And all have found that the advantage lies in the ability of bilinguals to metaprocess language, to think about the categories and relations in language. In one study, a group of bilingual Mexican-American four- to six-year-old children was compared to a group of age- and SES-matched peers on a number of metaprocessing tasks (Feldman & Shen, 1971). The bilingual children were found to be significantly better on an object constancy task, on the ability to switch common names of objects, and on the ability to place objects according to the relations expressed (for example, "The cup is in the box").

In another study (Ianco-Worrall, 1972), the ability of Afrikaans-and-English bilingual children and their monolingual (either Afrikaans or English) age peers was compared. Two age groups were included, four- to six- and seven- to nine-year-old children. It was found that the younger bilingual children were able to observe the semantic relation between two of the items in an array such as "cap," "cat," and "hat," whereas the younger monolingual children could only observe the phonological relation between "cap" and "can." Only the older monolingual children could see the semantic relation. The bilingual children also responded significantly more frequently to the question "Could we interchange X (for example "dog") for Y (for example, "cow")?" with "yes." However, they were no better than monolinguals in explaining why a common name was used or in answering questions about properties of objects when their names were changed (for example, "If we call a dog a cow, does this cow have horns or give milk?").

In another study, bilingual Hebrew-English and monolingual English and Hebrew five- to eight-year-old children were compared (Ben-Zeev, 1977). The bilingual children were significantly better in verbal transformations, in symbol substitution ("turtle" for "airplane"), and on the Ravens Matrices. There was no difference in the types of word associations they gave (paradigmatic or syntagmatic), and the bilinguals were worse on a test of English vocabulary than monolingual speakers. In a more recent study (Rosenblum & Pinker, 1983), a comparison was again made of bilingual (Hebrew-English) and monolingual (English) four- to approximately six-year-olds' ability to rename common objects and, also, to explain why one could rename. The children in each group were carefully matched on verbal ability, which may in part account for the results. In this study no differences were found in the renaming ability of the two groups or in the use of these names. However, monolinguals' explanations for renaming were concerned with the properties of objects whereas bilinguals provided social explanations. This difference, state the investigators, indicates that bilinguals have a greater awareness of the pragmatic conditions for particular word use. Overall, despite differences and sometimes contradictions among the findings of these studies, all of them point to cognitive advantages in abstract knowledge of words and use of words. With the exception of the Feldman and Shen study, all the children studied came from middle- and upper-middle-class families and the bilingual and monolingual children in each study came from similar cultural backgrounds.

Factors That Bias the Effect of Bilingualism on Cognitive Development

As pointed out by Cummins (1979), when the cognitive advantages of bilingualism are not found in populations of second-language acquirers (or those who presumably are in the process of becoming coordinate bilinguals), the factors often pointed to are the poor environments of these children and the poor education they have received. Cummins (1978) argues, along with Skutnabb-Kangas (1969), that these children do not show the cognitive advantage of bilingualism because they are, in fact, not truly bilingual. The suggestion is that children must reach some "threshold" level of native language knowledge and other language knowledge before the cognitive benefits of bilingualism can be observed. These researchers argue that instead of the second language adding to the child's language knowledge, this language-acquisition process subtracts from the knowledge already acquired. The instances in which this occurs are usually those in which low-status minority groups of children enter school and are required to acquire academic skills in a second language that is used by the majority.

Much of the research on coordinate bilinguals discussed above points to the ability of these bilinguals to engage in a number of language processing tasks with an accuracy of performance equal to that of compound bilinguals. One reason that has been suggested to account for the approximately equal competence in two languages of the coordinate bilinguals discussed previously, and the lesser competence in two languages by minority children, has been that in the first case the coordinate bilingual's native language is socially prestigious, while in the latter it is not (Lambert, 1975). One could also argue that there are differences in the level of language awareness achieved in the native language by these two groups of children. The minority children may not have had those language experiences which lead to the metaprocessing abilities that are required for further oral language development and written language development.

A final factor that might account for the differences in cognitive development in this group of second-language acquirers and the bilinguals discussed previously may be cultural background differences that place emphasis on different aspects of cognitive functioning. Such differences can place at a disadvantage those whose society has a different set of values for effective performance than that of the school (Cole and Scribneer, 1977). This may be the factor that plays the most important role in the further linguistic and cognitive development of this group of children and children who use a minority dialect. This position, however, is arguable. It has been found in several studies that minority children do better in some contexts than in others. For example, Finnish students fail academically in Sweden but succeed in Australia (Skutnabb-Kangas, 1984). Ogbu (1981) points out that Burkumin students fail in Japan but succeed in the United States. These findings tell us that minority children from different language backgrounds can succeed in some contexts, and, therefore, that their failures in other contexts are not due to differences in cultural aspirations for education but, rather, in the way they are educated.

Much of the early research on the cognitive performance of Black English speakers on standard tests of intelligence and language development were concerned with the validity of those tests in terms of the dialect in which they were written. Early studies attempted to compare the performance of children who were Black English speakers on tests written in that dialect and on standard versions. It was found that performance did not differ on the dialect versions of these tests, and that children who spoke Black English were able to comprehend the mainstream dialect (Quay, 1971; 1972).

A longitudinal study of patterns of cognitive development in white and black children was carried out (Hall & Kaye, 1980). The children were six to nine years old and came from black and white middle- and low-SES families. Several aspects of their cognitive performance were assessed. Their memory span for digits and their free recall of words were tested. They were given the Ravens Matrices and the Peabody Picture Vocabulary Test; they were engaged in learning tasks that involved paired associate learning, matrices training, and transfer; and they were given a matrices proficiency test and reading tests. The investigators state that the assessments were designed to tap memory, intelligence, learning, and transfer. The main finding of the study was that there was a difference in the readiness of the groups. This finding was supported by the fact that the low-income black children were behind the white middle-class children at six years, but progressed at the same rate up until nine years. Importantly, there were very few differences in the memory performance of the groups. Most differences were in the measured intelligence of the groups, and there were inconsistent differences among the groups in learning. These findings indicate that there were no differences between the groups in the capacity to learn, only differences in performance.

These findings concerning the cognitive processing of the four groups of children point to the fact that there are various ways of measuring cognitive behaviors, and that low-income children from a minority group do comparatively well on some measures of this processing and not on others. There have been a number of studies examining the cognitive behaviors of various cultural groups (for example, Dasen, 1980; Cole & Scribner, 1977). These studies indicate that, regardless of experience, some cognitive processes are shared by all groups, and these processes, therefore, develop similarly across groups. However, a larger number of behaviors are based on the particular experiences of a group. Formal education, for example, is a particular experience that very markedly affects cognitive behaviors (Cole & D'Andrade, 1982). It is in those areas in which groups differ in experience that differences between groups in cognitive behaviors are found. Minority children may be academically disadvantaged in two ways, then. Their particular cultural experiences may make them less ready for the culture of the school (Heath, 1983), and, because of this lack of readiness, they may be less able to take advantage of the school experience. This is particularly true of children whose native language, as well as culture, varies from that of the school.

Preschool experiences can vary among minority groups (Steward & Steward, 1973). When the preschool experiences of these low-income minority children are somewhat similar to those of middle-class majority children, they are well able to take advantage of schooling. A study of black low-income preschool siblings of second graders reading on grade level and those reading below grade level indicated that this is the case (Norman-Jackson, 1982). The results of the study were that the MLU was significantly greater and the development of mature language significantly more rapid in the preschool siblings of successful readers, compared to that of the siblings of poor readers. There was a significant difference in the amount of verbal interaction with and verbal stimulation from older siblings in the two groups, although there was no difference between the groups in measured intelligence, verbal interaction with parents, or parent-encouraged, child-initiated interaction. Five years later the school performance of the two groups was assessed. The children who had had successful readers as older siblings were successful readers; those with unsuccessful readers as siblings were also unsuccessful readers. One parental input factor that made a difference was that preschool children who later turned out to be unsuccessful readers had parents who discouraged child-initiated interaction significantly more frequently. Such results indicate that preschool communication interaction experience, regardless of its source, can have a positive effect on later acquisition of written language.

Assessment and Educational Implications

Assessment Procedures

Throughout this chapter there have been comments about assessments used to determine the linguistic and cognitive functioning of bilingual children, second-language acquirers, and nonmainstream dialect users. These assessment procedures have been used with these — and all — children for a number of reasons other than determining their linguistic and cognitive status. They have been used to determine the "normalcy" of these children, to recommend various educational and clinical interventions, and to assess the effect of these interventions. A very real question arose about the "fairness" of current frequently used tests to determine their cognitive functioning. These same questions arose about their linguistic functioning. Both sets of tests are based on norms for white middle-class mainstream children. Despite questions about "fairness," these tests continued to be used.

Various suggestions have been made about appropriate procedures for the assessment of the speech and language functioning of minority children. In a review article (Evard & Sabers, 1979), some procedures for developing tests, revising tests, and using standard tests with different ethnic-racial groups to assess their speech and language were discussed. One way the reviewers suggest to avoid the biases of standard tests is to develop tests that are based on a community's language and cultural norms. Some examples of such tests are the Austin Spanish Articulation Test (Learning Concepts, 1974) and the Developmental Assessment of Spanish Grammar (Toronto, 1976). Another method is to revise a standard test. The reviewers point to the method used by Balban (1975). In this instance a standard test (The North Western Syntax Screening Test) was modified for black children by replacing the pictures to represent black culture and by having a speaker of Black English record the sentences used. The third way to avoid bias is to develop local norms for tests so that such tests can be used with children in the community.

Procedures for assessing the linguistic and cognitive functioning of these children in natural situations has also been recommended by a number of researchers (for example, Labov, 1970; Nerlove, Roberts, Klein, Yarbrough, & Habicht, 1974). Assessment in a test situation, it is argued, does not provide the information needed to predict development. A counterargument is that tests are needed to predict success in school. Some interesting findings about the language status of a group of bilingual children recommended for assessment for special needs by their classroom teachers and their subsequent development highlights some of the benefits of testing in natural situations (Damico, Oller, & Storey, 1983). Analysis of a language sample obtained from these children indicated that traditional measures of language "normalcy," such as morphology and syntax — aspects that are usually measured on standard tests — did not successfully predict the children's performance on an achievement test seven months later nor teachers' ratings of the children's language development and socialization at that time. The degree of the children's pragmatic difficulties, as determined by nonfluencies, revisions, delays, lack of specificity of referential terms, abrupt topic shifts, inappropriate responses, and need for multiple repetition of prompts, was a much better predictor of later achievement, language development, and socialization. One could argue that the so-called pragmatic problems of the children also indicate lexical and semantax difficulties. However, one cannot argue against the fact that in this study a sample of natural language functioning provided more useful information about a child's subsequent development than did the structural features of their language, features usually measured on tests. Information obtained from naturalistic observations also provides very important information for intervention (Ripich & Spinelli, 1985). These data indicate the very real limitations of standard test results as a basis for determining particular educational and clinical interventions.

Educational Implications

The results of the many studies that have indicated cognitive advantage in bilingual children have led to educational and parental acceptance of what has been termed "total immersion programs." These programs provide early education (kindergarten and first grade) entirely in a second language. One of the most successful of these programs is one that began in 1965 in Montreal, Canada (Tucker, 1975). Children in this program are native speakers of English and are acquiring French as a second language. The children are immersed in French in kindergarten. In first grade they are taught reading, writing, and mathematics in French. In grade two they are exposed to English language arts as one course; the rest of the curriculum is in French. Gradually English is introduced into the curriculum so that by grade eight the curriculum is approximately 70 percent English and the balance is in French. Continuous monitoring of these children's knowledge of the two languages and their academic performance in the two languages indicates that they achieve much greater knowledge of the second language than do students exposed to traditional programs of second-language teaching. They also do as well as their monolingual age and ability level peers in academic performance in the two languages.

The results of this educational experiment indicate that children who are using a status language and who are then exposed to a second language on entering school can do very well under conditions of total immersion. In fact, they appear to do well when they are exposed to more than one other language (Genesee & Lambert, 1983). These children need not be from middle-class homes. A recent review of the results of several immersion programs throughout the country indicate, on the whole, that children in these programs are doing well, at least in the early grades (Genesee, 1985). These students are acquiring Spanish, French, or English as a second language, and assessments indicate that they are doing well in academic performance in their own and the second language. However, the situation appears to be very different for many minority group children. Total immersion (or regular education) programs seem to result in the academic failure of minority group children discussed previously. Such programs also appear to result in the very high dropout rate among language minority youth (Steinberg, Blinde, & Chan, 1984). For these children, bilingual education programs of various kinds have been recommended.

There are a number of different types of bilingual programs now in existence in the United States. There are "transition" bilingual programs that present early education (reading, writing, and math) in the native language of the child and continue such instruction until the child can function well academically using the English language. There are special alternative programs that provide the child with special instruction in English until the child is able to function well in the classroom using English. This instruction may or may not be given in the child's native language. Such a program is, obviously, quite different in content and philosophy from transition programs. Some programs provide early education in two languages to children who are minority- and majority-language speakers. Some of the successful immersion programs in this country are of this kind.

The effectiveness of various bilingual programs has been a matter of some controversy. Results of some assessments that have been carried out have indicated that transitional programs do not result in minority language students performing as well as majority language students in English or in other academic areas (Baker & deKanter, 1981). There has been a great deal of criticism concerning evaluations of the effectiveness of bilingual programs. The difficulty of equating subjects and programs on a number of variables in these evaluations make the results of such evaluations questionable (Willig, 1982). The social variables that play a role in successful second-language acquisition by minority students is a factor not often considered in program evaluations (Cummins, 1985), and such variables, as discussed previously, can play an all-important role in such acquisition. Recent research on minority language children's acquisition of competence in their own language and English indicate the importance of using the child's native language and of teacher sensitivity to cultural variables in the design of classroom activities (Hakuta, 1986; Wong-Fillmore, Ammon, McLaughlin, & Ammon, 1985).

Cummins (1986) has summarized those factors that can lead to the academic success, in English, of children from different cultural and language backgrounds. These are:

1. The incorporation of minority students' language and culture into the school program.
2. Community — in particular, parent — participation in children's education.
3. Curricula designed to engage children as active learners of the language.
4. Advocacy for these children on the part of those who assess them.

As discussed previously, there appear to be wide individual differences in those factors that can lead to the academic success of individual children from different language and cultural backgrounds. Cummins's summary suggests that there may be universals in educational policy that can, in general, lead to academic success by minority children.

Sensitivity in terms of the design of classroom activities also plays a very important role in the education of children who speak a nonmainstream dialect. Some of the problems may arise because of cultural differences in the communication interaction of these children and of the school in which they find themselves. There are differences in their attitudes toward school that may be a product of their experiences in school and, in this way, also affect school performance. The attitude of teachers toward children with a minority dialect and/or minority language can also have a marked effect on their school performance. One study carried out in the early 1970s points to the very marked effect that teacher attitude, as reflected in teaching strategies, can have on a very important academic accomplishment, learning to read (Piestrup, 1973). In this study, the reading instruction in fourteen predominantly black classrooms was tape recorded. Potential dialect conflicts were excerpted from these recordings and six teaching styles defined. These were labelled the Vocabulary Approach, Decoding Approach, Standard Pronunciation Approach, White Liberal Approach, Black Artful Approach, and the Interrupting Approach. The children were also given a sentence repetition task to measure their dialect use, and reading test scores were obtained from school records. The results of the study are indicated in Figure 11-3. In the figure the mean reading and dialect scores for the children in each type of teaching group are shown.

As shown in Figure 11-3, the children in the Black Artful group did best, and the children in the Interrupting group did worst. There was no relation between dialect use and reading scores for any of the children. The finding of no relation between dialect use and reading was found in another study (Labov & Cohen, 1967). Reading and dialect scores, as shown in the figure, differed for the children in the six different teaching style groups. The differences between the groups appeared to lie in two dimensions of the teachers' styles: the involvement of the children directly in the reading task, and the mutuality of the communication by teachers and children. The contrast of the styles of the teachers in the groups that did best and worst make clear the differences between the groups in the two dimensions.

Teachers in the Black Artful group engaged the children in rhyming, encouraged them to participate by listening to their responses, attended to vocabulary differences, and taught the children to listen for standard English sound distinctions. These children learned to read with enthusiasm. Teachers in the Interrupting group had children repeat words spoken in the dialect many times, interpreted dialect pronunciations as reading errors, and presented standard English sounds for discrimination without ensuring accuracy of response. These children worked at decoding without appearing to understand what was read, some withdrew and spoke softly and seldom, and still others engaged in verbal play apart from the teacher. In summary, those teachers who expected the children to learn to read and engaged them in doing so had children who learned to read. Those teachers who believed that getting these children to produce and discriminate sounds according to the standard dialect was not

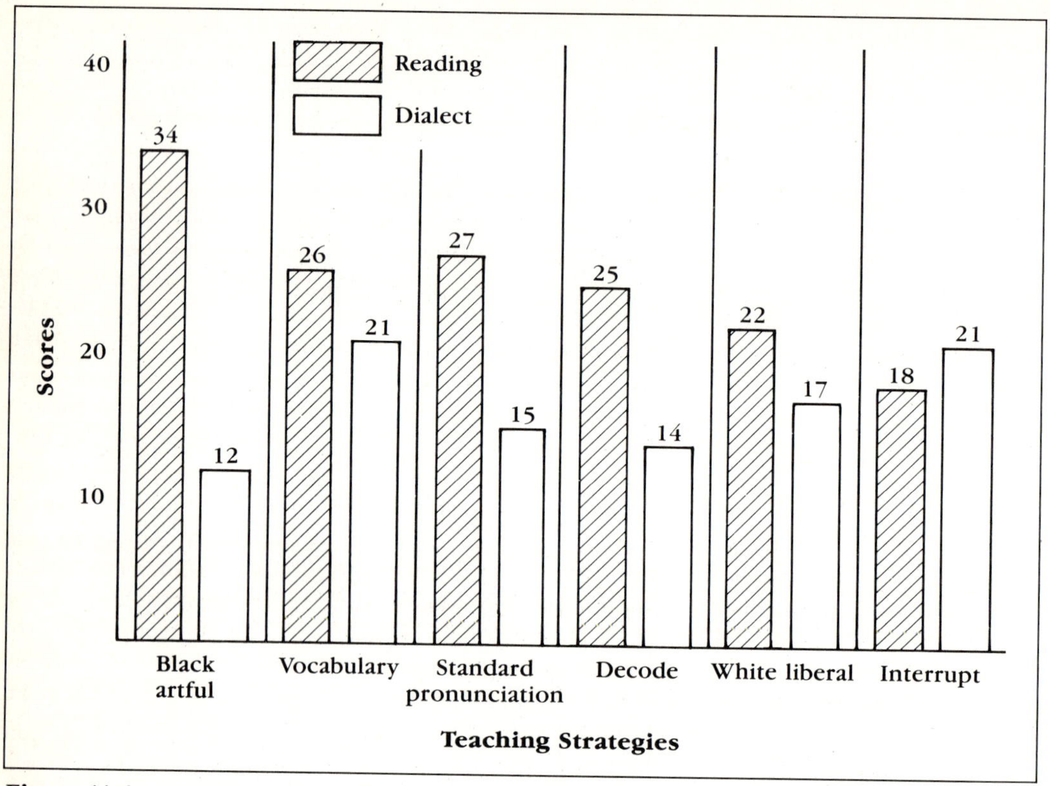

Figure 11-3 Mean reading and dialect scores of black children exposed to different teaching strategies.

only necessary but had to be done by repetition before they got at the task of learning to read, had children who did not learn to read. The results of research on educational approaches to teaching minority-dialect and minority-language children all indicate that the attitude of teachers, as exemplified by their teaching styles and strategies, has a very profound effect on what children learn.

Chapter Twelve
Language and Learning

The previous chapters in this book were concerned with why and how children acquire language, what they acquire and use to communicate with other members of their community, and some of the remarkable differences that exist in patterns of language development due to internal and external factors. This chapter is concerned with a different issue — how language is used to learn.

The role of language in learning has been viewed by varying theorists in differing ways. These views appear to be quite similar to those held by these theorists about learning in general. To those who are mediationists (elaborated S-R-R theorists), language plays an important role in learning as a mediator or labeller to help in recall. To cognitivists, language is just *one* of a group of means to represent and to internally manipulate experience. To Vygotskyites, language plays a primary role in learning because a culture's experience is conveyed to the child through language, and the child then uses language to modify this experience. There is one area of learning that all theorists would agree is based on language: the acquisition and development of reading and writing, or written language knowledge. However, many would suggest that reading and writing are not simply based on listening and speaking, but, rather, that the processes of reading and writing are based on particular uses of oral language knowledge, that is, metaprocessing.

In the first section of this chapter, we will look at theory and research concerning the role of language in learning about the world and about how one is expected to function in it. Three questions are addressed:

- Is language necessary for learning?
- In what specific ways does language play a role in learning?
- What are the educational implications of results of research on the role of language in learning?

The second section of the chapter will examine language development in the written mode. The questions to be addressed in that section are:

- What models are there presently to explain the relation between oral and written language development?
- How do the relations between the oral and written modes change developmentally?
- What written language problems may arise because of the relation between oral and written language development?

This section will end with a discussion of the educational implications of findings concerning the relation of oral and written language development.

The Role of Language in Learning

The question of whether or not language is necessary for learning seems to be best answered by "It depends." Some learning tasks require language, whereas others do not. It also appears to be the case that language is used in particular learning tasks only after some level of maturation has been achieved. Further, formal schooling appears to play a role in whether or not language will be used in some learning tasks. These facts make it impossible to provide a yes or no answer to the question. Those learning situations in which language is particularly required are those that involve recall and problem solving. Those learning situations in which language is not particularly required are those that involve recognition or motor performance. These latter behaviors are, presumably, dependent on imaginal representations of visual, auditory, and motor experiences. Another important role played by language is in controlling behavior, an aspect of social learning. The most important role of language in learning appears to be the opportunities to learn provided by communication interaction between the learner and the environment. These particular roles of language in learning have been examined in a number of studies.

Recall

The role of language in varying recall tasks has been observed in a large number of studies, and the results of these studies have been reported in a number of texts (for example, Carroll, 1986; Loftus & Loftus, 1976). These recall tasks range over the domains of (1) word or picture, (2) sequences of words or pictures/events, and (3) an episode or story. Language is said to play a role in the recall of language categories and relations and nonlanguage categories and relations — the role of providing meaningful labels for categories and events, which are then very useful in cuing recall. Language is used to encode information and is a pointer to the information needed to retrieve such categories and events. Figure 12-1 indicates the levels or units of processing for which language or nonlanguage representations are used to both encode and retrieve information.

Internal use of language →	Guide attention Recall items and events Plan and guide action Solve problems Control action Be creative Metaprocess
Communication interaction →	Knowledge of physical world Knowledge of social world Knowledge of pragmatic rules

Figure 12-1 Effects of internal use of language and communication interaction on specific aspects of learning.

It has been found that children do not begin to use language to recall until they reach a certain level of development. For example, it was found that vocal rehearsal of the names of pictures in an array interfered with the recall of these pictures by four- to six-year-olds, but enhanced the recall of seven-year-olds and adults (Conrad, 1972). The results of a study of sentence recall by five-year-old children and by adults indicated that children of five years recall sentences in terms of their imaginal representations, whereas adults do so in terms of their semantic (conceptual) representations (Kosslyn & Bower, 1974). Children judge that they have heard a sentence before because it is imaginally similar to one heard previously, although it is conceptually different. For example, when given the sentence "The big white sack looked exactly like a pillow," in the study trials and the sentence "The big white sack was really a pillow" in the test trial, 70 percent of the children judged that they had heard the sentence before, whereas only 15 percent of the adults did so.

There is evidence that semantic integration of pictures and sentences takes place after the child is eight years of age (Pezdek, 1980). There is an increase in the effect of verbal information on the recall of depicted events as the age (six, eight, and ten years) of subjects increases. There is evidence, as indicated in Chapter Six, that preschool children use internalized "scripts" to help them in conversation and in the *recall* of sequences of events (Nelson & Gruendel, 1979). It was hypothesized that these events may be coded either linguistically as scripts and stories or imaginally as a sequence of events. The data obtained in the studies discussed above suggest that in the preschool years such scripts are represented as a sequence of events and are only represented linguistically over the end of the early childhood years.

The results of studies of children's use of language in recall indicate that it is not until the middle childhood years that children use language to recall words and pictures and to recall sentences, but that language representations might be used to recall episodes and stories at a younger age. This difference in the age at which language is used to recall is probably due to the differences in the types of tasks. In episode and story recall, the child is calling upon stored representations of events. In word and picture and sentence recall, the child is in the process of learning how to apply memory strategies for the recall of unfamiliar items or events. This process begins as the child enters school and probably develops due to the experiences the child encounters in school (Cole & Scribner, 1977). Thus, education plays an important role in learning to use language to help in recall under certain circumstances.

Problem Solving and Controlling Behavior

Verbal labels have been found to be useful in drawing attention to the significant parameters of objects and events as well as in remembering them (White, 1970). Types of verbal instructions to the child can affect the recognition of the details of objects (Stein & Feldman, 1977). This result indicates that children can be led to attend or not attend to certain parameters by the language used in giving them instructions or in the instructions they give themselves. As discussed in Chapter Three, Vygotsky found that verbalization before and during the execution of a task helped the child to carry out the task (Vygotsky, 1962). A number of other researchers have also found this to be the case. In a study of the jigsaw-puzzle-solving behavior of preschoolers, it was found that children who used speech to guide their behavior made more puzzle-solving moves and completed the puzzle in a shorter period of time (Goodman, 1981). In a longitudinal study of the contexts in which early words are used, it was found that words such as "gone," "down," "in," "on," "there," "no," and "more" were initially used to encode the aim of an action (Gopnik, 1982). The experimenter concluded that language was being used to encode concepts that were being acquired. Another experimenter found that verbalization helped three-, four-, and five-year-olds to comply with commands by facilitating memory of the anticipated goals of action (Meacham, 1978). Finally, it has been found that verbalization is useful in delaying action or controlling impulsivity (Wozniak, 1972). These studies indicate that language is useful in planning, guiding, and remembering the goals of action or what the solution of the problem should be. It is also useful in the development of socially acceptable behavior. Impulsive behavior can be controlled by inner speech.

As discussed in Chapter Three, Piaget held that language was a product of logical thinking and, therefore, that language could play no role in the development of logical thinking. However, some studies have found that verbalization and verbal training help children on Piagetian tasks. One study found that when three- and four-year-old children were asked to identify another's view, verbally or by picture selection, verbalization led to substantially more correct responses (Ives, 1980). The experimenter concluded that linguistic processes were accessible for problem solving at an early age. Other researchers have found that when first- and second-grade children use general self-instruction, they do better than controls on the Matching Familiar Figures Test and in generalization to perspective taking (Schleser, Meyers, & Cohen, 1981). The results of yet another study indicated that frequent use of the verbal rule helped nonconservors to learn to conserve in some domains (Field, 1977). These data indicate that verbal guidance can be helpful in learning some logical operations.

Communication Interaction

All the above studies indicate that language is helpful or useful in performing certain cognitive activities that may be similar to those carried out in school. Language is crucial to still other cognitive and social activities. For example, it is through asking questions and receiving answers, in both the home and in the school, that the child acquires further knowledge of the physical structures and social organizations in the child's own society, in other societies, and about structures and organizations that existed in the past and those that might exist in the future. Testing of hypotheses about the physical and social world may take place by making statements about that world and getting responses to these statements. Sometimes this knowledge is acquired simply through demonstration (the action of others) or by one's own actions. However, very frequently in our society, it is acquired through communication interaction between the child and others, both children and adults, in the community (Ochs & Schieffelin, 1984). In a society such as ours, the school plays a vital role in acquisition of such knowledge.

In the discussion in Chapter Five of the effect of input on language development, both the role of caregiver and teacher input were discussed. The outstanding finding of research examining the effect of input was that the acknowledgements of vocal and nonvocal behaviors by caregivers and the opportunities given by them to take a turn were the two factors that were significantly related to language measures at age three (Liebergott, Schultz, & Menyuk, 1985). It was stated that input must play a crucial role in the child's acquisition of pragmatic rules, since societies differ from each other most markedly in these types of linguistic rules. It was also pointed out that the consensus of opinion was that teacher input could not and should not take the form of caregiver input. There were important additional language activities that should take place in school. Nevertheless, it was stressed that these activities should provide the child with the opportunity to learn more about language by participating in communication interaction with the teacher and classmates. These same principles have been found to apply in the acquisition of knowledge of the physical and social world, as well as in learning to read.

Heath (1985) discusses three types of teaching situations. The first is one in which the teacher as expert verbalizes task norms to the learner. The second is one in which the teacher as expert gives verbal directions. The third is one in which the teacher as expert works alongside the learner in an on-going stream of activity. In each of these situations certain types of communication interaction take place. In the first two, it is typical for the teacher to be the primary communicator. In the last one, there is much more interaction and a greater variety of types of communication, both of which provide the child with a greater variety of models as well as opportunities for interaction. The details of one experimental school program make clear the role that a number of researchers suggest the school can take in fostering this communication interaction and what effect such interaction may have on the development of reading.

The program that is discussed was designed to teach learning-disabled children to read (Cole & Hall, 1982). On average the children in the program were reading about two years below grade level. The program's curriculum was, in fact, composed of three curricula, each developed to teach reading comprehension. The labels given for the three are: (1) internalized problem solving, (2) guided anticipation of meaning, and (3) reciprocal teaching. Although the first two labels suggest that only the individual learner is actively engaged in the task of learning to read, all the curricula in the program emphasized an interactive learning framework.

Table 12-1 Features of the reciprocal teaching model.

1. Emphasis on meaning of text versus decoding.
2. Children read silently.
3. Focus on general strategies for approaching text.
4. Teacher models text interpretations.
5. Children have both question and answer practice.
6. Children have individual discrete turns.
7. Paragraph-sized segments introduced at once.
8. Teacher and expected student behavior guided by model of reading process.

A common theoretical assumption was shared by the three curricula: Learning takes place as the accomplishment of a task in a social situation in which communication interaction takes place. In order to learn how to comprehend text, there should be specially organized text material *and* special organizing teacher strategies. These special organizing teacher strategies, both planned and unplanned, had as a goal that students would take on tasks as their own and thereby participate in learning. In these situations, teachers shifted from being experts to being guides, from being guides to being coaches, and from being coaches to being learners along with the children. Use of microcomputers by the children probably enhanced their positive feelings of mastery of the learning situation. Although there were no remarkable changes in performance, posttests on those children available for testing indicated that, on the whole, their grades on report cards were better and they did better on standard tests of decoding and comprehension.

Some of the details of one of the curricula, reciprocal teaching, is listed in Table 12-1. This curriculum was selected for further discussion because its features put particular emphasis on the importance of communication interaction among the teacher and learners (as can be seen in feature 5). In the other two curricula, children simply answered questions, but did not ask them. Three features seem particularly important in the outline of the curriculum. The first is that reading should have a function; the second, that there are strategies that can be learned about ways in which to approach text; and the third, that the learner must be an active participant in learning.

Summary and Educational Implications

The role of language in learning is evident in both specific cognitive tasks and in general learning. Much of the emphasis in past research has been on the role of language in specific tasks. In these tasks verbal labels are useful in allowing learners to attend to the cues that differentiate objects and events. Such labels also help the learner to remember objects and events. Internalized scripts, schemas, and story grammars help in the recall of sequences of events and passages. Verbal self-instruction helps in the solution of a number of types of problems — in planning a sequence of action, for example, and in keeping in mind the goals of a sequence of actions. Talking aloud also helps in thinking about physical and social problems. Finally, self-instruction is used in controlling actions and thereby helps in situations where impulsivity may lead to academic or social failure.

Of much greater interest in recent research than these findings is the role of language in communication interaction that is consciously or unconsciously designed to teach the child about his or her physical and social world. In the past, research was conducted on the role of questioning in the child's acquisition of further knowledge about his or her world. The development and use of questions that allowed the child to learn more about categories of objects (what and who), actions (what doing and where), and both social and physical explanations (why and how) were the focus of this research (for example, Blank, 1975; Greenfield & Smith, 1976). More recently, there has been a great deal of research on the role of communication interaction between the child and other members of the community in teaching the child language and in the socialization of the child; that is, in teaching the child what roles he or she is expected to play in that society. There has also been a great deal of research on the particular role of the communication interaction that the child engages in in school with teachers and classmates on a child's ability to control the learning situation and to learn independently.

Two factors have been emphasized in this latter research. The first is congruence or incongruence between the child's communication interaction in the home and in the school. In the previous chapter, it was pointed out that teacher attitude toward children from different cultural and linguistic backgrounds can have either a positive or negative effect on the child's learning. The results of research cited in this chapter indicate the importance of an interactive framework in children's learning. This research emphasizes the importance of communication interaction between teacher and student. Therefore, in addition to teachers having positive attitudes about the learning abilities of culturally and linguistically different children, they must also be able to communicatively interact with these children. Otherwise the acquisition of further language, physical world, and social world knowledge might be impaired. The effects of language on learning in specific tasks and of communication interaction on learning in general are summarized in Table 12-2.

Table 12-2 Units of processing for which linguistic and nonlinguistic representations are used.

LANGUAGE UNITS	NONLANGUAGE UNITS
Word	Picture (of object or event)
Sentence	Relation among objects and events
Connected discourse (story, text)	Sequence of relations among objects and events (episodes)

This summary indicates that both use of language by the learner and communication interaction between the learner and others play an important role in learning. Language also — and very importantly — allows the learner to be imaginative and creative. Other representational codes that allow this creativity are mathematical, visual, and musical systems. Use of all these systems allows the user to generate objects and events that are totally unique. Use of these systems in imaginative and creative ways can add to the current body of knowledge about the physical and social world. Finally, language allows us to think and talk about language, cognition, and memory. These have been termed *metabilities* and involve awareness of the categories and relations in language and their use, awareness of the parameters of cognitive tasks and of strategies for use in these tasks, and awareness of the parameters of memory tasks and of strategies for remembering. Language is the vehicle of conscious awareness.

Since language plays these roles in learning, the problems of children with language disorders should extend beyond those they have with language. That is, children with language disorders should have difficulties in recall, planning and guiding action, controlling action, problem solution, creativity, and metaprocessing. Clearly, children who are severely mentally retarded and autistic children who are retarded do have problems in all areas, and they cannot take advantage of communication interaction. However, what the nature of their problem is — linguistic or cognitive — is unclear, given their general retardation. Many learning-disabled children and all children labelled as having a specific language impairment (SLI) are said to have normal intelligence, although there is a discrepancy between their verbal and nonverbal intelligence quotients (I.Q.s). In fact, the description for these diagnostic categories includes normal intelligence. Despite the normal measured intelligence of these children, striking differences between them and children without such disorders, in all areas in which language plays an important role, have been observed.

There is also evidence of poor classroom performance by SLI and learning-disabled children and the assumption has been that their poor performance is due to their inability to accurately and adequately process information in the classroom. The implication of this is that teaching them language and language use should have a profound effect on their learning as well as their language knowledge per se. Unfortunately, the impact of language intervention on learning in other areas has not, as a general rule, been carefully monitored. There are statements to the effect that when children have a better language system for *communication,* they advance both cognitively and socially. Some studies indicate that this might be the case (Ripich & Spinelli, 1985). This is an important issue, and future research may provide more direct answers to the question.

With children from different cultural and linguistic backgrounds, the problem is not lack of language knowledge. The problem these children have may lie in their lack of opportunity to *use* language for learning. Using language to remember unfamiliar items and events may be a product of education. It also may be a product of a particular society's favored method of processing information. Other means for remembering, planning, and problem solution do exist. Children from other cultures might not have the practice with the use of language to learn that children from the majority culture have. They, therefore, are less prepared to take on classroom tasks that require this use of language. The problem, however, may lie in the assumption rather than the fact that they do not use language to learn. In an observational study of Pueblo children, John-Steiner (1984) found that these children learned by verbal explanation as well as by demonstration, contrary to the opinion that these children learn only by demonstration.

Whether or not minority children use language to learn, it is clear that these children do not have to fill in gaps in their knowledge of their native language. Rather, they have to be given opportunities to use language to learn. The evidence, cited in the previous chapter, seems to indicate that positive results (particularly in learning to read) can be obtained when these children are taught to use their language knowledge. More evidence needs to be obtained about learning in other areas. Both groups of children, the specifically language impaired and the language-different, have a particular need to learn to metaprocess language.

Language Knowledge in Reading and Writing

The experiences children have with print in communication interactions provide them with knowledge about the possible relations between meaning and print. More fundamental to comprehending text, however, is the child's knowledge of the structures and uses of oral language. One may learn to read a second language without thorough oral language knowledge of that second language, but without oral language knowledge of any language, that would be impossible. Tarzan's acquisition of reading without any language is, of course, a piece of fiction (Burroughs, 1912). Producing written language, or writing, is also dependent on oral language knowledge. Recent research suggests that learning to read and write begins long before the child enters school.

Emergent Literacy

In the introductory chapter to their book *Emergent Literacy,* Teale and Sulzby (1986) summarize the history of thinking about the nature and the conditions for becoming literate. It is currently (and logically) held that literacy emerges from infancy on in our society. The very earliest stage of reading that is usually referred to in studies on the early acquisition of reading (for example, Durkin, 1966; Soderbergh, 1971) is *print awareness.* This awareness develops when children are exposed to print in familiar situations. The very important role of caregivers engaging their children in reading has been pointed to as the primary factor in the development of print awareness. Exposure to print and the routines of being read to lead the child to pointing to print and asking what it "says." In addition to making children aware of print, being read to helps the child to begin to develop knowledge of the structure of text. Thus, becoming literate begins long before the child is taught to read in school. Some studies that were referred to earlier have stressed the importance of the role of literacy experiences in the home on the development of written language knowledge (Heath, 1982; Michaels, 1981).

In addition to the importance of print awareness in becoming literate, writing during the preschool years also plays an important role. A number of researchers have pointed out that reading and writing can occur concurrently, and that writing and reading influence each other (Ferreiro & Teberosky, 1982). Perhaps they may influence each other in the way that speaking and comprehending can influence each other. Further, being able to read one's own writing can certainly influence both reading and writing (Sulzby, 1985). The motivational importance of reading one's own writing is clear and, in addition, such experiences provide the child with the very important notion of the *function* of literacy.

The term "literate," although often used, has different meanings for different users. The dictionary meaning for literate is (1) "educated, especially being able to read and write," and (2) "having or showing extensive knowledge, experience, or culture." The two definitions are related in that it has been the case, at least in the last century, that having extensive knowledge and culture is dependent on reading. Having such knowledge and culture is also dependent on oral language knowledge. However, these definitions of literacy do not point to the symbiotic relations between oral and written language knowledge.

Recent research indicates that literacy begins by the preschool child's engagement with print for important functions, such as being read to or reading one's own writing. It is argued here that a prerequisite to these early experiences leading to emergent literacy is knowledge of oral language. Communication interaction in the home that leads to oral language knowledge and use as well as literacy experiences play an important role in the child becoming a successful reader in school (Norman-Jackson, 1982). Long before the child enters school, he or she engages in native language communication. As we have seen, native language communication interaction literally begins in the cradle. At the end of the first year, the infant's vocalizations have become recognizable words, and infant and caregiver begin to engage in exchanges of information. At about one and a half to two years, infants are engaged in testing their knowledge of the world via language as well as interacting communicatively. Baby says "Wuzzat?" or "Wuzzat chu?" ("What's that — shoe?") not only to take part in conversation but also to get information about language (What is that thing called?) and to test recognition (Is that a shoe?). These experiences in language exploration are important in developing cognitive strategies for print processing in reading and writing.

Long before the child begins to read, then, one of the primary vehicles for conveying information about the world and about how to behave in the world is language. Our discriminations and perceptions of the physical and social world are tested and corroborated through language. In addition to the early "wuzzat," another example of the use of language to find out about the world is the two-and-a-half- to three-year-old's "whying" endlessly. This first begins to keep the conversation going ("That's a giraffe." "Why?" "Because that's its name." "Why?" "Because that's what we call that animal." "Why?" and on and on and on). Shortly thereafter, this conversational "why" becomes the genuine "why" of seeking information.

As stated, information about and testing knowledge of the world is primarily conveyed through oral language long before the child begins to read. In societies that are labelled nonliterate, this verbal language vehicle continues to be the primary one for conveying the customs, history, and mythology of the culture. Therefore, one can be literate in one sense of the word — that is, have extensive knowledge of at least one's own culture — without reading. However, knowledge of that world is highly dependent on oral language interaction. Knowledge of other people's worlds is dependent, in addition, on the ability to read. Although knowledge can by conveyed by pictures, as in television or graphic arts or through sound alone via radio, it is only when the information is conveyed through written language that there is the opportunity to reflect on it. In turn, being able to reflect allows us to organize and store information in more efficient ways that, in turn, enable us to retrieve the information and apply it appropriately. Information conveyed by person, radio, or television disappears too quickly for deep reflection.

In summary, knowledge of the world and knowledge of the uses of language is conveyed by communication interactions among children and caregivers during the first year of life. Such interactions are a necessary prerequisite to understanding the discourse conveyed in written language. Even though the child may learn to read and understand the words and sentences in a written text, it would be very difficult for the child to understand the content of a written text if it dealt with topics and relations that are foreign to the child.

Reading Beyond Print Awareness

The first definition of being literate is being able to read and write. The cognitive process of learning to read has been theorized about and researched for many centuries. Despite the amount of time devoted to this one (in our society, very important) ability, there is still a great deal of controversy about the nature of the process and about how the process should be taught. Chall (1967; 1983) has summarized current thinking on the way in which reading should be taught once the child enters school and on the unfolding of the process over a number of years, from reading in the first grade to college text reading. The developmental view that reading abilities mature over a long period of time and that there are dramatic changes in skills is an important one for researchers and teachers to be aware of. Much of the theorizing about the process has been based on either highly skilled readers or beginning ones.

It is in learning to read that native language structural knowledge plays a crucial role. A large number of researchers have suggested that the task of learning to read requires, at least initially, translations of written symbols into oral language categories and relations. This process, in turn, requires bringing to conscious awareness oral language categories and relations. Thus, oral language awareness during the beginning stages of word decoding and of reading for meaning are said to be required. The bases for this position lie in the results of several studies that have examined the awareness of language categories by good and poor readers.

Studies of the reading development of children who turn out to be good readers suggest that, even very early, only a few examples of a word are needed to establish what is called an "orthographic address" (Reitsma, 1983). Once this address is established, the child can directly access the whole word, phonologically and semantically. The strategy used to establish addresses for words has been described by some researchers as *integrative*. That is, parts of a word (perhaps the first and last sounds) may be decoded to get at the pronunciation of the word and, from that, its meaning (Bertelson, 1986). Thus, both whole words and parts of words are used to get at pronunciation and meaning. Such strategies require awareness of the relation between orthographic and phonological units of various sizes (Barron, 1986). Studies of poor readers have indicated that they are unaware of the phonological segments in words (Shankweiler & Liberman, 1972). Studies on the sentence and passage level indicate that poor readers, both adults and children, are unaware of some semantax relations in these contexts (Flood & Menyuk, 1983; Menyuk, 1981; 1983; 1985). Further support for this position comes from studies that have found that children who come to school knowing how to read can metaprocess language at a much more sophisticated level than nonreaders (Salus, 1982). Studies have also found that kindergarten children who are significantly worse than their age peers in metaprocessing turn out to be disabled readers at the end of first grade (Oppenheim, 1981).

As the child becomes a more sophisticated reader, translation of text into oral language categories becomes an automatic process. Figure 12-2 represents the steps in the process, from perception of text to comprehension of meaning. Two arrows depict the translation process: the first is solid, to indicate that at time 1 translation is required; the second is broken, to indicate that at time 2 translation is not required. At this point, recognition is automatic (LaBerge & Samuels, 1974). However, automaticity of recognition of text takes place only for text that contains words and structures that are familiar to the reader. The young reader will automatically recognize simple text but have difficulty with more complex text. With more complex text, translation or conscious awareness is required.

The process of going from translation to automatic recognition probably

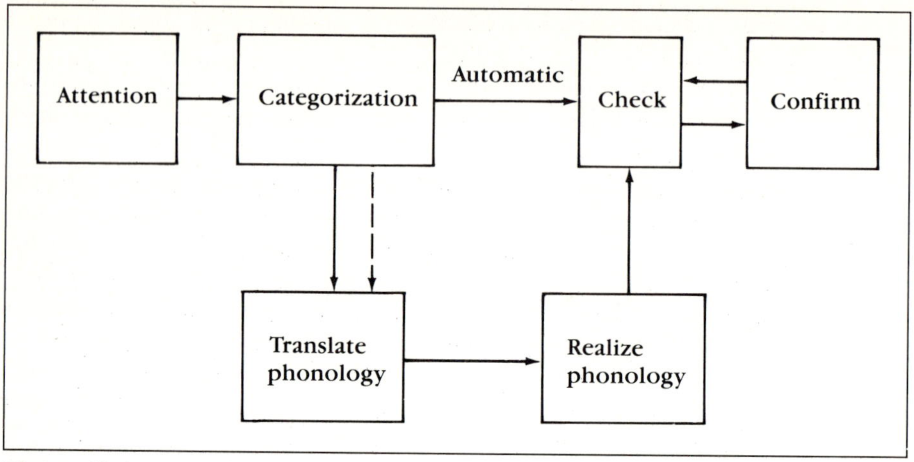

Figure 12-2 A model of the steps in the processing of written text.

takes place repeatedly over the school years. Children begin shifting to automatic processing with simple text in the early grades and with more complex text in the later grades. By the time most children enter school, they are competent users of their native language. They have a fairly extensive vocabulary and have unconscious knowledge of how to form words and sentences to convey different meanings. A four-year-old can be quite sophisticated in the structure of the sentences he uses. However, some four-year-olds are more advanced than others. For example, one four-year-old, in describing a picture, said, "There's a farmer sleeping in the field, and he doesn't see the crows eating his corn. When he wakes up, he'll be very mad that the scarecrow didn't scare the crows away." This child can form sentences that contain quite complex structures, such as anaphora, relative clauses, and complements. Other four-year-olds produce simpler sentences. The cultural background of the speaker does not necessarily dictate the level of language used. One four-year-old dialect speaker produced sentences such as "Ifn he do that, he gonna get what for. He don't got no call to take what he did." These sentences contain relative clauses, anaphora, and complements, as well. There is variation in the level of language sophistication attained by children as they enter school that is not determined by dialect use but, rather, by external or internal factors.

Despite this variation, most of the materials that these children will be required to read, initially, are theoretically well within their linguistic competence — for example, such sentences as, "Look, Tim. See the train go." However, the linguistic sophistication of children does not mean that learning to read will be simple. It is a task that challenges most children. Bringing to conscious awareness what is known unconsciously and matching the orthographic representations to available language categories is a challenging process. The requirements are twofold: first, having linguistic categories available;

and second, being able to match visual representations to native language categories by bringing them to conscious awareness.

Once children have learned to decode and recognize a few words, they begin to read connected discourse in text. Text processing requires what has been termed parallel processing. Such processing is quite similar to that proposed for oral language comprehension. The reader, in this case — like the speaker — uses information from all levels to comprehend the meaning of what is read. Information about letter-sound correspondences, letter-sequence-word correspondences, and the structure of the sequence of words is used to determine meaning. Use of the last type of information has been termed "psycholinguistic guessing" (Goodman, 1976).

In addition to linguistic knowledge, the child uses real-world knowledge and inferencing to comprehend and *remember* connected discourse. Throughout the school years, children's knowledge of their native language and of the real world increases. They are, therefore, able to read increasingly more complex materials. Multisyllabic words, such as "presentiment," appear in multiword complex sentences, such as "Before she opened the door, Alice had a presentiment that what lay before her was the beginning of a new chapter in her life." They read texts that become increasingly more complex in language and in ideas. They have to understand such phrases as "If the square of the hypotenuse . . ." As the child's knowledge of language and of the world increases in all aspects, she or he becomes capable of dealing with increasingly complex written materials.

Summary and Implications

In order to read, the child must have conscious knowledge of the language categories and relations that will allow translation of written symbols into native language categories and relations. The process then becomes automatic, with written materials that represent the child's available knowledge. When the materials are beyond children's linguistic knowledge, the children will be unable to read and comprehend correctly, although they may be able to decode some or all of the words in the text. Throughout the school years, if the material represents newly acquired linguistic knowledge, children will treat it in the same manner as they did when they first began to read. That is, they will bring the material to conscious awareness. Adults do exactly this when reading a passage that is difficult. They will stop, read it again, and perhaps mouth the words or read them aloud to achieve understanding. Later, the same material that the child needed to bring to conscious awareness, because it was not well learned, will be read automatically.

Reading supplies the child with new information about language. For example, the meanings of new words are learned from the context in which they appear in the text. New structural relations can appear in text as well. Engaging in the act of reading contributes to native language knowledge in two ways. First, it helps the child to become consciously aware of linguistic categories and relations. Reading exercises metaprocessing. Secondly, it adds to the store of native language knowledge by exposing the child to new words and relations among words. The first contribution is due to the fact that written symbols do not disappear in time, and, therefore, the child can think about the language that is represented in the text. There is a mutually nourishing relation that exists between native language knowledge and reading, once the child begins to read. Knowledge of the world conveyed through communication interactions during the early years of life and knowledge of the categories and relations in language per se play a crucial role in learning to read and becoming a sophisticated reader. However, once reading begins, it contributes to both world knowledge and knowledge of language. Beginning to read and reading materials that grow in complexity are both dependent on knowledge of the structure and use of language. Reading increases this knowledge as the child matures.

This process is now generally held to be the cognitive process by which children become literate. Many children are very ready in terms of literacy experiences and language development to take on the task of reading. Others are not. There are some children who do not become literate or who only become semiliterate. They mature into adults that are illiterate or only semiliterate. A review of adult literacy (Nickse, 1984) indicated the following:

1. Fifty percent of adults with yearly incomes under $5000 are functionally illiterate.
2. Over one-third of mothers who are receiving Aid to Families with Dependent Children (AFDC) are illiterate.
3. An estimated 13 percent of white, 56 percent of Hispanic, and 47 percent of black youth are illiterate.
4. Poor parents have less schooling than others, and so do their children — leading to intergenerational illiteracy.

These figures make clear that one of the primary causes of failing to learn to read is poverty. Minority-group children from the lowest SES families form the largest proportion of children who do not read. Some children in these groups do not have adequate educational facilities because of their geographical location. However, the reasons for a large majority of failures appear to be that the communication interaction that takes place in the home does not prepare the child for the acquisition of reading, and the communication interaction in the school does not compensate for this lack. These children, on entrance to school, may not have had a great deal of experience in communication interaction in a wide variety of settings. They may not have developed an easy ability to think and talk about language. They may not be children who, from an early age on, have tested their knowledge of language overtly by being engaged in language games. Their experiences may not have led to the ability to think and talk about language nor to their knowing about and talking about a wide variety of experiences. What they have not experienced in the preschool years makes them less prepared for learning to read.

Despite the fact that all children have not had the same degree of experience in thinking and talking about language and in thinking and talking about the world, all children who are developing normally have developed intuitive knowledge of language and are able to communicate effectively in their native language. They are, therefore, capable of bringing this intuitive knowledge to conscious awareness. A study cited in the previous chapter corroborates this (Piestrup, 1973). All the children in the study came from an inner-city black neighborhood and, presumably, had similar preschool experiences. Children in several classrooms did not learn to read. Children who were successful readers at the end of first grade had a teacher who, first, assumed they could learn to read and, second, engaged them in language tasks which brought their intuitive knowledge to conscious awareness, and who taught them to consciously apply this knowledge to written symbols. This research points to the fact that even though some children have had an insufficient amount of preschool experience in language use — which makes them less able to learn to read — they can be taught to think and talk about language, and their knowledge can be widened and talked about.

Another reason why normally developing children may have difficulty in learning to read is that they may not have developed sufficient knowledge of the language they are required to read. Second-language acquirers fall into this category. Some second-language acquirers have no problems in learning to read in their second language. However, minority-group children who are called on to learn to read in a second language have many of the same problems as minority-group dialect speakers. Therefore, they also are not ready to learn to read. They also need to be made consciously aware of the categories and relations in their native language and to have their knowledge widened and discussed. They are certainly not ready to learn to read in a foreign language. This process would require translation of the written word into an unavailable second-language word and then translation of that word into the native language synonym or equivalent word. This requirement imposes an additional difficult learning task on these children and does not address their particular needs in learning to read — the needs to become consciously aware of their language categories and relations and more familiar with the topics dealt with in written materials.

A group of children analogous to second-language acquirers are deaf children; specifically, deaf children of hearing parents. These children often reach school age with neither a good grasp of oral language knowledge nor a good grasp of sign language. Research does indicate that deaf children who are exposed to sign language from birth do better in reading and in spelling and mathematics than deaf children without this early experience (Brasel & Quigley, 1977). Deaf children without sign language experience read, on average, at the fourth-grade level. In this case, as with other groups of children, a solid native language base is required for the acquisition of written language. Clearly, the traditional methods of teaching reading that rely heavily on the development of correspondences between written symbols and speech sound categories do not work well with deaf children. Apparently, successful deaf readers have learned alternate routes to getting at the meaning of text. They may use pattern recognition in unique ways. Hearing readers can use the initial letter or letters of a word and its overall *shape* to make good guesses as to what the word is (Haber & Haber, 1981). It is possible that deaf children who read well become experts at this.

Thus far, the acquisition of reading by children who are successful in learning to read and by children who have problems has been discussed. All of these children are developing normally. In Chapter Ten, children with impaired language were discussed. All children with such impairments have problems in learning to read, not just learning-disabled children. Less markedly impaired than those who are labelled language disordered is a group of children who are thought to be developing normally but who are doing so at a slower than average rate. These are children who do not learn to read at the usual age, but, rather, at seven, eight, or even nine years. Their problem is not lack of sufficient language interaction. These children are in families that provide them with rich linguistic experiences. Research indicates that although these children appear to communicate as well as their peers, they are still at the developmental stage of representing language primarily in terms of visual imagery (Jorm, 1979). With these children, for example, the word "cat" brings up only a visual image of the object the word represents. They have yet to represent words phonologically. Such representation occurs earlier in most children and they then go on to learn to read in first grade. Clearly, children who have not developed phonological representations are not ready to engage in the task of decoding when they are confronted with it in the first grade. These children do learn to read when they are ready. This is because they learn in situations where this is made possible. In other contexts these children would simply be reading failures. Another way of dealing with this problem is to explore different ways of presenting reading material so that it is more congruent with children's processing style. Rebus materials, which are composed of pictures and letters, is one such way.

Once a child learns to read successfully, many of the strategies that have been observed in skilled readers are also observed in the child. Children very early begin to use "psycholinguistic guessing" while simultaneously listening and looking at the text and self-correcting when errors are observed. Children who are read to have knowledge of story grammar at an early age. They use this grammar to interpret and predict the organization of the text they are exposed to. Even children as young as six years give evidence of their awareness of the importance level of prose information in their recall of such information (Young & Schumacher, 1983). Their interest in and prior knowledge of the topic of the text influences comprehension of that text and, also, their ability to make inferences from the text as they read (Danner & Matthews, 1980). Thus, as soon as some skill is achieved in reading, children use the same strategies as do skilled readers in their approach to the text. They, like skilled readers, are more or less able to apply the strategies, depending on the complexity of the language of the text, the familiarity of the topic of the text, and its organization and cohesiveness.

Findings concerning the acquisition of reading and its development suggest that most children are ready to take on the reading task. They can become consciously aware of the language that is represented in the text they read, and they have had a lot of experience in listening to organized text and are therefore ready to apply organizational schema to the reading task. Finally, they have a great deal of familiarity with the real and fantasy topics of the written material they will be exposed to because of the topics of prior communication interactions and because of the materials read to them. They have both knowledge of the appropriate vocabulary and of the concepts or main ideas of the various topics. The educational implications of these findings are that children who are not ready in any one of these three areas need to be *made* ready, and, by and large, this is what takes place in the educational setting. This task, however, becomes difficult, when the children have cultural backgrounds, dialects, and languages that are different from those of the school or have some learning disabilities. Despite these circumstances, children with learning disabilities due to external factors — and, perhaps, some slowness — can learn to read, by becoming active participants in situations that make them more ready to consistently apply the strategies they have either acquired spontaneously or have been taught. It is most crucial that children who have reading difficulties because of internal factors be made ready to become aware of language units and the relations of these units to units of orthography (Trumbull, 1984).

Writing

As any freshman composition teacher knows, writing seems to have become a task that is alien to many students. There have been serious efforts over this past decade to develop teaching techniques that engage the very young child in writing in the hopes that early acculturation to the task will overcome many of the problems that students of all ages appear to have. There appears to be a mutually sustaining contribution between the writing and the reading processes. This is similar to the oral language learning that takes place by both speaking and listening. It is also over the past decade that the role of language development and of language processing in writing has begun to be carefully examined. The questions that have been asked in studies examining the relation between spoken language knowledge and writing are:

- What are the similarities and differences in telling and writing?
- What are the differences between good and poor writers at varying ages?

There appear to be two aspects of the development of writing. One is the development of the mechanics of writing skills, the development of spelling and of fluency in writing. Thus, there have been numerous studies that indicate that older writers write more (are more fluent) than younger writers, and that good readers are more fluent in writing than poor readers. The other aspect of the development of writing that has been examined is the nature of the cognitive and linguistic requirements of the task of writing (Flowers & Hayes, 1977; Graves, 1975). It is the role of language knowledge in writing development and in successful writing that is discussed here. However, it should be kept in mind that factors outside of language knowledge play a role in writing development and in fluency and creativity in writing. Those other factors are very similar to those found to be important in the development of reading: real-world knowledge; cognitive processes, such as problem solution; and the development of metacognitive strategies, such as monitoring the meaningfulness and grammaticality of the material being processed. Writing, like reading, requires metalinguistic processing. There is a very large literature on these topics.

Sometimes before the child enters school — and many times after the child enters school and becomes involved in generating written material — a process termed "invented spelling" takes place (Chomsky, 1970; Reed, 1965). This process appears to be somewhat analogous to the cognitive decoding process observed in the beginning stages of reading for some readers. That is, in the beginning of the decoding process, the child relates the written symbols to a phonological representation and then to a semantic representation. In the case of invented spelling, the inverse takes place. The child attempts to relate the speech sounds in a word to orthographic representations. In both processes the child brings to conscious awareness knowledge of the speech-sound categories and speech-sound sequence rules of the language. Evidence of this is found in the products of invented spelling. These invented spellings take into account such facts as: (1) vowels are nasalized before nasal sounds ("band" is spelled "bad"); (2) words can end with a single sound ("bottle" and "butter" are spelled "botl" and "butr"); and (3) some vowel sounds have a one-to-one relation between their sound and their spelling representation by letter ("gate" is spelled "gat"), whereas other vowel sounds have a many-to-one relation. They can be grouped on the basis of their similarities in sound and represented by a single letter ("pot" and "pat" are both spelled "pat"). These beginning stages of writing words suggest that initial writing, as well as reading, of words is based on phonological representations for some children. It also seems to be the case that initial sentence writing is based on conscious knowledge of lexicon and semantactic rules. Writing connected discourse is, however, based not only on knowledge of how connected discourse takes place in conversation and in story telling, but also of how it takes place in text.

Several researchers have examined the relation between the development of connected discourse in speaking and in writing, and they have come to somewhat different conclusions concerning the relation. There is a great deal of agreement about the fact that speaking and writing are different from each other, based on a number of features. Some of the features are:

- Writing is limited to societies that have represented their language orthographically, whereas speaking is universal.
- Writing takes place with an absent audience, whereas speaking takes place with a present audience.
- Writing requires inclusion or consideration of contextual information, whereas speaking is produced in context.
- Writing results in a permanent product, whereas speaking fades away.
- Writing is usually planned self-conscious behavior, whereas speaking usually takes place spontaneously.

Because of these differences between writing and speaking, the form as well as the function of writing and speaking can differ. Despite the differences however, it is usually the case that oral language knowledge places limitations on what is produced orthographically. For example, we usually produce in written materials only those lexical items that we have knowledge of, and we produce only those structures that we have knowledge of. Therefore, despite the fact that written language is usually less redundant in word use than is spoken language, this is a product of having more time to retrieve lexical items and to check for redundancy rather than an indication of different lexicons for writing and speaking. Chafe (1982) pointed out that there might be differences in the structures produced in writing and speaking because of the differences in the conditions for production. Because spoken language is produced more rapidly than written language, spoken products contain more nongrammaticalities, fuzziness, and fragments than written language.

Lexical and semantactic differences between speaking and writing appear to be greater or smaller as a function of the purpose of the spoken and written discourse. There have been studies which indicate that many of the types of differences observed between spoken and written language disappear when the purpose of the discourse becomes similar (for example, Beaman, 1984; Redeker, 1984). There appear to be similarities between telling and writing stories and between lecturing on and writing on a topic. That is, spontaneity can exist in writing as well as speaking, and planned behavior can exist in speaking as well as writing. There are, however, overall differences in the style or register of writing as compared to speaking because of the usual differences in the communicative goals of the two forms of language and the channel in which they are produced. Tannen (1982) analyzed the spoken and written narratives of university students and came to the conclusion that genre, topic, function, and absence or presence of audience lead to the differences in the styles of the two types of communication. Thus, although written language production is highly dependent on native language knowledge, the writer has to acquire additional knowledge about style, not necessarily about form.

One basis for the development of this ability is the development of metaprocessing of language. While one is writing, access to lexical items and the relational structures of the language needs to take place. This accessing is necessary for planning writing, monitoring it on-line, and reviewing it during the editing process. Younger children appear to have difficulty in accessing the linguistic categories and structures as they write, despite the increased time that writing allows. Very early writing represents a stream of speech without segmentation of word units. Bissex (1980) presents examples of this occurrence in his book on his child's acquisition of written language knowledge, entitled *Gnys at Wrk: A Child Learns to Read and Write.* As children mature and increase their ability to metaprocess language, such accessing during writing becomes easier. For skilled writers it becomes automatic, just as recognition of text becomes automatic in skilled readers. However, speaking and writing become less alike over time (Perera, 1986).

There are children who are comparatively delayed in achieving metaprocessing of varying aspects of language, primarily because of the external factor of different experiences with and through language. Because of this delay they may have difficulty in learning to read and to write. One basis, then, for being able to write in a style suitable for written discourse is metaprocessing of language. Some children are delayed in the development of this ability. Reading also helps the development of metaprocessing of language. Thus, children who are delayed in metaprocessing will be delayed in reading. And they will therefore be further delayed in metaprocessing, which will cause them difficulties in accessing language during the writing process and limit their ability to develop appropriate writing styles. Figure 12-3 shows the dependency relations that exist between oral language development and reading and writing. As indicated in Figure 12-3, reading and writing development are mutually dependent.

It is not simply accessing language categories and structures that leads to the development of writing styles, it is also familiarity with the writing styles themselves that leads to fluent writing — or, at least, to the style of writing that is considered literate in our culture. This is all-important in determining which structures and categories *should* be selected or accessed under certain conditions. Children learn how to do this by being exposed to written material. Again, children who have had little experience in reading or being read to will have difficulty with writing because of their comparative lack of knowledge of different writing styles. They will, in particular, have difficulty in acquiring the writing style that is valued in the school (Michaels & Collins, 1984).

Kroll (1981) has suggested that there are four phases in which oral language and writing get further and further apart. In the first phase the two are very closely tied, as the child learns to represent phonological knowledge orthographically and masters the physical aspects of handwriting. This, he says, is achieved by age seven. The next phase is one of consolidation. The child

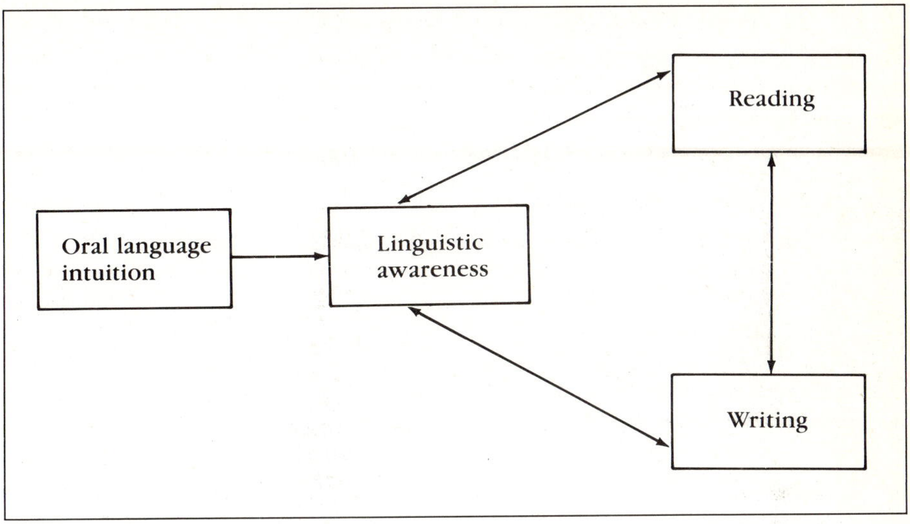

Figure 12-3 Interdependencies between oral language knowledge and reading and writing.

uses the same structures in writing that are used in speech and in much the same proportions. This is accomplished by age nine or ten, or well into the middle childhood period when there is awareness of even complex structures in the language. The next phase is differentiation, when writing is said to take on its own grammar. Kroll suggests that this begins at varying ages. The final phase is integration. The writer sometimes selects from her or his speaking register those forms that will engage the reader in a conversational exchange, and at other times maintains the differences between the spoken and written register.

There have been few studies that have compared good and poor writers while keeping constant a number of the variables that have been said to affect writing style and form. One such study made clear the diversity of factors that play a role in the development of good writing. Gordon (1986) compared the writing of five good and five poor writers. All the children in the study were girls in grades ten, eleven, and twelve. They were white and they came from low-SES families. Their writing was evaluated by their teachers. For the study, they were asked to tell a story and write a story about a frightening or dangerous experience. The order of telling or writing was randomized for each subject. Their spoken and written stories were then analyzed in a number of ways — segmentation, narrative style, lexicon, syntax, and amount of density of information as indicated by the number and organization of propositions. Labov's (1972) analysis of narrative style was used to analyze the written and spoken stories. This analysis examines the proportion of narrative and non-narrative clauses and evaluations within narrative clauses by the use of intensifiers, comparators, correlatives, and explicatives.

The results of the analysis indicated a number of differences between the good and poor writers.

1. Poor writers write less than good writers, but speak as much.
2. Both good and poor writers segmented their spoken stories in similar ways, but poor writers did not use paragraphing to segment their written stories.
3. Good writers maintained or added to the proportion of narrative clauses and evaluation of narrative clauses that were in their speech, but poor writers reduced the proportion in their writing.
4. Poor writers had less lexical diversity both in their speech and in written stories than did good writers.
5. The syntactic structures in the writing of good writers increased in complexity, but the complexity of the syntactic structures used by poor writers was the same in both speech and writing. Good writers used more subordination in their speech.
6. Good writers increased the density of their propositions in writing, but poor writers did not.

The experimenter concluded that poor writers do not write as much as good writers because of their difficulties in doing on-line selection of appropriate language. They write less well than they speak, in terms of the narrative style they use when writing. They, unlike good writers, do not incorporate in their written stories the use of nonfinite clauses or complements that use participles for modification. Finally, they are less able than good writers in terms of lexical knowledge in both speech and writing.

Some Educational Implications

The results of research on emergent literacy suggest that it is extremely important that children be exposed to literacy experiences as early as possible. These experiences take place in a number of ways. One early experience is communication interaction in which the child begins to be aware of the categories and relations in language. Another is exposure to reading adults who act as models for the child both passively, as they read to themselves, and actively, as they read to the child. These early experiences should involve the child in active processing of print and include both reading and writing. With continued exposure to print, the child begins to be aware of orthography — meaning relations in familiar contexts (for example, stop signs, names on cereal boxes, and some words in familiar books). Later she or he recognizes them in decontextualized situations. It has been suggested that teachers should be aware that some children come to school with only contextualized notions of print (Heath, 1983). This fact can be used to gradually shift the child from contextualized to decontextualized reading. If given the opportunity, the child engages in production of text and reads her or his own text. The functions of literacy become very clear in these circumstances.

If children have not had the opportunity to engage in such activities in the home, the experiences need to be provided in the school. The child needs to be exposed to literacy experiences and, in addition, to opportunities for engaging in metaprocessing of language. Such opportunities involve awareness of the varying units of spoken language, and later, of the relation of varying units of language to print units. Such experiences allow the child to approach text in a number of productive ways. The child has the notion that written materials provide information and that this information can be obtained by a number of strategies. These include using contextual information and decoding to get at meaning. If difficulties arise in this process, it has been suggested that reciprocal teaching experiences can help overcome some of the difficulties. These experiences allow the child to actively participate in the reading process. There is communication interaction between the teacher and learner, and the learner is encouraged to ask questions about the learning process and the text.

Throughout the process of acquisition of written language knowledge, the child is engaged in writing as well as reading experiences. Research on the differences between early and later writing (Kroll, 1981) and between good and poor writers (Gordon, 1986) has suggested to researchers that intervention should involve:

1. Lexical expansion.
2. Development of syntactic fluency.
3. Development of awareness of appropriate lexical and structural selection.
4. Increased exposure to different text styles.

The first and second recommendations speak to the development of less redundancy and greater fluency in writing. The third recommendation emphasizes the fact that training is needed, first, to develop awareness of appropriate use of lexical items and semantax structures, and then to apply them automatically when writing, if such awareness and automaticity does not develop spontaneously. Finally, more experience in reading is needed to develop appropriate and flexible styles in writing.

The research results obtained in studies of writing (and the interventions suggested) once again point to the importance of the child's intuitive and conscious native language knowledge in learning about and using written language. Experience — in this case, exposure to written materials — provides the data for application of this knowledge and for its modification. Very young writers and children who are relatively poor writers have less intuitive knowledge of language than others and are less able to metaprocess the knowledge they do have. This makes them less able to comprehend the nature of different writing styles and, of course, to reproduce these styles. However, these difficulties can be overcome.

References

Abrahamsen, A., Cavallo, M., and McCluer, J. 1985. Is the sign advantage a robust phenomenon? *Merrill Palmer Quarterly* 31: 177–98.

Ackerman, B. 1981. Performance bias in children's interpretations of ambiguous communications. *Child Development* 52: 1224–30.

———. 1982. Contextual integration and utterance interpretation: the ability of children and adults to interpret sarcastic utterances. *Child Development* 53: 1075–83.

———. 1983. Children's judgments of the functional acceptability of referential communications in discourse contexts. *J. of Child Language* 10:151–66.

Aitchison, J. 1983. Review of *Roots of language,* by Derek Bickerton. *Language and Communication* 3: 83–97.

Akiyama, M. 1985. Denials in young children. *Child Development* 56: 95–102.

Anglin, J. 1970. *The growth of word meaning.* Cambridge, MA.: M.I.T. Press.

Anderson, E., Dunlea, A., and Kekelis, L. 1984. Blind childrens' language: resolving some differences. *J. of Child Language* 11: 645–64.

Anderson, E., and Kekelis, L. 1982. Effects of visual impairment on early mother — child communication. Paper presented at the 7th Annual Boston University Language Development Conference, Boston, October, 1982.

Anisfeld, M., and Tucker, R. 1967. English pluralization rules of six-year-old children. *Child Development* 38: 1201–17.

Antinucci, F., and Miller, R. 1976. How children talk about what happened. *J. Child Language* 3: 167–89.

Aram, D., Ekelman, B., and Nation, J. 1984. Preschoolers with language disorders: 10 years later. *J. Speech and Hearing Research* 27: 232–44.

Aram, D., Ekelman, B., and Whitaker, H. 1985. Spoken syntax in children with acquired unilateral hemisphere lesions. Paper presented at Tenth Annual Boston University Language Development Conference, Boston. October, 1985.

Ardery, G. 1980. On coordination in child language. *J. Child Language* 7: 305–20.

Asch, S., and Nerlove, H. 1960. The development of double function terms. In *Perspectives in psychological theory: Essays in honor of Heinz Werner,* eds. B. Kaplan and S. Wapner. New York: International Universities Press.

Aslin, R., Pisoni, D., and Jusczyk, P. 1983. Auditory development and speech perception in infancy. In *Handbook of child psychology,* eds. M. Haith and J. Campos. Vol. 2, 4th ed. New York: John Wiley & Sons.

Atkinson-King, K. 1973. Children's acquisition of phonological stress constraints. *UCLA Working Papers,* No. 25.

Au, K., and Jordan, C. 1981. Teaching reading to Hawaiian children. In *Culture in the bilingual classroom: Studies in classroom ethnography,* eds. H. Trueba, G. Guthrie, and K. Au. Rowley, MA: Newbury House.

Baer, D., and Guess, D. 1973. Teaching productive noun suffixes to severely retarded children. *American Journal of Mental Deficiency* 77: 498–505.

Baker, K., and de Kanter, A. 1981. *Effectiveness of bilingual education: A review of the literature.* Washington, D.C.: Office of Planning Budget and Evaluation, U.S. Dept. of Education.

Balaban, M. 1975. A receptive measure of syntax in Black Dialect. Paper presented at Annual Convention of American Speech and Hearing Association, Washington, D.C.

Banker, M. 1985. An examination of apical stop consonants in normally developing and language-disordered children. Unpublished doctoral dissertation, Boston University.

Baratz, J. 1969. A bidialectal test for determining language proficiency in economically disadvantaged children. *Child Development* 40: 889–902.

Barnes, S., Gutfreund, M., Satterly, D., and Wells, G. 1983. Characteristics of adult speech which predict children's language development. *J. of Child Language* 10: 65–84.

Barron, R. 1986. Word recognition in early reading: A review of the direct and indirect access hypothesis. *Cognition* 24: 93–119.

Barton, D. 1976. Phonemic discrimination and the knowledge of words in children under three years. *Papers and Reports on Child Language,* 11, Linguistics. Stanford, CA.: Stanford University.

Bates, E. 1976. Pragmatics and sociolinguistics in child language. In *Normal and deficient child language,* eds. D. Morehead and A. Morehead. Baltimore: University Park Press.

Bates, E., Benigni, L., Bretherton, I., Camaioni, L., and Volterra, V. 1979. *The emergence of symbols: Cognition and communication in infancy.* New York: Academic Press.

Bates, E., Camaioni, L., and Volterra, V. 1975. The acquisition of performatives prior to speech. *Merrill Palmer Quarterly* 21: 205–26.

Bates, E., MacWhinney, B., Caselli, C., Descovi, A., and Venza, F. 1984. A cross-linguistic study of the development of sentence interpretation strategies. *Child Development* 55: 351–54.

Bateson, M. 1969. The interpersonal context of infant vocalizations. *Quarterly Progress Reports,* M.I.T., Research Laboratory of Electronics no. 100 (Jan. 15), 170–76.

Beaman, K. 1984. Coordination and subordination revisited: Syntactic complexity in spoken and written narrative discourse. In *Coherence in spoken and written discourse,* ed. D. Tannen. Norwood, N.J.: Ablex.

Beilin, H. 1975. *Studied in the cognitive basis of language development.* New York: Academic Press.

Bell, C., and Flavell, J. 1984. Development of the ability to distinguish communicative intention and literal message meaning. *Child Development* 55: 920–28.

Bell, R., and Ainsworth, M. 1972. Infant crying and maternal responsiveness. *Child Development* 43: 1171–90.

Ben-Zeev, S. 1977. The influence of bilingualism on cognitive strategy and cognitive development. *Child Development* 48: 1009–18.

Berko-Gleason, J. 1958. The child's learning of English morphology. *Word* 14: 150–77.

Bernstein, M. 1983. Formation of internal structure in a lexical category. *J. Child Language* 10: 381–400.

Bertelson, P. 1986. The onset of literacy: Liminal remarks. *Cognition* 24: 1–30.

Bever, T. 1971. The nature of cerebral dominance in speech behavior of child and adult. In *Acquisition of language: models and methods,* eds. R. Huxley and E. Ingram. London: Academic Press.

Bialystok, E., and Ryan, E. 1985. Toward a definition of metalinguistic skill. *Merrill Palmer Quarterly* 31: 235–52.

Bickerton, D. 1981. *Roots of language.* Ann Arbor, Mich.: Karma.

Billow, R. 1975. A cognitive developmental study of metaphor comprehension. *Developmental psychology* 11:415–23.

Bissex, G. 1980. *Gnys at wrk: A child learns to read and write.* Cambridge, MA.: Harvard U. Press.

Blank, M. 1975. Mastering the intangible through language. *Annals of the New York Academy of Sciences* 263: 44–58.

Bloom, L. 1970. *Language development: Form and function in emerging grammars.* Cambridge, MA.: M.I.T. Press.

Bloom, L., Lifter, K., and Hafitz, J. 1980. Semantics of verbs and the development of verb inflection in child language. *Language* 56: 386–412.

Bloom, L., Lightbown, P., and Hood, L. 1975. Structure and variation in child language. *Monographs of the Society for Research in Child Development* 40 (Serial No. 160).

Bloom, L., Tackeff, J., and Lahey, M. 1984. Learning to in complement constructions. *J. Child Language* 11: 391–406.

Blumstein, S. 1986. On acoustic invariance in speech. In *Invariance and variability in speech processes,* eds. J. Perkell and D. Klatt. Hillsdale, N.J.: Lawrence Erlbaum Assoc.

Boggs, S. 1978. The development of verbal disputing in part-Hawaiian children. *Language in Society* 7: 325–44.

Bondurant, J., Romeo, D., and Kretschmer, R. 1983. Language behaviors of mothers of children with normal and delayed language. *Language, Speech and Hearing Services in the Schools* 14: 233–42.

Bonvillian, J., Orlansky, M., and Novack, L. 1983. Developmental milestones: sign language acquisition and motor development. *Child Development* 54: 1435–55.

Bowerman, M. 1973. *Early syntactic development: A crosslinguistic study with special reference to Finnish.* Cambridge, England: Cambridge University Press.

———. 1974. Learning the structure of causative verbs: a study in the relationship of cognitive, semantic, and syntactic development. *Stanford Papers and Reports on Child Language Development* 8: 142–78.

Bowerman, M. 1979. The acquisition of complex sentences. In *Language Acquisition,* eds. P. Fletcher and M. Garman. Cambridge, England: Cambridge University Press.

Braine, M. 1971. On two types of models of the internalization of grammar. In *The ontogenesis of grammar,* ed. D. Slobin. New York: Academic Press.

———. 1976. Children's first word combinations. *Monographs of the Society for Research in Child Development* Vol. 41, No. 1, Serial No. 164.

Braine, M., and Hardy, J. 1982. On what case categories there are, why they are, and how they develop. In *Language acquisition: State of the art,* eds. E. Wanner and L. Gleitman. Cambridge, England: Cambridge University Press.

Braine, M., and Wells, R. 1978. Case-like categories in children: the actor and more related categories. *Cognitive Psychology* 10: 100–122.

Brasel, K., and Quigley, S. 1977. Influence of certain language and communication environments in early childhood in the development of language in deaf individuals. *J. Speech and Hearing Research* 20: 95–107.

Bresnan, J. 1978. A realistic transformational grammar. In *Linguistic theory and psychological reality,* eds. M. Halle, J. Bresnan, and G. Miller. Cambridge, MA.: M.I.T. Press.

Bricker, W., and Bricker D. 1974. An early language training strategy. In *Language perspectives: Acquisition, retardation and intervention,* eds. R. Schiefelbusch and L. Lloyd. Baltimore: University Park Press.

Bridges, A. 1984. A preschool child's comprehension of agency. *J. Child Language* 11: 593–610.

Bristow, D., and Fristoe, M. 1984. Learning of Blissymbols and manual sign. *J. of Speech and Hearing Disorders* 49: 145–51.

Bronckart, J., and Sinclair, H. 1973. Time tense and aspect. *Cognition* 2: 107–30.

Brown, A., Campione, J., and Barclay, C. 1979. Training self-checking routines for estimating test readiness: generalization from list learning to prose recall. *Child Development* 50:501–12.

Brown, H. 1980. *Principles of language learning and teaching.* Englewood Cliffs, N.J.: Prentice-Hall, Inc.

Brown, R. 1973. *A first language: The early stages.* Cambridge, MA.: Harvard University Press.

Bruner, J. 1957. On perceptual readiness. *Psychological Review* 64: 123–52.

Bruner, J., Goodnow, J., and Austin, G. 1956. *A study of thinking.* New York: Wiley.

Buium, N., Rynders, J., and Turnure, J. 1974. Early maternal linguistic environment of normal and Down's syndrome language-learning children. *Amer. J. of Ment. Def.* 79: 52–58.

Burroughs, E. 1912. *Tarzan of the Apes.* New York: Frank A. Mansey Co.

Bushnell, E., and Maratsos, M. 1984. Spooning and basketing: children's dealing with accidental gaps. *Child Development* 55: 893–902.

Calculator, S. 1985. Describing and teaching discourse problems in mentally retarded children: The myth of mental retardese. In *School discourse problems,* eds. D. Ripich and F. Spinelli. San Diego, CA: College Hill Press.

Callanan, M., and Markman, E. 1982. Principles of organization in young children's natural language hierarchies. *Child Development* 53: 1093–1101.

Campbell, B. 1970. The roots of language. In *Biological and social factors in psycholinguistics,* ed. J. Morton. Urbana, Ill.: U. of Illinois Press.

Carey, S. 1978. The child as word learner. In *Linguistic theory and psychological reality,* eds. M. Halle, J. Bresnan, and G. Miller. Cambridge, MA.: M.I.T. Press.

———. 1982. Semantic development, state of the art. In *Language acquisition: State of the art,* eds. E. Wanner and L. Gleitman. Cambridge, England: Cambridge University Press.

———. 1986. Are children fundamentally different kinds of thinkers and learners than adults? In *Thinking and learning skills,* eds. S. Chipman, J. Segal, and R. Glaser. Vol. 2. Hillsdale, N.J.: Lawrence Erlbaum Assoc.

Carroll, D. 1986. *Psychology of language.* Monterey, CA.: Brooks/Cole Pub. Co.

Carroll, J. 1979. Psychometric approaches to the study of language abilities. In *Individual differences in language ability and language behavior,* eds. C. Fillmore, D. Kempler and W. Wong. New York: Academic Press.

Carter, A. 1979. Prespeech meaning relations: an outline of one infant's sensori — motor morpheme development. In *Language acquisition,* eds. P. Fletcher and M. Garman. Cambridge, England: Cambridge University Press.

Casby, M., and Ruder, K. 1983. Symbolic play and early language development in normal and mentally retarded children. *Journal of Speech and Hearing Research* 26: 404–11.

Cazden, C. 1974. Suggestions from studies of early language acquisition. In *Language and the language arts,* eds. J. DeStefano and S. Fox. Boston: Little, Brown & Co.

———. 1983. Play with language and metalinguistic awareness: one dimension of language experience. In *Early childhood development and education,* eds. M. Donaldson, R. Grieve, and C. Pratt. New York: The Guilford Press.

Chafe, W. 1982. Integration and involvement in speaking, writing, and oral literature. In *Spoken and written language: Exploring orality and literacy,* ed. D. Tannen. Norwood, N.J.: Ablex.

Chai, D. 1967. Communication of pronominal referents in ambiguous English sentences for children and adults. *U. Michigan Center for Growth and Development,* Report No. 13.

Chall, J. 1983. *Learning to read: the great debate.* 2nd ed. New York: McGraw-Hill Book Co.

———. 1983. *Stages of reading development.* New York: McGraw-Hill Book Co.

Chao, Y. R. 1973. The cantian idiolect: an analysis of the Chinese spoken by a twenty-eight-month child. In *Studies of child language development,* eds. C. Ferguson and D. Slobin. New York: Holt, Rinehart & Winston, Inc.

Chomsky, C. 1969. *The acquisition of syntax in children from five to ten.* Cambridge, MA.: M.I.T. Press.

———. 1970. Reading, writing and phonology. *Harvard Educational Review* 40: 287–309.

———. 1980. Developing facility with language structure. In *Discovering language with children,* ed. G. Pinell. Urbana, Ill.: Natl. Council of Teachers of English.

Chomsky, N. 1965. *Aspects of a theory of syntax.* Cambridge, MA.: M.I.T. Press.

———. 1980. On binding. *Linguistic Inquiry* 11: 1–80.

Chomsky, N., and Lasnik, H. 1977. Filters and control. *Linguistic Inquiry* 8: 425–504.

Clark, C. 1981. Learning words using traditional orthography and the symbols of Rebus, Bliss, and Carrier. *J. Speech and Hearing Disorders* 46: 191–96.

Clark, E. 1981. On the acquisition of antonyms in two semantic fields. *J. Verbal Learning and Verbal Behavior,* 1972, 11: 750–58.

———. 1981. How children learn to create new words. In *The child's construction of language,* ed. W. Deutsch. London: Academic Press.

———. 1982. The young word-maker: A case study of innovation in the child's lexicon. In *Language Acquisition: The state of the art,* eds.

E. Wanner and L. Gleitman. Cambridge, England: Cambridge University Press.

———. 1983. Meanings and concepts. In *Handbook of child psychology,* eds. J. Flavell and E. Markman. Vol. III. New York: John Wiley & Sons.

Clark, H., and Clark, E. 1977. *Psychology and language.* New York: Harcourt Brace Jovanovich, Inc.

Clark, R. 1978. The transition from action to gesture. In *Action, gesture and symbol: The emergence of language,* ed. A. Lock. London: Academic Press.

Cole, M., and D'Andrade, R. 1982. The influence of schooling on concept formation: Some preliminary conclusions. *Quarterly Newsletter of the Laboratory of Comparative Human Cognition, University of California, San Diego* 4: 19–26.

Cole, M., and Hall, W., eds. 1982. A model system for the study of learning disabilities. *Quarterly Newsletter of the Laboratory of Comparative Human Cognition, University of California, San Diego* 4: 39–66.

Cole, M., and Scribner, S. 1977. Developmental theories applied to cross-cultural cognitive research. *Annals of the New York Academy Of Sciences* 285: 366–73.

Collins, A., and Quillian, M. 1969. Retrieval from semantic memory. *J. Verbal Learning and Verbal Behavior* 8: 204–47.

Collins, A., and Loftus, E. 1975. A spreading activation theory of semantic processing. *Psychological Review* 82: 407–28.

Cometa, M., and Eson, M. 1978. Logical operation and metaphor interpretation: A Piagetian model. *Child Development* 49: 649–59.

Conrad, R. 1972. The developmental role of vocalizing in short-term memory. *J. Verbal Learning Verbal Behavior* 11: 521–33.

Conti-Ramsden, G., and Friel-Patti, S. 1983. Mothers' discourse adjustments to language-impaired and non–language-impaired children. *J. of Speech and Hearing Disorders* 48: 360–67.

Coon, R., Lipscomb, T., and Copple, C. 1982. Effect of listener feedback on the messages of kindergarten children in a referential communication task. *J. Applied Developmental Psychology* 3: 337–46.

Cooper, J. 1982. Residual impairments in children with a history of acquired aphasia. Unpublished doctoral dissertation, U. of Washington.

Cowan, N., Suomi, S., and Morse, P. 1982. Echoic storage in infant perception. *Child Development* 53: 984–90.

Cromer, R. 1972. The learning of linguistic surface structure cues to deep structure by educationally subnormal children. *Amer. J. of Ment. Def.* 77: 346–53.

———. 1974. Receptive language in the mentally retarded: Processes and diagnostic distinctions. In *Language perspectives: Acquisition, retardation and intervention,* eds. R. Schiefelbusch and L. Lloyd. Baltimore: University Park Press.

Cross, T. 1977. Mothers' speech adjustments: The contribution of selected child-listener variables. In *Talking to children: Language input and acquisition,* eds. C. Snow and C. Ferguson. Cambridge, England: Cambridge University Press.

Cruttendon, A. 1985. Intonation comprehension in ten-year-olds. *J. Child Language* 12: 643–61.

Crystal, D. 1975. *The English tone of voice.* London: Edward Arnold.

Cummins, J. 1978. Educational implications of mother-tongue maintenance in minority-language children. *The Canadian Modern Language Review* 34: 395–416.

———. 1979. Linguistic interdependence and the educational development of bilingual children. *Review of Educational Research* 49: 222–51.

———. 1985. In search of independent variables: Historical analysis of bilingual children's academic achievement. Paper presented at Biennial Meeting of the Society for Research in Child Development, Toronto, Canada, April, 1985.

———. 1986. Empowering minority students: A framework for intervention. *Harvard Educational Review* 56: 18–36.

Curtiss, S. 1974. The linguistic development of Genie. *Language* 50: 528–54.

———. 1981. Dissociation between language and cognition: Causes and implications. *J. of Autism and Developmental Disorders* 11: 15–30.

Curtiss, S., Fromkin, V., and Yamada, J. 1978. The independence of language as a cognitive system. Paper presented at the 3rd Annual

Boston University Language Development Conference, Boston, October, 1978.

Damico, J., Oller, J., and Storey, M. 1983. The diagnosis of language disorders in bilingual children: Surface-oriented and pragmatic criteria. *J. Speech and Hearing Disorders* 48: 385–94.

Danner, F., and Matthews, R. 1980. When do young children make inferences from prose. *Child Development* 51: 906–8.

Dasen, P. 1980. Psychological differentiation and operational development: A cross-cultural link. *Quarterly Newsletter of the Laboratory of Human Cognition, University of California, San Diego* 2: 81–86.

Demorest, A., Meyer, C., Phelps, E., Gardner, H., and Winner, E. 1984. Words speak louder than actions: understanding deliberately false remarks. *Child Development* 55: 1527–34.

Denckla, M., and Rudel, R. 1976. Naming of object-drawings by dyslexic and other learning-disabled children. *Brain and Language* 3: 1–15.

Dennis, M. 1980. Capacity and strategy for syntactic comprehension after left or right hemidecortication. *Brain and Language* 10: 287–307.

De Boysson-Bardies, B. 1986. Acoustic investigations of cross-linguistic variability. In *Precursors of Early Speech,* eds. B. Lindblom and R. Netterstrom. New York: Stockton Press.

DePaulo, B., and Bonvillian, J. 1978. The effect on language development of the special characteristics of speech addressed to children. *J. of Psycholinguistic Research* 7: 189–211.

Derwing, B., and Baker, W. 1979. Recent research in the acquisition of English morphology. In *Language acquisition,* eds. P. Fletcher and M. Garman. Cambridge, England: Cambridge University Press.

DeTore, B. 1978. An investigation of the resolution of anaphora in written discourse. Unpublished doctoral dissertation, Boston University.

DeVilliers, J., and DeVilliers, P. 1974. Competence and performance in child language: Are children competent to judge? *Journal of Child Language* 1: 11–22.

Diaz, R. 1985. Bilingual cognitive development and addressing three gaps in the literature. *Child Development* 56: 1376–88.

Donahue, M. 1978. Form and function in mother-toddler conversational turn taking. Unpublished doctoral dissertation, Boston University.

———. 1985. Communicative style in learning-disabled children. In *School discourse problems,* eds. D. Ripich and F. Spinelli. San Diego, CA.: College Hill Press.

Donahue, M., and Bryan, T. 1983. Conversational skill and modelling in learning-disabled boys. *Applied Psycholinguistics* 4: 251–78.

Donahue, M., Pearl, R., and Bryan, T. 1982. Learning-disabled children's syntactic proficiency in a communication task. *J. Speech and Hearing Research* 47: 397–403.

———. 1983. Conversational competence in learning-disabled children. In *Advances in learning and behavioral disabilities,* eds. H. Bialer and K. Gadow. Vol. 3. Greenwich, Conn.: J.A.I. Press.

Dore, J. 1975. Holophrases, speech acts, and language universals. *J. of Child Language* 2: 21–40.

Dore, J., Franklin, M., Miller, R., and Ramer, A. 1976. Transitional phenomena in early language acquisition. *J. of Child Language* 3: 13–28.

Dorval, B., and Eckerman, C. 1984. Developmental trends in the quality of conversation achieved by small groups of acquainted peers. *Monographs of the Society for Research in Child Development,* Vol. 29, No. 2, Serial No. 206.

Dulay, H., and Burt, M. 1975. A new approach to discovering universal strategies of child second-language acquisition. In *Developmental psycholinguistics: Theory and applications,* ed. D. Dato. Washington, D.C.: Georgetown University Press.

Durkin, D. 1966. The achievement of preschool readers: Two longitudinal studies. *Reading Research Quarterly* 1: 5–36.

Edwards, M. 1974. Perception and production in child phonology: The testing of four hypotheses. *J. Child Language* 1: 205–20.

Eilers, R. 1980. Infant speech perception. In *Child phonology,* eds. G. Yeni-Komshian, J. Kavanaugh, and C. Ferguson, Vol. 2. New York: Academic Press.

Eilers, R., Gavin, W., and Oller, D.K. 1982. Cross-linguistic perception in infancy: Early effects of linguistic experience. *J. Child Language* 9: 289–302.

Eilers, R., and Oller, D.K. 1976. The role of speech discrimination in developmental sound substitutions. *J. Child Language* 3: 319–29.

Eilers, R., Oller, D.K., and Benito-Garcia, C. 1984. The acquisition of voicing contrasts in Spanish- and English-learning infants and children: A longitudinal study. *J. Child Language* 11: 313–36.

Eimas, P. 1975. Speech perception in early infancy. In *Infant perception,* eds. L. Cohen and P. Salapatek. New York: Academic Press.

Eimas, P., Siqueland, E., Jusczyk, P., and Vigorito, J. 1971. Speech perception in infants. *Science* 171: 303–6.

Eisenberg, A., and Garvey, C. 1981. Children's use of verbal strategies in resolving conflicts. *Discourse Processes* 4: 149–70.

Ervin-Tripp, S. 1971. Social background and verbal skills. In *Language acquisition: Models and methods,* eds. R. Huxley and E. Ingram. London: Academic Press.

Evard, B., and Sabers, D. 1979. Speech and language testing with distinct ethno-racial groups: A survey of procedures for improving validity. *J. Speech and Hearing Disorders* 44: 271–81.

Fasold, R. 1969. Tense and the form *be* in Black English. *Language* 45: 763–76.

Fein, D., Skoff, B., and Mirsky, A. 1981. Clinical correlates of brain stem dysfunction in autistic children. *J. Autism and Developmental Disorder* 11: 303–15.

Feldman, C., and Shen, M. 1971. Same-language-related cognitive advantages of bilingual five-year-olds. *J. of Genetic Psychology* 118: 235–44.

Ferguson, C. 1986. Discovering sound units and constructing sound systems: It's child's play. In *Invariance and variability in speech processes,* eds. J. Perkell and D. Klatt. Hillsdale, N.J.: Lawrence Erlbaum Assoc.

Ferreiro, E., and Teberosky, A. 1982. *Literacy before schooling*. Exeter, N.H.: Heinemann Educational.

Field, D. 1977. The importance of the verbal content in the training of Piagetian conservation skills. *Child Development* 48: 1583–92.

Fillmore, C. 1968. A case for case. In *Universals in linguistic theory,* ed. E. Bach. New York: Holt, Rinehart & Winston.

Flavell, J. 1966. Role taking and communication skills in children. *Young Children* 21: 164–77.

Flavell, J. 1985. *Cognitive development*. Englewood Cliffs, N.J.: Prentice-Hall, Inc.

Flavell, J., Botkin, P., Fry, C., Wright, J., and Jarvis, P. 1968. *The development of roletaking and communication skills in children*. New York: John Wiley & Sons.

Flavell, J., Speer, J., Green, F., and August, D. 1981. The development of comprehension monitoring and knowledge about communication. *Monographs of the Society for Research in Child Development,* Vol. 46, No. 5, Serial No. 192.

Fletcher, P. 1979. The development of the verb phrase. In *Language Acquisition,* eds. P. Fletcher and M. Garman. Cambridge, England: Cambridge University Press.

Flood, J., and Menyuk, P. 1983. The development of metalinguistic awareness and its relation to reading. *J. Applied Developmental Psychology* 4: 65–80.

Flood, J., and Salus, P. 1984. *Language and the language arts*. Englewood Cliffs, N.J.: Prentice-Hall, Inc.

Flower, L., and Hayes, J. 1977. Problem-solving strategies and the writing process. *College English* 39: 449–61.

Fodor, J., Bever, T., and Garrett, M. 1974. *The psychology of language*. New York: McGraw-Hill Book Co.

Foley, W., and Van Valin, R. 1984. *Functional syntax and universal grammar.* Cambridge, England: Cambridge University Press.

Foorman, B., and Kinoshita, Y. 1983. Linguistic effects on children's encoding and decoding performance in Japan, United States and England. *Child Development* 54: 69–77.

Forster, K. 1978. Assessing the mental lexicon. In *Explorations in the biology of language,* ed. E. Walker. Hassocks, England: Harvester Press.

Fowler, A., Gelman, R., and Gleitman, L. 1980. A comparison of normal and retarded language as a function of MLU. Paper presented at 5th Annual Boston University Language Development Conference, Boston, October, 1980.

Fox, S. 1980. Promoting growth in oral language. In *Discovering language with children,* ed. G. Pinnell. Urbana, Ill.: Natl. Council of Teachers of English.

Fraiberg, S., and Adelson, F. 1973. Self-representation in language and play: Observations of blind children. *The Psychoanalytic Quarterly* 43: 539–62.

Fromkin, V., and Rodman, R. 1978. *An introduction to language.* 2nd ed. New York: Holt, Rhinehart & Winston.

Furrow, D., Nelson, K., and Benedict, H. 1979. Mother's speech to children and syntactic development: Some simple relations. *J. of Child Language* 6: 423–42.

Furrow, D., and Nelson, K. 1984. Environmental correlates of individual differences in language acquisition. *J. of Child Language* 11: 523–34.

Furth, H. 1973. *Deafness and learning: A psychosocial approach.* Belmont, CA.: Wadsworth Pub. Co. Inc.

Galburda, A., and Kemper, T. 1979. Cytoarchitectonic abnormalities in developmental dyslexia: A case study. *Annals of Neurology* 6: 94–100.

Garcia, E. 1983. Becoming bilingual during early childhood. *Intl. J. of Behavioral Development* 6: 375–404.

Gardner, H. 1974. Metaphors and modalities: How children project polar adjectives onto diverse domains. *Child Development* 45: 84–91.

Gardner, R., and Gardner, B. 1975. Evidence for sentence consitutents in the early utterances of child and chimpanzee. *J. Exper. Psychol. Gen.* 104: 244–67.

Garman, M. 1979. Early grammatical development. In *Language acquisition,* eds. P. Fletcher and M. Garman. Cambridge, England: Cambridge University Press.

Garnica, O. 1973. The development of phonemic speech perception in early childhood. In *Cognitive development and the acquisition of language,* ed. T. Moore. New York: Academic Press.

Garvey, C., and Hogan, R. 1973. Social speech and social interaction: Egocentrism revisited. *Child Development* 44: 562–68.

Geer, S., Gleitman, H., and Gleitman, L. 1972. Paraphrasing and remembering compound words. *J. Verbal Learning and Verbal Behavior* 11: 348–55.

Genesee, F. 1985. Second-language learning through immersion: A review of United States programs. *Review of Educational Research* 55: 541–61.

Genesee, F., and Lambert, W. 1983. Trilingual education for majority-language children. *Child Development* 54: 105–14.

Geschwind, N. 1965. Disconnection syndromes in animal and man. *Brain,* 88 (Part 2): 237–94.

Gibson, E., and Spelke, E. 1983. The development of perception. In *Handbook of child psychology,* eds. J. Flavell and E. Markman. 4th ed. Vol. 3. New York: John Wiley & Sons.

Gilbert, J., and Johnson, C. 1977. Temporal and sequential constraints on six-year-olds' phonological productions: some observations on "ambliance" phenomenon. *J. Child Language* 5: 101–12.

Gleitman, L., Gleitman, H., and Shipley, E. 1972. The emergence of the child as a grammarian. *Cognition* 1: 137–64.

Gleitman, L., Newport, E., and Gleitman, H. 1984. The current status of the motherese hypothesis. *J. of Child Language* 11: 43–79.

Glucksberg, S., and Danks, J. 1975. *Experimental psycholinguistics.* Hillsdale, N.J.: Lawrence Erlbaum Assoc.

Goffman, E. 1974. *Frame analysis.* New York: Harper & Row.

Goldin-Meadow, S., and Feldman, H. 1977. The development of language-like communication without a language model. *Science* 197: 401–3.

Goldsmith, S. 1977. Reading disability: some support for a psycholinguistic base. Paper presented at 2nd Annual Boston University Language Development Conference, Boston, October, 1977.

Golinkoff, R., Hirsh-Pasek, K., Lavallee, A., and Baduini, C. 1985. What's in a word: The young child's predisposition to use lexical contrast. Paper presented at 10th Annual Boston University Conference on Language Development, Boston, October, 1985.

Goodman, G., Haith, M., Guttentag, R., and Rao, S. 1983. Automatic processing of word meaning: Intralingual and interlingual interference. *Child Development* 56: 103–18.

Goodman, K. 1976. Reading: A psycholinguistic guessing game. In *Theoretical models and processes of reading,* eds. H. Singer and R. Rudel. Newark, Del.: International Reading Assoc.

Goodman, S. 1981. The integration of verbal and motor behavior in preschool children. *Child Development* 52: 280–89.

Goodhart, W. 1984. Morphological complexity: ASL and the acquisition of sign language in deaf children. Unpublished doctoral dissertation, Boston University.

Gopnik, A. 1982. Words and phrases: Early language and the development of intelligent action. *J. Child Language* 9: 303–18.

Gopnik, A., and Meltzoh, A. 1986. Relations between semantic end cognitive development in the one-word stage: The specificity hypothesis. *Child Development* 57: 1040–53.

Gordon, S. 1986. Oral discourse and literate prose. Unpublished doctoral dissertation, Boston University.

Graham, N., and Gulliford, R. 1968. A psychological approach to the language deficiencies of educationally subnormal children. *Educational Review* 20: 136–45.

Graybeal, C. 1981. Memory for stories in language-impaired children. *Applied Psycholinguistics* 2: 269–83.

Green, M. 1985. The development of metaphoric comprehension and preference. Unpublished doctoral dissertation, Boston University.

Greenbaum, I. 1985. Nonverbal differences in communication styles between American Indian and Anglo elementary classrooms. *American Educational Research J.* 22: 101–15.

Greene, R. 1982. Now you mean it now you don't: an explanatory study of children's sensitivity to consistent and discrepant message meanings as judged by normal, learning-disabled and math-depressed boys. Unpublished doctoral dissertation, Boston University.

Greenfield, P., and Smith, J. 1976. *The structure of communication in early language development.* New York: Academic Press.

Grice, H. 1975. Logic and conversation. In *Syntax and semantics, Vol. 3: Speech Acts,* eds. P. Cole and J. Morgan. New York: Seminar Press.

Grosjean, F. 1985. The bilingual as a competent but specific speaker-hearer. *The J. of Multilingual & Multicultural Development* 6: 467–77.

Grosjean, F., and Soares, C. 1986. Processing mixed language: Some preliminary findings. In *Language processing in bilinguals: Psycholinguistic and neurophysiological perspectives,* ed. J. Vaid. Hillsdale, N.J.: Lawrence Erlbaum Assoc.

Guess, D., Sailor, W., and Baer, D. 1974. To teach language to retarded children. In *Language perspectives: acquisition, retardation and intervention,* eds. R. Schiefelbusch and L. Lloyd. Baltimore: University Park Press.

Gumperz, J. 1975. Sociolinguistics and communication in small groups. *Working Paper No. 33,* Language Behavior Research Laboratory, University of California at Berkeley.

Gumperz, J. 1979. Individual and social differences in language use. In *Individual differences in language ability and language behavior,* eds. C. Fillmore, D. Kempler, and W. Wang. New York: Academic Press.

Guttentag, R., Haith, M., Goodman, G., and Hauch, J. 1984. Semantic processing of unattended words by bilinguals: A test of the input switch mechanism. *J. Verbal Learning and Verbal Behavior* 23: 178–88.

Haber, R., and Haber, L. 1981. The shape of a word can specify its meaning. *Reading Research Quarterly* 16: 334–45.

Haith, M. 1980. *Rules that babies look by.* Hillsdale, N.J.: Lawrence Erlbaum Assoc.

Hakuta, K. 1978. A report on the development of the grammatical morphemes in a Japanese girl learning English as a second language. In *Second language acquisition,* ed. E. Hatch. Rowley, MA.: Newbury House.

———. 1986. *Mirror of language: The debate on bilingualism.* New York: Basic Books.

Hall, V., and Kaye, D. 1980. Early patterns of cognitive development. *Monograph Society for Research in Child Development* 45, Serial No. 184.

Hall, W., and Freedle, R. 1973. A developmental investigation of standard and nonstandard English among black and white children. *Human Development* 16: 440–64.

Halliday, M. 1975. *Learning how to mean: exploration in the development of language.* London: Edward Arnold.

Hamburger, H., and Crain, S. 1984. Acquisiton of cognitive compiling. *Cognition* 17: 85–136.

Hamp, E. 1978. Problems of multilingualism in small linguistic communities. In *International dimensions of bilingual education,* ed. J. Alatis. Washington, D.C.: Georgetown University Press.

Hardy, J., and Braine, M. 1981. Categories that

bridge between meaning and syntax in five-year-olds. In *The child's construction of language,* ed. W. Deutsch. London: Academic Press.

Hayes, C. 1955. *The ape in our house.* New York: Harper & Bros.

Heath, S. 1982. What no bedtime story means: Narrative skills at home and school. *Language and Society* 11: 49–77.

———. 1983. *Ways with words.* Cambridge, England: Cambridge University Press.

———. 1985. The cross-cultural study of language acquisition. *Papers on Research in Child Language Development,* Vol. 24. Stanford, CA.: Stanford University.

Hedrick, D., Prather, E., and Tobin, A. 1975. *Sequenced inventory of communication development.* Seattle: Washington University Press.

Heider, E., and Olivier, D. 1972. The structure of the color space in naming and memory for two languages. *Cognitive Psychology* 3: 337–54.

Hirsh-Pasek, K., Golinkoff, R., Beaubien, F., Fletcher, A., and Cauley, K. 1985. In the beginning: One-word speakers comprehend word order. Paper presented at 10th Annual Boston University Language Development Conference, Boston, October, 1985.

Hockett, C. 1963. The problems of universals in language. In *Universals of language,* ed. J. Greeberg. Cambridge, MA.: M.I.T. press.

Hoh, H., and Hatch, E. 1978. Second-language acquisition: A case study. In *Second language acquisition,* ed. E. Hatch. Rowley, MA.: Newbury House.

Holzman, M. 1974. The verbal environment provided by mothers for their very young children. *Merrill-Palmer Quarterly* 20: 31–42.

Horgan, D. 1978. The development of the full passive. *J. Child Language* 5: 65–80.

Hsu, J., Cairns, H., and Fiengo, R. 1985. The development of grammars underlying children's interpretation of complex sentences. *Cognition* 20: 25–48.

Hunt, K. 1974. How little sentences grow into big ones. In *Language and the language arts,* eds. J. Destefano and S. Fox. Boston: Little, Brown & Co.

Hyams, N. 1986. Core and peripheral grammar and the acquisition of inflections. Paper presented at 11th Annual Boston University Conference on Language Development, Boston, October, 1986.

Hymes, D. 1964. Directions in ethno-linguistic theory. *American Anthropologist* 16: 6–56.

———. 1971. Sociolinguistics and the ethnography of speaking. In *Social anthropology of language,* ed. E. Ardener. London: Tavistock.

Ianco-Worrall, A. 1972. Bilingualism and cognitive development. *Child Development* 43:1390–1400.

Iglesias, A. 1985. Cultural conflict in the classroom: The communicatively different child. In *School discourse problems,* eds. D. Ripich and F. Spinelli. San Diego, CA.: College Hill Press.

Ingram, D. 1974. Phonological rules in young children. *J. Child Language* 1: 49–64.

Ives, W. 1980. Preschool children's ability to coordinate spatial perspectives through language and pictures. *Child Development* 51: 1303–6.

Jackendoff, R. 1978. Grammar as evidence of conceptual structure. In *Linguistic theory and psychological reality,* eds. M. Halle, J. Bresnan, and G. Miller. Cambridge, MA.: M.I.T. Press.

Jaffe, B. ed. 1977. *Hearing loss in children.* Baltimore: University Park Press.

Jakobson, R. 1968. *Child language, aphasia, and phonological universals.* The Hague, Netherlands: Mouton.

Jakobson, R., Fant, G., and Halle, M. 1963. *Preliminaries to speech analysis.* Cambridge, MA.: M.I.T. Press.

Jenkins, J., and Palermo, D. 1964. Mediation processes and the acquisition of linguistic structure. In *The acquisition of language,* eds. U. Bellugi and R. Brown. *Monographs of the Society for Research in Child Development.* Vol. 10, Serial No. 92: 141–69.

John-Steiner, V. 1984. Learning styles among Pueblo children. *Quarterly Newsletter of the Laboratory of Comparative Human Development, University of California, San Diego* 6: 57–62.

Johnston, J. 1982. Narratives: a new look at communication problems in older language-disordered children. *Language Speech and Hearing Services in Schools* 13: 144–56.

Johnston, J., and Weismer, S. 1982. Mental rotation abilities in language-disordered children. *J. Speech and Hearing Research* 26: 397–403.

Jorm, A. 1979. The cognitive and neurological basis of developmental dyslexia. *Cognition* 7: 19–29.

Jusczyk, P. 1982. Auditory versus phonetic coding of speech signals during infancy. In *Perspectives in mental representation: experimental and theoretical studies of cognitive processes and capacities,* eds. J. Mehler, M. Garrett, and E. Walker. Hillsdale, N.J.: Lawrence Erlbaum Assoc.

———. 1986. Toward a model of the development of speech perception. In *Invariance and variability in the speech process,* eds. J. Perkell and D. Klatt. Hillsdale, N.J.: Lawrence Erlbaum Assoc.

Kahmi, A., Catts, H., Koenig, L., and Lewis, B. 1984. Hypothesis testing and nonlinguistic symbolic abilities in language-impaired children. *J. Speech and Hearing Disorders* 49: 169–76.

Kahmi, A., and Johnston, J. 1982. Toward an understanding of retarded children's linguistic abilities. *J. Speech and Hearing Research* 25: 435–45.

Kail, R. 1979. *The development of memory in children.* San Francisco, CA.: Freeman.

———. 1984. *The development of memory in children,* 2nd ed. New York: W.H. Freeman Co.

Kail, R., and Hagen, J. 1977. *Perspectives in the development of memory and cognition.* Hillsdale, N.J.: Lawrence Erlbaum Assoc.

Kanter, R. 1980. The acquisition of classifiers in American Sign Language. *Sign Language Studies* 36: 233–82.

Kaplan, E., and Kaplan, G. 1970. The prelinguistic child. In *Human development and cognitive processes,* ed. J. Eliot. New York: Holt, Rhinehart & Winston.

Karmiloff-Smith, A. 1978. The interplay between syntax, semantics, and phonology in language-acquisition processes. In *Recent advances in the psychology of language: Language development and mother-child interaction,* eds. R. Campbell and P. Smith. New York: Plenum Press.

———. 1979. Language development after five. In *Language acquisition,* eds. P. Fletcher and M. Garman. Cambridge, England: Cambridge University Press.

Katz, J., and Jusczyk, P. 1980. Do six-month-olds have perceptual constancy for phonetic segments? Paper presented at Intl. Conference on Infant Studies, New Haven, Conn., April, 1980.

Keil, F., and Batterman, N. 1984. A characteristic to defining shift in the development of word meaning. *J. of Verbal Learning and Verbal Behavior* 23: 221–36.

Kent, R. 1983. The segmental organization of speech. In *The production of speech,* ed. P. MacNeilage. New York: Springer-Verlag.

Kent, R., and Bauer, H. 1985. Vocalization of one-year-olds. *J. Child Language* 12: 491–526.

Kinsbourne, M. 1975. The ontogeny of cerebral dominance. *Annals of the New York Academy of Sciences* 263: 244–50.

Kipling, R. 1894. *The jungle book.* London: Harcourt.

Kirsner, K., Smith, M., Lockhart, R., and King, M. 1984. The bilingual lexicon: Language-specific units in an integrated network. *J. Verbal Learning and Verbal Behavior* 23: 519–39.

Knights, R., and Bakker, D. 1976. *The neuropsychology of learning disorders.* Baltimore: University Park Press.

Kosslyn, S., and Bower, G. 1974. The role of imagery in sentence meaning: A developmental study. *Child Development* 45: 30–38.

Kramer, P., Koff, E., and Luria, Z. 1972. The development of competence in an exceptional language structure in older children and young adults. *Child Development* 43: 121–30.

Krashen, S. 1975. The critical period for language acquisition. *Annals of the New York Academy of Sciences* 263: 211–24.

Kroll, B. 1981. Developmental relationships between speaking and writing. In *Exploring speaking-writing relationships: Connections and contrasts,* eds. B. Kroll and R. Vann. Urbana, Ill.: Natl. Council of Teachers of English.

Kubilius, A. 1979. A developmental investigation into low-ability and high-ability reader's comprehension of intersentential elipsis in written discourse. Unpublished doctoral dissertation, Boston University.

Kuder, J. 1984. Lexical organization and free recall in learning-disabled, mentally retarded and normal children. Unpublished doctoral dissertation, Boston University.

Kuhl, P. 1985. Categorization of speech by infants. In *Neonate cognition: beyond the blooming, buzzing confusion,* eds. J. Mehler and R. Fox. Hillsdale, N.J.: Lawrence Erlbaum Assoc.

———. 1986. Reflections on infants' perception and representation of speech. In *Invariance and variability in the speech process,* eds. J. Perkell and D. Klatt. Hillsdale, N.J.: Lawrence Erlbaum Assoc.

Kuhl, P., and Meltzoff, A. 1982. The bimodal perception of speech in infancy. *Science* 218: 1138–41.

Kuhl, P., and Miller, J. 1978. Speech perception by the chinchilla: Identification functions for synthetic VOT stimuli. *J. Acoustical Society of America* 63: 905–17.

LaBerge, D., and Samuels, S. 1974. Toward a theory of automatic information processing in reading. *Cognitive Psychology* 6: 293–323.

Labov, W. 1966. *The social stratification of English in New York City.* Center for Applied Linguistics, Washington, D.C.

———. 1970. The logic of nonstandard English. In *Language and poverty,* ed. F. Williams. Chicago: Markham Pub. Co.

———. 1972. The transformation of experience in narrative syntax. In *Language in the inner city,* ed. W. Labov. Philadelphia, PA.: University of Pennsylvania Press.

———. 1973. Modes of mitigation and politeness. In *Language society and education: A profile of Black English,* ed. J. DeStefano. Worthington, Ohio: Charles A. Jones Publ. Co.

———. 1986. Sources of inherent variations in the speech processes. In *Invariance and variability in speech processes,* eds. J. Perkell and D. Klatt. Hillsdale, N.J.: Lawrence Erlbaum Assoc.

Labov, W., and Cohen, P. 1967. Systematic relations of standard and nonstandard rules in the grammars of Negro speakers. *Project Literacy Reports.* No. 8. 66–82. Utica, N.Y.: Cornell University.

Lackner, J. 1968. A developmental study of language behavior in retarded children. *Neuropsychologia* 6: 301–20.

La France, M., and Mayo, C. 1976. Racial differences in gaze behavior during conversations. *J. Personality and Social Psychology* 33: 547–52.

Lambert, W. 1972. *Language, psychology and culture. Essays by Wallace E. Lambert.* Stanford, CA.: Stanford University Press.

———. 1975. Culture and language as factors in learning and education. In *Education of immigrant students,* ed. A. Wolfgang. Toronto: Ontario Institute for Studies in Education.

Lambert, W., and Rawlings, C. 1969. Bilingual processing of mixed language associative networks. *J. Verbal Learning and Verbal Behavior* 8: 604–9.

Landau, B., and Gleitman, L. 1985. *Language and experience.* Cambridge, MA.: Harvard University Press.

Lane, H. 1976. *The wild boy of Aveyron.* Cambridge, MA.: Harvard University Press.

Langner, J. 1970. Werner's theory of development. In *Carmichael's manual of child psychology,* ed. P. Mussen. Vol. 1. New York: John Wiley & Sons.

Layton, T., and Sharifi, H. 1979. Meaning and structure of Down's syndrome and nonretarded children's spontaneous speech. *Amer. J. of Ment. Def.* 83: 439–45.

Learning Concepts. 1975. *Austin Spanish articulation test.* Austin, Texas: Learning Concepts.

Lenneberg, E. 1966. Natural history of language. In *Genesis of language,* eds. F. Smith and G. Miller. Cambridge, MA.: M.I.T. Press.

———. 1967. *The biological foundations of language.* New York: John Wiley & Sons.

Lenneberg, E., Nichols, I., and Rosenberger, E. 1964. Primitive stages of language development in mongolism. In *Proceedings of the Association for Research in Nervous and Mental Disease,* 42nd Annual Meeting, New York.

Leonard, L. 1972. What is deviant language? *J. Speech and Hearing Disorders* 37: 427–46.

———. 1979. Language impairment in children. *Merrill Palmer Quarterly* 25: 205–32.

Leonard, L., Miller, J., and Brown, H. 1980. Consonant and syllable harmony in the speech of language-disordered children. *J. Speech and Hearing Disorders* 45: 336–45.

Leonard, L., Wilcox, M., Fulmer, K., and Davis, G. 1978. Understanding in direct requests: an investigation of children's comprehension of pragmatic meanings. *J. of Speech and Hearing Research* 21: 528–37.

Leopold, W. 1939. *Speech development of a bilingual child: A linguist's record.* Vol. 1. Evanston, Ill.: Northwestern University Press.

———. 1947. *Speech development of a bilingual child: a linguist's record.* Vol. 2. Evanston, Ill.: Northwestern University Press.

Levy, C. 1977. Linguistic and nonlinguistic processing by children with normally developing and impaired language. Unpublished doctoral dissertation, Boston University.

Levy, J. 1979. Strategies of linguistic processing in human split-brain patients. In *Individual differences in language ability and language behavior,* eds. C. Filmore, D. Kempler, and W. Wang. New York: Academic Press.

Levy, Y. 1983. It's frogs all the way down. *Cognition* 15: 75–93.

Liberman, A. 1970. The grammars of speech and language. *Cognitive Psychology* 1: 301–23.

Liberman, A., Cooper, F., Shankweiler, D., and Studdert-Kennedy, M. 1967. Perception of the speech code. *Psychological Review* 74: 431–61.

Liberman, I., Shankweiler, D., Fisher, F., and Carter, B. 1974. Explicit syllable and phoneme segmentation in the young child. *J. Experimental Child Psychology* 18: 201–12.

Liebergott, J., Menyuk, P., Schultz, M., Chesnick, M., and Thomas, S. 1984. Individual variation and mechanisms of interaction. Paper presented at 8th biennial *Southeastern Conference on Human Development,* Atlanta, Ga., April, 1984.

Liebergott, J., Schultz, M., and Menyuk, P. 1985. A prescriptive manual for parents and teachers of children at risk for language disorders. *Final report on U.S. Department of Education, Office of Special Education and Rehabilitation Services,* Field-initiated research grant G008006727.

Lieberman, P. 1974. *On the origins of language.* New York: MacMillan.

———. 1986. On the genetic basis of linguistic variation. In *Invariance and variability in the speech processes,* eds. J. Perkell and D. Klatt. Hillsdale, N.J.: Lawrence Erlbaum Assoc.

Limber, J. 1973. The genesis of complex sentences. In *Cognitive development and the acquisition of language,* ed. T. Moore. New York: Academic Press.

Lindfors, J. 1980. *Children's language and learning.* Englewood Cliffs, N.J.: Prentice-Hall, Inc.

Loban, W. 1976. *Language development: Kindergarten through grade twelve.* Urbana, Ill.: Natl. Council of Teachers of English.

Locke, J. 1983. *Phonological acquisition and change.* New York: Academic Press.

Loftus, G., and Loftus, E. 1976. *Human memory: The processing of information.* Hillsdale, N.J.: Lawrence Erlbaum Assoc.

Long, M. 1981. Input, interaction and second-language acquisition. In *Native language foreign language acquisition,* ed. H. Winitz. *Annals of the New York Academy of Sciences* 379: 259–78.

Loritz, D. 1981. Children's knowledge of advanced phonics rules. Unpublished doctoral dissertation, Boston University.

Lujon, M., Minaya, L., and Sankoff, D. 1984. The universal consistency hypothesis and the prediction of word order acquisition stages in the speech of bilingual children. *Language* 60: 343–71.

Luria, A. 1976. *Cognitive development: Its cultural roots and social foundation.* Cambridge, MA.: Harvard University Press.

Lust, B., and Mervis, C. 1980. Development of coordination in the natural speech of young children. *J. Child Language* 7: 279–304.

Mack, M., and Lieberman, P. 1985. Acoustic analysis of words produced by a child from 46 to 149 weeks. *J. of Child Language* 12: 527–50.

Macken, M., and Barton, D. 1980. The acquisition of voicing contrasts in Spanish: a phonetic and phonological study of word initial stop consonants. *J. of Child Language* 7: 433–58.

Mackworth, N., Grandstaff, N., and Pribram, K. 1972. Prolonged orientation to pictorial novelty in speech-disordered children. In *Papers and reports in child language development,* ed. D. Ingram. No. 4. Stanford, California: Institute of Childhood Aphasia, Stanford University.

MacNamara, J. 1972. The cognitive basis of learning in infants. *Psychological Review* 79: 1–13.

MacWhinney, B. 1978. The acquisition of morphophonology. *Monographs of the Society for Research in Child Development.* Vol. 43, Serial No. 174, Nos. 1 and 2.

Magnusson, E. 1983. The phonology of language-disordered children: Production perception and awareness. *Travaux de L'Institut de Linguistique de Lund.* Lund, Sweden: CWK Gleerup.

Malgady, A. 1977. Children's appreciation and interpretation of riddles. *Child Development* 48: 1734–38.

Malsheen, B. 1980. Two hypotheses for phonetic clarification in the speech of mothers to children. In *Child phonology,* eds. G. Yeni-Komshian, J. Kavanaugh, and J. Jenkins. Vol. 2. New York: Academic Press.

Mandler, J. 1983. Representation. In *Handbook of child psychology,* eds. J. Flavell and E. Markman. Vol. 3. New York: John Wiley & Sons.

Mandler, J., and DeForest, M. 1979. Is there more than one way to recall a story? *Child Development* 50: 886–89.

Mandler, J., Scribner, S., Cole, M., and DeForest, M. 1980. Cross-cultural invariance in story recall. *Child Development* 51: 19–26.

Mann, V., Liberman, I., and Shankweiler, D. 1980. Memory for sentences and word strings in relation to reading ability. *Memory and Cognition* 8: 329–35.

Maratsos, M. 1973. Non-egocentric communication abilities in preschool children. *Child Development* 44: 697–700.

———. 1974. How preschool children understand missing complement sentences. *Child Development* 45: 700–6.

———. 1979. Learning how and when to use pronouns and determiners. In *Language acquisition,* eds. P. Fletcher and M. Garman. Cambridge, England: Cambridge University Press.

———. 1983. Some current issues in the acquisition of grammar. In *Handbook of child psychology,* eds. J. Flavell and E. Markman. Vol. 3. New York: John Wiley & Sons.

Marler, P. 1963. Inheritance and learning in the development of animal vocalizations. In *Acoustic behavior of animals,* ed. A. Busnel. Amsterdam: Elsevier Pub. Co.

Marslen-Wilson, W., and Tyler, L. 1980. The temporal structure of spoken language understanding. *Cognition* 8: 1–71.

Mazeika, E. 1971. A comparison of the phonologic development of a monolingual and bilingual (Spanish-English) child. Paper presented at Biennial Meeting of the Society for Research in Child Development, Minneapolis, Minn., April, 1971.

McCune-Nicolich, L. 1981. Toward symbolic functioning: Structure of early pretend games and potential parallels with language. *Child Development* 52: 785–97.

McDonald, L., and Pien, D. 1982. Mother conversational behavior as a function of interaction intent. *J. of Child Language* 9: 337–58.

McGhee, P. 1979. *Humor: its origin and development.* San Francisco: Freeman.

McNeill, D. 1970. *The acquisition of language: The study of developmental psycholinguistics.* New York: Harper & Row.

———. 1971. The capacity for the ontogenesis of grammar. In *The ontogenesis of grammar,* ed. D. Slobin. New York: Academic Press.

Meacham, J. 1978. Verbal guidance through remembering the goals of action. *Child Development* 49: 188–93.

Meltzoff, A. 1986. Imitation and intermodal representation in early infancy. In *Precursors of early speech,* eds. B. Lindblom and R. Zetterstrom. New York: Stockton Press.

Meltzoff, A., and Borton, R. 1979. Intermodal matching by human neonates. *Nature* 282: 403–4.

Menn, L. 1976. Pattern, control, and contrast in beginning speech: a case study in the development of word form and word function. Unpublished doctoral dissertation. University of Illinois, Champaign-Urbana.

———. 1981. Theories of phonological development. In *Native language and foreign language acquisition,* ed. H. Winitz. *New York Academy of Sciences Annals,* 379.

Menyuk, P. 1963. A preliminary evaluation of grammatical capacity in children. *J. Verbal Learning and Verbal Behavior* 2: 429–39.

———. 1964*a*. Alternation of rules in children's grammar. *J. Verbal Learning and Verbal Behavior* 3: 480–88.

———. 1964*b*. A comparison of the grammar of children with functionally deviant speech. *J. Speech and Hearing Research* 7: 109–21.

———. 1967. Children's perception of a set of words. *Quarterly Progress Reports, Research Laboratory of Electronics, M.I.T.* No. 84, 254–57.

———. 1968. Children's learning and reproduction of of grammatical and nongrammatical phonological sequences. *Child Development* 39: 844–60.

———. 1969. *Sentences children use.* Cambridge, MA.: M.I.T. Press.

———. 1971. *The acquisition and development of language.* Englewood Cliffs, N.J.: Prentice-Hall, Inc.

———. 1972. Speech-sound categorization

within sets. *Quarterly Progress Reports, Research Laboratory of Electronics, M.I.T.* No. 105, 119–23.

———. 1974. Early development of receptive language: From babbling to words. In *Language perspectives: Acquisition, retardation and intervention,* eds. R. Schiefelbusch and L. Lloyd. Baltimore: University Park Press.

———. 1975*a*. The language-impaired child: Linguistic or cognitive impairment. *Annals of the New York Academy of Sciences* 263: 59–69.

———. 1975*b*. Children with language problems: What's the problem? In *Developmental psycholinguistics: Theory and application,* ed. D. Dato. Washington, D.C.: Georgetown University Press.

———. 1976. That's another funny, awful way of saying it. *J. of Education,* Boston University 158: 25–38.

———. 1977. *Language and maturation.,* Cambridge, MA.: M.I.T. Press.

———. 1978. Linguistic problems in children with developmental dysphasia. In *Developmental dysphasia,* ed. M. Wyke. London: Academic Press.

———. 1980. The role of context in misarticulations. In *Child phonology,* eds. G. Yeni-Komshian, J. Kavanaugh, and C. Ferguson. Vol. I. New York: Academic Press.

———. 1981. Syntactic competence and reading. In *Language learning and reading disabilities: A new decade,* eds. J. Stark and S. Wurtzel. City University of New York, New York: Queens College.

———. 1983. Language development and reading. In *Pragmatic issues: Assessment and intervention,* eds. T. Gallagher and C. Prutting. San Diego, CA.: College Hill Press.

———. 1984. Continuities and discontinuities in language development over the first two years. In *Language and cognition,* ed. L. Raphael. New York: Plenum Press.

———. 1985*a*. Wherefore metalinguistic skills. *Merrill-Palmer Quarterly* 31: 253–59.

———. 1985*b*. Early communication and language behavior. In *In the beginning: development during the first two years of life,* eds. J. Rosenblith and J. Simms-Knight. Monterey, CA.: Brooks Cole.

———. 1986*a*. Language development in a social context. *The Journal of Pediatrics* 109: 217–24.

———. 1986*b*. Predicting speech and language problems with persistent otitis media. In *Otitis media and child development,* ed. J. Kavanaugh. Parkton, MD.: York Press.

Menyuk, P., and Bernholtz, N. 1969. Prosodic features and children's language production. *Research Laboratory of Electronics Quarterly Progress Reports, M.I.T.* No. 93. 216–19.

Menyuk, P., and Flood, J. 1981. Linguistic competence, reading and writing problems, and remediation. *Bulletin of the Orton Society* 31: 13–28.

Menyuk, P., and Klatt, D. 1968. Children's production of initial consonant clusters. *Research Laboratory of Electronics Quarterly Progress Reports, M.I.T.,* No. 91. 205–13.

Menyuk, P., Liebergott, J., and Schultz, M. 1986. Early vocalization in premature and full-term infants: predicting speech and lexical development. In *Precursors to early speech,* eds. B. Lindblom and R. Zetterstrom. New York: Stockton Press.

Menyuk, P., and Looney, P. 1972*a*. A problem of language disorder: length versus structure. *J. Speech and Hearing Research* 15: 264–79.

———. 1972*b*. Relationships among components of the grammar in language disorder. *J. Speech and Hearing Research* 15: 395–406.

Menyuk, P., and Menn, L. 1979. Early strategies for the perception and production of words and sounds. In *Language acquisition,* eds. P. Fletcher and M. Garman. Cambridge, England: Cambridge University Press.

Menyuk, P., Menn, L., and Silber, R. 1986. Early strategies for the perception and production of words and sounds. In *Language Acquisition, 2nd Edition,* eds. P. Fletcher and M. Garman. Cambridge, England: Cambridge University Press.

Merino, B. 1983. Language loss in bilingual Chicano children. *J. Applied Developmental Psychology* 4: 277–94.

Michaels, S. 1981. "Sharing time": Children's narrative styles and differential access to literacy. *Language in Society* 10: 49–76.

Michaels, S., and Collins, J. 1984. Oral discourse styles: Classroom interaction and the acquisition of literacy. In *Coherence in written and spoken discourse,* ed. D. Tannen. Norwood, N.J.: Ablex.

Miller, G. 1962. Some psychological studies of grammar. *American Psychologist* 17: 748–62.

Miller, J., and Chapman, R. 1981. The relation between age and mean length of utterances in morphemes. *J. Speech and Hearing Research* 24: 154–61.

Miller, J., Chapman, R., and MacKenzie, H. 1981. Individual differences in the language acquisition of mentally retarded children. Paper presented at Biennial Meeting of the Society for Research in Child Development, Boston.

Miller, J. O., and Eimas, P. 1983. Studies in the categorization of speech by infants. *Cognition* 13: 135–65.

Mishler, E. 1975. Implications of teacher strategies for language and cognition: Observations in first grade classrooms. In *Functions of language in the classroom,* eds. C. Cazden, V. Johns, and D. Hymes. New York: Teachers College Press.

Molfese, D., and Molfese, V. 1979. Hemisphere and stimulus differences as reflected in the cortical responses of newborn infants to speech stimuli. *Developmental Psychology* 15: 205–11.

Moorhead, D., and Moorehead, A. 1974. From signal to sign: A Piagetian view of thought and language during the first two years. In *Language perspectives: Acquisition, retardation and intervention,* eds. R. Scheifelbusch and L. Lloyd. Baltimore: University Park Press.

Morse, P. 1978. Infant speech perception: Origins, processes and alpha centauri. In *Communication and early cognitive abilities: Behavioral assessment,* eds. F. Minifie and L. Lloyd. Baltimore: University Park Press.

Morse, P., and Snowden, C. 1978. An investigation of categorical speech discrimination by rhesus monkeys. *Percept. Psychophys.* 17: 9–16.

Morton, J. 1982. Disintegrating the lexicon: an information-processing approach. In *Perspectives on mental representation,* eds. J. Mehler, E. Walker, and M. Garrett. Hillsdale, N .J.: Lawrence Erlbaum Assoc.

Mounty, J. 1986. Nativization and input in the language development of two deaf children of hearing parents. Unpublished doctoral dissertation, Boston University.

Myerson, R. 1976. A study of children's knowledge of certain word formation rules and the relationship of this knowledge to various forms of reading. Unpublished doctoral dissertation, Harvard University.

Nakazima, S. 1962. A comparative study of the speech development of Japanese and American English in childhood. *Studia Phonologica* 3: 27–39.

Naremore, R., and Dever, R. 1975. Language performance of educable mentally retarded and normal children at five age levels. *Journal of Speech and Hearing Research* 18: 82–95.

Nas, G. 1983. Visual word recognition in bilinguals: evidence for a cooperation between visual and sound-based codes during access to a common lexical store. *J. Verbal Learning and Verbal Behavior* 22: 526–34.

Nelson, K. 1973. Structure and strategy in learning to talk. *Monographs of the Society for Research in Child Development* Vol. 38. Serial No. 149.

———. 1981. Individual differences in language development: Implications for development and language. *Devel. Psychol.* 17: 170–87.

Nelson, K., and Gruendal, J. 1979. All morning it's lunch time: A scriptal analysis of children's dialogues. *Discourse Processes* 2: 73–94.

———. 1981. Generalized event representations: Basic building blocks of cognition development. In *Advances in developmental psychology,* eds. M. Lamb and A. Brown. Vol. 1. Hillsdale, N.J.: Lawrence Erlbaum Assoc.

Nelson, K.E., and Bonvillian, J. 1978. Early language development: conceptual growth and related processes between two and four and a half years of age. In *Child Language,* ed. K. Nelson. Vol. 1. New York: Gardner Press.

Nelson, K.E., Danninger, M., Bonvillian, J., Kaplan, B., and Baker, N. 1983. Maternal adjustments and nonadjustments as related to children's linguistic advances. In *The development of oral and written languages: Readings in developmental and applied linguistics,* eds. A. Pelligrini and T. Yawky. New York: Ablex.

Nerlove, S., Roberts, J., Klein, R., Yarbrough, L., and Habicht, J. 1974. Natural indicators of cognitive development: An observational study of rural Guatemalan children. *Ethos* 2: 265–95.

Nettlebladt, U. 1983. Developmental studies of dysphonology in children. *Travaux de L'Institut de Linguistique de Lund.* Lund, Sweden: CWK Gleerup.

Neville, H. 1980. Event-related potentials in

neuropsychological studies of language. *Brain and Language* 11: 300–18.

Nikse, R. 1983. Adult literacy in the United States: Issues and responses. Unpublished paper. Boston University, School of Education.

Nippold, M., and Fly, S. 1983. Metaphoric understanding in preadolescents having a history of language acquisition difficulties. *Language Speech and Hearing Services in the Schools* 14: 171–80.

Norman-Jackson, J. 1982. Family interactions, language development and primary reading achievement of Black children in families of low income. *Child Development* 53: 349–58.

Ochs, E., and Schieffelin, B. 1984. Language acquisition and socialization: Three developmental stories. In *Culture theory: Essays on mind self and emotion,* eds. R. Shweder and R. Levine. Cambridge, England: Cambridge University Press.

Ogbu, J. 1978. *Minority education and caste.* New York: Academic Press.

Oken, M. 1984. The development of naming skills in normal and language-deficient children. Unpublished doctoral dissertation, Boston University.

Oller, K. 1986. Metaphonology and infant vocalization. In *Precursors of early speech,* eds. B. Lindblom and R. Zetterstrom. New York: Stockton.

Oller, K., and Eilers, R. 1983. Speech identification in Spanish- and English-learning two-year-olds. *J. Speech and Hearing Research,* 26: 50–53.

Olsen-Fulero, L. 1982. Style and stability in mother conversational behavior. *J. of Child Language* 9: 543–64.

Oppenheim, P. 1981. Selected relationships between linguistic processing skills and reading. Unpublished doctoral dissertation, Boston University.

Ornitz, E. 1978. Neuropsychologic studies. In *Autism: A reappraisal of concepts and treatment,* eds. M. Rutter and E. Schopler. New York: Plenum Press.

Osgood, C. 1966. Language universals and psycholinguistics. In *Universals of language,* ed. J. Greenberg. Cambridge, MA.: M.I.T. Press.

Oviatt, S. 1982. Inferring what words mean: Early development of infants' comprehension of common object names. *Child Development* 53: 274–77.

Paivio, A. 1968. A factor-analytic study of word attributes and verbal learning. *J. Verbal Learning and Verbal Behavior* 7: 41–49.

———. 1969. Mental imagery in associative learning and memory. *Psychol. Review* 76: 241–63.

———. 1971. *Imagery and verbal processes.* New York: Holt, Rinehart & Winston.

Perera, K. 1986. Language acquisition and writing. In *Language acquisition,* 2nd ed., eds. P. Fletcher and M. Garman. Cambridge, England: Cambridge University Press.

Pezdek, K. 1980. Life-span differences in semantic integration of pictures and sentences in memory. *Child Development* 51: 720–29.

Phillips, J. 1973. Syntax and vocabulary of mother's speech to young children: Age and sex. *Child Development* 44: 182–85.

Piaget, J. 1926. *The language and thought of the child.* New York: Harcourt, Brace Jovanovich, Inc.

———. 1970. Piaget's theory. In *Carmichael's manual of child psychology,* ed. P. Mussen. Vol. 1. New York: John Wiley & Sons.

Piatelli-Palmarini, M., ed. 1980. *Language and learning: The debate between Jean Piaget and Noam Chomsky.* Cambridge, MA.: Harvard University Press.

Piestrup, A. 1973. Black dialect interference and accommodation of reading instruction in first grade. *Monographs of the Language Behavior Research Laboratory.* No. 4. U. of California, Berkeley.

Pinker, S. 1981. A theory of the acquisition of lexical interpretive grammars. In *The mental representation of grammatical relations,* ed. J. Bresnan. Cambridge, MA.: M.I.T. Press.

———. 1984. *Language learnability and language development.* Cambridge, MA.: Harvard University Press.

Platt, C., and MacWhinney, B. 1983. Error assimilation as a mechanism in language learning. *J. Child Language* 10: 401–14.

Potter, M., So, K., Von Eckardt, B., and Feldman, L. 1984. Lexical and conceptual representation in beginning proficient bilinguals. *J. Verbal Learning and Verbal Behavior* 23: 23–38.

Prawat, R., and Wildfong, S. 1980. The influence of functional context on children's labelling responses. *Child Development* 51: 1057–60.

Premack, D. 1985. "Gavagai!" or the future history of the animal language controversy. *Cognition* 19: 207–96.

Prizant, B., and Duchan, J. 1981. The function of immediate echolalia in autistic children. *J. Speech and Hearing Disorders* 46: 241–49.

Quay, L. 1971. Language dialect, reinforcement, and the intelligence test performance of Negro children. *Child Development* 42: 5–15.

———. 1972. Negro dialect and Binet performance in severely disadvantaged black four-year-olds. *Child Development* 43: 245–50.

Quill, K. 1985. The nature of semantic knowledge in autism. Unpublished doctoral dissertation, Boston University.

Rapin, I., and Wilson, B. 1978. Children with developmental language disability: Neurological aspects and assessment. In *Developmental Dysphasia,* ed. M. Wyke. London: Academic Press.

Redeker, G. 1984. On differences between spoken and written language. *Discourse Processes* 7: 43–55.

Redlinger, W., and Park, T. 1980. Language mixing in young bilinguals. *J. Child Language* 7: 337–52.

Reed, D. 1965. A theory of language, speech, and writing. *Elementary English,* 42: 845–51.

Reitsma, P. 1983. Printed-word learning in beginning readers. *J. Experimental Child Psychology* 36: 321–39.

Reynolds, R., and Ortony, A. 1980. Some issues in the measurement of children's comprehension of metaphorical language. *Child Development* 51: 1110–19.

Ricks, D., and Wing, L. 1975. Communication and the use of symbols in normal and autistic children. *J. Autism and Childhood Schizophrenia* 5: 191–221.

Rintell, E. 1980. Language variation and pragmatic ability: The influence of context on the production of speech acts by second-language learners. Unpublished Ph.D. dissertation, Boston University.

Ripich, D., and Spinelli, F. 1985. *School discourse problems.* San Diego, CA.: College Hill Press.

Robinson, E., and Robinson, W. 1982. The advancement of children's verbal referential communication skills: The role of metacognitive guidance. *Intl. J. of Behavioral Development* 5: 329–56.

Robinson, R. 1981. Equal recovery in child and adult brain? *Developmental Medicine & Child Neurology* 23: 379–82.

Rondal, J. 1983. Maternal speech to normal and Down's syndrome children matched for MLU. Minneapolis: University of Minnesota Research, Development and Demonstration Center in Education of Handicapped Children.

———. 1985. *Adult–child interaction and the process of language acquisition.* New York: Praeger Publishers.

Rosenblum, T., and Pinker, S. 1983. Word magic revisited: Monolingual and bilingual children's understanding of the word object relationship. *Child Development* 54: 773–80.

Ryan, J. 1975. Mental subnormality and language development. In *Foundations of language,* eds. E. Lenneberg and E. Lenneberg. Vol. 2. New York: Academic Press.

Sachs, J., and Truswell, L. 1978. Comprehension of two-word instructions by children in the one-word stage. *J. Child Language* 5: 17–24.

Salapatek, P. 1977. Stimulus determinants of attention in infants. In *International encyclopedia of psychiatry, psychology, psychoanalysis and neurology,* ed. B. Wolman. Vol. 10. New York: Van Nostrand Rheinhold.

Salus, M. 1982. The syntax and metalinguistic skills of children who read early. Unpublished doctoral dissertation, Boston University.

Salzinger, K. 1967. The problem of response class in verbal behavior. In *Research in verbal behavior and some neurophysiological implications,* eds. K. Salzinger and S. Salzinger. New York: Academic Press.

Satz, P., Rardin, D., and Ross, J. 1971. An evaluation of a theory of specific dyslexia. *Child Development* 42: 2009–21.

Saville-Troike, M. 1984. What really matters in second-language learning for academic achievement? *Tesol Quarterly* 18: 199–219.

Schankweiler, D., and Liberman, I. 1972. Misreadings: A search for causes. In *Language by ear and by eye,* eds. J. Kavanaugh and I. Mattingly. Cambridge, MA.: M.I.T. Press.

Schleser, R., Meyers, A., and Cohen, R. 1981. Generalization of self-instructions: Effects of general versus specific content, active rehearsal, and cognitive level. *Child Development* 52: 335–40.

Schlesinger, I. 1977. The role of cognitive development and linguistic input in linguistic development. *J. Child Language* 4: 1–35.

Schmidt, C., and Paris, S. 1983. Children's use of successive clues to generate and monitor inferences. *Child Development* 54: 742–59.

Schopler, E., and Mesibov, G. 1985. *Communication problems in autism.* New York: Plenum Press.

Schuman, J. 1975. Affective factors and the problem of age in second-language acquisition. *Language Learning* 25: 209–35.

Schwartz, R., Leonard, L., Folger, M., and Wilcox, M. 1980. Early phonological behavior in normal speaking and language-disordered children. *J. Speech and Hearing Disorders* 45: 357–77.

Schwartz, R., and Solot, C. 1980. Response patterns characteristic of verbal expressive disorders. *Language Speech and Hearing Services in Schools* 11: 139–44.

Scollan, R., and Scollan, S. 1979. *Linguistic convergence: An ethnography of speaking at Fort Chipewyan, Alberta.* New York: Academic Press.

———. 1981. *Narrative, literacy, and face in interethnic communication.* Norwood, N.J.: Albex Press.

Sebeok, T. 1972. *Perspectives on zoosemiotics.* The Hague, The Netherlands: Mouton.

———. 1981. The ultimate enigma of "clever Hans": the union of nature and culture. In *The clever Hans phenomenon: communications with horses, whales, apes, and people. Annals of New York Academy of Sciences,* eds. T. Sebeok and R. Rosenthal. 364: 199–205.

Segalowitz, N., and Lambert, W. 1969. Semantic generalization in bilinguals. *J. Verbal Learning and Verbal Behavior* 8: 559–66.

Seidenberg, M., and Pettito, L. 1979. Signing behavior in apes: A critical review. *Cognition* 7: 177–215.

Selman, R. 1971. Taking another's perspective: Roletaking development in early childhood. *Child Development* 42: 1721–34.

Shankweiler, D., and Liberman, I. 1972. Misreading: A search for causes. In *Language by ear and by eye,* eds. J. Kavanaugh and I. Mattingly. Cambridge, MA.: M.I.T. Press.

Shantz, C., and Wilson, K. 1972. Training communication skills in young children. *Child Development* 43: 693–98.

Shatz, M., and Gelman, R. 1973. The development of communication skills: modifications in the speech of young children as a function of listener. *Monographs of the Society for Research in Child Development.* Vol. 28, No. 5, Serial No. 152.

Sheldon, A. 1974. The acquisition of relative clauses in English. *Indiana Linguistics Club Papers,* Bloomington, Indiana.

Sherman, J. 1984. The acquisition of control in complement sentences: defining syntactic and lexical constraints. Paper presented at Applied Psycholinguistics Colloquium, Boston University, April, 1984.

Shultz, T., and Pilon, R. 1973. Development of the ability to detect linguistic ambiguity. *Child Development* 44: 728–33.

Shvachkin, N. 1973. The development of phonemic speech perception in early childhood. In *Studies of child language development,* eds. C. Ferguson and D. Slobin. New York: Holt, Rinehart & Winston.

Siegel, G. 1963. Adult verbal behavior with retarded children labelled as "high" or "low" in verbal ability. *Amer. J. of Ment. Def.* 3: 417–24.

Sigel, I., McGillicuddy-DeLisi, A., Flaugher, J., and Rock, D. 1982. Parents as teachers of their own learning disabled children. *Final report on U.S. Department of Education, Office of Special Education, Grant G007902000.*

Sinclair-De-Zwart, H. 1969. Developmental psycholinguistics. In *Studies in cognitive development: Essays in honor of Jean Piaget,* eds. D. Elkind and J. Flavell. New York: Oxford University Press.

———. 1973. Language acquisition and cognitive development. In *Cognitive development and the acquisition of language,* ed. T. Moore. New York: Academic Press.

Singer, J., and Flavell, J. 1981. Development of knowledge about communication skills: children's evaluation of explicitly ambiguous messages. *Child Development* 52: 1211–15.

Skinner, B.F. 1957. *Verbal behavior.* New York: Appleton-Century-Crofts.

Skutnabb-Kangas, T. 1979. *Language in the process of cultural assimilation and structural incorporation of linguistic minorities.* Rosslyn, VA.: Natl. Clearinghouse for Bilingual Education.

———. 1984. *Bilingualism or not: The education of minorities.* Clevedon, Eng.: Multilingual Matters.

Slobin, D. 1966*a*. Grammatical transformations and sentence comprehension in childhood and adulthood. *J. Verbal Learning and Verbal Behavior* 5: 219–27.

———. 1966*b*. Soviet psycholinguistics. In *Present-day Russian psychology: A symposium by seven authors,* ed. N. O'Connor. Oxford, England: Pergamon Press.

———. 1973. Cognitive prerequisites for the development of grammar. In *Studies of child language development,* eds. C. Ferguson and D. Slobin. New York: Holt, Rinehart & Winston.

———. 1979. *Psycholinguistics* 2nd ed. Glenview, Ill.: Scott, Foresman & Co.

———. 1981. The origin of grammatical encoding of events. In *The child's construction of language,* ed. W. Deutsch. London: Academic Press.

———. 1982. Universals and particulars in the acquisition of language. In *Language acquisition: State of the art,* eds. E. Wanner and L. Gleitman. Cambridge, England: Cambridge University Press.

———. 1985. Cross-linguistic evidence for the language making capacity. In *The cross-linguistic study of language acquisition,* ed. D. Slobin. Hillsdale, N.J.: Lawrence Erlbaum Assoc.

Slobin, D., and Bever, T. 1982. Children use canonical sentence schemas: A cross-linguistic study of word order and inflections. *Cognition* 12: 229–65.

Smit, A., and Bernthal, J. 1983. Performance of articulation-disordered children on language and perception measures. *J. Speech and Hearing Research* 26: 124–36.

Smith, B., and Oller, K. 1981. A comparative study of premeaningful vocalizations produced by normally developing and Down Syndrome infants. *J. Speech and Hearing Disorders* 46: 46–51.

Smith, E., Shoben, E., and Rips, L. 1974. Structure and process in semantic decisions. *Psychol. Review* 81: 214–41.

Smith, N. 1973. *The acquisition of phonology: A case study.* Cambridge, England: Cambridge University Press.

Snow, C. 1972. Mother's speech to language-learning children. *Child Development* 43: 549–65.

Snow, C., and Ferguson, C., eds. 1977. *Talking to children: Language input and acquisition.* Cambridge, England: Cambridge University Press.

Snow, C., and Hoefnagel-Hohle, M. 1978. The critical period for language acquisition. *Child Development* 49: 1114–28.

Soderburgh, R. 1971. *A linguistic study of a Swedish pre-school child's gradual acquisition of reading ability.* Stockholm: Almqvist & Wiksell.

Sonnenschein, S. 1982. The effects of redundant communications on listeners: When more is less. *Child Development* 53: 717–29.

Somerfelt, A. 1968. Phonetics and sociology. In *Manual of Phonetics,* ed. B. Malmberg. Amsterdam: North Holland Publishing Co.

Stampe, D. 1969. The acquisition of phonetic representation. In *Papers from the Fifth Regional Meeting, Chicago Linguistic Society,* eds. R. Binick, A. Davison, G. Green, and S. Morgan.

Stark, R. 1979. Prespeech segmental feature development. In *Language acquisition,* eds. P. Fletcher and M. Garman. Cambridge, England: Cambridge University Press.

Stein, A. 1976. A comparison of mother's and father's language to normal and language-deficient children. Unpublished doctoral dissertation, Boston University.

Stein, N., and Feldman, S. 1977. The effects of different modes of verbalization on the recognition of object details in pictures. *Child Development* 48: 1544–51.

Steinberg, L., Blindes, P., and Chan, K. 1985. Dropping out among language-minority youth. *Rev. Ed. Res.* 55: 541–61.

Stemmer, N. 1971. Some aspects of language acquisition. In *Pragmatics of natural languages,* ed. Y. Bar-Hillel. Dodrecht, Holland: D. Reidel Pub. Co.

Stevens, K. 1972. The quantal nature of speech: Evidence from articulatory and acoustic data. In *Human communication: A unified view,* eds. P. Denes and E. David. New York: McGraw-Hill.

Steward, M., and Steward, D. 1973. The observation of Anglo-Mexican and Chinese-American mothers teaching their young sons. *Child Development* 44: 329–37.

Straight, S. 1980. Auditory versus articulatory phonological processes. In *Child phonology,* eds. G. Yenikomshian, J. Kavanaugh, and C. Ferguson. Vol. 1. New York: Academic Press.

Strand, K. 1982. The relation of metamemory to memory performance in normal and language-impaired children. Unpublished doctoral dissertation, Boston University.

Strange, W. 1986. The role of speech input in speech perception. In *Otitis-media and child development,* eds. J. Kavanaugh and J. Jenkins. Parkton, MD.: York Press.

Strange, W., and Broen, P. 1980. Perception and production of approximant consonants. In *Child phonology,* eds. G. Yeni-Komshian, J. Kavanaugh, and C. Ferguson. Vol. 2. New York: Academic Press.

Sulzby, E. 1985. Kindergartners as writers and readers. In *Advances in writing research,* Vol. 1: *Children's early writing development,* ed. M. Farr. Norwood, N.J.: Ablex.

Swain, M. 1977. Bilingualism, monolingualism and code acquisition. In *Bilingualism in early childhood,* eds. W. Mackey and T. Anderson. Rowley, MA.: Newbury House.

Tager-Flusberg, H. 1981. Sentence comprehension in autistic children. *Applied Psycholinguistics* 2: 5–24.

———. 1985*a*. Constraints on the representation of word meaning: Evidence from autistic and mentally retarded children. In *The development of word meaning,* eds. S. Kuczaj and M. Barrett. New York: Springer-Verlag.

———. 1985*b*. The conceptual basis for referential word meaning in children with autism. *Child Development* 1167–78.

Tallal, P., and Piercy, M. 1978. Defects of auditory perception. In *Developmental Dysphasia,* ed. M. Wyke. London: Academic Press.

Tallal, P., and Stark, R. 1980. Speech perception of language-delayed children. In *Child Phonology,* eds. G. Yenikomshian, J. Kavanaugh, and C. Ferguson. Vol. 2. New York: Academic Press.

Tallal, P., Stark, R., Kallman, C., and Mellits, D. 1984. A reexamination of some nonverbal perceptual abilities of language-impaired children as a function of age and sensory modality. *J. Speech and Hearing Research* 24: 351–57.

Tannen, D. 1982. Oral and literate strategies in spoken and written narrative. *Language* 58: 1–21.

Tarone, E., Cohen, A., and Dumas, G. 1976. A closer look at some interlanguage terminology: A framework for communication strategies. *Working Papers in Bilingualism.* No. 9. April, 1976.

Teale, W., and Sulzby, E. 1986. *Emergent Literacy.* Norwood, N.J.: Ablex.

Terrace, H. 1979. Is problem-solving language? *J. Exper. Anal. Behav.* 31: 161–75.

Tfouni, L., and Klatzky, R. 1983. A discourse analysis of deixis: pragmatic cognitive and semantic factors in comprehension. *J. Child Language* 10: 123–33.

Thomas, D., Campos, J., Shucard, D., Ramsey, D., and Shucard, J. 1981. Semantic comprehension in infancy: A signal detection analysis. *Child Development* 52: 798–803.

Tomikawa, S., and Dodd, D. 1980. Early word meanings: Perceptually or functionally based? *Child Development* 51: 1103–9.

Trevarthen, C. 1986. Facial, vocal and gestural signs for motivation for speech in infants. In *Precursors of early speech,* eds. B. Lindblom and R. Zetterstrom. New York: Stockton Press.

Truby, H., Bosma, J., and Lind, J. 1965. Newborn infant cry. *Acta Paediatrica Scandinavica.* Supplement 163.

Trumball, E. 1984. Metalinguistic skills: Can they be taught? Unpublished doctoral dissertation, Boston University.

Tucker, R. 1975. The acquisition of knowledge by children educated bilingually. In *Developmental psycholinguistics: Theory and application,* ed. D. Dato. Washington, D.C.: Georgetown U. Press.

Tyler, L. 1983. The development of discourse mapping processes: The on-line interpretation of anaphoric expressions. *Cognition* 13: 309–41.

Urwin, C. 1978. Early language development in blind children. *British Psychological Society, Division of Learning and Child Psychology, Occasional Papers.* Vol. 17.

Vihman, M. 1985. Language differentiation in the bilingual infant. *J. Child Language* 12: 297–324.

Volterra, V., and Taeschner, T. 1978. The acquisition and development of language by bilingual children. *J. Child Language* 5: 311–26.

Vosniadou, S., Ortony, A., and Reynolds, R. 1982. Children's enactment of metaphors in the context of a story: A developmental study of the acquisition of metaphorical meaning. Paper presented at the 7th Annual Boston

University Conference on Language Development. Boston, October, 1982.

Vygotsky, L. 1962. *Thought and language.* Cambridge, MA.: M.I.T. Press.

———. 1978. *Mind in society,* eds. M. Cole, V. John-Steiner, S. Scribner, and E. Souberman. Cambridge, MA.: Harvard University Press.

Wada, J., Clarke, R., and Hamm, A. 1975. Cerebral hemispheric asymmetry in humans. *Arch. Neurol.* 32: 239–46.

Wales, R. 1979. Deixis. In *Language Acquisition,* eds. P. Fletcher and M. Garman. Cambridge, England: Cambridge University Press.

Walters, J. 1978. Variation of language use in the language acquisition of bilingual children. Unpublished doctoral dissertation, Boston University.

Watson, K. 1975. Transferable communicative routines: strategies and group identity in two speech acts. *Language in Society* 4: 53–72.

Watson, L. 1979. Maternal self-repetition as a function of child feedback. Unpublished doctoral dissertation, Boston University.

Watson, R. 1985. Toward a theory of definition. *J. Child Language* 12: 181–97.

Wehren, A., DeLisi, R., and Arnold, M. 1981. The development of noun definition. *J. Child Language* 8: 165–75.

Weiner, P. 1972. The perceptual-level functioning of dysphasic children: A follow-up study. *J. Speech and Hearing Research* 15: 423–38.

Weinreich, U. 1966. On the semantic structure of language. In *Universals of language,* ed. J. Greenberg. Cambridge, MA.: M.I.T. Press.

Wells, G. 1983. Talking with children: The complementary roles of parents and teachers. In *Early childhood development and education,* eds. M. Donaldson, R. Grieve, and C. Pratt. New York: The Guilford Press.

Werner, H., and Kaplan, E. 1950. Development of word meaning through verbal context: An experimental study. *J. of Psychology* 29: 251–57.

Werner, H., and Kaplan, B. 1964. *Symbolic formation.* New York: John Wiley & Sons.

Wertsch, J. 1979. From social interaction to higher psychological process: A clarification and application of Vygotsky's theory. *Human Development* 22: 1–22.

White, S. 1970. The learning theory approach. In *Carmichael's manual of child psychology,* ed. P. Mussen. Vol. 1. New York: John Wiley & Sons.

Whitehurst, G., and Merkur, S. 1977. The development of communication: Modelling and contrast failure. *Child Development* 48: 993–1001.

Whitehurst, G., Sonnenschein, S., and Ianfolla, B. 1981. Learning to communicate from models: Children confuse length with information. *Child Development* 52: 507–13.

Wiig, E. 1984. Language disabilities in adolescents: A question of cognitive strategies. *Topics in Language Disorders,* March, 41–58.

Wiig, E., and Semel, E. 1980. *Language assessment and intervention for the learning-disabled child.* Columbus, Ohio: Charles-Merrill.

Wilbur, R. 1979. *American sign language and sign systems.* Baltimore, MD.: University Park Press.

Wilcox, J., and Webster, E. 1980. Early discourse behavior: An analysis of children's response to listener feedback. *Child Development* 51: 1120–25.

Willig, A. 1982. The effectiveness of bilingual education: Review of a report. *NABE Journal* 6: 1–19.

Wing, L., and Gould, J. 1979. Severe impairments of social interaction and associated abnormalities in children: Epidemiology and classification. *J. Autism and Severe Developmental Disorders* 9: 11–29.

Winner, E., Rosenstiel, A., and Gardner, H. 1977. The development of metaphoric understanding. *J. Learning Disabilities* 10: 147–49.

Wittelson, S. 1977. Early hemisphere localization and interhemisphere plasticity. In *Language development and neurological theory,* eds. S. Segalowitz and F. Gruber. New York: Academic Press.

Wolf, M. 1983. Word retrieval process and reading in children and aphasics. In *Children's Language,* ed. K. Nelson. Vol. 3. New York: Gardner Press.

Wolfram, W. 1973. Sociolinguistic implications for education sequencing. In *Language society and education: A profile of Black English,* ed. J. DeStefano. Worthington, Ohio: Charles A. Jones Publishing Co.

Woods, B. 1981. *Children and communication: Verbal and non-verbal message development.* Englewood Cliffs, N.J.: Prentice-Hall Inc.

Wong-Fillmore, L. 1979. Individual differences in second-language acquisition. In *Individual differences in language ability and language behavior,* eds. C. Fillmore, D. Kempler, and W. Wong. New York: Academic Press.

Wong-Fillmore, L., Ammon, P., McLaughlin, B., and Ammon, M. 1985. *Learning English through bilingual instruction.* Roslyn, VA.: Natl. Clearinghouse for Bilingual Education.

Woods, B., and Carey, S. 1979. Language deficits after apparent clinical recovery. *Annals of Neurology* 6: 405–9.

Wozniak, R. 1972. Verbal regulations of motor behavior. *Human Development* 15: 13–57.

Yoder, D., and Miller, J. 1972. What we may know and what we can do: Input toward a system. In *Language intervention with the retarded: Developing strategies,* eds. J. McLean, D. Yoder, and R. Schiefelbusch. Baltimore: University Park Press.

Young, D., and Shumacher, G. 1983. Context effects in young children's sensitivity to the importance level of prose. *Child Development* 54: 1446–56.

Zimin, S. 1978. Sex of speaker and addressee in degree of deference used to request and apologize by first- and second-language users. Unpublished doctoral dissertation, Boston University.

Index of Authors

Index of Subjects